Citrix® MetaFrame™ for Windows® Terminal Services: The Official Guide

STEVE **KAPLAN**
MARC **MANGUS**

Osborne/**McGraw-Hill**

New York   Chicago   San Francisco
Lisbon   London   Madrid   Mexico City   Milan
New Delhi   San Juan   Seoul   Singapore   Sydney   Toronto

Osborne/**McGraw-Hill**
2600 Tenth Street
Berkeley, California 94710
U.S.A.

For information on translations or book distributors outside the U.S.A., or to arrange bulk purchase discounts for sales promotions, premiums, or fund-raisers, please contact Osborne/**McGraw-Hill** at the above address.

Citrix® MetaFrame™ for Windows® Terminal Services: The Official Guide

234567890 FGR FGR 01987654321

ISBN 0-07-212443-1

Publisher
  Brandon Nordin
Associate Publisher and
Editor-in-Chief
  Scott Rogers
Acquisitions Editor
  Wendy Rinaldi
Project Editors
  Judith Brown
  Jennifer Malnick
Copy Editor
  Judith Brown
Proofreader
  Karen Mead

Indexer
  Jack Lewis
Computer Designers
  Roberta Steele
  Lauren McCarthy
  Jim Kussow
Illustrators
  Beth Young
  Michael Mueller
  Robert Hansen
Cover Design
  Dodie Shoemaker
Series Design
  Peter F. Hancik

This book was composed with Corel VENTURA™ Publisher.

Steve Kaplan
To my wife, Lisa, my son, Ryan, and my daughter, Alexis. They provided encouragement and good cheer during my 10 months of long nights and early mornings holed up in my study writing the book (connected to the office over Citrix MetaFrame, of course).

Marc Mangus
To my love, Dawndee, for always telling me I could do it.

ABOUT THE AUTHORS

Steve Kaplan is the CEO and cofounder of RYNO Technology. Steve has been a columnist for both *Solutions Integrator* and *Reseller Management*. He has had articles published in several other magazines, both within and outside the computer industry. He is the author of a thin-client comic book and an early PC DOS user's manual, and developed a DOS-based point-of-sales program. Steve is a frequent speaker on ASP solutions and has spoken at events such as Citrix Summit and Crossroads 2000. He holds a B.S. in business administration from UC Berkeley and a master's degree in management, with an emphasis on both marketing and finance, from Northwestern's J. L. Kellogg Graduate School of Management.

Marc Mangus is the Vice President and Chief Technology Officer for RYNO Technology. He was formerly Director of Information Services at Wink Communications, where the network he implemented was named one of the top 100 in the country by *Wired* magazine. Marc has worked in IT for 13 years, managing technology within companies as well as without as a consultant. Marc is certified in Oracle, Sybase, and AT&T UNIX. He holds a B.A. in business management from Saint Mary's College in Moraga, California.

CONTENTS

Part II

Designing a Corporate ASP Solution

Part III

Implementing a Corporate ASP Solution

FOREWORD

first visited coauthor Steve Kaplan in the late 1980s when I was vice president of marketing for an imaging and workflow software company. Steve's system integration company was one of our first Northern California value-added resellers. In those days, most of us in the imaging and workflow industry were excited about the vast promise of this new Windows-based technology. We believed it had the potential to significantly enhance corporate productivity and eliminate a lot of paper from the office.

Imaging, though, never made it into the mainstream, and workflow is still looking for its market position. Industry players underestimated the demands that distributed PC–based computing would make upon an organization's computing resources. Administrators tend to spend so much time supporting end-user hardware and PC configuration issues that they do not have the bandwidth to explore productivity-enhancing technologies such as imaging and workflow.

Moving applications from the distributed desktop to the server frees administrators from the drudgery of PC support issues. It also significantly improves the management of organizational expenditures for PC upgrades and administration. As a result, administrators are more likely to have both the time and monetary resources necessary to focus on using technology to make their organizations more efficient and competitive.

Once an organization's IT department decides to embrace server-based computing, they must address a range of technical, educational, cultural, political, and internal marketing challenges. Over 8000 members of the Citrix Solutions Network have helped us build the server-based computing industry by designing and installing solutions that successfully meet these challenges.

Although Kaplan's integration company abandoned imaging years ago, it is now one of a select group of top-notch Citrix Platinum-authorized resellers. In this book, coauthors Steve Kaplan and Marc Mangus present the culmination of years of best practices gleaned from setting up hundreds of Citrix MetaFrame and Microsoft Terminal Server systems. They have written openly about their innovative methodologies and approaches. If you are considering implementing a server-based computing solution for an enterprise of any size, you should read this book.

Mark B. Templeton
President, Citrix Systems, Inc.

ACKNOWLEDGMENTS

Many people contributed to this book. Rob Ruzika of Citrix Consulting helped us to define and to refine our material, while several engineers at Citrix helped to review it or promote it, including Arlo Paranhos, Jason Gradel, and Matt McGrigg. Mike Graff and Bob Chapman of Citrix helped us understand how to sell this technology to organizations at the enterprise level, as did Bob (Darth) Schwartz and Tony Davi of Wyse.

We would like to thank RYNO's Vice President, Alan Kaplan, for having the tenacity and dedication to make this technology work on an enterprise scale for one of the world's 1000 largest companies. The methodologies Alan developed are referenced throughout the book. RYNO's engineering team was essential to refining and contributing to these methodologies and making their own large projects successful. Without them, this book would never have been written. Bob Britz and the RYNO consulting team also contributed to building our knowledge base for the book, and the rest of our staff kept us in business so we could write it.

Wendy Rinaldi, Executive Editor at Osborne/McGraw-Hill, provided invaluable vision, guidance, encouragement, and occasional motivation (bottom-kicking). Judith Brown and Monika Faltiss contributed outstanding editing.

Tony Woo of Mainstream wrote much of the content of Chapter 3 on Terminal Services. Tony used to be a Citrix trainer, and his firm has a great reputation for providing outstanding training around the country in Terminal Services and Citrix MetaFrame.

Denton Gentry gave invaluable technical input on the wonderful worlds of networking and security, as well as astute corrections to the general text. Eric Mann provided help with the numerous checklists throughout the book.

And, where would we be without our customers? Some, like Sean Finley, Tony Kloeppel, and Bob Miller of ABM, or Rob Hutter of Westaff and Rob Lawrence of Palo Alto Medical Group, actually contributed to, or reviewed, our book. Others, like John Forberg and Steve Steinbrecher of Contra Costa County, Tony Chavez of Mechanics Bank, Lee Wines of Bank of Walnut Creek, and Jeff Doan of Pacific Gulf Properties, were early enterprise adapters of Citrix WinFrame and provided us with our initial foundation for building an enterprise server-based computing business.

We would particularly like to thank Anthony Lackey of ABM Industries. Anthony's brilliant work in financial modeling and internal marketing methodologies played a very important part in the book. When we started working on the thin-client design for ABM, Anthony was Director of MIS. Big companies tend to like to work with big integrators (one reason being that it gives them someone with resources to sue in the event of project failure). But Anthony chose our small regional firm over several contending international consulting firms because he liked what he saw in our focus on this technology. We started this book while the project was still in process, and we couldn't be 100 percent sure it would have a happy ending. Fortunately, ABM ended up saving many millions of dollars a year, and Anthony was promoted to VP of Electronic Services and Chief Technology Officer (CTO).

Though we had a lot of help with this book, any mistakes of commission or omission are solely our own.

INTRODUCTION

I n a server-based computing environment, Windows applications execute on central server farms running Microsoft Windows 2000 Terminal Services and Citrix MetaFrame. Users see only screen prints of their applications displayed on a wide variety of devices, ranging from handheld units to Windows terminals to traditional PCs. This new computing paradigm also goes by several other names, including application serving, thin-client computing, ASP services, and simply Terminal Services. By reducing or eliminating the requirements for both PC upgrades and remote-office servers, organizations minimize their ongoing capital expenditures. They realize much bigger savings from being able to slash administration costs. And perhaps most important, organizations gain strategic benefits from the ability to quickly deploy applications to anyone, anywhere, anytime.

> *Server-based computing is great. It's happening. It's part of our strategy.*
> —Steve Ballmer, Microsoft President,
> from the *Wall Street Journal,* July 21, 1999

EVOLUTION OF AN INDUSTRY

Server-based computing exploded from a 3 percent share of the networking market in 1997 to a 23 percent share by the end of 1999. Citrix launched the industry in the late 1980s when they introduced a multiuser OS/2 product called WinView. Today, Citrix is one of the world's largest software companies and one of the fastest growing U.S. firms of any kind. The server-based computing industry is enormous and includes scores of Windows terminal choices, bandwidth management devices, wireless connectivity options, and thousands of software partners, resellers, and consultants. Microsoft's incorporation of Terminal Services into Windows 2000 is further expediting its replacement of conventional client-server computing as the new corporate networking standard.

> **NOTE:** Some readers may take exception to our declaration of server-based computing as the new networking standard. We firmly believe that its overwhelming economic advantages make this transition inevitable. Organizations that do not embrace the much greater efficiencies and strategic benefits that server-based computing enable will be at a competitive disadvantage.

Terminal Services and MetaFrame provide the enabling technology for the majority of the ASP (Application Service Provider) movement. When implementing Terminal Services for the enterprise, an IT department acts as an ASP to the organization's remote offices and users.

In an enterprise implementation of Terminal Services, most applications execute at one or more central data centers rather than on individual PCs. This entails a paradigm shift back to mainframe methodologies, procedures, and discipline, while still utilizing technology and environmental aspects unique to the PC world. It requires a much more resilient, reliable, and redundant network infrastructure than in a conventional client-server WAN. A myriad of decisions must be made about building this infrastructure as well as about ancillary items such as choosing the right Windows terminals, prioritizing WAN traffic, and migrating from legacy systems.

GENESIS OF THIS BOOK

We started selling Citrix OS/2 multiuser software as a remote-access solution in 1995, but it took us almost a year to figure out the thin-client implications. One of our solutions consultants, Sean Thomas, was studying the attributes of the new NT 3.51 version of the Citrix product called WinFrame. "You know," he said, "I don't think our clients are going to need servers at all in their remote offices. In fact, they won't even have to upgrade their PCs."

The lightbulb finally went on, and we became evangelists of thin-client computing, as it was exclusively called back then. In those early days, though, the concept of going back to centralized computing was still very unfamiliar, particularly to people without a systems background. There were only a couple of Windows terminal manufacturers, and most software companies had no clue as to whether their products would run over Citrix.

We typically found it difficult to explain the new paradigm to IT people, and often extremely challenging to convince a CFO or a board of directors. The most common refrain we heard was, "It sounds too good to be true." We created a thin-client comic book to help IT managers present a humorous but informative explanation to the people controlling the budget.

NOTE: When we created the comic book, we sent a copy to Mark Templeton, then CEO of Citrix. He was out of town and his administrative assistant opened his mail and read the comic book. When he returned, she told him, "Now I finally understand what we do."

Today, Citrix software is commonplace and is used by 100 percent of the Fortune 100 companies. Surprisingly, though, it only has a 3 percent to 5 percent penetration within these firms. Citrix often is initially introduced into a company to solve a particular business problem, such as remote access or deploying an ERP application or facilitating the opening of a remote office. Gradually, the software spreads throughout the organization as more departments discover its advantages.

This pattern had been true with most of our Citrix implementations until 1998. At that point, we were awarded the project to design an enterprise implementation of server-based computing for all PC users in 210 offices and at the headquarters of ABM Industries, a Fortune 1000 company. We found a surprising dearth of knowledge about how to handle enterprise server-based computing tasks such as setting up 1000 printers of all different makes and models, building an economic disaster recovery solution, and implementing a back-end file services model that could store terabytes of data yet be simple to administer.

Through research and discussions with engineering teams at companies such as Citrix, Microsoft, Network Appliance, Cisco, Packeteer, and Wyse, we came up with what we felt to be a very innovative and robust technical design for an enterprise server-based computing implementation. But that was only part of the story. We had to work with our customer to help build a financial justification. There were myriad cultural and political issues to address when undergoing such a massive paradigm shift. Project management, change control, and migration strategies all required development and execution.

The project was a huge success by any measure, as ABM was able to reduce their PC/LAN support personnel expense by more than half and yet garner higher ratings from users. The methodologies we developed have continued to work well for us as we now commonly implement large-scale server-based computing solutions for both private and public organizations. We wanted to help expand the industry by continuing to share our knowledge and educate potential users. There was just too much information, though, to pack into a comic book. Fortunately, Citrix and Osborne/McGraw-Hill saw the merit in what we were doing and felt that it would be a good entry into their "Official Guide" series of books.

> *I first saw Citrix when a demonstration of the product was done for us at our headquarters. After about 10 minutes, I excused myself and nearly ran from the room back to my office. I picked up the phone and called the chairman of the board. "Martinn, I've just seen our future, and it's thin!"*
>
> —Anthony Lackey,
> VP Electronic Services and CTO, ABM Industries

COMPOSITION OF THIS BOOK

This book provides the framework to design and implement a successful enterprise server-based computing environment. Our focus is on using Terminal Services and MetaFrame to accommodate hundreds or thousands of users running the majority of their desktop applications from one or more data centers. We address the myriad technical, design, and implementation issues involved in constructing this environment. We assume that readers already have a good working knowledge of networking and system administration for Windows NT or Windows 2000.

The book is divided into three parts. Part I is an overview of enterprise server-based computing. This section reviews Windows 2000 Terminal Services and MetaFrame and includes justifications for enterprise deployments. Part II covers the design of a Corporate ASP solution and ranges from planning and internally selling the project to providing guidelines for data center and WAN architecture, file services, remote access, security, network management, and thin-client devices. Part III covers the deployment of server-based computing and includes project management, installation, automation, server farms, profiles, policies and procedures, printing, and migration methodologies.

In Appendix A we present a methodology for building a spreadsheet-based financial model to analyze the comparative benefits of thin-client versus fat-client computing. Appendix B includes a suggestion for creating an ASP-like billing model for charging users for application hosting.

We include "Notes," "Tips," and "Cautions" to supply additional detail to the text. A Note is meant to provide information when the general flow of the discussion is concentrating on a different area or is not as detailed as the Note. A Tip is a specific way to do or implement something being discussed. A Caution is meant to alert the reader to a potential problem.

Writing a book about such a rapidly evolving technology poses a challenge. For instance, we only had the time and space to briefly cover two of the most exciting new Citrix developments: NFuse and MetaFrame for UNIX. Fortunately, the methodologies and approaches we describe should be relatively timeless, and should prove very useful as you begin your own enterprise server-based computing project.

WHO SHOULD READ THIS BOOK

The primary audience for this book is likely to be the technical IT staff of any organization considering, or using, Terminal Services as an alternative to conventional client-server computing. As a compendium of best practices for enterprise deployment of Terminal Services, it should also appeal to the engineers and consultants of the 8500 Citrix integration companies and 21,000 Microsoft Solution Providers. IT and project managers can benefit from the sections on change control, customer care, and migration strategies.

CIOs, CFOs, and champions of organizational efficiency can profit from the sections on justifying the migration to a server-based computing architecture. The book covers both business benefits and economic savings. It also addresses common concerns about Terminal Services along with potential solutions.

> *I find the idea of implementing a fat-client network disgusting.*
> —Alan Kaplan, CTO, RYNO Technology
> (from a statement made to coauthor
> Steve Kaplan in early 1998)

INTERACTIVE INFORMATION

We welcome your feedback and will incorporate appropriate suggestions into further releases of the book. You can contact Steve Kaplan at skaplan@ryno.com, Marc Mangus at mmangus@ryno.com, or you can discuss your ideas on the book forum at www.ryno.com.

PART I

Overview of Enterprise Server-Based Computing

CHAPTER 1

Introducing the Corporate ASP Alternative

Server-based computing utilizing Microsoft Terminal Services and Citrix ICA (Independent Computing Architecture) is at the core of the ASP (Application Service Provider) movement. This chapter introduces the concept of enterprise server-based computing, which we refer to as building a Corporate ASP. We'll look at the business benefits of server-based computing, including rapid application deployment, improved information access, improved productivity, reduced risk, and enhanced growth. We consider the many economic benefits of server-based computing and the major industry trends that are accelerating its acceptance. The main components of a Corporate ASP as well as justifications for implementing one are analyzed. Finally, we discuss the process of designing a Corporate ASP, which we will build upon in the chapters that follow.

THE CORPORATE ASP

Application Service Providers host applications at data centers. Customers access these applications through data lines or through the Internet, typically for a monthly fee. When an organization builds an enterprise server-based computing solution, the Information Technology (IT) department hosts applications for their users in a manner similar to commercial ASPs. We, therefore, refer to an enterprise server-based computing environment as a Corporate ASP. The Corporate ASP model is a particularly useful one because it can position the IT department as a profit center. In this environment, building a robust, reliable, and scalable architecture is essential. The Corporate ASP model also emphasizes the necessity of running the server-based computing data centers like mainframe shops, with control over changes, limited access, and well-defined policies and procedures.

A Corporate ASP has many other similarities with the mainframe model of computing. For example, IT control of the desktop and application standards, reduced infrastructure costs, and much lower staffing requirements are attributes shared with the mainframe environment. Unlike the mainframe model, though, Corporate ASP users do not have to wait six months in an MIS queue in order to have IT produce a report for them. Instead, they can create it themselves in minutes by using Excel or any application to which IT gives them access.

A Corporate ASP thus combines the best of both the mainframe and PC worlds. It incorporates the inexpensive desktop-computing cost structure of the mainframe model while allowing users the flexibility and versatility they are used to having with their PCs. The matrix in Figure 1-1 compares server-based computing with both mainframe and PC-based computing with respect to cost and flexibility.

JUSTIFICATION FOR SERVER-BASED COMPUTING

If economics were the only factor involved in making IT decisions, the Corporate ASP model would already be the computing standard. In reality, a myriad of educational, historical, cultural, and political factors influence an organization's decision of whether or

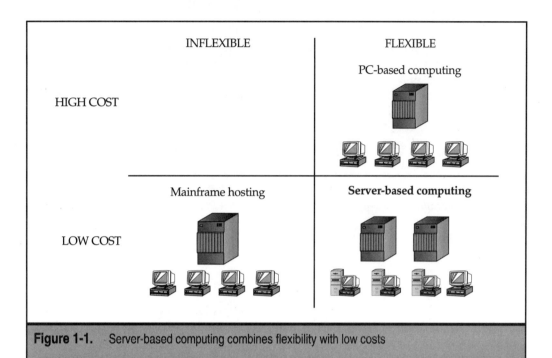

Figure 1-1.   Server-based computing combines flexibility with low costs

not to implement server-based computing. Different departments, for example, may control their own budgets and have their own IT staffs. They may resist ceding computing control to a centralized corporate IT department. Users who distrust a network's reliability because of a history of frequent downtime are going to be extremely reluctant to place all of their computing eggs in the IT department's basket.

Applications Driving Server-Based Computing

Early "killer" applications that people just couldn't do without, such as VisiCalc and desktop publishing, drove the initial sale of PCs and Macs. Today, we are seeing applications similarly driving the stampede into constructing Corporate ASPs. An organization's existing PCs, for example, may be inadequate to run a popular application such as Office 2000. Rather than expending the huge amounts of money and labor required to upgrade or replace existing PCs, an organization can implement a Corporate ASP and simply publish the Office 2000 icon to all users.

Enterprise Resource Planning (ERP) applications such as SAP, PeopleSoft, and JD Edwards are particularly effective in leading organizations to implement server-based computing. This was the case for California's Contra Costa County when the Department of Information Technology received a mandate to implement PeopleSoft for the county's 360 human resources (HR) users. The county was faced with replacing many dumb terminals and upgrading most of the remaining PCs. They also would have had to undergo expensive bandwidth upgrades to 60 different buildings. Instead, the county set up a MetaFrame server farm to deploy PeopleSoft, Kronos Time & Billing, Microsoft Office, Lotus Notes, and other applications to all HR users without requiring any PC or bandwidth upgrades. IBM's version of Windows terminals, called Network Stations, replaced the dumb terminals and low-end PCs.

Business Benefits Driving Server-Based Computing

As a community bank, it is imperative for us to offer superb customer service at all locations. Citrix MetaFrame enables our employees at the branches to utilize our sophisticated systems at headquarters without the requirement for implementing an expensive wide area network infrastructure.

—Lee Wines,
Executive Vice President, Bank of Walnut Creek

Server-based computing inevitably slashes the cost of information processing. And certainly, reduced cost is usually at the heart of any server-based computing initiative, but it may not be the most important factor. More important considerations may involve broad strategic goals such as faster time to market, improved productivity, lowered risk, improved information access, or faster organizational growth.

Rapid Application Deployment

The ability to rapidly deploy applications to all users throughout the enterprise enables organizations to provide faster responses to their customers or bring new products to market more quickly.

Access to Corporate Applications and Databases

A need for corporate-wide access to an Enterprise Resource Planning (ERP) application such as PeopleSoft, or to a Customer Resource Management (CRM) package such as Siebel, may be driving the server-based computing initiative. The need to remotely access databases ranging from accounting to CAD sometimes may act as the catalyst.

Improving User Productivity

Organizations often document their cost of providing help desk support. They seldom quantify, though, the amount of lost productivity as users either struggle to fix the problem themselves or wait for the help desk to handle it. Users may also waste other employees' time by asking for help from them instead of from IT. Other productivity losses occur when users have to stop work because their personal computers or applications are being upgraded. Incompatible software versions sometimes make it necessary to do time-consuming data conversions in order to share information with other employees.

Server-based computing enhances productivity by significantly reducing the downtime associated with PCs. Employees are more effective because they can see "their" desktop no matter which PC or Windows terminal they use and no matter where they use it.

Users at remote offices are more productive because a Corporate ASP enables them to access the same network services—such as e-mail, color printing, and network faxing—as headquarters users.

> *The typical Windows PC…is still a headache to use. Crashes, unexpected failures, and generally inconsistent and irritating behavior are daily occurrences.*
>
> —Walter Mossberg,
> *The Wall Street Journal*, October 28, 1999

Reducing Risk of Significant Economic Loss

A PC-based computing environment can expose an organization to large fines because of the difficulty of preventing unlicensed software use. Even worse, the corporate information is much more susceptible to loss or to theft because it is stored on hard drives of individual PCs and servers distributed throughout the enterprise. In a server-based computing environment, all of the corporate information is housed in corporate data centers, where it is secure, managed, backed up, and redundant.

A PC-based computing environment typically has limited redundancy. A catastrophe at headquarters can leave hundreds or thousands of employees unable to do their work. Failure of a server in a remote office can mean a day or more of downtime until a replacement unit can be secured and installed. Server-based computing makes it affordable to build redundancy into the corporate data center, and to build redundant data centers. This enables much better continuity protection for all headquarters and remote-office users than is practical in a PC-based computing environment.

Facilitating Growth

A Corporate ASP enables faster organizational growth by making it easy either to open remote offices or to assimilate offices of acquired companies into an organization's electronic information system. Servers do not need to be configured and set up in the remote offices. Users only need low-bandwidth connectivity to the data center, and IT can then publish application icons to their desktops.

Other Business Benefits of Server-Based Computing

While perhaps not enough on their own to warrant construction of a Corporate ASP, the following server-based computing capabilities make a strong case when considered together.

Electrical Power Savings

Using Windows terminals greatly reduces power consumption. The bigger the company, the more PCs replaced, the larger the savings. You could potentially save thousands of dollars every year on electricity bills. Many Windows terminals draw 50 watts while most modern PCs draw 250 watts.

Telecommuting   Since users see only screen prints of applications that use very little bandwidth, employees can effectively telecommute by dialing into the network or by coming in through the Internet. A cable modem or DSL connection will often enable speeds equivalent to those obtained when using a fat-client PC at headquarters.

Embracing Corporate Standards   Under server-based computing, control of the desktop shifts from the user to the IT staff, making it relatively effortless to implement corporate software standards. This reduces inefficiencies resulting from data-sharing problems and helps to eliminate duplication of work. It also enables IT to present a common user interface, whether Windows or browser based.

Reducing Virus Risk   Eliminating or restricting users' ability to add software via their local floppy or onto their local hard drive means that the network antivirus software should eliminate most computer virus problems.

Eliminating the PC as a Status Symbol   Identical performance for everyone means that the PC loses its value as an organizational status symbol. The *personal* computer becomes the corporate computer. This eliminates the common, and very inefficient, tendency to shuffle PCs between users as new units are introduced.

Homogenizing Clients   New PCs, old PCs, PCs with older operating systems, UNIX workstations, Macs, Windows terminals, and even many handheld devices can all run the latest Windows applications over Terminal Services.

Eliminating the Need for Local Data Backup   Many organizations rely on users and remote office administrators to do their own data backups, or they contract this function out to third-party services. A Corporate ASP eliminates the time, risk, and expense associated with distributed data backups.

Improving Remote User Support   The shadowing features of Citrix software enable the help desk to see users' desktops for both troubleshooting and training purposes.

Eliminating Theft of Fat-Client PCs   As organizations increasingly utilize Windows terminals instead of desktops and laptops, they remove the attraction for thieves to steal the devices since they are both inexpensive and useless without being attached to a server-based computing network.

Helping to Prevent Theft of Intellectual Property   Since users see only screen prints of data, IT can more easily prevent employees from copying corporate information files. This can be important in staffing industries, for example, where applicant databases constitute the company assets and are frequent targets of theft by dishonest employees.

Eliminating Games and Other Personal Programs   If desired, IT can completely eliminate the ability to load games or other productivity-sapping personal programs.

Making Applications Web Ready   Using the Citrix Application Launching and Embedding (ALE) capabilities, IT can quickly and inexpensively make existing applications Web ready.

Economic Savings Promoting Server-Based Computing

Server-based computing requires a much more elaborate data center architecture than that of a distributed PC-based computing model. Nonetheless, a Corporate ASP environment is far less expensive to build and maintain because of the savings achieved from four areas: personal computers, remote-office infrastructures, bandwidth, and topologies.

Personal Computers

> *Thin continues to be in. A study by Gartner Group's Datapro unit has found that enterprises that have deployed networks based on thin clients...tend to extend those installations to other parts of the enterprise. "The staffing required to support fat client PCs is at least five times greater than for Windows terminals or PCs that are configured as Windows terminals," said Peter Lowber, the Datapro analyst who authored the report.*
>
> —*InternetWeek,* June 1, 1999

Since administration is the largest component of a PC's total cost of ownership, server-based computing saves organizations huge amounts of money by reducing IT staffing requirements. The deputy CIO of California's Contra Costa County, John Forberg, says that they have a network administrator who supports 500 thin-client users. This compares to a fat-client PC-based computing average of around one administrator per 100 users. Forberg commented that server-based computing enabled the county to upgrade a PeopleSoft ERP package for hundreds of users literally over lunch.

Personal computers tend to have a maximum life span of only a few years for most organizations. Upgrading a PC is an enormously expensive task that includes not only the cost of the machine and its operating system software, but also the expense of ordering, delivering, and configuring the PC. Data files often need transferring from the old unit to the new one, and the company suffers from downtime during the process. In a Corporate ASP environment, personal computers no longer require upgrading since applications are processed on central server farms. New users can receive inexpensive Windows terminals that are set up in minutes.

In an attempt to lower administration expenses, many organizations are utilizing Microsoft Windows NT at the desktop to "lock down" the PCs. One IT department went to the extent of placing faceplates over all newly purchased PCs to prevent access to the CD-ROM and floppy drives. They then disabled drive mapping to the C: drive. They even put a lock on the back of the cases to prevent users from opening them. Of course, a server-based computing environment provides the ultimate in desktop lockdown, without the enormous effort and expense and continued upgrades required in the PC-based computing paradigm.

Remote-Office Infrastructures

In a PC-based computing environment, even small remote offices often require not only file servers, but also e-mail servers, SQL database servers, and possibly other applications servers. An example of a PC-based computing environment in a remote office is shown in Figure 1-2. The remote offices also require associated peripheral software and hardware, such as network operating systems software, tape backups, tape backup software, antivirus software, network management software, and uninterruptible power supplies. Someone needs to administer and maintain these remote networks as well as ensure that data is consistently synchronized or replicated with data at headquarters.

In a Corporate ASP model, remote-office servers and their peripherals can usually be eliminated entirely by simply running all users as thin clients to a central server farm. Both powerful and low-end PCs, Windows terminals, Macintoshes, and UNIX workstations can be cabled to a low-bandwidth hub and then connected with a router to the corporate data center through a leased line, frame relay cloud, or even through the Internet. Figure 1-3 shows a typical small remote office in a Corporate ASP environment.

TIP: Here is an important question to ask when comparing server-based computing with PC-based computing: do you want your corporate data sitting on hard drives of individual PCs and servers distributed throughout your enterprise, or do you want it all to reside at your corporate data center where it is protected, backed up, redundant, and managed in a secure environment?

Bandwidth

It is not uncommon for an ERP package such as JD Edwards' One World to require 128KB of bandwidth or more per user, making it very expensive to connect remote-office users in a PC-based computing environment. A Corporate ASP utilizing Microsoft Terminal Services and MetaFrame requires only around 10KB to 20KB of bandwidth per concurrent user to run a Citrix ICA session. Rather than building local area network (LAN) infrastructures that require data replication with headquarters, the low Terminal Services bandwidth requirements usually make it much more economical for remote-office users simply to run all of their applications from the corporate data center. With the addition of Citrix ICA encryption technology, users can often use the Internet as an even less expensive bandwidth medium for enabling server-based computing.

Topologies

Fat-client PCs increasingly require faster LAN bandwidth of 100MB or more to every desktop. Users of PCs and Windows terminals operating in a server-based computing

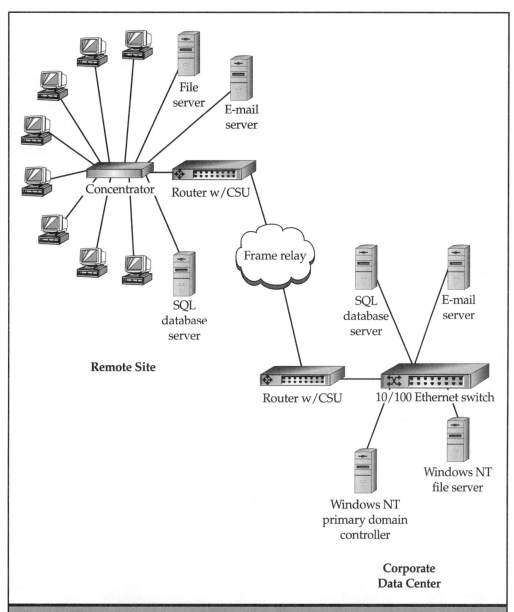

Figure 1-2. Typical remote office in a PC-based computing environment

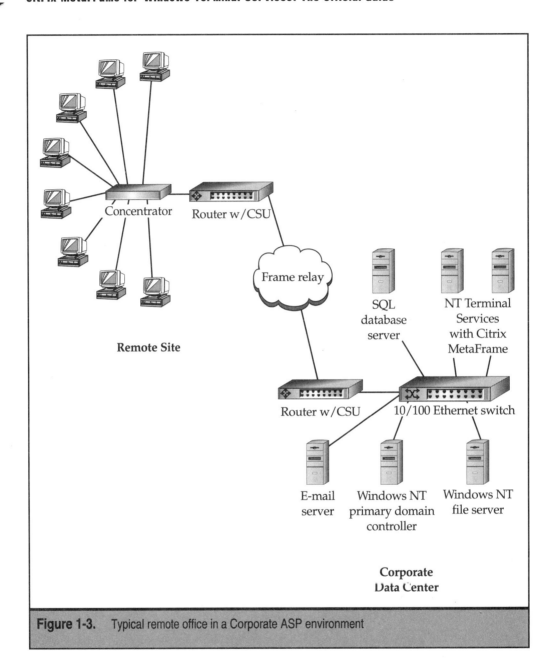

Figure 1-3. Typical remote office in a Corporate ASP environment

environment see only low-bandwidth screen prints. Although a fast server backbone is a must, legacy topologies of older 10MB Ethernet can typically continue to be used to connect workstations with no degradation in performance.

Industry Trends Accelerating Server-Based Computing

Three major industry trends will ensure that the explosion of server-based computing will not only continue, but also accelerate. These trends are based upon laws of both technology and economics: Moore's Law, Metcalf's Law, and the law of supply and demand.

Moore's Law

Gordon Moore, a cofounder of Intel, discovered decades ago that the number of transistors per square inch doubles roughly every 18 months. Moore's Law means that server performance doubles roughly every 18 months without corresponding increases in cost. As more powerful MetaFrame servers support ever more thin-client users, the economics become even more favorable toward centralizing most organizational computing. For example, suppose a company wants to deploy an application that would normally require an upgrade of all existing PCs. The option of purchasing one MetaFrame server, today, instead of 100 new desktops is certainly going to be attractive. But within a couple of years, a similarly priced MetaFrame server will likely handle 200 concurrent users or more. This makes the hardware cost savings of the server-based computing solution even more enticing.

Metcalf's Law

> *One thing is certain. Over the next decade, computer speeds will rise about a hundredfold while bandwidth increases a thousandfold or more. Under these circumstances, the winners will be the companies that learn to use bandwidth as a substitute for computer processing.*
> —George Gilder, *Forbes ASAP*

Bob Metcalf invented Ethernet and cofounded 3Com. George Gilder says that Metcalf's Law of the Telecosm refers to receiving *n* squared potential value when connecting any number of *n* machines in a network. In other words, as corporations exploit the rapidly dropping cost of bandwidth and server-based computing technology to connect users in remote offices, they will realize exceptional, and often unexpected, benefits. The exponential value of Metcalf's Law is not in the additional network links per se, but the myriad different ways in which the new users will use existing corporate information to create new information. Remote-office users can then utilize corporate databases and network resources as if they were working at headquarters. A greater sense of community is enabled throughout the organization, and different divisions can share common information and best practices much more easily.

Law of Supply and Demand

PC-based computing is extraordinarily labor intensive. It is not uncommon for network administrators to spend up to 80 percent of their time solving end-user issues such as hardware failures, deleted icons or INI files, and problems resulting from loading applications or software utilities. This has resulted in a shortage of network administrators relative to the demand for properly skilled labor, which in turn has created a rapid escalation of salaries for IT personnel. Just obtaining a valued certification such as becoming a Microsoft Certified Systems Engineer (MCSE) can easily add $10,000 to an administrator's salary. The rising cost of networking talent makes the huge administration savings obtained from server-based computing even more attractive.

A server-based computing environment requires far fewer network administrators than does the PC-based computing alternative. Server-based computing virtually eliminates the need for time-consuming desktop troubleshooting. System administrators no longer have to handle the same desktop problems over and over again. The ability to standardize on all applications makes application troubleshooting easier as well. Administrators can also "shadow" a user's session, which lets them see and control the user's PC screen, mouse, and keyboard.

Rather than spending the majority of their time on unpleasant, unchallenging, and unrewarding end-user support issues, administrators can now have the time to work on implementing more interesting technologies such as e-commerce and workflow. This helps IT managers retain good administrators while making their organizations more efficient and competitive.

Corporate ASP Concerns

When considering implementation of a Corporate ASP, it is important to address concerns about network infrastructure reliability and single points of failure. We have also discussed Corporate ASPs as if the only option were to utilize both Microsoft Terminal Services and Citrix MetaFrame software. We need to address concerns about using only these technologies.

Network Unreliability

The Corporate ASP may be a new concept for your organization, but it is dependent upon your existing network infrastructure. It is senseless to take on a Corporate ASP project unless your organization is willing to make the necessary investment to bring your network infrastructure up to an extremely reliable and stable condition.

A history of network unreliability may have created the perception that users require their own departmental servers or must keep applications on their local hard drives to enable continued productivity in the event of network failure. In reality, users are becoming so dependent upon network applications, such as e-mail and browsing, that network failure means a loss of productivity in any case. Beyond this misperception, it is more prudent to spend a smaller amount of corporate resources building a redundant and reliable network than it is to devote a large amount of resources to maintaining an extremely inefficient PC-based contingency plan. Server-based computing saves so much money on the client side that organizations should easily have the financial resources required to build world-class data centers and network infrastructures.

Single Point of Failure

Concentrating all of your former PC-based computing into a central data center leaves your remote offices, in particular, exposed to potential downtime risks that they formerly did not face. These risks can be partially mitigated by building reliability and redundancy into the data center that go well beyond anything the remote offices could do on their own. Establishing a secondary redundant data center enables remote offices to continue working even in the event of a major catastrophe at the main production data center. In a PC-based computing environment, the remote offices are extremely unlikely to have access to a redundant "hot site" that could enable their users to keep working should their own server setup meet with disaster. Finally, redundant bandwidth connections should be implemented to enable at least key remote-office employees to keep working in the event of a communications failure. These topics are discussed more thoroughly in Chapters 5 and 6.

Everything Is Going Web Based Anyway

Software manufacturers are increasingly writing Web-based interfaces to their applications that may eventually obviate the need for a traditional Terminal Services/MetaFrame hosting environment. Today, however, it is a Windows world. Most users prefer the dynamic and robust Windows interface to the static Web-server HTML interface. Additionally, a browser requires a deceptively fat client in order to accommodate complex Java scripts and browser plug-ins.

Citrix is committed to deploying all applications effectively through a thin client. It makes more sense to invest in server-based computing technology that will work for both Windows and Web-based applications, than it does to continue investing in a bloated PC-based architecture that is inefficient today and will be even more inefficient in the future.

Microsoft Is Going to Make MetaFrame Obsolete

As with other Microsoft independent software vendors (ISVs), the challenge for Citrix is to continue adding value to Terminal Services. Thus far, they have unquestionably succeeded. Constructing an enterprise server-based computing environment today without benefiting from the load balancing, application publishing, management utilities, and many other MetaFrame enhancements would be both impractical and unwise. MetaFrame and the accompanying Citrix support are an integral part of any serious Corporate ASP. If, in the future, Microsoft or some other vendor makes MetaFrame unnecessary, then only the software investment is lost. Although the cost of the MetaFrame software is not insignificant, it pales in comparison to the savings that will be realized from implementing a Corporate ASP.

A Corporate ASP is a serious and complex undertaking utilizing relatively new technology on constantly changing platforms. It is imperative that sacrifices not be made in the quality of the data center and networking infrastructure. This is also true for the MetaFrame component. Delaying the decision to implement a Corporate ASP in order to see what the future may bring means the continuation of huge unnecessary expenditures in the present.

COMPONENTS OF A CORPORATE ASP

A Corporate ASP has three major components: one or more data centers, clients (at both headquarters and at remote offices and possibly at home offices), and wide area network connectivity.

Data Center

The data center is the heart of a corporate ASP. Not only are all server-based computing applications and corresponding data hosted in the data center, but 100 percent of the application processing occurs within the data center as well. The major data center components include the MetaFrame server farm, file servers and/or Storage Area Network (SAN) systems, other application servers, host systems, a fast server backbone, and a backup system. Figure 1-4 shows a sample data center running a Corporate ASP.

MetaFrame Server Farm

Application execution occurs on the servers running Microsoft Terminal Services and Citrix MetaFrame. Because of the high demands made on these servers as well as the challenges involved in configuring them to run multiple applications without DLL conflicts or other problems, it is prudent to utilize at least two load-balanced servers at all times in a Corporate ASP environment. The MetaFrame load-balancing software is recommended over other solutions because of its ability to share server resources while providing good redundancy. If a user should be disconnected from the server, when she logs back in, MetaFrame load-balancing software will find the server in the farm where the user's session is running and reconnect her to it. Note that data is never stored on the MetaFrame servers. Data is always stored on back-end file servers, application servers, or SAN systems.

File Servers

The file server or servers run a network operating system such as NT or Novell. The servers feed files to the MetaFrame server farm, maintain directory services, and sometimes handle printing functions. For larger Corporate ASPs, a separate high-end print server should be dedicated to handle the printing function, as described in Chapter 17. NT or Novell servers have less overall performance demands than the Terminal Services/MetaFrame server farm, which must run multiple simultaneous applications, but it is still a good idea to build in redundancy and utilize multiple clustered file servers. This topic is discussed more thoroughly in Chapter 7.

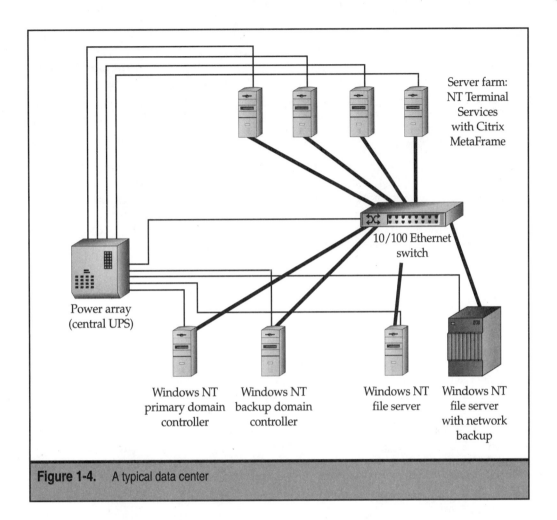

Figure 1-4.   A typical data center

Storage Area Networks and Network-Attached Storage Systems

A Storage Area Network (SAN) can include clustered file servers, RAID arrays connected through a controlling server, or any storage scheme that relies on a host to pass data and control traffic. A Network-Attached Storage (NAS) device is disk storage that connects directly to a network via a LAN interface such as Ethernet or FDDI. Popular SAN devices include products by companies such as Hewlett-Packard, IBM, and EMC. NAS vendors include Network Appliance and EMC. Either SAN or NAS enable very fast data access, and many models have storage capacity measured in terabytes. Since most, if not all, of the organization's data will be hosted in the data center, such a storage scheme is often essential. In some Corporate ASPs, a SAN or NAS will supplement the file servers, allowing organizations to store and access large amounts of data more efficiently. In others, the SAN or NAS may take the place of clustered back-end file servers and still provide mainframe-like reliability and redundancy along with superior performance and scalability. The best solution for your organization depends on both your application environment and user file-sharing needs. This topic is discussed more thoroughly in Chapter 7.

Application Servers

The rule of thumb is to have your MetaFrame server farm located wherever your data is stored. E-mail servers, SQL database servers, and all other application servers ideally should be located within the data center. At a minimum, they must be connected to the file servers and MetaFrame server farm through a very fast backbone. In a server- based computing environment, the MetaFrame server farm is hosting virtual NT desktops for users throughout the organization. While users see only screen prints of the applications at their workstations or Windows terminals, real data is traveling back and forth between the MetaFrame server farm and the file servers and application servers. An inadequate server backbone will cause an immediate data traffic jam that will result in performance degradation for all users.

Host Systems

Mainframe and minicomputer systems should be housed in the data center where they can be managed along with the Terminal Services hosting infrastructure. This enables organizations to leverage both their data center environmental resources and their support staffs.

Server Backbone

A very fast backbone should connect the MetaFrame server farm, the back-end file servers, and all other servers in the data center. This backbone should be either switched 100MB Ethernet, FDDI, ATM, or switched gigabit Ethernet. As with all data center components, a redundant server backbone is desirable. This topic is discussed more thoroughly in Chapter 6.

Backup System

A backup system should enable automatic backups of all servers. Tapes should be rotated off-site. Remote electronic data backups by companies such as Evault can add still another layer of redundant data protection. This topic is discussed more thoroughly in Chapter 7.

Number of Data Centers

The number of data centers utilized depends upon many variables, including bandwidth availability and business and geographic segregation. For instance, if a corporation's European operations utilize entirely different software than the U.S. businesses, and bandwidth is expensive between the continents, separate data centers make more sense than a single, central one. In general, though, savings will be greater when data centers are fewer. This is a result of the economies of scale realized by centralizing as much server-based computing hardware, software, and administration labor as possible. This topic will be discussed more thoroughly in Chapter 5.

Data Center Redundancy

A single data center, despite internal redundancy, leaves a corporation's headquarters and remote operations vulnerable to a single point of failure. One strategy for mitigating this risk is to utilize multiple data centers with fail-over capabilities. Another strategy is to use one corporate data center, and then contract with a disaster recovery provider to maintain a geographically distant facility that mirrors the MetaFrame farm and other crucial components of the corporate data center. This topic is discussed more thoroughly in Chapter 5.

Clients

Corporate ASP users will often work at headquarters, at remote offices, and at home. At times, they will be in hotels or at customer sites. They will utilize PCs, laptops, Windows terminals, and handheld devices. Increasingly, they will use specialty display devices that incorporate the Citrix ICA protocol to take advantage of the inexpensive computing capabilities provided by server-based computing. Clients are covered in Chapters 8 and 11.

Personal Computers

PC users can access applications hosted at the data center in multiple ways. When PCs have a full-time connection to the data center (through Ethernet frame relay or the Internet), MetaFrame enables application publishing. Employees see icons of both local applications (if any) and applications hosted on the MetaFrame server farm to which they have access. These icons can be part of their start-up file, and it is not obvious whether they represent local applications or applications hosted by the server farm. Users who run all applications from the server farm may receive their entire desktop as a published application. The lower the number of local applications accessed by a PC user, the less administration costs are borne by the IT staff. This topic is discussed more thoroughly in Chapter 16.

Laptops

Laptops typically run local applications when disconnected from the network. When connected to the network by a dial-up connection, laptop users will commonly launch a MetaFrame desktop. Extra training will help ensure that laptop users do not confuse local applications with hosted applications. We have found that many employees of companies with Corporate ASPs end up abandoning laptops except when on planes or in motels. They find it less cumbersome to simply use a PC or Windows terminal at both the office and at home.

Windows Terminals

Nearly every major PC manufacturer, including Hewlett-Packard, IBM, Compaq, and Dell, now makes Windows terminals. Many specialty companies, including Maxspeed, Netier, Boundless, Boca, and market leader Wyse Technology, focus on building Windows terminals. Figure 1-5 shows two popular Windows terminals: Wyse on the left and IBM on the right. Windows terminals are typically display devices with no moving parts of any kind. Some models have no local operating system and boot right to the Citrix ICA client. Others utilize Windows CE, a version of Windows NT, or even LINUX. Increasingly, Windows terminals have built-in local host emulation and, sometimes, browsing in order to off-load these character display functions from the MetaFrame server farm.

Because Windows terminals tend to have mean times between failure measured in decades, their maintenance expense is extremely low. If a Windows terminal does fail, IT simply delivers a replacement unit to the user. The user plugs in the Windows terminal, turns it on, and sees his or her desktop. Windows terminals significantly reduce the cost of supporting telecommuters. Unlike PCs, Windows terminals do not allow users to destroy their unit configuration by loading games or screen savers or other potentially damaging software. This makes the Windows terminal a particularly ideal device for telecommuters who may have families that like to share any personal computers in the home. Windows terminals are discussed more thoroughly in Chapter 11.

Figure 1-5. Windows terminal setups by Wyse (left) and IBM (right)

Other ICA Clients

Most UNIX workstations and Macintoshes can access MetaFrame servers by running the Citrix ICA client. Many handheld units such as Hewlett-Packard's Jornada and Symbol System's modified Palm Pilot are capable of running an ICA client. Manufacturers such as Compaq are building wireless laptops that run only as an ICA connection to a MetaFrame server farm.

Increasingly, expect to see manufacturers come up with specialty ICA devices. For instance, a time clock system could be built as a Windows terminal using buttons instead of a keyboard. Employee time stamping could then be directly entered into the corporation's Windows-based time and billing system.

Using a Browser Interface

As the Internet's pervasiveness continues to grow, more organizations prefer to utilize browser interfaces. With MetaFrame, organizations can use their browser to launch published applications from the server farm. MetaFrame's NFuse feature also enables an organization's customers to launch authorized applications through a browser. For example, a MetaFrame-enhanced browser interface enables users to launch Windows applications from the browser. Different users with different logins will see different applications. This topic is discussed more thoroughly in Chapter 8.

Wide Area Network Connectivity

MetaFrame requires between 10KB and 20KB of bandwidth per user session. This does not include additional bandwidth for large print jobs or for downloading or uploading files to and from a fat-client PC. When remote office applications are hosted at a corporate data center, they are completely dependent upon access to the MetaFrame servers for all of their processing. A Corporate ASP must include both adequate and reliable bandwidth connections along with redundant contingencies.

A frame-relay circuit is probably the most popular connectivity method to multiple remote offices, though organizations increasingly utilize virtual private networks or straight Internet connectivity. Telecommuters, in particular, are using inexpensive fixed-fee Internet accounts to connect to corporate data centers. Bandwidth management is often desirable in order to prioritize ICA traffic. Bandwidth management devices from manufacturers such as Packeteer, NetReality, Cisco, and Sitrara Networks will prevent a user's large print job or file download, for example, from killing performance for the remaining users at a remote office. This topic is discussed more thoroughly in Chapter 6.

DESIGNING A CORPORATE ASP

A successful Corporate ASP implementation depends upon a comprehensive project design. A detailed and in-depth plan needs to address all aspects of the server-based computing migration, including data centers, disaster recovery, bandwidth, systems management, policies and procedures, security, applications, migration strategies, clients, and support. Unanticipated problems will occur even with the best-laid plans. Diligent work up front, though, will minimize any potential for big disasters and help ensure a successful implementation.

Installing a Corporate ASP is like putting in a mainframe system with the additional headache of a potentially less stable platform. Terminal Services may be far more desirable and even more stable than a distributed PC-based computing environment, but it requires much effort to match the reliability commonly found on mature host platforms such as Hewlett-Packard's HP/9000 or IBM's AS/400. PC users are often particularly unforgiving of server-based computing problems because they are initially reluctant to give up the "personal" part of their personal computers.

The considerable technical and cultural challenges make in-depth project planning absolutely essential to a successful Corporate ASP implementation. The first step is to set up a proof-of-concept pilot to ensure that the crucial applications will run acceptably within a server-based computing environment. Next, assemble a project planning team to prepare a project definition document. The definition document will include the project goals, scope, roles, risks, success criteria, and milestones. The third step involves a comprehensive infrastructure assessment that will both ensure support for a Corporate ASP implementation and enable a meaningful planning process. Finally, a comprehensive design plan for migrating from a PC-based to a server-based computing environment will serve as a roadmap for the project managers and implementation teams. These steps are covered more thoroughly in Chapter 4.

ABM INDUSTRIES' CORPORATE ASP IMPLEMENTATION

Deploying JD Edwards in our fat-client PC environment would have been prohibitively expensive. The tremendous cost advantages of a Corporate ASP enabled us to deploy all applications and networking services to our users around the country, even to those working in small offices or at customer facilities. We replaced our disparate and often overlapping regional IT processing with a unified corporate IT department and approach.

—Anthony Lackey,
VP Electronic Services and CTO, ABM Industries

According to Citrix, ABM Industries was the first Fortune 1000 company to deploy a Corporate ASP for all of its users throughout the enterprise. With annualized revenues in excess of $1.6 billion and more than 55,000 employees, ABM provides outsourced facility services to thousands of customers in hundreds of cities across North America. Management had decided to implement the client-server version of JD Edwards' One World accounting system for all divisions. This would have required upgrading hundreds of PCs and many remote-office bandwidth connections. In addition, the company had nearly 1,000 PCs that were non-Y2K compliant. Rather than continue the endless spiral of PC upgrades, Anthony Lackey, then Director of Information Technology, built a strong case for embracing server-based computing throughout the enterprise.

ABM's rollout began only after months of in-depth design, planning, and pilot testing. They moved their data center from a San Francisco high-rise to a hosting facility that offered the advantages of high security and access to a much broader communications infrastructure. A redundant data center hot site was set up in New Jersey as part of a disaster recovery contract with a business continuity firm.

Thirty top-end Quad Xeon MetaFrame servers in the data center support over 2,000 concurrent users at headquarters and across the country. A Cisco gigabit backbone connects the MetaFrame server farm and other servers. All users store their personal and shared files on a Network Appliance filer—a Network-Attached Storage device. More than a terabyte of information is stored on this virtual NT file server. Eighty percent of ABM's users work on Wyse WinTerms, while the rest use a mix of laptops and desktop computers running the Citrix ICA client software. Figure 1-6 shows a schematic of the ABM Corporate ASP.

ABM Industries performed a detailed and conservative cost analysis that projected minimum five-year savings of $19 million from switching their first 2,500 users to server-based computing. The ABM Industries project will be referenced throughout the book as a case study showing the technical and cultural implications of migrating a large organization entirely to server-based computing.

ABM is hardly alone in its enthusiasm for server-based computing as the corporate standard. At the September 1999 Citrix iForum user conference in Orlando, Florida, the CIO of Federal Express, Rod Carter, gave a keynote speech. He announced that Federal Express was up to 6,000 thin-client users and planned to be at 20,000 by the end of the year.

The excitement in this new, exploding industry was evident at iForum. By the end of 1999, 100 percent of the Fortune 100 firms and over 80 percent of the Fortune 500 used Citrix software. As organizations embrace server-based computing on an enterprise scale, they significantly lower the cost of their IT infrastructure while enhancing their data processing capabilities. This gives them an advantage over competitors still mired in cumbersome and expensive PC-based computing environments.

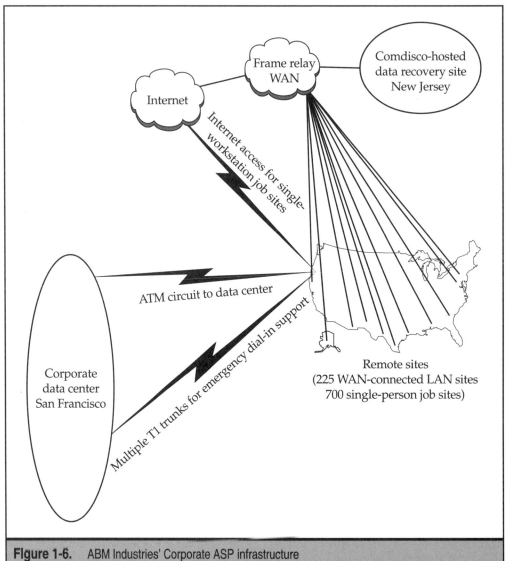

Figure 1-6.   ABM Industries' Corporate ASP infrastructure

CHAPTER 2

Citrix MetaFrame

Metaframe is a complementary product to the MultiWin-enhanced Microsoft operating system products. MetaFrame goes well beyond the basic function set provided in TSE and Windows 2000. It adds significant features to the MultiWin technology that facilitate its use within heterogeneous computing environments for application delivery across bandwidth-restricted connections to a broad diversity of clients.

In this chapter we discuss the evolution of the MetaFrame product and dissect its Independent Computing Architecture (ICA) protocol. We also cover the enhancements that MetaFrame brings to Terminal Services, including

▼ Application publishing

■ Enhanced administration capabilities

■ Universal access to applications, regardless of client type

■ Support for application load balancing

■ Support for enterprise-class application services

▲ The ability to act as an application portal via browsers

THE EVOLUTION OF METAFRAME

Many people have observed that the Microsoft NT operating system developed from a single-user operating system architecture and continued, for nearly a decade, to be limited in certain applications by that fact. NT provided real-time multiprocessing capabilities comparable to those of rival UNIX operating systems, but did not provide functions within its OS kernel to support concurrent multiuser access to applications hosted on NT platforms.

Given the dominant business computing architecture of the late 1980s and early 1990s, which featured increasingly capable desktop computers (so-called *fat-client* PCs) that provided much of the processing of client-server applications, it may well be that the need for multiuser computing platforms (similar in concept to mainframe computing environments) was not of primary concern to Microsoft designers. In Microsoft's preferred computing model, information processing was conceived as inherently distributed and individualized: desktop computers were viewed as "peers" of server platforms. In fact, most early server host systems were little more than highly configured PCs, typically featuring many of the same hardware components.

There was an interest in some niche areas for a server platform that would "host" applications and share them among several connected client devices, configured as dumb terminals. One such application was remote access: a technique by which one or more off-site users could access an application located on a corporate local area network (LAN). Ideally, the remote user would be able to perform useful work as though seated at a terminal directly attached to the LAN.

However, the mainstream architecture for business computing did not involve shared application use. Instead, a combination of Windows-based desktop computers, emphasizing locally stored and executed individual applications, and UNIX- or NT-based servers (or both) interconnected via a LAN, supporting client-server computing, dominated the scene.

Multiuser Windows—MultiWin

The idea behind server-based computing on Windows NT can be traced to the X Window System developed by MIT in 1984. By utilizing powerful UNIX servers, remote X Window clients can send keyboard and mouse input to server-based applications running on central servers. The X Window System on the server then tracks output from the applications and updates the appropriate remote client session.

The founder and chairman of Citrix Systems, Ed Iacobucci, originally conceived the idea of allowing different types of computers to run the same applications, even though they might not have the same operating system or adequate local resources. While working as head of the joint Microsoft/IBM design team on the OS/2 project, he approached both companies with the idea, but neither firm was interested. Iacobucci then formed Citrix Systems in 1989, and the technology behind the current Terminal Services was developed—MultiWin. MultiWin rode on top of the OS/2 kernel and allowed multiple simultaneous OS/2 sessions and desktops in a protected memory area for each individual user.

WinView

In 1993, Citrix shipped its first OS/2-based multiuser operating system, called WinView. WinView used the MultiWin technology and one of the first incarnations of a remote display client, called Independent Computing Architecture (ICA). Citrix first worked to deliver multiuser extensions to the OS/2 operating system and subsequently worked on the delivery of applications across Novell and TCP/IP networks. Despite prevailing personal and client-server computing models, developers at Citrix believed that multiuser computing had a future, especially as applications moved off the desktop and "into the network." They convinced Microsoft that a market for multiuser NT could be cultivated and secured a license to add multiuser extensions to the NT operating system.

WinFrame

Whether or not Microsoft shared the Citrix Systems vision of the future, the license agreement was certainly a "win-win" for Microsoft. With the multiuser extensions provided by Citrix in the form of WinFrame, Microsoft would be able to answer criticisms from UNIX advocates regarding a purported "deficiency" of its server operating systems: they provided little or no support for multiuser computing requirements. If Citrix visionaries were correct, and a market for multiuser computing platforms could be cultivated, Microsoft would have a solution to offer that market.

Citrix WinFrame is a combination of Microsoft Windows NT 3.51 Server and Citrix MultiWin technology. WinFrame was a major upgrade to the OS/2-based WinView. At the time of its release, Windows 3.1 (and later, Windows 95) had become the desktop standard, and WinFrame surpassed WinView as a tool for installing and executing the standard corporate end-user applications.

Thin-Client Computing

In the mid-1990s, the case for multiuser NT was reinforced by the findings of analysts such as the Gartner Group regarding the total cost of ownership of Windows PCs. Analysts claimed that fat-client PCs cost firms between $7,000 and $13,000 per PC per year in maintenance and support. This position touched off a firestorm of industry activity, mainly from longtime Microsoft rivals. The so-called SONIA set—an acronym for Sun Microsystems, Oracle Corporation, Netscape Communications, IBM, and Apple Corporation—led the charge to displace Microsoft PCs from corporate desktops, substituting their own "network computer" in its place. Despite the obvious self-interest inherent in the SONIA value proposition, and the subsequent failure of the network computer to take hold in the market, the underlying tenet of the SONIA argument took hold. The Citrix concept of *thin-client computing* was introduced to the lexicon of modern business computing.

Thin-client computing advocates held that, as server capabilities grew, it was only natural for server hosts to become "fatter" and for desktop platforms to become "thinner." Application software, advocates argued, should reside on application servers, rather than individual PCs. Placing applications on a server would make them accessible by means of a variety of inexpensive client devices. The advent of the Internet and World Wide Web at about the same time reinforced this perspective. Many people adopted a view of computing in which all applications would be accessed via a universal, hardware-agnostic client such as a Web browser.

Citrix Systems Synonymous with Thin

Citrix Systems, with its Independent Computing Architecture, emerged from the discussion of thin computing as the undisputed leader in a market it had long helped to facilitate. In an ICA-based solution, WinFrame-based application servers could host Windows-compliant applications, while end users, equipped with any of a broad range of client devices (whether network computers or Windows PCs), could access and use the applications over a network connection. Integral to the WinFrame approach was a remote presentation services protocol capable of separating the application's logic from its user interface, so that only keystrokes, mouse clicks, and screen updates would travel the network. With the ICA protocol, Citrix claimed, the user's experience of the server-hosted application would be comparable in all respects to that of an application executing on the end user's own desktop PC.

Terminal Services and MetaFrame

Increased interest in the WinFrame solution encouraged Microsoft to license MultiWin, the core technology of WinFrame, from Citrix Systems in 1997 and to integrate the technology into its own operating systems soon after. As explained in Chapter 3, Microsoft first implemented MultiWin in a special Terminal Services Edition (TSE) of its NT 4.0 OS. The implementation was not completely in accord with Citrix Systems' ICA vision, however.

Microsoft Remote Desktop Protocol (RDP)

A major difference in the TSE implementation of MultiWin was its client system. TSE developers limited the variety of clients that could be connected to the server to Windows PCs and specially designed terminals built to work with the Terminal Server environment. Moreover, the Microsoft Terminal Server Client program used a different protocol from the one used by Citrix ICA—one developed originally for use with Microsoft's NetMeeting, called the Remote Desktop Protocol (RDP). Although standards based (RDP is built on the International Telecommunications Union's (ITU) T.120 protocol), the protocol further narrowed the list of clients that would work with TSE.

Introduction of MetaFrame

Citrix released MetaFrame in 1998 to resolve these issues and to add value to the TSE solution. Unlike WinFrame, which had been a stand-alone product and a "replacement" operating system for NT, MetaFrame was an add-on to the Microsoft NT 4.0 TSE platform. One reason for the MetaFrame product was to continue to meet the needs of WinFrame customers who were interested in migrating their NT 3.51–based WinFrame environments to newer NT 4.0 TSE–based environments but who were afraid of losing application server connections with non-RDP clients. MetaFrame added ICA client and protocol support back into the Microsoft multiuser operating system offering.

From 1998 forward, MetaFrame has been steadily enhanced to work with both NT Server, Terminal Server Edition, and also with Microsoft's Windows 2000 Advanced Servers, which incorporate TSE technology. MetaFrame complements Microsoft NT 4.0 TSE and Windows 2000 Advanced Server functionality with enterprise-class application management capabilities. Native capabilities provided with TSE technology are limited to network and session load management. MetaFrame adds tools for managing where applications reside and the resources they use, and for balancing the application load across "application server farms." MetaFrame also enhances the ability to manage sessions from the user's standpoint—to manage the configuration of sessions so that users enjoy a customized experience.

MetaFrame also provides the means to publish Windows applications to Web pages on intranets and the public Internet. Application access can be delivered directly to the end user via a browser, or to a Web server, where various applications can be combined into an "application portal."

With MetaFrame, access to applications can be provided across a variety of networks, including wide area networks, remote access dial-up connections, local area networks, the Internet, and wireless nets. Over 200 types of clients, including Windows PCs, Windows terminals, UNIX workstations, handheld devices, network computers, and numerous others, are supported as ICA clients. These features improve dramatically on the RDP client support inherent in NT 4.0 TSE and Windows 2000 Advanced Server.

INDEPENDENT COMPUTING ARCHITECTURE (ICA)

Citrix Independent Computing Architecture is restored to Microsoft MultiWin implementations through the use of MetaFrame. To understand more fully what ICA contributes to Microsoft server-based computing, an overview of ICA may be useful.

ICA is an architecture for server-based computing that competes with and/or complements other architectures such as Microsoft's Remote Desktop Protocol (RDP) and Sun Microsystem/X-Open's X Window protocol. What all of these architectures share is a goal to provide a means to extend resources, simplify application deployment and administration, and decrease the total cost of application ownership.

With all of these server-based computing architectures, applications are deployed, managed, supported, and executed completely on a server. Client devices, whether fat or thin, have access to business-critical applications on the server without application rewrites or downloads.

For everything that ICA, RDP, and the X Window System have in common, they vary significantly from each other at the component level. The three primary components of any server-based computing architecture are

▼ A multiuser operating system that allows multiple concurrent users to log on and run applications in logically separate, protected sessions on a single server

■ A remote presentation services protocol that separates application logic from its user interface and provides efficient delivery across a network to client devices

▲ Centralized application and client management utilities that facilitate application deployment, access, performance tuning, and security

The way these component functions are provided by ICA, RDP, and the X Window System differs significantly. Table 2-1 summarizes the differences. Of the three competing approaches, a persuasive argument can be made that the ICA architecture is the most robust. At the server, ICA provides functionality to separate an application's logic from its user interface so that the interface can be efficiently transported to client devices over standard network protocols and popular network connections.

Function	ICA Citrix Systems, Inc.	RDP Microsoft Corp.	X Window System X Consortium
Application server	MS Windows NT Server 4.0 TSE or Windows 2000 Advanced Server, plus MetaFrame: "MetaFrame Application Server."	MS Windows NT Server 4.0 TSE or Windows 2000 Advanced Servers. Terminal Server is an NT or Windows 2000 service.	Numerous UNIX operating systems.

Table 2-1. High-Level Comparison of ICA, RDP, and the X Window System

Function	ICA Citrix Systems, Inc.	RDP Microsoft Corp.	X Window System X Consortium
Presentation services protocol	ICA Network Protocol, which can adapt its performance characteristics to operate efficiently over both high- and low-bandwidth networks (for example, offers compressed mode operation for remote devices connected via low-bandwidth pipes and uncompressed mode operation for locally attached devices). ICA also supports shadowing, which lets an administrator take control of a thin-client device.	Officially protocol independent, but products ship with the Remote Desktop Protocol, an ITU standards–based network protocol. The only supported transport protocol is TCP/IP over WAN, LAN, or remote access networks. According to Microsoft, RDP is tuned for high-bandwidth enterprise networks.	X is optimized for communication via high-bandwidth pipes with locally attached client devices. It does not perform well in remote-computing situations.
Client support	Over 200 clients supported, including 16- and 32-bit Windows PCs, Windows terminals, Windows CE devices, network computers, and a wide range of non-Windows clients. Web browsers are also supported.	Windows 16- and 32-bit PCs and Windows CE devices, including Windows terminals, are the only supported clients. Web browser support promised in upcoming edition (RDP 5.0).	Supports X terminals or emulation clients only. Third-party software is available to extend client support to other devices.

Table 2-1.   High-Level Comparison of ICA, RDP, and the X Window System *(continued)*

ICA Presentation Services Protocol

As depicted in Figure 2-1, the ICA presentation services protocol transports only keystrokes, mouse clicks, and screen updates to the client. The protocol has been demonstrated to consume less than 5 kilobits per second of network bandwidth, enabling even the latest 32-bit applications to be operated remotely across low-bandwidth links while delivering performance comparable to local execution on existing PCs, Windows-based terminals, network computers, and a host of evolving business and personal information appliances.

> *Citrix MetaFrame enables us to deploy Windows applications to our students in both a very cost-effective and expeditious manner. This is true whether they are working on a PC or Windows terminal on campus or working off-site using an Internet connection.*
>
> —Tony Holland,
> Director of Computing Services, Stanford Business School

The performance of applications on the client side can be improved through the replacement of the Remote Desktop Protocol with the ICA protocol. The ICA protocol was designed with low-bandwidth connections in mind, making it a robust performer on both large- and small-capacity links. Moreover, the ICA protocol responds dynamically to changing network, server, and client operating conditions. It takes advantage of network and server resources that are available and adapts automatically when conditions are more restrictive, often without generating any noticeable changes in the end user's experience. Much of the performance of the ICA protocol can be attributed to the use of intelligent caching and data compression techniques, and to technologies such as SpeedScreen.

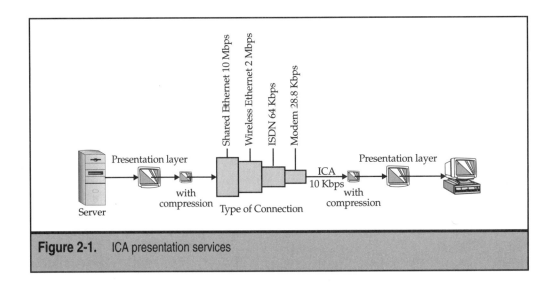

Figure 2-1. ICA presentation services

SpeedScreen

SpeedScreen is a technology for improving the performance of application delivery across ICA links. It accomplishes this by reducing the amount of data that must traverse an ICA connection as an end user interacts with a MetaFrame server-based application. SpeedScreen targets the repainting function of a hosted application. With many applications, entire screens are repainted with each keyboard entry (or mouse click) made by the end user. SpeedScreen uses an intelligent agent technology to compare information previously transmitted to the ICA client with information that is about to be transmitted, then transmits only the changed information. This is visually represented in Figure 2-2. By limiting repaint operations to specific sections of a screen affected by user interaction, the amount of traffic that must traverse the connection is dramatically reduced.

With some applications, bandwidth consumption may be reduced by as much as 30 percent through the implementation of SpeedScreen, while total packets transmitted may be reduced by 60 percent. The result is lower latency in the network and better application performance—especially across low-bandwidth connections—for the end user.

Connectivity Options

A broader range of connectivity options are supported by MetaFrame and ICA than by RDP, so a more diversified set of users can access and utilize hosted applications. Figure 2-3 depicts the connectivity options enabled by ICA, which include dial-up, ISDN, multiple LANs, wireless LANs, numerous WANs, and the Internet. RDP, by contrast, is limited in its support only to TCP/IP LAN environments.

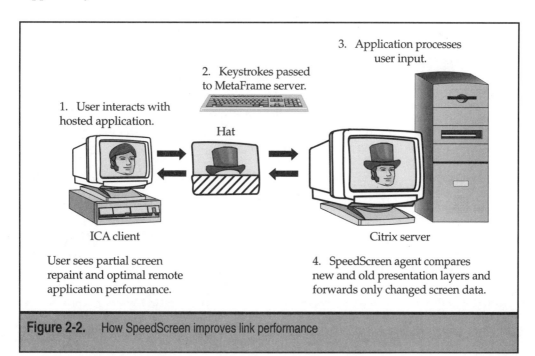

Figure 2-2. How SpeedScreen improves link performance

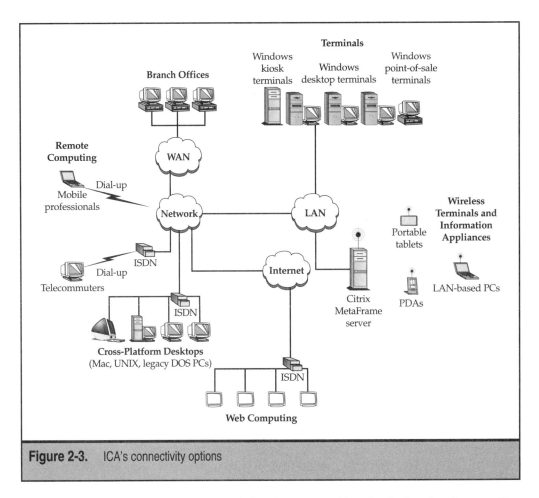

Figure 2-3. ICA's connectivity options

Additionally, using MetaFrame and the ICA protocol breaks the barriers imposed by RDP to extending application access beyond Windows PCs. The ICA protocol supports more than 200 clients, providing flexibility in access options far surpassing that of RDP.

The ICA Client Environment

In addition to the contributions of MetaFrame and the ICA protocol to application delivery performance, MetaFrame also enhances the basic multiuser client-server environment supported by Microsoft through its Windows NT TSE and Windows 2000 products. MetaFrame embodies numerous innovations designed to facilitate a broad range of hosted application environments. Considerable effort has been invested by MetaFrame designers to enable all applications, whether remote or local, to operate and interoperate as though they were local to the end user. This approach increases the user's comfort level and decreases the need for training.

The MetaFrame ICA Desktop

The MetaFrame ICA desktop is designed to provide a user experience that is on a par with a Windows PC running locally installed and executed applications. MetaFrame enables complete access to all local system resources, such as full 16-bit stereo audio, local drives, COM ports, and local printers, if available.

The mapping of local resources can be performed automatically or by means of administrative utilities. Specialized client capabilities such as modem dial-up are also supported.

Additionally, mapped resources can be shared with the MetaFrame server, if desired. Configuration of these mappings is built into the standard Windows NT device redirection facilities. The client mappings appear as another network that presents the client devices as share points to which a drive letter or printer port can be attached.

Seamless Window

Of course, not all MetaFrame implementations utilize a full-fledged "remote desktop" model (one in which there are no applications locally installed on the client). Indeed, in many environments where MetaFrame is deployed, clients are themselves Windows PCs configured to provide a mixture of some locally installed applications and some remotely hosted applications. Seamless Window is a feature of MetaFrame designed to accommodate this scenario.

Seamless Window is a shorthand expression referring to the capability of the Citrix ICA Win32 client to support the integration of local and remote applications on the local Windows 95, Windows 98, or Windows NT 4.0 desktop. When configuring a connection to the MetaFrame server, an administrator or user can simply select the Seamless Window option to enable this function.

With Seamless Window, the user can gain access to hosted applications without having to load a remote desktop environment. While connected in a MetaFrame server session, the user can gain access to local applications using the Windows task bar. Icons for both local and remote applications can be installed on the local Windows desktop, and both local and remote application windows can be cascaded on the local desktop.

Multiple Keyboards   The Seamless Window environment supports the definition of multiple keyboards to facilitate command entry in local and remote application environments. This prevents specially mapped key combinations used by MetaFrame (such as ALT+TAB) from interfering with similar key combinations used by locally executing applications.

Windows Clipboard   Seamless Window supports the use of the Windows clipboard in conjunction with both local and MetaFrame-hosted applications. Users can cut, copy, and paste information between applications running remotely on the server or locally from the desktop. Rich text format cut-and-paste is fully supported.

TIP: The local/remote clipboard is part of MetaFrame's overall solution set. It can be used independently of Seamless Window or Program Neighborhood.

Program Neighborhood

Building on the concept of a Seamless Window environment, MetaFrame also delivers an easy-to-use method for accessing remotely hosted applications. Similar in concept to the Microsoft Windows Network Neighborhood, MetaFrame pushes links to published applications into a client-based Program Neighborhood facility.

In operation, Program Neighborhood presents application sets to MetaFrame client users. An *application set* is a user's view of the applications published on a given MetaFrame server or server farm, which that user is authorized to access. A single user-authentication operation (usually launched when the user launches either the Program Neighborhood or a MetaFrame-hosted application displayed in the Start menu or as an icon on the local desktop) identifies the user to all MetaFrame servers. Based on the user's individual or group account parameters, the Program Neighborhood is populated with an application set containing each application configured for the specific user account or user group. Published applications appear as icons and are preconfigured with such properties as session window size and colors and supported level of encryption, audio, and video appropriate to the user and his or her client device.

Program Neighborhood technology is especially useful as a means to publish hosted applications quickly that are intended for use by groups of users. Users can click on the Program Neighborhood icon on their Windows desktop (or click on the corresponding entry in their Windows Start menu) to review a list of hosted applications that are available for use. No special client configuration is required to launch and use these published applications.

Management Features

From a client management perspective, MetaFrame brings to the administrative tool kit the Automatic ICA Client Update utility and a tool to facilitate rapid application deployment, ReadyConnect. Together, these features can save administrators many hours of tedious client configuration tasks.

The Automatic ICA Client Update utility provides the means to update Citrix ICA client software centrally, from the MetaFrame server itself. The latest versions of ICA client software are identified by the administrator, who then uses the update tool to schedule download and installation on appropriate client devices. This utility reduces the need to travel from client to client throughout the enterprise in order to install and configure the latest version of ICA client software. With it, organizations will realize greater levels of cost efficiency and reduced cost of administration and ownership.

ReadyConnect enables client connections to be predefined at the server. By capturing ICA client connection data, including phone numbers, IP addresses, server names, and other connection options, applications can be mass deployed throughout the enterprise with speed and agility. Users can access applications across predefined connection points through a simple point-and-click operation.

ICA Browser Management

MetaFrame provides enterprise-class stability to application servers and server farms through its ICA browser management functionality. This is explained in greater detail in Chapter 6, but a brief discussion is included here.

In ICA terminology, *browsing* refers to a technique for exchanging information about servers, applications, links, and clients and for keeping this data synchronized between devices participating in a server-centric computing architecture. In other words, browsing is the glue that holds the ICA infrastructure together. Without it, efficient server-based computing would be impossible.

Every MetaFrame server runs the ICA browser service. One MetaFrame server is "elected" the master browser, while all other MetaFrame servers on the network are member browsers. The details of this election process are provided in Chapter 15. In operation, the ICA browser service on each MetaFrame server uses directed packets to communicate with other ICA browser services running on all other MetaFrame servers.

The master browser maintains a comprehensive browse list and periodically obtains updates from the member browsers on other MetaFrame servers in the same network. If MetaFrame servers are deployed on multiple networks, each network, as defined by its transport protocol (TCP/IP, IPX, and NetBIOS), has its own master browser.

The master browser acts as a central information store within its MetaFrame server network. ICA clients must locate the master browser to get the address of a server or published application. The ICA client can locate the master browser by sending out broadcast packets. Alternatively, if the address of a MetaFrame server is specified in the Citrix ICA client software itself, or in an ICA file, the ICA client locates the master browser by sending directed packets to the specified address. The ICA client requests the address of the master browser from any MetaFrame member browser service.

During application session operations, ICA clients query the master browser service to obtain a list of MetaFrame servers and published applications. When an application is launched by a client, the browser service acts behind the scenes to provide necessary information for selecting the server host and accessing the hosted application. MetaFrame servers also use the ICA browser service to pool licenses and share administrative and performance information.

Typically, little intervention is required for ICA browsing to work efficiently. However, MetaFrame provides a master browser manager so that administrators can control certain operating parameters in browser operations. With the manager, administrators can dictate which server is the master server. They can also set the locations for backup ICA browsers and ICA gateways (see the next section), and change update and refresh intervals for browser data collection operations. Administrators can also configure which servers will attempt to become the master browser. The master browser manager interface is intuitive and easy to use.

As previously stated, each physical network of MetaFrame servers has one master browser. If the current master browser on a network ceases operation, a new master browser election is held, and a new browser service is dubbed the master browser. This comparatively simple process helps to provide high reliability for the ICA browser service within a network.

However, in a growing number of MetaFrame implementations, MetaFrame servers reside on different networks within the enterprise. Each has its own master browser. Providing access to applications on different networks could prove to be a difficult proposition if it were not for ICA gateways.

ICA Gateways

An ICA gateway enables MetaFrame servers or ICA clients to communicate with MetaFrame servers on a different network. The ICA gateway, described in greater detail in Chapter 15, enables the master browsers on different networks to share information about available MetaFrame servers and published applications. Information about established ICA gateways is stored in each master browser service. This redundancy helps to provide resiliency should one master browser service cease operation.

To enable ICA gateways to work correctly, network routers must pass ICA browser traffic between subnets. ICA gateways on TCP/IP networks use directed UDP datagrams to port 1604. Routers on TCP/IP networks must be configured to route UDP datagrams between network subnets. For ICA gateways to function on IPX networks, routers must be configured to route raw IPX packets.

The MetaFrame master browser manager provides administrators with the means to configure both ICA gateways and backup ICA gateways for optimized operation. Once established, ICA gateways will automatically adapt to changes, such as new master browser elections.

LOAD BALANCING

Load balancing is a concept familiar to many administrators of Microsoft Terminal Service Edition servers, but it has a special meaning in the context of MetaFrame server operation. To see the differences, a quick review of Microsoft's Network Load Balancing is appropriate.

With Microsoft's NT Server 4.0 TSE and Windows 2000 operating systems, multiuser computing capabilities are viewed as a service, much like SQL services or SNA services. Due to this orientation, Microsoft's approach to balancing system load across multiple servers focuses less on the nature and requirements of the load itself (application sessions in the case of multiuser computing) than on the distribution of the session load across multiple systems. In effect, clients are presented with a virtual IP address representing multiple servers with replicated resources and services. As each server reaches a load threshold, incoming client session requests are forwarded to a server with available resources. Approximately 32 servers can be included in a load-balancing strategy, facilitating between 125 to 500 users on each 500MHz, four-CPU server system.

MetaFrame takes load balancing from the server level to the application level. Citrix adds features such as automatic session reconnection and enhanced manageability to TSE services, fine-tuning the concept of load balancing considerably.

With MetaFrame load balancing, an application can be published for execution on any or all MetaFrame servers in a server farm. When an application or desktop session that has been configured for multiple servers is launched by an ICA client, MetaFrame load balancing selects which server will run the application based on a set of tunable parameters. Administrators have access to load-balancing tunables—essentially the calculations used by the ICA browser to determine server loads—via a Load Balancing Administration utility.

Load Balancing Administration Utility

Administrators can use the Load Balancing Administration utility to set basic load-balancing parameters such as the number of users on a system that represents full utilization of the system. Administrators can also set a weight governing the importance of user load characteristics in load-balancing calculations.

For a finer level of granularity in load-balancing management, the utility provides a set of graphical slide switches for setting the relative weights or importance of factors such as

▼ **Pagefile usage**   The ratio of the current pagefile size to the allowed minimum free space left in the pagefile.

■ **Swap activity**   The number of times per second the pagefile is accessed.

■ **Processor usage**   The percentage of time the server processor is busy.

■ **Memory load**   The ratio of available memory to total physical memory on the server.

■ **Sessions**   The ratio of total configured ICA connections to free ICA connections.

▲ **Overall adjustment**   The overall calculated load of a server. By default, this is set at no adjustment, but it can be raised or lowered.

Using these slide switches, administrators adjust the importance of each factor. A factor's setting determines how much its load influences the overall system load calculation relative to the other factors. For example, if User Load is set to "Very Important" and all other factors are set to "Not Important," the User Load calculation will be the sole factor used to determine overall system load.

Importance settings are accorded equal status in MetaFrame load-balancing calculations. Raising the importance of one factor does not influence how important any other factor is in the overall calculation. For example, if each factor is set at the same importance rating, all factors are given the same weight.

Load Balancing in a Mixed Citrix Environment

MetaFrame load balancing supports mixing WinFrame 1.7 or later and MetaFrame servers in a single server farm. Applications that are intended to be load balanced must be installed on each server in the server farm, and they must be designated as load-balanced applications at the time they are published on the MetaFrame environment (see the next section).

NOTE: Sessions that use RDP are not counted for the User Load or Sessions calculations. If Citrix MetaFrame ICA and Microsoft RDP connections are mixed in the same server environment, servers should be configured to use advanced factors such as Processor Usage and Memory Load to calculate load levels.

Of course, load balancing presumes the existence of a load to balance. The load in server-based computing is defined in terms of application sessions: users access server-hosted applications across a data communications link.

APPLICATION PUBLISHING

Application publishing refers to the installation and configuration of applications on a multiuser server (or server farm) so they can be accessed readily by users. MetaFrame enhances the basic application publishing capabilities of TSE by providing a Published Application Manager to facilitate the process of fielding an application.

The objective of the Published Application Manager is not only to ease the burden of administrators, but also to shield users from the complexities of setting up applications for use on their clients. When an application is published using the Published Application Manager utility, user access is simplified in three ways:

▼ **Application addressing** Instead of connecting to a MetaFrame server by its IP address or server name, users can connect to a specific application by whatever name has been assigned to the application itself. Connecting to applications by name eliminates the need for users to remember which servers contain which applications.

■ **Application navigation** With applications published under MetaFrame, the user does not need to possess knowledge of the Windows NT 4.0 or Windows 2000 desktop (Windows NT Explorer or Program Manager) to find and start applications after connecting to MetaFrame servers. Instead, published applications present the user with the desired application in an ICA session.

▲ **User authentication** Instead of logging on and logging off multiple MetaFrame servers to access applications, Program Neighborhood allows users to authenticate themselves a single time to all servers and obtain immediate access to all applications configured for their user group or specific user name. Also, publishing applications for the special Anonymous user group allows user authentication processes to be eliminated completely. This can be a useful time-saver when publishing applications for general use by all users on the network.

User Accounts

The publishing of an application using MetaFrame usually begins with the consideration, not of the application itself, but of the users who will operate the application once it is published. MetaFrame application publishing provides ICA session access to two types of user accounts: anonymous and explicit.

The total number of users, whether anonymous or explicit, who can be logged onto the MetaFrame server at the same time is contingent upon an organization's licensed user count and on server and link limitations. These limitations need to be clearly understood before proceeding with application publishing.

Anonymous User Accounts

During MetaFrame installation, the Setup program creates a special user group called "Anonymous." By default, this Windows NT user group contains 15 user accounts with account user names in the format Anon000 through Anon014. Anonymous users are afforded guest permissions by default.

If an application that is to be published on the MetaFrame server is intended to be accessed by guest-level users, the application can be configured using the Published Application Manager to allow access by anonymous users. When a user starts an anonymous application, the MetaFrame server does not require an explicit user name and password to log the user onto the server, but selects a user from a pool of anonymous users who are not currently logged on. Anonymous user accounts are granted minimal ICA session permissions, including

▼ Ten-minute idle (no user activity) time-out

■ Logged off on broken connection or time-out

■ No password required

▲ Password cannot be changed by user

Anonymous user accounts do not have a persistent identity. That is to say, no user information is retained when an anonymous user session ends. Any desktop settings, user-specific files, or other resources created or configured by the user are discarded at the end of the ICA session. Because of the inherent permission limitations of anonymous user accounts, the 15 anonymous user accounts created during MetaFrame installation usually do not require any further maintenance.

Explicit User Accounts

Explicit users, which are created and maintained via the MetaFrame User Manager for Domains, have a "permanent" existence. Their desktop settings, security settings, and so on, are retained between sessions for each user in a user profile.

Explicit users can be of any user class and are generally created for a specific purpose. Their access permissions may be changed over time by using the MetaFrame User Manager utility.

Identifying what groups of users will have access to an application that is about to be published will aid in server and link resource planning and may even expedite the publishing process. Administrators can capitalize on group settings and extend application access to multiple users concurrently. Conversely, using the Anonymous group is a handy way to make general-purpose applications available to the broadest possible user community in the least amount of time.

Application Publishing Security

As implied in the above discussion, in addition to considering the user population for an application, administrators also need to consider the security requirements of applications they are planning to publish. MetaFrame provides additional methods, beyond those of Microsoft operating systems, for securing access to applications published on the MetaFrame server.

Limiting Users to Published Applications

Users of a specific connection type (dial-up, for example) can be restricted to running published applications only. By allowing users to access predefined applications only, unauthorized users are prevented from obtaining access to the Windows desktop or a command prompt. This type of security may be obtained by using the Advanced Connection Settings dialog box in the Connection Configuration utility supplied with MetaFrame.

Limiting Applications

Published Application Manager lets you restrict an application to specified users or groups of users. This is possible only with respect to explicit user access.

Internet Firewalls

MetaFrame supports Internet firewalls that can be used to restrict Internet access to the MetaFrame server, as shown in Figure 2-4.

TIP: Many Web professionals recommend that organizations either disassociate their Web sites from their production systems, or take strong measures to restrict external access. Any system accessible through the Internet is by definition a security risk and may provide unauthorized access to production data and processes. Therefore, unless the organization has very robust security, Web servers should be kept on a separate network loop outside the organization's firewall.

User Names and Passwords

Users can be required to enter a user name and password in order to execute an application. This feature, again, can only be used with explicit user accounts.

ACLcheck Utility

An ACLcheck utility is supplied with MetaFrame that examines the security ACLs associated with MetaFrame files and directories. This utility can be used to report on any potential security exposures.

Application Execution Shell

The Application Execution Shell (App) in MetaFrame allows administrators to write application execution scripts that perform actions before and after application execution. These scripts can be used in connection with other security utilities to check the security of MetaFrame servers and clients.

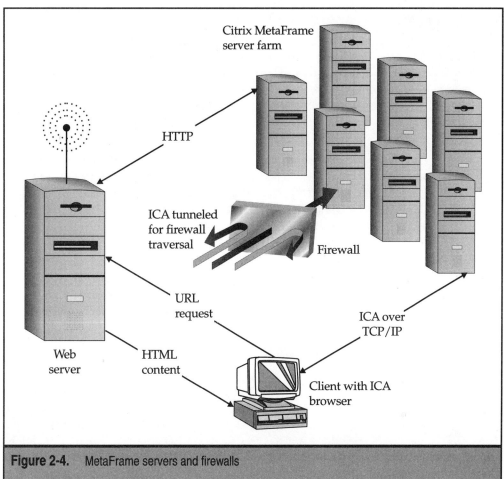

Figure 2-4.   MetaFrame servers and firewalls

SecureICA

For applications utilizing sensitive data, administrators should also consider a product from Citrix Systems, SecureICA Services, which provides RSA RC5 encryption of data traversing the network between the ICA client and the MetaFrame server.

The Published Application Manager

Once the application user community and necessary security safeguards have been identified and provided, the Published Application Manager can provide an efficient method for publishing the application itself. Not only does it make application publishing a more manageable and less time-consuming task, it also facilitates the management of applications once they are published.

Publishing Windows Applications

To publish a standard Windows application, the administrator should select the appropriate server or server farm, then launch an application publishing wizard supplied in the Published Application Manager. The wizard leads the administrator through the setup and configuration process. The result is an application that will be pushed automatically to the Program Neighborhood facility of clients whose users are permitted to access the application.

> **NOTE:**   Published Application Manager includes the Windows NT domain's scope of management to provide backward compatibility and interoperability with existing Citrix server installations (WinFrame 1.7 and MetaFrame 1.0) that contain existing published applications. Using Published Application Manager to publish applications in this scope results in applications that are not enabled for automatic configuration of Program Neighborhood sessions.

Other Publishing Capabilities

In addition to standard applications, MetaFrame can be used to publish video files, Citrix Installation Management Services (IMS), and load-balanced applications. In each case, wizard-based setup and configuration routines aid the administrator in fielding the application expeditiously.

Changing Properties of Published Applications

Once applications are published, their properties may need to be changed after a time. For all common changes—such as changing the user list, changing the MetaFrame server list, and renaming the published application—and many others, the Published Application Manager provides utilities and wizards to guide administrators through the procedure. The Manager also provides utilities to disable and enable published applications and to delete published applications.

Change the Command Line and Working Directory for the Application   This modification alters the path information for the application's executable IMS script (for Citrix IMS applications), or Citrix Video Information file (for published videos). You can also edit or add parameters to the command line when applicable.

Change Program Neighborhood Settings   You can change Program Neighborhood settings that are applied to this application when accessed by a Program Neighborhood. This applies only to applications that are created and deployed in a MetaFrame server farm.

METAFRAME AS AN APPLICATION PORTAL

In these days of electronic business and the Internet, companies are also porting applications to extranets and to the Internet, where they can be used by business partners and even consumers. MetaFrame facilitates this objective with NFuse, which utilizes Application Launching and Embedding (ALE).

Application Launching and Embedding (ALE)

MetaFrame includes an ALE wizard enabling published applications to be embedded into Web pages. The ALE wizard generates all necessary Hypertext Mark-up Language (HTML) code required to deliver application access through a Web page. Once the code is implemented in a Web page, the application may be accessed via an ActiveX Control for Microsoft Internet Explorer, a plug-in for Netscape Navigator, or in a Java applet for any Java-enabled device.

With ALE, administrators can instantly integrate Windows-based applications into intranet, extranet, or Internet Web sites, extending the reach of business applications while saving time and money. The embedded application looks, feels, and performs as if it were running locally, even though it is executing on a MetaFrame server located behind a Web server and firewall.

NFuse

Building on ALE functionality, Citrix also provides an add-in product for MetaFrame called NFuse. NFuse enables users to integrate applications and data that is published using ALE into customized portals for the end user, who accesses applications via Web technology.

Using NFuse, the presentation layer elements of multiple applications can be combined on a single page for exposure to the end user as a single, unified application. A simple wizard is provided to aid the administrator in defining the portal contents, which may include applications hosted on standard MetaFrame servers and MetaFrame for UNIX servers. Support for MetaFrame for UNIX enables the NFuse portal to be used to integrate both Windows and UNIX-based applications and data.

NFuse portals can be customized to meet the needs of individual users, who access their applications in accordance with a user or group account login, or general purpose portals can be fielded for access by anonymous users. Either way, the portals, like other MetaFrame applications, are managed via the same set of MetaFrame utilities used to manage and control other applications published via MetaFrame.

SHADOWING

In addition to providing tools for managing application publishing, MetaFrame delivers a utility targeted at reducing administrative costs by enabling the remote support of users of published applications. Session Shadowing enables the administrator (or help desk personnel) to remotely join, or take control, of another user's ICA session. When activated, Session Shadowing displays the user's screen on the administrator's console. Optionally, the administrator can assume control of the remote user's mouse and keyboard.

In addition to facilitating help desk and troubleshooting processes, Session Shadowing can also be used in online interactive teaching and call center applications.

Configuring Session Shadowing

Session Shadowing is configured at the time of connection configuration. The shadowing settings in the Advanced Connection Settings dialog box control the behavior of shadowing for all sessions on the connection. Setting options include

▼ **Enabled**   Specifies that sessions on the connection can be shadowed

■ **Disabled**   Specifies that sessions on the connection cannot be shadowed

■ **Input On**   Allows the shadower to input keyboard and mouse actions to the shadowed session

▲ **Notify On**   Specifies that the shadowed user gets a message asking if it is OK for the shadowing to occur

Session Shadowing Initiation

The initiation of Session Shadowing is accomplished via the MetaFrame Server Administration utility. This utility is also used to disconnect and reconnect sessions, send messages to users, reset connections, terminate processes, and to obtain statistical information about the operation of the server-centric infrastructure. To begin shadowing, the administrator displays a list of sessions, selects one to shadow, and then selects Start Shadowing from the utility menu.

APPLICATION COMPATIBILITY SCRIPTS

Of course, there is no such thing as a panacea in information technology. MetaFrame has its limitations. Some features, such as Program Neighborhood, are not available to all ICA clients. Moreover, some applications—even those written for Windows 95 or NT—do not "work and play well" with MetaFrame (or Terminal Services). The latter is especially important. Some applications, designed for a single-user desktop, do not operate smoothly in a multiuser operating system. In some cases, the applications are not segmented for sharing. In other cases, the application seeks to write user data into one location and cannot understand multiple user datasets and directories.

The work-around for application incompatibilities in a Microsoft NT Server TSE environment is application compatibility scripts. In Windows 2000, software vendors have been provided with much stricter guidance regarding the enabling of applications for multiple user operation. Citrix posts the latest application compatibility scripts for popular applications on their Web site at www.citrix.com/support/ftp_ims.html#appcompat.

METAFRAME LICENSING

The MetaFrame license is more than an agreement describing the cost to the user and revenue to the vendor. Licenses are pooled by the MetaFrame servers themselves and used to calculate authorized use of the product. In short, if the license provides for 15 users to connect to a MetaFrame server, user number 16 will be locked out by the server.

Citrix delivers MetaFrame licenses in three ways: shrink wrap method, corporate licensing, and ASP licensing.

> *Gartner Group estimates that 80 percent of the world's 500-plus ASPs will be using Citrix software within five years—up from about 50 percent today.*
> —BusinessWeek Online, May 22, 2000

Shrink Wrap Method

Administrators can purchase the base product and licenses for 15 concurrent users. When originally announced, the suggested retail price for a MetaFrame 1.8 software license for 15 concurrent users and a one-year enrollment in the Citrix Subscription Advantage program was $5995. Subscription Advantage customers receive automatic delivery of enhancements, updates, and maintenance releases to the base server software and installed system management services.

As configurations expand, bulk user packs can be purchased to meet changing needs. At the time of the MetaFrame 1.8 announcement, additional MetaFrame user licenses could be added in increments of 5, 10, 20, or 50 concurrent users for $995, $1995, $3990, or $9975, respectively.

Corporate Licensing

Corporate licensing programs are available for large license quantities. In addition, special pricing is available for corporate customers who adopt a "long-term strategic use" posture. In this case, cumulative purchases drive discounts.

ASP Licensing

Citrix is also endeavoring to drive the Application Service Provider market forward by designing some attractive "pay as you grow" options that will encourage the use of MetaFrame as a key infrastructure component for commercial application delivery services.

RESOURCE MANAGEMENT SERVICES

Citrix Systems offers an additional product for use with MetaFrame that is the only application and systems management product designed specifically for the Citrix application software and Microsoft multiuser Windows NT environments. This product, Resource Management Services (RMS), equips administrators with a full-featured management tool suite for analyzing and tuning Citrix application servers and Microsoft Windows 2000 Servers, NT Server 4.0, and Terminal Server Edition systems.

RMS is discussed in more detail in Chapter 10, but the key features are summarized here:

▼ **Application and system audit trail creation** RMS works with most ODBC-compliant databases to capture user connections and disconnections, to track connection durations, and to record what applications are used during user sessions. Administrators can view the percentage of time applications that are in use as opposed to just being loaded, and application resource requirements can be recorded to assist administrators with capacity planning. Graphs may be created to display system usage, and users' favorite applications may be displayed ranked by use count.

■ **Comprehensive system monitoring** RMS alerts administrators and help desks to potential system problems before they impact users. More than 30 real-time performance counters are analyzed and displayed with green, yellow, or red status indicators on the RMS console. In effect, administrators may view the health of multiple MetaFrame, WinFrame, and Terminal Server systems from a single console. They may set custom thresholds for each performance counter and designate a method for receiving alerts in the event that a threshold is exceeded. RMS alerts can be sent via a pager or an e-mail message. Expert advice for eliminating performance bottlenecks is available from the product's extensive knowledge base.

▲ **Support for charge-back systems** In a centralized computing environment, charge-back or departmental billing systems are used to bill end-user departments for their use of central computer systems. With RMS, fees may be set per minute of connection time, memory utilization, and/or processor utilization. Users may be assigned to cost centers. Billing reports may be constructed to show resources used, session start time, session elapsed time, and applications executed.

Resource Management Services' data collection service runs in the background of each application server that is being monitored. Graphical analysis tools make this product easy to learn and use. Using RMS, administrators can create graphs depicting historical performance of any given Citrix MetaFrame server. These, in turn, enable the administrator to respond proactively to operational trends, to optimize system performance, and to deliver maximum availability to the end user.

INSTALLATION MANAGEMENT SERVICES

Citrix Installation Management Services (IMS) is designed to automate the application installation process and facilitate application replication across MetaFrame servers throughout the enterprise. Through the use of IMS, applications can be distributed across multiple servers in minutes rather than days or weeks. IMS is described in more detail in Chapter 14, but a brief overview is included here.

IMS contains two components: the Packager and the Installer. With the Installer deployed to all Citrix servers in the enterprise, the Packager makes replicating applications a simple two-step "package and publish" process.

The Packager provides the administrator with an easy-to-use wizard that supports the step-by-step process of installing and configuring an application. The result is a "package" that contains all application files and a "script" that describes the application setup process.

To "push" an application to Citrix servers equipped with the Installer, simply publish the script to those servers. The application will then be seamlessly distributed and automatically installed onto Citrix servers across the enterprise.

IMS is especially useful in organizations utilizing multiple MetaFrame servers, or having numerous and frequently updated applications. In these settings, the automation offered by IMS can yield significant cost and administrative time savings.

Installation Management Services works with both MetaFrame and WinFrame servers as well as all Citrix-supported client platforms. The Packager runs on its own PC. The Installer runs as a background service on each Citrix server and is completely transparent to the user.

IMS also helps to sort out uninstall issues associated with many applications. For example, with many uninstall programs, application components can be left behind on the server. With IMS, the Installer component tracks every application component installed and completely uninstalls the components when the administrator elects to "unpublish" the application on a specific server. This simplifies the relocation of applications from one server to another.

VIDEOFRAME

For a variety of reasons, more and more companies are turning to digital audio and video *streaming* as a method for communicating with employees, partners, and consumers. Streaming is analogous to traditional application execution: a digital audio or video file is executed, and its output—whether aural or visual information—is directed across a network to a client system that uses driver software (specifically, a CODEC) to interpret the stream and "play" its contents to the end user by using installed equipment.

Citrix offers a technology called VideoFrame to support audio and video file streaming within an ICA environment. VideoFrame uses the extremely efficient Citrix Video CODEC and ICA Streaming Channel technologies to support high-clarity, true-color, full-motion video. It dynamically scales streams according to available bandwidth, making it appropriate for use across a variety of link types.

VideoFrame integrates with MetaFrame's Program Neighborhood, enabling organizations to deploy multimedia files with the same speed and manageability as other published applications. Client support is initially restricted to 32-bit clients; however, Citrix Systems reports that the product, which is an add-on to the MetaFrame environment, will soon be available to clients on multiple platforms. This will give organizations the ability to deploy audio and video content within heterogeneous computing environments.

The Citrix Video CODEC, used by clients to play the stream from a VideoFrame server, can be used with third-party content creation tools. Since the multimedia content is streamed from a server, rather than residing on the end-user client device, requirements for playback (such as large hard disks) are eliminated.

One frequent application for VideoFrame is corporate training. Streaming video of training presentations can be deployed to users throughout the enterprise as MetaFrame hosted applications. Streams can be pushed directly to the desktop, then executed at the user's convenience or in accordance with network bandwidth availability. Just as easily, older training files can be removed from the desktop when they become outdated.

METAFRAME FOR UNIX

Based in part on the success and popularity of MetaFrame in the Windows application hosting environment, Citrix recently announced a new MetaFrame product aimed at the hosting of UNIX, X Window, and Java applications—MetaFrame for UNIX Operating Systems. The product, which at present supports the Sun Microsystems Solaris Operating System, offers the same value as MetaFrame for Windows, but with a UNIX/Java twist: universal client access over any network connection to any UNIX or Java application.

At the core of the MetaFrame for UNIX product is a modified X11R6.3 server. This does not replace the X11 server supplied with most UNIX operating systems. X11R6.3 is specifically used to enable ICA-connected sessions running on the MetaFrame for UNIX server. MetaFrame for UNIX runs all standard X11 applications using the modified X server rather than the native X11 server.

In operation, the modified X11 server talks to a UNIX-ported ICA stack (Winstation Driver, Protocol Driver, and Transport Driver), which performs an X-to-ICA conversion. This is key to delivering applications seamlessly to clients from all MetaFrame platforms.

In addition to the modified X11 server and ported ICA stack, MetaFrame for UNIX also provides an ICA browser for use in load balancing and client browsing, a "listener" to intercept incoming ICA connections, and a "Frame Manager," which manages all the sessions currently running on the server.

The same core functionality used by MetaFrame for UNIX to deploy X11 and other applications hosted on UNIX servers can also be applied to Java applications. At first, this capability may seem redundant: in theory, Java applications are already portable to any device. In reality, however, Java client-side application deployment still confronts numerous challenges.

Downloading Java applications entails the use of the available client-server network protocol, which is often not optimized for low-bandwidth connections. This results in the major complaint about Java applications—that they are sometimes incredibly slow to download for operation. Operating the Java application, which is executed locally on a server, over a bandwidth-optimized ICA connection provides a higher performance solution to this issue.

Java applications also fall prey to peculiarities in the Java Virtual Machine that runs on the client system. Not all JVMs are the same, and it is often the case that a Java application that runs perfectly in one JVM behaves very differently in another. By executing Java applications within the server's JVM environment, this difficulty goes away.

Utilizing a single, server-based JVM also saves time and money when developing and testing Java applications developed in-house. Once the application is working in the server JVM, it can be deployed instantly to any ICA client device.

It should also be noted that the Java Virtual Machine is typically a large piece of software. Although the development of an embedded JVM is under way, ultra-thin-client devices lack capacity to run a JVM that offers sufficient features or performance. This issue is removed through the use of the MetaFrame for UNIX Operating Systems solution.

In summary, MetaFrame for UNIX Operating Systems can be an important adjunct to Windows-based MetaFrame servers in heterogeneous server environments. MetaFrame for UNIX servers can be included in server farm and load-balancing schemes, and applications hosted on MetaFrame for UNIX systems may be published individually or as part of integrated NFuse portals for integrated access by end users.

CHAPTER 3

Windows Terminal Services

When installing a Terminal Services solution into an enterprise, the methodology for administering and maintaining the system has more in common with a host-based or mainframe computing model than with a distributed PC model. In the traditional, centralized host architecture, dumb terminals provide a simple, character-based interface between the user and the host. Users can log on, run programs, read and write shared files, direct output to shared printers, and access shared databases. Furthermore, each dumb terminal session functions independently from other terminal sessions because the host operating system handles the communication between the host applications and the remote dumb terminal users.

The primary difference between Terminal Services and a centralized mainframe or host architecture is the graphical nature of the Windows operating system. Host environments have traditionally been character oriented, requiring only a small amount of network traffic to travel over the communication lines between the host and the terminal. With Terminal Services, all of the graphical screen output and related input/output comprising mouse movements, keyboard commands, and screen updates must flow between the desktop client and the server.

In this chapter, we cover NT 4.0 Terminal Server Edition (TSE) as well as Windows 2000 Terminal Services. We discuss the many facets of the Remote Desktop Protocol (RDP) and the differences between versions 4.0 and 5.0. We cover Terminal Services in the enterprise, including migration, domain considerations, and application considerations. Finally, we discuss licensing for both Terminal Server Edition and for Windows 2000 Terminal Services.

TERMINAL SERVICES FAMILY

Terminal Services allows multiple users to log onto a server, have their own desktop environment, and execute programs that stay resident. User logons effectively get their own protected memory space for applications and data. Users can have a Windows desktop and run Windows-based applications without the need to load the applications on their local PC. A server running Terminal Services can host ten, or even hundreds, of concurrent users. In this chapter we will use the generic term *Terminal Server* to refer to either a server running Windows 2000 with Terminal Services enabled, or a server running TSE.

The client computing device used to communicate with the Terminal Server can be a PC or a specially designed terminal made to work with the Terminal Server display protocol. The PC or terminal runs a relatively small program that enables a logon and accepts redirected screen output from the Terminal Server. The Microsoft Terminal Services client program relies on a protocol originally developed for Microsoft's NetMeeting, called Remote Desktop Protocol (RDP). RDP is based on the International Telecommunications Union's (ITU) T.120 protocol. The T.120 protocol is a standard multichannel conferencing protocol that is tuned for enterprise environments and supports session encryption.

Windows NT 4.0 Server was Microsoft's standard file, print, and application server for business computing before the release of Windows 2000. Windows NT 4.0 is commonplace in the information technology infrastructures of corporate computing today. On the end-user desktop, Windows NT 4.0 Workstation is often chosen over Windows 95 or 98 because of its enhanced security and performance with 32-bit Windows (Win32) applications.

Windows NT 4.0 Server, Terminal Server Edition

Microsoft's Windows NT 4.0 Server, TSE, is the implementation of Citrix MultiWin on the Windows NT 4.0 Server platform. Because of the MultiWin-inspired kernel of TSE, users can log onto virtual Windows NT 4.0 sessions with the same desktop and application look and feel of Windows NT 4.0 Workstation. With TSE, Microsoft created a separate code base for the operating system in order to overcome some of the memory management limitations of Windows NT 4.0 Server and to generally tune it for multiuser access.

Microsoft includes their Terminal Server client, which is the client portion of the Remote Desktop Protocol, with TSE. The RDP client supports a variety of Windows desktops over TCP/IP networking, including Windows for Workgroups 3.11, Windows 95 and 98, Windows CE, Windows NT Workstation, and Windows 2000 Professional.

TSE Internals

In order to achieve the multiuser capabilities required in TSE, the Citrix MultiWin technology needed to be integrated into the Windows NT 4.0 Server kernel. This integration meant that several components, services, and drivers have been added or modified in the original Windows NT 4.0 Server core operating system. Windows NT 4.0 components such as the Virtual Memory Manager (VMM) and Object Manager (OM) have been modified to perform in a multiuser environment.

Virtual Memory Manager   The VMM maps virtual addresses in the process's address space to physical pages in the computer's memory. In Windows NT, a process's address space is divided into two 2GB address ranges: *user* (process-specific addresses) and *kernel* (system-specific addresses). For the user address space, the VMM provides an individualized view of the physical memory to each process, ensuring that a call for system resources (a thread) within a process can access its own memory, but not the memory of other processes.

SessionSpace   The kernel address space is common for all processes within the system, thus providing a consistent means for accessing all kernel services. The fact that all processes share the kernel address space resulted in kernel resource limitations when supporting multiple interactive sessions on a single server. In TSE, these limitations were addressed by creating a special address range in the kernel, called *SessionSpace*, which can be mapped on a per-session basis. Each process is associated with a SessionSpace via a *SessionID*. When a remote user connects to Terminal Server, a new SessionID is generated, and all of the processes created for that connection inherit that SessionID and unique session space, as shown below. Other process groups, with a different SessionID, point to a separate set of memory-mapped objects and physical pages at the same virtual address.

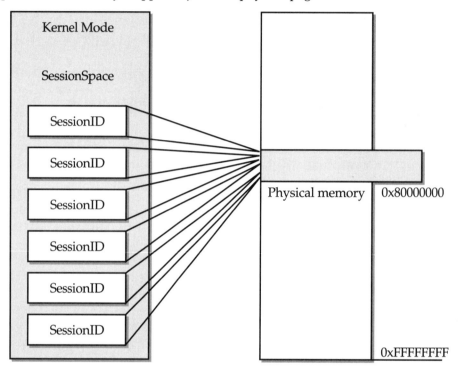

The Windows NT 4.0 Terminal Server makes all objects required for multiuser capability virtual so that the applications and system programs from different user sessions do not collide. Every object name created within a session is appended with a unique identifier number associated with the individual user session (SessionID) that created it. For example, if a user starts an application in the first session on the Terminal Server, the session would be seen as *session1* and the application seen as *application1*, as seen in Figure 3-1.

The Remote Desktop Protocol is designed to support TCP/IP over LAN or WAN communication links. Due to the multisession nature of the protocol, a special user mode extension (RDPWSX), as depicted in Figure 3-2, is needed to receive all incoming client packets. RDPWSX manages LPC sessions and calls WINLOGON to authenticate them. In addition, RDPWSX will validate the client license with the license server and negotiate client-server encryption keys.

Upon successfully establishing a session, the MultiWin subsystem gains control over session management. A virtual session is created by localizing a copy of WIN32K.SYS with all the necessary device drivers. The TERMDD (Terminal Server Device Driver) then provides the run-time environment of a session-specific protocol driver in order to service multiple client session requests.

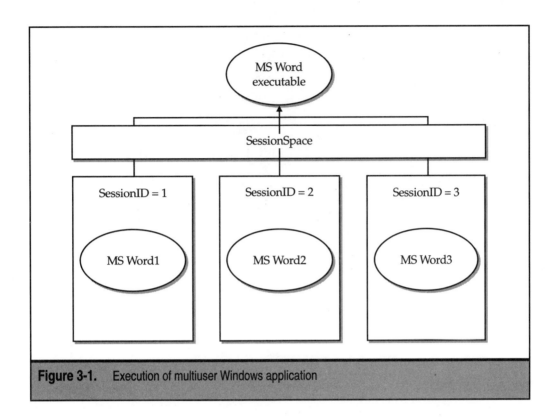

Figure 3-1.   Execution of multiuser Windows application

To support the mouse and keyboard commands sent to each session's copy of the WIN32K.SYS subsystem, the RDPWD (Remote Desktop Winstation Driver) is loaded.

The console session is always the first to load, and it is assigned a special client connection ID of 0. The console session launches at system startup with system-configured Windows NT display, mouse, and keyboard drivers loaded. The Terminal Server service calls the Windows NT session manager (SMSS.EXE) and loads the RDP user mode protocol extension RDPWSX to create two idle client sessions right after the creation of the console session. These two idle sessions listen on TCP service port 3389 for RDP protocol packets from the client.

Code Sharing   Terminal Server also implements memory *code sharing* (also known as Copy on-Write Page Protection). This feature allows one copy of executable code, such as Microsoft Word, to be loaded into physical memory, and to have multiple users run the same copy of the program code. If a user loads a private copy of a Word document, a separate memory space will be set aside and marked as read/write under the protection of Virtual Memory Manager. No other process can access this private memory space. This is extremely useful and efficient when a large number of users are using the same programs.

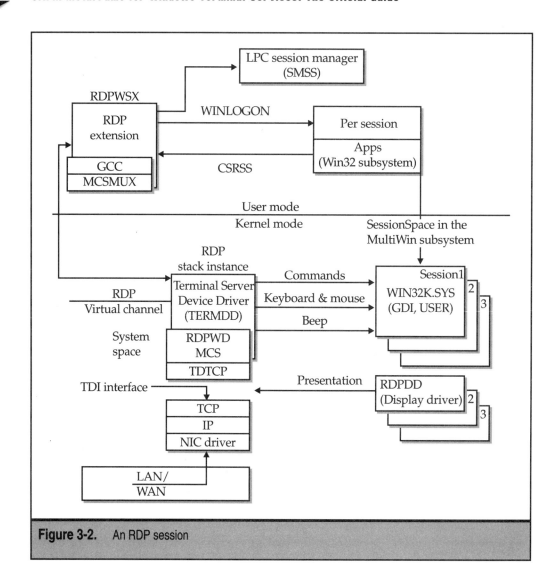

Figure 3-2. An RDP session

NOTE: Code sharing cannot be utilized in 16-bit applications, since they need to run inside a separate DOS VDM (Virtual DOS Machine). For this reason, approximately 20 percent more memory is used by 16-bit and DOS applications than by comparable 32-bit applications. In order to properly size the RAM requirement, a live functional test should be conducted to observe the total working set of memory consumed by a specific application, because many 32-bit applications contain 16-bit code.

Windows 2000 Terminal Services

In Windows 2000 Terminal Services, SessionSpace remains. The layout on the memory map has been modified to further tune the system and enable a common layout for all Windows 2000 systems, whether or not Terminal Services has been installed. The main modification is that SessionSpace has been reduced to 60MB and starts at the memory address location A0000000. Moving SessionSpace up to A0000000 allows all system drivers (WIN32K.SYS), video drivers, and printer drivers to be loaded in a common virtual address location, whether they are accessed through a Terminal Services session or on a session without Terminal Services. Microsoft redesigned the memory mapping to eliminate the need for a separate version of the operating system to support Terminal Services, as was necessary with Windows NT 4.0 Server and TSE.

A new Windows NT service, called appropriately Terminal Services (TERMSRV.EXE), is the controlling process in the Terminal Server architecture. It is primarily responsible for session management, initiation, and termination of user sessions and session event notification. The Terminal Server service is entirely protocol independent, so it can function using RDP or a third-party add-on protocol such as ICA from Citrix.

> *During our evaluation of Windows 2000 Terminal Services and MetaFrame, we noticed an improved performance and stability over the NT 4.0 product.*
>
> —Rob Lawrence,
> Systems Engineer, Palo Alto Medical Foundation

A user mode protocol extension provides assistance to the Terminal Server service. It is the responsibility of this component to provide protocol-specific functions and services, such as licensing, session shadowing, client font enumeration, and so forth. Each Terminal Server session protocol (for example, RDP and ICA) has its own protocol extension, providing a variety of services.

NOTE: For RDP, this user mode extension is called WSXTSHAR.DLL.

REMOTE DESKTOP PROTOCOL (RDP)

In this part of the chapter, we describe in more detail how the Remote Desktop Protocol performs session management and other functions.

Session Connection

When a client initiates a session, the TCP/IP transport driver passes the request to the TERMDD program on the Terminal Server. TERMDD then passes the request to RDPWSX, which in turn signals the Terminal Server service to create a thread to handle the incoming session request. In addition, RDPWSX is responsible for initiating session negotiation with the client and capturing all necessary client information, such as compression, encryption level, client version number, and license details. As each client connection is accepted and assigned an idle SessionSpace, a new idle session is created within 0.2 seconds. The session manager also executes the client-server run-time subsystem process (CSRSS.EXE), and a new SessionID is assigned to that process. The CSRSS process then invokes the Windows Logon (WINLOGON.EXE) and the graphic device interface (GDI) module (WIN32K.SYS) to render the initial logon screen information and present it to the particular user SessionID, as shown in Figure 3-3.

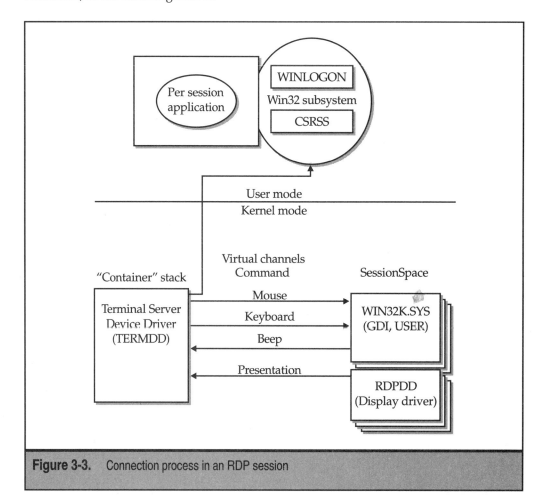

Figure 3-3.   Connection process in an RDP session

NOTE: Under heavy session logon activity, a Registry setting can increase the two idle session numbers. The values are contained in the following key: HKEY_LOCAL_MACHINE\System\CurrentControlSet\Control\ Terminal Server\IdleWinstationCount\.

Session Disconnection

When a user disconnects from an active session without logging off, the GDI stops taking commands from the user by stopping all drawing operations from reaching the display driver. A disconnected desktop object is created and represented in the Terminal Server Connection Configuration (TSCC) application, as shown in Figure 3-4.

The disconnected object continues to prevent any graphical input or output to take place. During the disconnection time-out period, the RDP stack is unloaded, but TERMDD is still active because WIN32K.SYS maintains an active handle to it for keyboard and mouse control. Before the time-out period expires, the user can be reconnected to the same session. The session disconnect process is shown in Figure 3-5.

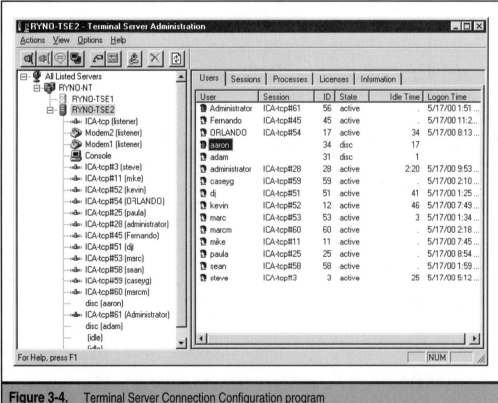

Figure 3-4. Terminal Server Connection Configuration program

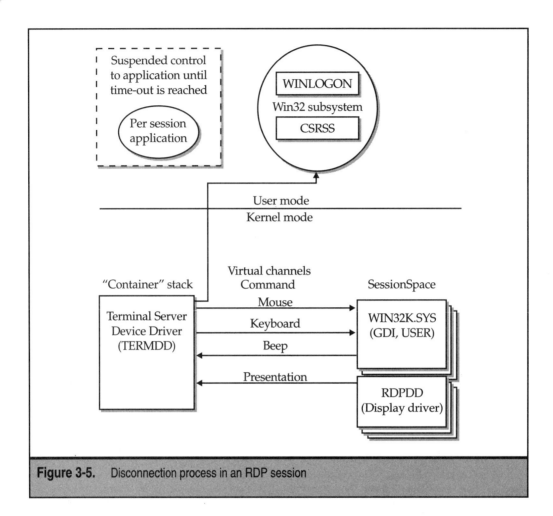

Figure 3-5. Disconnection process in an RDP session

Session Reconnection

When a user initiates a connection to the **same server**, a brand-new connection is first created. The RDP stack is loaded, and SessionSpace is assigned. The user is presented with a logon screen. Thus far, the process is identical to a new session connection. However, when WINLOGON scans the userid and determines that the user has a disconnected session, TERMDD is instructed to perform a session reconnection. The user session is then switched back to the disconnected session.

Data Transmission

RDP packets are formed in the presentation layer of the Open System Interconnect (OSI) model. The packets are encrypted and frames packaged according to the requirements of the network protocol. Currently, only TCP/IP is supported by RDP. The RDP data content may include keyboard input and mouse movement coordinates, as well as graphical bitmaps and printer redirection output. The return RDP packet goes in reverse through the same protocol stack, is decrypted, unwrapped, and the TCP/IP header information is stripped for the specific client session. Some of the data transmission optimization features of RDP include the following:

▼ **Intelligent encoding**   The redrawing of graphical images can be encoded to tell the client to redraw changes only since the last refresh took place. In other words, only the changes are sent.

■ **Glyph and bitmap caching**   The RDP client automatically reserves a minimum of 1.5MB of memory space to cache the required set of glyphs needed in the display of common text. Bitmaps of different sizes are also cached in memory. Whenever a command is issued from the RDP server, the client can redraw the required text and bitmaps very quickly by extracting the elements from cache.

▲ **Bulk compression**   A client-side option optimizing a low-speed connection will turn on bulk compression, which can reduce the packet count by 50 percent.

Image Display

RDP uses a highly efficient encoding algorithm to encapsulate screen data, similar to the X Window protocol. Most common or repetitive drawings are sent as a command rather than an actual bitmap. This method greatly reduces the amount of data required to paint a new screen or refresh an old one. Microsoft has published the exact bandwidth requirements to paint a common Windows screen, but lab tests from Mainstream Networks show that RDP 4.0 may use up to 40 Kbps on a dial-up connection (with compression) and even more on a LAN. There is a significant improvement in bandwidth utilization on the Windows 2000 version of RDP—version 5.

RDP updates the screen as follows: A user starts an application, which informs the GDI where and how to draw the application window. The GDI relays the command to the RDP display driver (RDPDD) by way of standard Win32 API calls. This is the same process used in a Windows NT system without Terminal Services, and is similar to the way a print job is rendered. The main API calls that are sent to RDP include the following:

▼ **TextOut( )**   This call results in the display of text information on a client screen. GDI informs RDP of the location and the glyphs (a graphical representation of a character). RDP tells the client which glyph to cache and which cache entry to use next time the same text is called for.

■ **PatBlt( )**   Pattern Block Transfer is used by RDP to tell the client how to draw a block of color. This translates into a small command and is the alternative to sending a block of bitmaps and consuming a large amount of bandwidth.

▲ **LineTo( )**   This command allows RDP to tell the client the beginning and ending coordinates of a 3D beveling line. The line can be used to form boxes. This command can be as small as 6 bytes to complete a line drawing.

Windows 2000 Graphical Enhancements

RDP version 5.0 not only improves the protocol communication efficiency, it also expands its feature set and offers some of the benefits contained in the ICA protocol.

▼ **Session shadowing**   This feature allows an administrator or authorized person to take over the screen, keyboard, and mouse movement of any user session running to the same physical machine. Session shadowing in version 5.0 is backward compatible with version 4.0 clients.

■ **Clipboard redirection**   The RDP version 5.0 protocol synchronizes the server-side application clipboard to the client-side clipboard buffer. This allows applications running on the Terminal Server to cut and paste data to applications running on the client workstation.

■ **Client printer autocreation**   Local client COM and LPT ports can be remapped automatically from the server. The local default printer will be created in the Terminal Server session, and print jobs produced by applications running in a server session will be printed on the client's local default printer.

▲ **Bitmap cache**   Windows 2000 RDP provides additional persistent bitmap cache over version 4.0, which only used RAM cache. Upon successful bitmap transmission, the server instructs the client where to store persistent cache information. When the same data is needed again, only the location coordinate for this bit is sent to the client. This improvement is especially important in low-speed dial-up connections.

Windows 2000 Terminal Services Client Architecture

A Terminal Services client using RDP supports three different operating system platforms:

▼ The Win32 platform, which includes Windows 2000, Windows NT, Windows 95, 98, and the upcoming Windows Millennium version

■ The Win16 platform, which includes Windows and Windows for Workgroups 3.11

▲ The WinCE platform, which includes many new thin-client devices with WinCE running as the embedded operating system

The design goals are to minimize bandwidth utilization, minimize memory usage, and speed up screen transmission. RDP version 5.0 represents a striking improvement over version 4.0 in both speed and features. Planned for the next release is the ActiveX control component embedded inside the client architecture, which will enable direct Web access to applications.

Table 3-1 shows a comparison of some of the major features of RDP versions 4.0 and 5.0.

Feature	Description	RDP 4.0	RDP 5.0
Clients	32-bit clients for Windows 95, 98, NT, 2000	Yes	Yes
		Yes	Yes
	16-bit client for Windows 3.11	Yes	Yes
	Windows CE–based clients	No	Future*
	Browser client		
Transport protocol	TCP/IP	Yes	Yes
Audio	System beeps	Yes	Yes
Local printer redirection	Print to client-attached printer	No	Yes
Local drive mapping	Local client drive access from session	No	Yes
Cut and paste	Cut and paste between server session and client session	No	Yes
Load balancing	Provide high availability**	Yes	Yes
Remote control	Shadowing client session with control	No	Yes
Bitmap caching	Bitmap caching in memory	Yes	Yes
	Bitmap caching to disk	No	Yes
Preconfigured client	Predefined client with IP address, server name, and connection information	No	Yes

*Browser access for RDP 5.0 will be offered through an ActiveX control, currently in beta testing.

**Load balancing for Terminal Services is provided through Windows Load Balancing Services (WLBS). WLBS is available as an add-on for TSE and as a standard service in Windows 2000 Advanced Server.

Table 3-1.   RDP Version 4.0 vs. 5.0

RDP Client Software Architecture

The RDP client software is installed on the server under the directory SystemRoot%System32\Tsclient. The client disk creator program under Start >Programs >Administrative Tools >Terminal Server Client Creator will make the necessary disk set for distribution to RDP clients.

When the Terminal Server client starts, the user interface calls the core API to set up a session with a server name or IP address. The default TCP/IP port is set to 3389. The security layer in turn calls the network layer to set up a socket with the goal of establishing a connection to the server. Once the TCP/IP connection is set up, the security layer starts to negotiate an encryption level with the server. Then the core protocol will negotiate bitmap cache and printer and COM port redirection. Upon successful negotiation, an active session is launched, and the user is presented with the Windows logon screen.

Client Caching   Client cache is negotiated during session setup. By default, 1.5MB of RAM is set for bitmap caching. In addition, version 5.0 will set up persistent caching to improve communication speed over slow links. When a bitmap is to be sent to the client, the RDP display driver (RDPDD) compresses the bitmap image, then sends the bitmap across the network. RDPDD also instructs the client in which cache cell to store the bitmap. When the client requests the same bitmap again, the server simply sends the cache cell reference number to the client.

The RDP client employs yet another technique to make use of screen cache in a shadowing session. Windows drop-down menus make up much of the display. Most frequently used menus are cached in RAM when being activated the first time. Further clicking on the same menu display will be retrieved from RAM and not sent across the network.

RDP Client Encryption   RDP supports three levels of encryption: low, medium, and high. Low-level encryption uses a 40-bit algorithm on client data being sent to the server. Medium-level encryption uses a 40-bit algorithm to encrypt data flow from both directions. Finally, high-level encryption uses a 128-bit two-way algorithm on both client and server. Terminal Services configuration on the server determines the lowest level of encryption allowed. For example, if the server enforces high level 128 bit encryption, then only a 128-bit encryption client can connect to the server. However, if the server only requires 40-bit encryption, then both 128-bit and 40-bit clients are able to connect.

RDP Client Remote Control   A new feature on RDP version 5.0, session shadowing, allows administrators to view and take control of another user's session running on the same server. By setting special permissions in the Terminal Services Connection Configuration program, help desk personnel can use the session shadowing feature to assist users by taking over their screen. Use the Terminal Services Manager found in Administrative Tools to highlight the desired user, and click on the Remote Control option.

TIP: Remote control cannot take over the server console session; neither can the server console take control over any virtual session. The screen resolution and color depth of the shadowing session should be equal to or higher than the session being shadowed.

In a shadowed session connection, TERMDD establishes a *shadow pipe* in which RDP packets are sent to both the shadowing and the shadowed sessions, as shown in Figure 3-6. In this way, input is accepted from both sessions, and results are returned to both sessions.

NOTE: If an administrator wants to shadow a session from the server console, an RDP virtual session has to be launched first, using the Terminal Services server as the "client." From inside the virtual client session, the administrator can then shadow a session.

RDP Client Session Administration   The Terminal Services Connection Configuration (TSCC) program can be used to control keyboard and mouse inactivity time-outs. The same interface can also automatically reset a disconnected session when the disconnect time-out value expires. By default, these two values are not set. This means no time-out will be triggered when a user leaves the client session unattended or the session is otherwise disconnected. For security reasons and to conserve server resources, it is strongly recommended that you set a reasonable value for both of these parameters, as shown in Figure 3-7.

NOTE: The systemwide session control in Figure 3-7 has the connection time-out set for 1 hour, the disconnection time-out set for 10 minutes, and the idle time-out set for 1 hour. These settings should be sufficient for most disconnect situations. Adjustments to these values should be made according to company policy and user behavior.

For the settings in Figure 3-7, if a session detects no keyboard or mouse input for one hour, the session is disconnected. In this case, a user needs to log onto the system again to connect to the suspended session, and no data loss is likely. If a user fails to log on within two hours after the one-hour inactivity time-out, the system will reset the disconnected session, and any data not saved will be lost.

TERMINAL SERVICES IN THE ENTERPRISE

In this part of the chapter, we discuss some issues you will encounter when adding Terminal Services to your enterprise.

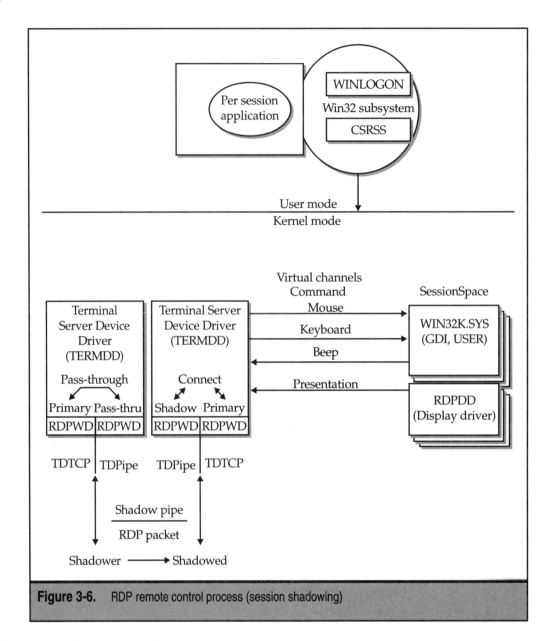

Figure 3-6. RDP remote control process (session shadowing)

Domain Considerations

The standard principles for installing a Terminal Server apply equally to TSE and Windows 2000 Terminal Services. If Active Directory is installed on the network, simply join the Active Directory Domain. There is no longer a Primary Domain Controller (PDC) or Backup Domain Controller (BDC) in Active Directory setup. A PDC Emulator will be created in the Windows 2000 Domain Controller (DC) when a Windows NT Domain client

Advanced Connection Settings ☒

┌─ Logon ─────────────────────────────────────┐
   ⦿ Disabled   ⦾ Enabled

┌─ Timeout settings (in minutes) ──────────────┐

   Connection [60]   ☐ No Timeout
                      ☐ (inherit user config)

   Disconnection [10] ☐ No Timeout
                       ☐ (inherit user config)

   Idle [60]   ☐ No Timeout
                ☐ (inherit user config)

┌─ Security ───────────────────────────────────┐
   Required encryption [Low   ▾]
   ☐ Use default Windows NT Authentication

┌─ AutoLogon ─────────────────────────┐
   User Name [   ]
   Domain [   ]
   Password [   ]
   Confirm Password [   ]
                Prompt for Password ☐
       ☑ (inherit client config)

┌─ Initial Program ───────────────────┐
   Command
   Line   [   ]
   Working
   Directory [   ]

   ☑ (inherit client/user config)
       ☐ Only run Published Applications

┌─ User Profile Overrides ────────────┐
   ☐ Disable Wallpaper

[OK]
[Cancel]
[Help]

On a broken or timed-out connection, [disconnect. ▾] the session. ☑ (inherit user config)
Reconnect sessions disconnected [from any client. ▾]   ☑ (inherit user config)
Shadowing [is enabled: input ON, notify ON. ▾]   ☑ (inherit user config)

Figure 3-7.   Setting time-out values for RDP session

attempts to log on. Therefore, it is possible to mix TSE servers with Windows 2000 servers running Terminal Services.

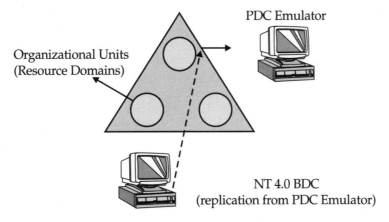

PDC Emulator

Organizational Units
(Resource Domains)

NT 4.0 BDC
(replication from PDC Emulator)

Integration with a Windows NT 4.0 PDC

When using a Windows 2000 server as a Terminal Server, Active Directory should not be installed. If there is an existing Windows NT 4.0 PDC, simply configure the Windows 2000 Server as a stand-alone server, or join the existing domain as a member server. When users log onto Windows 2000, the server will be authenticated against the Windows NT 4.0 PDC. For more information on security, refer to Chapter 9.

Migrating to Windows 2000 from an Existing Windows NT 4.0 PDC

If a Windows 2000 server is installed in an existing network that employs Backup Domain Controllers (BDCs), the new Windows 2000 server operates as a "mixed mode" Domain Controller. In this case, the Windows 2000 DC will be migrated first to Active Directory and will emulate a Windows NT 4.0 PDC. The old PDC-to-BDC security database synchronization will continue until all BDCs are migrated to Active Directory and "mixed mode" has been switched to "native mode."

NOTE: Fastlane's NT/MG is an excellent tool for migrating to Windows 2000. This software provides fallback capability if your migration encounters a problem. NT/MG records all changes to the domain, and changes can be "undone" if needed. You can test-drive a copy at www.fastlanetec.com.

Application Considerations

Most applications are written to run on a single-session platform such as Windows 95, 98, or Windows NT Workstation with a single user. Terminal Services requires significant changes to be made to the kernel and operating system to accommodate multiuser access. Because of these changes, both programmers and administrators must fully understand the issues and possible solutions in order to configure the system so that single-session applications can be executed in a multisession environment. We discuss some of the problems and possible solutions in this section.

Terminal Services makes special demands on how an application is written and how the application uses the Windows NT operating system. The Windows NT Registry is used by many programs to store variables during an installation, changes while the program executes, and changes that normally occur when users with differing logons access the application. On a typical Windows NT Workstation, an application may put data into the HKEY_LOCAL_MACHINE Registry hive, assuming only one user will access the application at a time. On Terminal Server, this could prove disastrous, as changes to this Registry hive would affect all users of this Terminal Server, not just the user executing the application making the change.

Many problems occur with applications that store local data constructs in global locations. In addition to separating global and local information in the Registry, global and local file-based data constructs should also be maintained separately. For example, user preference files should not be stored in a main system directory (\WinNT) or program directory (\Program Files). Instead, preference files or other user-specific local data should be stored in the user's home directory or a user-specified directory. This consideration also applies to temporary files used to store interim information (such as cached data) or to pass data on to another application. User-specific temporary files must also be stored on a per-user basis.

Some specific issues that would cause an application to fail in a multiuser environment include

▼ **Incorrect Registry entries**   Many applications write a global INI file to the system root for user-specific information. Thus, when one user changes or opens the INI file, other users may not be able to access the same file. Some applications add shortcuts to the installer's menu only during installation; other users may not see the shortcut. Still, many applications point the data files, temporary files, or cache files to the same location for all users. In this situation only one user can run the application at a time.

■ **Changed object name**   An object created in a session is named differently. The application may not be able to find the object using the expected name or location.

▲ **Incorrect file and object rights access**   An application normally locates libraries and executables in the Windows NT %SystemRoot% directory. Multiple users accessing the same file may create file-locking problems.

The following are some other application problems and issues to be aware of within a multiuser Terminal Services environment:

▼ *Do not assume computer name, MAC address, or IP address equates to a single user.* In the traditional distributed Windows client-server architecture, one user is logged onto one computer at a time. Thus, the computer name or Internet Protocol (IP) address assigned to either a desktop or server computer equates to one user. In the Terminal Services environment, the application can only see the IP or NetBIOS address of the server. Applications that use the computer name or IP address for licensing or as a means of identifying an iteration of the application on the network will not work properly in the Terminal Services environment because the server's computer name or IP address can equate to many different desktops or users.

▲ *MS-DOS and 16-bit Windows applications require more RAM than native 32-bit Windows applications.* Windows runs an emulation layer called the Virtual DOS Machine (VDM) as a process on the 32-bit operating system. Although this memory requirement may not show up as performance degradation on a high-powered desktop computer running the latest Windows operating system with 64MB of RAM, it may easily show up on a system running Terminal Services due to the multiplier effect of many user sessions.

Multiuser Application Issues

You may encounter several possible issues when running applications under Terminal Services that were not designed to run in a multiuser environment. Some of the important ones are summarized here. We will discuss these and other application-related issues in more detail in Chapter 15.

Application Compatibility Scripts

Many of the issues discussed so far have been addressed by the creation of application compatibility scripts. After installing an application, an administrator is required to run the corresponding script to resolve the issues mentioned. As of this writing, there are only 27 scripts included with Windows 2000 Advanced Server. Before an application can be certified for Windows 2000, Microsoft requires that it be multiuser compatible. We hope to see more scripts from third-party vendors. Application compatibility scripts are located in the %SystemRoot%\Application Compatibility Scripts\Install folder.

DOS and 16-Bit Windows Programs

For best performance, run 32-bit Windows applications whenever possible. Win32 allows code sharing and thus runs more efficiently in a multiuser environment. If additional users need to access the same Win32 application code, a pointer is created that shares the same code from the original copy loaded in the kernel and user modes. Code sharing cuts down the total amount of memory usage when multiplying a large number of sessions. On the other hand, 16-bit Windows and DOS applications need to run in their own VDM, and so no code sharing is possible. Also, Win16 applications often require 16- to 32-bit conversion programs ("thunking" and "context switching") that increase resource utilization even further.

Effective Use of the Registry

In a multiuser environment, applications should store common information pertaining to systemwide operation in the HKEY_LOCAL_MACHINE section of the Registry. Such information includes the path used to load application components, and what components are needed during execution. User-specific information, such as the locations of custom dictionaries (CUSTOM.DIC) and user templates (NORMAL.DOT), should be stored in HKEY_CURRENT_USER. Some applications incorrectly store information meant to be user specific in HKEY_LOCAL_MACHINE.

The application compatibility script addresses this issue by mapping an unused drive letter to the home directory of each user. REG.INI then changes pointers to this drive to each user's home directory environment variable. In this way, each user gets his own copy of an initialization file.

TIP: A utility in the Exchange Server Resource Kit, named PROFGEN.EXE, resolves common pointer issues that cause each user to try to open the same e-mail post office box when a mandatory profile is used. This utility can be useful when enabling many users running Terminal Services to access the same Exchange server.

Application Install and Execute Modes

During installation, an application writes user-specific keys to the Administrator's HKEY_CURRENT_USER Registry hive. Information such as Document Path and Autosave Path are missing from other users' HKEY_CURRENT_USER keys because they did not install the application. These keys are crucial in successfully using the application. Terminal Services provides a global Install mode to address this situation. During installation, the system is placed under Install mode by entering the command **change user /install** at the command prompt. All user-specific keys generated by the application under the software hive are shadowed by a key hive under the location in HKEY_LOCAL_MACHINE\SOFTWARE\Microsoft\WindowsNt\CurrentVersion\TermialServer\Install.

This key hive is appropriately called the *shadow key*. After installation is fully completed, the system can be switched back into normal execution mode by entering the command **change user /execute** at the command prompt. In the Execute mode of operation, the shadow key information is written back into each user's software key hive when the system finds that the keys are missing.

The same command addresses missing INI and DLL files in the case of 16-bit applications. These files are copied into each user's Windows directory (normally, C:\WTSRV or C:\WINNT). This also applies to 32-bit applications if they use INI files.

User-Specific Application Data

Some settings, such as "DocumentPath" in the HKEY_CURRENT_USER "Microsoft Word" subkey, may only be created the first time the application is run. Therefore, the installer must execute the application in global Installation mode right after finishing the initial installation. By doing this, the system will generate these values and record them in the shadow key so that they can later be copied into each user's HKEY_CURRENT_USER Registry hive.

Sometimes an application creates a path pointer to a common location for all users. For example, the Microsoft Office installation program sets a document template pointer to C:\Program Files\Microsoft Office\Template. When multiple users try to update or open the same file, errors will occur. To address this situation, the administrator needs to search the Registry and change the pointer to each user's home folder, such as H:\Office 97\Template, then create the correct directory structure for each user in the logon script

(%SystemRoot%\System32\usrlogon.cmd). A simple statement such as the one below will accomplish this task:

```
IF NOT EXIST H:\OFFICE 97\TEMPLATE MD H:\OFFICE 97\TEMPLATE
```

A similar problem occurs when all users are directed to use the same cache files. The cache file pointer is set to a common location, such as C:\Temp\Cache. When multiple users attempt to write to the same location, the application will often halt, corrupt the cache, or simply crash the server. Again, the solution is to change the pointer in HKEY_LOCAL_MACHINE and HKEY_CURRENT_USER, then create the corresponding directory structure in each user's home directory to support an individual application cache.

File Security

Applications often store files in the system root directory. Security is normally set to Read-Only for regular users. When a user attempts to write to a file stored in this directory, execution of the application may fail. You can track down the particular file and re-assign security to it by using the FILEMON utility. A better method is to relocate the file to each user's Windows directory.

Application COM/DCOM Objects

The same application may create identical objects for multiple sessions. To separate the same object created by different sessions, a logon ID is appended to each object name. Session objects created in this way are called *user global objects* and are only visible inside the session in which they were created. If an object is created from the console, there will be no logon ID appended to the object name. This type of object is called a *system global object*. Because of this distinction, application objects to be used for multiple sessions should be generated as system global objects and installed from the console instead of a user session.

Memory Utilization

Some applications do not return memory to the system upon exit. This situation is exacerbated in a multiuser environment, and often causes the system to crash. The possible solution is to clear the memory by rebooting the system at a regular interval. The frequency of the reboot depends on how active the memory utilization is. A daily reboot may be necessary when memory utilization is high.

DCOM Compliance

Most programs use traditional Open Database Connections (ODBC) to access network objects, such as a data source in a SQL database. To allow a common interface for communication between all system programs (objects) across a network, Microsoft developed the Distributed Component Object Model (DCOM).

In order to be certified by Microsoft as Windows 2000 compatible, an application must support DCOM. This ensures that software components can communicate and share functions over a network in an efficient and reusable manner. TSE inherited a subset of DCOM functionality from Windows NT 4.0. Therefore, some applications written for Windows NT 4.0 may not function properly under TSE's multiuser environment. Microsoft has addressed this issue in Windows 2000. All DCOM activation modes are fully supported, as shown below:

- ▼ **Run as Activator**   Local activation is the same whether Terminal Services is enabled or not. The server is activated on the same session as the activator.

- ■ **Remote Activation**   When DCOM is activated remotely, the process is launched in a WindowStation with a special SessionID = 0, not a session corresponding to the user. This modification preserves the activation activity of a remote call.

- ■ **Run as Named User**   The application is configured in the Registry to run as a specified user. Local and remote activation of DCOM behaves in the same way.

- ■ **Run as Windows NT-Based Service**   The application is configured to run as a service. This type of service is not tied to any session.

- ▲ **Run as Interactive User**   This application is configured to run in the security context of the user.

LICENSING

Both Terminal Server RDP clients and Citrix ICA clients require two licenses to connect to a Terminal Server session. The first license is the standard Microsoft Client Access License (CAL) for accessing Windows NT files and print services. The License Manager enforces licenses in two different ways: per seat and per server.

TIP: If the License Manager refuses a connection because of insufficient per-server count, the event will be recorded as event 201 in the Event Log.

The second license required to enable a client connection is a Windows NT Workstation license. If the RDP client is running on a computer with Windows NT 4.0 (Server, Workstation, or TSE) or Windows 2000 Professional, it is not necessary to purchase an additional license. Windows NT 4.0 TSE does not enforce licensing; it simply logs license-related events in a file called HYDRA.MDB in %SystemRoot%\System32\lserver. A client license is recorded under HKEY_LOCAL_MACHINE\Software\Microsoft\ MSLicensing.

NOTE: Terminal Server Manager creates seven JET.TMP files for each new client. These are temporary files, and the system is responsible for removing them. If the system is shut down abnormally, many of these will be left over in the \System32 directory. These files should be deleted manually.

Windows 2000 Licensing

Windows 2000 enforces the use of the Terminal Services CAL. During any attempt to connect to a session, both the standard CAL and the RDP CAL will be checked. If either license is missing or invalid, the connection is refused.

Windows 2000 server comes with a license services server that tracks and allocates RDP CAL licenses to clients at connection time. The license server needs to be installed on a Windows 2000 Domain Controller and activated through Microsoft License Clearing House. When a client requests a connection to a Windows 2000 server, the request is forwarded to the central license server for validation. The license server uses the user name and computer name to check for an existing license. If none is available, a new license will be issued to the client, and the connection is completed. If the license pool is exhausted, the connection is refused. A temporary license can be enabled that will expire after 90 days.

NOTE: There is a special provision for an Internet CAL. This license mode allows 200 anonymous, concurrent users to access Terminal Services.

Licensing and Terminal Services Execution Modes

Windows 2000 Terminal Services can be installed in two different modes. The *remote administration* mode does not require an RDP CAL. The purpose of this mode is to allow administrators to do server maintenance remotely. Therefore, certain restrictions apply to running in this mode. Only two concurrent client sessions are permitted. Server application compatibility services are also disabled, such as the global Install mode.

PART II

Designing a Corporate ASP Solution

CHAPTER 4

Preparing Your Organization for a Corporate ASP

Constructing a Corporate ASP demands extensive planning and resources. In addition to the technical challenges, political and cultural factors inevitably play a part in a server-based computing implementation. This chapter covers the steps involved in building a Corporate ASP. We start the process with a small proof-of-concept pilot program to ensure application compatibility with Terminal Services. We then look at putting together a feasibility committee to define the project's scope and objectives as well as to seek executive sponsorship and determine financial justification. A guide to performing an infrastructure assessment is followed by a project planning outline. Finally, we talk about using videos and other techniques to create a "buzz" and to help sell the Corporate ASP concept internally.

The steps involved in planning a Corporate ASP are as follows:

1. Establish a nonproduction proof-of-concept pilot program.
2. Establish a production proof-of-concept pilot program.
3. Assemble a feasibility committee.
4. Recruit an executive sponsor.
5. Justify the project financially.
6. Assemble a project planning team.
7. Create a project definition document.
8. Perform an infrastructure assessment.
9. Generate a project design plan.
10. Expand the pilot to beta stage.
11. Sell the project internally.

THE PROOF-OF-CONCEPT PILOT PROGRAM

Applications are the driving force behind server-based computing, and it makes little sense to go through all of the expense and trouble of planning a Corporate ASP until you know your organization's applications will run adequately within this environment. An inexpensive proof-of-concept pilot program enables you to see the performance of your applications running together on Terminal Services. It also enables you to more accurately gauge the server resources required to implement an enterprise server-based computing rollout.

Start with a Nonproduction Pilot Program

Although you may ultimately wish to run all of your organization's applications within a Corporate ASP, the decision to implement server-based computing generally depends upon successfully running a small number of critical applications. These are the applications that should first be loaded on a server running Terminal Services and MetaFrame offline. If the results are not acceptable, adjustments to the applications or operating system may be required. Once the crucial applications are running well over MetaFrame, other less crucial applications can be added if desired.

TIP: If Corporate ASP users will be using foreign language versions of Windows 2000 Terminal Services and MetaFrame, a separate proof-of-concept pilot program should be set up for each language since different hot fixes and patches are often required.

Expand to a Production Pilot Program

Once the offline pilot program is stable, you can expand it to include a small number of pilot users. Great care, though, should go into the selection of these participants. A natural inclination of IT people is to choose from two types of users. The first type is a user who has an immediate computing need that the pilot program will solve, such as a requirement for an upgraded PC. The second type of user is someone who is known to be difficult because he is particularly demanding or requires constant help. The thinking here is that if server-based computing can make a difficult user happy, it can make anyone happy. Using these selection criteria, though, is toying with disaster. A pilot program is likely to have some bugs that require working out. The wrong participant may loudly complain about the problems of working with Terminal Services. If the complaining reaches the ears of an executive, the whole Corporate ASP initiative could be killed. The organization would lose the opportunity for all of the savings and benefits from server-based computing because of poor selection of participants.

Pilot users should be a representative sample of those who will ultimately use Terminal Services, but they should be friendly to the concept and understanding about the likelihood of encountering initial problems until IT works them out. Avoid choosing people for any reason other than testing the server-based computing concept. For instance, making someone a pilot user to avoid purchasing a new PC for that user is a bad idea.

We also recommend limiting a pilot program to the minimum number of participants necessary to get a representative sample of the type of users who will be on the production system. This makes it much more manageable. Once the pilot program has been proven successful, it can always be expanded into a beta implementation with more users.

Hybrids or Pure Thin Clients

When a user continues to run one or more applications on his or her local PC, this is called operating in hybrid mode. If pilot participants will be operating in hybrid mode, make sure their desktops are set up so that they know whether they are in a local session or in a MetaFrame session. This can be accomplished using application publishing (as explained in Chapter 15).

Even if Windows terminals are not in your organization's Corporate ASP plans, we recommend securing one for the pilot program. Since a Windows terminal is completely dependent upon server-based computing to operate, installing one contributes to a deeper understanding of the new paradigm. You may find that the Windows terminal "brick" has uses that you hadn't previously considered, such as serving as an employee's home "PC."

CAUTION: If you are going to have pilot users run legacy PCs, make sure the PCs are high-quality, reliable models (though they do not need to be powerful machines). In one of the authors' projects, a teacher became frustrated because her extremely cheap PC's keyboard broke when she was made a pilot MetaFrame user. Unfortunately, she had grown attached to her low-end keyboard, and despite our best efforts, we could not convince her that her keyboard's failure had nothing to do with Terminal Services. She ended up poisoning the entire project by warning the other teachers not to let MetaFrame into their classrooms "because it breaks keyboards."

Remote-Office Users

If your pilot users are in a remote office and are connected by limited bandwidth, it is essential that you instruct them in proper usage. You do not want them, for instance, to back up files from their local hard drives to the MetaFrame server at headquarters. This will chew up bandwidth and may cause performance degradation for other users in the remote office. As discussed in Chapter 6, you might also consider setting up bandwidth management as part of your pilot program in order to ensure adequate WAN performance.

TIP: Even if you have no intention of putting headquarters users onto Terminal Services, you should consider setting up at least one corporate IT person as part of the pilot program. Again, this will help to foster understanding of the server-based computing concept and enable your IT staff to experience it firsthand.

Document Performance

Document your expectations of the pilot program before you begin. Decide up front upon the success metrics, and after the pilot program, create a report on whether success metrics were met. Document any problems encountered along with their solutions. Document any open issues along with the actions being taken to resolve them.

Pilot Server(s)

Ideally, two load-balanced servers will be utilized for the production pilot program in order to provide redundancy. In most cases, though, organizations will probably use only one server in order to keep expenses lower during the proof-of-concept phase. The server should still be close enough to your expected production rollout model to make the results meaningful. For instance, using a Hewlett-Packard server with only two CPUs and half the RAM of your ultimate intended Hewlett-Packard MetaFrame server is probably OK. Using a different brand with different CPU and memory configurations is not a good idea.

Applications

If you are running anything other than 32-bit applications, be prepared for less than optimal performance. Make users aware of what they can expect of various applications. Use products such as Citrix Resource Management Services (RMS) in order to test application performance under simulated greater usage. If performance is less than expected, try removing questionable applications to see if a particular product is causing problems.

THE FEASIBILITY COMMITTEE

Once the proof-of-concept pilot program has proven that the necessary applications run together acceptably within Terminal Services, it is time to determine whether an enterprise server-based computing deployment makes sense for the organization. The decision process of whether to implement a Corporate ASP should include an evaluation of the proposed project's impact on the organization from operational, financial, cultural, and political perspectives.

A feasibility committee made up of IT personnel and employees from other appropriate departments should assess the merits of migrating to server-based computing. The first task of the feasibility committee will be to broadly define the project's scope along with its benefits. The committee must then evaluate the strategic fit of a Corporate ASP within the organization. The next steps include finding an executive sponsor and preparing a financial justification for the project. The committee's resulting report can then be utilized to help guide the planning team's work should the Corporate ASP project move forward.

Project Scope

Server-based computing might be limited to deployment of a single application, or it may encompass the entire desktop. It might be utilized only in certain departments or regions, or it may be implemented as the new corporate standard. In general, the more extensively an organization implements a Corporate ASP, the more money they will save compared with using PC-based computing. (In Chapter 1 we covered the composition of these savings as well as many other benefits of a Corporate ASP.) The feasibility committee must determine whether a complete enterprise rollout is practical or whether a scaled-back implementation would be more appropriate.

Corporate Culture Considerations

The economies achieved from implementing server-based computing inevitably make it much less expensive than decentralized PC-based computing. A hidden potential cost, though, is the turmoil that may result from introducing such huge changes into the computing environment.

Centralized Standards

The nature of PC-based computing makes it difficult for organizations to enforce IT standards. Typically, corporate IT is unaware of many applications that users run locally or departmentally. Although a Corporate ASP does offer IT the flexibility to allow users to run local applications, it also makes it easy to lock down desktops. Since greater lockdown equates to less administration, IT will tend to exploit this advantage. Even if IT decides to host only a few critical corporate applications, these particular programs now will be outside the direct control of users.

In many organizations, greater IT control is taken for granted as an advantage. Banks, for instance, typically have a tradition of mainframe hosting and readily embrace computing standards for PC users. A software development firm, on the other hand, may decide that the creative benefits of unbridled individual computing outweigh the lower costs obtained from enforcing centralized standards.

The feasibility committee needs to evaluate whether standardization is an acceptable condition within their organizational environment.

Understanding User Perceptions of the Network Infrastructure and IT

The distribution of economic and IT resources mandated by distributed processing often results in a network infrastructure that is plagued with performance and reliability problems. In these environments, users will be reluctant to give up control of their desktops to IT.

NOTE: The feasibility committee must call attention to a networking infrastructure that suffers from performance or reliability problems, but this does not mean that the Corporate ASP project should be abandoned. On the contrary: As long as IT can fix the existing problems, an uncompromising first review presents an opportunity to build rapid project acceptance. IT should initially implement smaller Terminal Services beta projects that deliver better reliability and performance to thin-client users than to their fat-client peers. This strategy can create rapid enthusiasm for the new technology and, in turn, help enable IT to plan an enterprise-wide implementation of server-based computing.

Political Considerations

In many organizations, the disparate nature of distributed processing has led to control of IT budgets by different departments or divisions. Creating a Corporate ASP is a costly endeavor that affects users throughout the organization. The feasibility committee needs to determine whether the organization will be able to marshal the resources to implement such an encompassing project.

Reduced IT Staff

Gartner Group reports that the staffing required to support a fat-client environment is at least five times greater than the staffing required to support a thin-client environment. A Corporate ASP implementation can eliminate the need for remote office IT personnel or even for entire regional IT departments. It is the job of the feasibility committee to evaluate whether the corporate culture will permit elimination of unnecessary network administration, help desk personnel, and PC technician positions.

IT Staff Salaries

Since the majority of organizational processing under a Corporate ASP takes place at central data centers, the network administrators must be quite skilled. They may require higher salaries than their peers in many distributed processing environments, perhaps even higher than their managers. The feasibility committee must assess whether these types of administrators are already on staff and, if not, whether the organization's salary structure will allow for hiring them.

TIP: A Corporate ASP is too encompassing, and too vital to efficiency (and eventual savings), to allow for skimping on anything in the data center—including the people who run it. If higher wages for a select network administrator would wreak havoc on the IT department's existing salary structure, consider alternative solutions, such as outsourcing the position.

Finding an Executive Sponsor

> *Gaining an executive sponsor and executive support is without question the single most important thing I did for this project. The challenges that would follow during the next nine months would have been difficult, if not impossible, to overcome without the complete backing of the most senior folks in our company.*
>
> —Anthony Lackey,
> VP Electronic Services and CTO, ABM Industries

Many people simply resist change, particularly if they feel they are giving something up. A server-based computing paradigm is very different from traditional PC-based computing and is bound to cause some disharmony. Executive sponsorship is essential for the successful implementation of a Corporate ASP. Upper management must make it absolutely clear that the enterprise server-based computing initiative is something that will happen and that everyone is expected to make work. Ideally, the CIO and selected other executives should switch from PCs to Windows terminals in order to show their complete support for the project.

Justifying a Corporate ASP Financially

As the feasibility committee members discuss the scope and organizational ramifications of a Corporate ASP, they are likely to become more aware of the enormous savings and benefits it will provide. In order for the project to move forward, they need to convey this information to management. Most corporate decision makers are going to require an in-depth financial analysis of the specific impacts of migrating to server-based computing. They will primarily be interested in the estimated cost of the project and the return on the required investment. A reasonable time frame over which to calculate these figures usually ranges from three to five years.

Although it may seem both very difficult and impractical to estimate project costs without first doing a detailed infrastructure assessment and in-depth planning, this is not the case. The components of a Corporate ASP are not difficult to estimate on a broad range. And since the resulting savings over PC-based computing are likely to be enormous, broad estimates are all that is required for a revealing financial analysis.

We recommend taking a three-pronged approach to building a financial analysis, and we give examples in Appendix A. First, present the hard cost savings. This can be done by comparing the estimated costs of staying with PC-based computing over a period of three to five years versus the estimated costs of implementing a Corporate ASP. Hard costs include easily identified expenditures such as hardware purchases and help desk personnel salaries. In most cases, the hard savings alone will more than justify the entire project. This will isolate the feasibility committee from detractors who might try to take shots at the financial analysis.

Next, present the estimated soft cost savings. These are real savings, but their quantification may be harder to agree upon. For instance, how much does it really cost the organization when users suffer downtime as their PCs are upgraded? The model presented in Appendix A shows how these types of savings can be estimated. Presenting them as part of the financial analysis gives management a better idea of the ultimate economic impact of migrating to a Corporate ASP.

The last component is a list of the expected benefits from a Corporate ASP. These benefits can sometimes be quantified, but often have just as big an impact if they are listed without numerical assignations. As described in Chapter 1, the business benefits of a Corporate ASP often have more strategic importance to the organization than the hard and soft savings combined.

THE PROJECT PLANNING TEAM

Once an executive sponsor has been identified and management has accepted the feasibility committee's financial analysis of implementing a Corporate ASP, a planning team can be assembled.

The project planning team will be made up primarily of IT staff, including hands-on technical people. It should also include some members from the feasibility committee and possibly representatives from multiple departments or divisions. This will help ensure that the organization's enterprise goals are met with this enterprise deployment. Each member's role and expected contributions should be defined. Accountability should be established.

Server-Based Computing Consultants

Since a Corporate ASP rides on top of NT technology, many organizations are inclined to plan the entire process internally and use only existing staff. This is probably not an optimal utilization of resources. We recommend seeking out Citrix specialists who have designed and implemented multiple large-scale server-based computing migrations. The experience they bring to the table should pay for their fees many times over.

NOTE: Citrix has stratified its reseller channel into three categories: silver, gold, and platinum. Platinum resellers represent approximately the top one percent of all resellers. They must have a minimum of six Citrix certified engineers on staff, and they are the most likely segment to have the resources and experience to successfully implement an enterprise server-based computing project. Of course, you should carefully check the references and ascertain the capabilities of any consultants you engage.

The Project Definition Document

The first task of the planning committee is to prepare a document defining project goals, scope, roles, and risks along with success criteria and milestones. This will be a living document that will guide the planning team through the infrastructure assessment, design, and implementation stages. As expectations, requirements, and conditions change, the planning definition document will serve as a touchstone for keeping the project on track.

Project Goals

While saving money is likely to be an important objective, the strategic advantages and other benefits described in Chapter 1 may be even more important considerations. Clearly defined project goals serve as a benchmark as the Corporate ASP rolls out.

Project Scope

The preliminary work done by the feasibility committee combined with management's reaction to the financial analysis enable the planning committee to identify the parameters of the Corporate ASP. In particular, the committee must select the applications to be run as part of the Corporate ASP along with expectations for stability and for upgrades during the implementation process. Adding a new application, for example, requires extensive testing as well as the creation of a new server image. What's known as *scope creep* is inevitable, and guidelines need to be established for an approval process when requests for additional applications or features are made. Allowances must also be made for delays caused by these changes.

Project Roles

Keeping the project's executive sponsor closely informed of progress will help garner upper management support when needed. The project also requires both an IT owner and a high-level business owner who can intercede to work through problems that will arise. A project manager needs to be assigned along with a backup project manager who can make decisions in the event the project manager is unavailable. Outlining escalation procedures for contacting the appropriate decision maker in the event that the project manager is unable or unwilling to solve a problem helps to keep things on track. If the rollout is large enough, both a quality assurance person and a training coordinator should be assigned to the project as well.

Project Risks

Identifying risks such as scope creep, unavailability of resources, and lack of user acceptance helps the committee include strategies for reducing risk of project failure. Contingency plans should also be included.

Criteria for Success

Identifying the criteria by which the project will be judged a success enables the planning and implementation teams to better focus their energies. If user satisfaction is a requirement for success, for example, user surveys should be designed along with a mechanism for their distribution, collection, and tabulation. We recommend simple electronic forms allowing users to grade the Corporate ASP project on items such as performance, functionality, and reliability. Figure 4-1 shows a sample of the Lotus Notes–based survey forms that ABM e-mailed to their users.

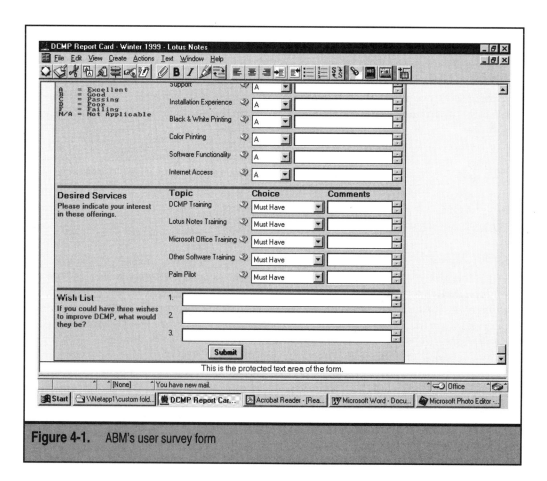

Figure 4-1.   ABM's user survey form

Project Milestones

The infrastructure assessment and upgrade, design document, beta implementation, enterprise rollout, and both administrator and user training are examples of project milestones.

INFRASTRUCTURE ASSESSMENT

To produce a meaningful Corporate ASP planning document, a detailed infrastructure assessment must first be completed. This assessment includes identifying the appropriate contacts for each category and conducting meetings with them.

Another purpose behind the infrastructure assessment is to discover and remedy any infrastructure problems prior to a server-based computing rollout. In a PC-based computing environment, employees are often used to things being sloppy. Although the network might have some performance or downtime problems, users tend to be somewhat understanding because they commonly save files to their local hard drives anyway. When users destroy their PC configurations by adding a software utility or deleting an INI file, they often ask a peer for help rather than making an embarrassing support call to IT. Since users work on *their* personal computers and departments run *their* own servers, they are less likely to complain to IT staff or management even when problems arise that are not of their making.

In a server-based computing environment, employees' *personal* computers become *corporate* computers. While vastly more efficient from an organizational standpoint, users lose the status conferred by having ever more powerful PCs. They are more likely to complain about problems that they would never have mentioned in a PC-based computing environment. Since users are completely dependent upon a central server farm for the majority, or all, of their applications, any instability or performance problems in the network infrastructure will instantly be amplified. The new technology will often be blamed for the existing infrastructure problems. Back-end file servers, the data center server backbone, and wide area connectivity all need to be running flawlessly or the enterprise deployment of server-based computing will be in jeopardy of failing.

The Application Environment

The Corporate ASP is really about delivery of applications. It is therefore crucial that all relevant information about the Corporate ASP applications is identified.

Application Database Sources

List the source of any database information utilized by applications, including the database application, the host system, and its geographical location.

Operating Under Terminal Services

Describe whether manufacturer support exists for running each application under Terminal Server or Windows 2000 Terminal Services. List any manufacturer requirements for this environment as well as any caveats.

Application Composition

Describe the language of each application as well as whether it is client or server or telnet.

Application Architecture

Determine whether or not the application is built for a multiuser environment.

> **TIP:** Custom applications can be particularly tricky. You will want to make sure that the applications use Microsoft multiple user architecture that utilizes roaming profiles. This means that the applications are user specific; users have their own settings and will not be sharing settings (HKEY_CURRENT_ USER versus HKEY_LOCAL_MACHINE). The applications should also have subordinate files, such as log files or temp files, that can be redirected to the user's Windows directory and/or Temp directory. A program that is not user specific but has global settings means that a user making setting switches will affect all users on that server. If the application is not written as user specific, you will need to lock those keys in the registry to prevent users from changing them.

Manufacturer Support Contracts

If manufacturer support contracts exist for any of the applications, include the relevant information along with phone numbers and the appropriate identification authorization.

Application Requirements

List specific operating conditions for each application, including

- ▼ Memory requirements
- ■ Disk space requirements
- ■ Sound requirements
- ■ Drive mapping requirements
- ■ Any patches or service packs
- ▲ Location of the install files

Application Issues

List any application issues that could affect performance within a Corporate ASP. For instance, if an application tends to cause blue screens when running in a PC-based computing environment, the planning committee must be aware that similar problems are likely to occur under server-based computing.

Application Packaging

Describe how the application is distributed to users within the existing PC-based computing environment. How often is the application revised? How is it packaged? For instance, can users install updates with a single mouse click?

Internal Application Support

Identify any internal support contacts for all internal and line-of-business applications. Identify any internal application owners who are responsible for deploying new versions of applications.

The Hardware Environment

The planning process will be based upon knowledge about the existing hardware environment for servers and host systems. Because Corporate ASP users will likely require far more central storage for their data, existing storage subsystems are a particularly important element to consider.

The Data Center Environment

Evaluating existing data center sites for power, cooling, and physical security will let the project planning team assess whether they are adequate for hosting the Corporate ASP data center(s).

The System Management Environment (SME)

Evaluating the existing SME enables the planning committee to incorporate it into the server-based computing design. This includes identifying any existing tools for measuring metrics, such as HP OpenView or Tivoli.

The Support Structure and Processes

Determining the different levels of support resources available will help the planning team arrive at a strategy for providing support during the Corporate ASP implementation. Also define the way support calls are placed and relayed. What help desk package is in use, if any? How is a PC call handled versus an operating system issue? Are any service level agreements (SLAs) currently defined? How is support localized in remote offices?

The Testing Environment

Creating a testing environment is crucial to implementing and successfully maintaining a Corporate ASP. The planning team needs to know if a current formalized testing environment exists and if testing labs are available.

Changing Control Procedures

What change control policies and procedures are in place today? What kind of approval process is required for making changes? Does a database application exist for recording all changes to critical systems? Is there a quality assurance group?

TIP: In many organizations, the IT administrators learned their trade on a PC rather than in a host systems environment. They may be used to making changes on the fly and not recording the changes they make. This approach will cause a Corporate ASP to fail. A mainframe shop mentality with rigorous change control is essential for success.

The Training Environment

Is there a formalized training group? Are classrooms available? What kind of training is commonly used for IT people? For end users?

The NT Server Environment

Identifying components such as protocols used, the existing domain structure, naming conventions, and partitioning is essential information for planning a Terminal Services infrastructure.

Network Architecture

Defining the existing network architecture is crucial to designing a solid Corporate ASP infrastructure, including routers, switches, protocols, policy servers, bandwidth allocation policies, remote office servers, existing redundancy options, and remote access capabilities. Any existing network reliability or performance problems such as client latency issues need to be identified and ultimately resolved prior to the server-based computing rollout.

The Security Environment

In order for the planning committee to design the proper secure Terminal Services environment, they need to know the following: What firewalls are in place? How is dial-up security currently handled? What internal policies are in place on NT servers? How is lockdown of NTFS partitions handled? Is there a security group?

The Backup Environment

Increased data consolidation within a Corporate ASP will likely require increased storage systems and, therefore, new backup systems. The planning committee needs to know what kind of data backup mechanisms and backup policies exist today.

The Printing Environment

Printing is a big issue under Terminal Services, and the existing environment needs to be defined. Does printing take place through locally attached printers or only on the network? What network protocols are used? What are the types and number of printers? What print drivers are required? Are print servers used in remote offices today?

The Client Environment

Define the client environment of the Corporate ASP participants. This includes categories of users, their location, and whether they have access to a local server. Also describe the details of the specific clients, such as device (PC, laptop, UNIX workstation, handheld), model, local O/S, and any existing performance or reliability issues.

THE PROJECT DESIGN PLAN

The project plan incorporates all aspects of the Corporate ASP design. This plan includes both the project definition document and results of the infrastructure assessment. The financial analysis performed by the feasibility committee should be fine-tuned throughout the planning process until the final planning document includes a solid estimate for project costs.

The planning document should clearly convey the organization's server-based computing migration strategy and be suitable for presentation to both executives and auditors. It discusses the various options that the planning team considered for each major component of the project, along with the rationale behind the team's ultimate decision.

The project plan also serves as a roadmap for the project managers and implementation team as they work to institute a Corporate ASP environment. Detailed explanations of the design plan are discussed in the remaining chapters in this part of the book. An overview of the design plan follows.

Terminal Services Design

Designing the Terminal Services environment will be difficult for organizations unfamiliar with the basics of server-based computing. We recommend that the appropriate IT personnel take courses in Terminal Services, MetaFrame, and Advanced MetaFrame before beginning the design process.

Application Architecture Design

Define the strategy both for deploying the Corporate ASP and for handling legacy applications that will not be supported. Users may be allowed, for instance, to run legacy applications locally as long as they want. Alternatively, they may be given a deadline for transitioning to corporate-approved and -supported applications. (Application strategies are covered in more detail in Chapter 15.)

Data Center Architecture Design

The planning team needs to determine the number of data centers, based upon demographic, geographic, disaster recovery, and business requirements. They must evaluate site considerations, including power, cooling, fire suppression, and physical security. They also must evaluate options for either hosting the centers internally or using co-location centers, such as AT&T or Exodus. (Data center architecture is discussed more thoroughly in Chapter 5.)

Disaster Recovery Design

Since users are completely dependent upon a Corporate ASP for all of their processing, disaster recovery is an extremely important component. Fortunately, server-based computing makes a real-time disaster recovery solution far more practical and affordable than in a PC-based computing environment. (A variety of disaster recovery options are discussed in Chapter 5.)

Network Backbone Design

Each data center requires a high-speed backbone connecting the MetaFrame server farm with other servers in the data center. Small organizations may be able to get by with 100 Mbps switched Ethernet. Large firms will likely require ATM or switched gigabit. Redundant network interface cards (NICs) and switches should be incorporated as part of the design. (The network backbone is discussed more thoroughly in Chapter 6.)

Server Farm Architecture Design

The findings from the proof-of-concept pilot program will enable the planning committee to select server quantity, type, sizing, and configuration for the Terminal Services implementation. Citrix Resource Management Services (RMS) and NT Performance Monitor can help determine server scalability. Other tools can simulate server loads. If DOS or 16-bit applications will be run, extra servers may be required for a multitiered server farm. Likewise, support for multiple languages will necessitate additional servers for each language. (Server farm architecture is discussed more thoroughly in Chapter 15.)

File Services Design

When users store all of their data at corporate data centers, unique problems arise in handling file services efficiently. The project team should evaluate the different options, including server clustering of general-purpose file servers, Storage Area Networks (SANs), and Network-Attached Storage (NAS). Archive systems and backup software and services must also be selected. (File services are covered in detail in Chapter 7.)

Print Server Architecture Design

Printing tends to be the most difficult and time-consuming part of an enterprise server-based computing implementation. Decisions must be made about the configuration of one or more central print servers at each data center as well as the type and quantity of print servers in remote offices. Just a few of the other printer-related decisions the team will have to make include integration of host system printing, local PC printing, printer autocreation to create temporary printer assignments for mobile users, trusted print sources, lockdown of registries, and control over printer access. (Printing is discussed in detail in Chapter 17.)

User Profiles Design

Most Terminal Services implementations utilize either mandatory or roaming profiles, but we recommend that organizations use scripting to enable desktop lockdown while allowing users the flexibility to select default drives and printers. (We present our scripting techniques in Chapter 16.)

ICA Browser Design

The ICA browser maintains data on Citrix servers and published applications. Decisions must be made about whether to set up a server as a dedicated ICA master browser, the number of backup browsers, whether to use ICA gateways, and load-balance tuning.

Login Script Design

To minimize administration, there should be one script that works for both fat and thin clients. Additionally, login scripts should be designed to run very quickly and efficiently.

Automation Design

You will want to automate application installation and updates, server imaging processes, and client installations using products such as Citrix Installation Management Services (IMS) and Norton Ghost. (Automation design is covered in Chapter 14.)

NT Design

Designing an NT infrastructure to support Terminal Services is a key part of the planning process. The following components are included.

Domain Model Design

When designing large enterprise infrastructures, it is easy to design a domain that entails frequent and inefficient replication. For a server-based computing environment, we generally recommend a single master domain model to separate authentication of users and groups from authentication of resources.

WINS Architecture Design

Under server-based computing, WINS is less likely to be required.

Backup Architecture Design

If the infrastructure assessment reveals inadequate backup systems to handle the demands of centralized data storage, the archive systems and backup software and services require selection. (Backup systems are explained in Chapter 7.)

Back-End Database Design

The size and configuration of a back-end database in a server-based computing environment, where all users will be hitting one database at one time, will often be different from a distributed database model, where several database servers are located across the enterprise. The distributed servers would handle a relatively small number of users and have replicated data back to a central point. The server-based computing model might require far more powerful database server(s) or clustered servers at the data center, depending on usage, as well as middleware application changes.

Network Design

A sound network infrastructure is vital to supporting a Corporate ASP environment. In addition to remedying any shortfalls discovered during the infrastructure assessment, the following issues should be addressed.

Topologies

Because the MetaFrame ICA client uses such little bandwidth, the composition of the topology to the desktop is generally not of great importance as long as it is reliable. In most cases, 4 Mbps Token Ring will deliver the same performance as switched 100 Mbps.

WAN Architecture

A Corporate ASP environment requires a robust, scalable, and highly reliable WAN design because remote office users are completely dependent upon the MetaFrame servers at the corporate data centers. The planning team must evaluate the different connectivity options, including the Internet and redundancy options. During the transition from PC-based to server-based computing, residual traffic will chew up an inordinate amount of bandwidth. The project plan must allow for this temporary increased bandwidth requirement during the migration process. (Bandwidth management, including packet prioritization, is often essential in order to ensure adequate performance in a Terminal Services wide area network. Wide area connectivity is discussed more thoroughly in Chapter 6.)

Policies and Procedures Design

As is the case with the mainframe model of computing, clearly defined policies and procedures are essential for Corporate ASP success. Adding an application or making a small change to a central router can have severe consequences for hundreds or thousands of Corporate ASP users. Although we continue to emphasize the numerous advantages of an enterprise server-based computing environment, it does require that the days of the network cowboy come to an end.

> *Having been raised, from an MIS perspective, in the midrange and micro eras of computing, my staff had a hard time rethinking the way they do things. For example, while "maintenance windows" were commonplace in the days of the mainframe, they've seemingly disappeared in the PC era. My network technicians were used to shutting a system down minutes after announcing it. We all had to relearn what the MIS personnel we replaced 10 to 15 years ago knew as second nature.*
>
> —Anthony Lackey,
> VP Electronic Services and CTO, ABM Industries

Data Center Policies and Procedures Design

The planning document should include the organization's strategy for managing environmental changes.

TIP: Depending upon the current policies and procedures as revealed in the infrastructure assessment, new requirements may be necessary. For example, a workflow-enabled database should track all changes by administrators and implementers to the Terminal Services infrastructure.

User Policies and Procedures Design

Decisions must be made about data access, device access, and adding new devices. For example, will users be allowed to access local devices from an ICA session? If so, this policy can have unanticipated ramifications, such as security concerns when users access their local drives from a Citrix session. (Policies and procedures are discussed more thoroughly in Chapter 16.)

Client Design

The planning committee should identify the different client categories and the levels to which they are expected to utilize Corporate ASP services. They must further decide how to specifically set up the clients, and how to configure user desktops. Choices must be made regarding policies for local browsing, emulation, drive mappings, PC local operating systems, local hardware peripherals, and integration with handheld devices such as Palm Pilots. If Windows terminals will be used, the planning team must evaluate the different options and choose the brand and models most appropriate for their organization. (Client implementation is discussed more thoroughly in Chapter 11.)

Client Operating Systems

A primary benefit of centralized computing is the standardization of applications. While standard client equipment and operating systems make administration easier, one of the most compelling strengths of server-based computing is its ability to effectively manage a heterogeneous environment. Still, different operating systems do have different ramifications for functionality under Terminal Services.

User Interface Design

Users can launch entire MetaFrame desktops, or simply click on icons generated through Citrix Program Neighborhood. Citrix NFuse enables application publishing to a browser interface.

Integration with Local Devices

Design strategies must be included for client integration with local printers, handheld units, scanners, bar code readers, and cash drawers.

UNIX Workstation Client Design

MetaFrame enables UNIX workstation users to run Windows applications without requiring a separate PC. UNIX Integration Services (UIS) adds the functionality of the X Window protocol. An ICA client is also available for most major UNIX versions.

Data Organization Design

When users migrate to Terminal Services, policies will need to be set about where their data will be stored for different applications (central server storage versus local storage). Creating broad policies that extend across all Corporate ASP users will greatly facilitate the ability of help desk personnel to provide prompt support.

Client Application Design

Different application strategies may be appropriate for different categories of users. For instance, mobile users will likely have some local applications, while office users may have none.

Other Client Design Considerations

Groups, drive mappings, and login script strategies must be designed for the different categories of users.

Remote Access Design

The project planning team needs to choose the appropriate remote access strategy, whether using leased lines, frame relay, dial-up lines, or the Internet. (Remote access design considerations, including connection and redundancy strategies, profiles, and gateway routing, are detailed in Chapter 8.)

Security Design

A security strategy must be incorporated into the project plan. Citrix SecureICA should be considered along with the Internet Protocol Security (IPSec). Firewall integration, account management, auditing, and the Terminal Services Registry should all be included. (Security is discussed more thoroughly in Chapter 9.)

The Systems Management Environment

If the infrastructure assessment indicates that a network management package is already utilized as part of the existing PC-based computing environment, the planning team should extend it to encompass the Corporate ASP. The team should also decide on how the existing network management package, or a new one, can best be configured to work with server-based computing packages such as Citrix Resource Management Services. (Network management environments are covered in detail in Chapter 10.)

Metrics Design

As part of the systems management environment, the planning team should determine which metrics are to be collected and analyzed in order to develop strategies for expansion and for limiting bottlenecks. Citrix Resource Management Services is a good tool to use in this capacity, though it may overlap with existing utilities such as HP OpenView or Tivoli.

General Implementation Design

The implementation plan should cover training, user communications, data migration, project management, change management, and customer care.

Training Plan

A training plan needs to be designed for support personnel, system administrators, and end users.

TIP: Once end users are set up to access their desktop through Citrix, you can coordinate a more formal introductory training class by using the MetaFrame shadowing capabilities. The trainer can have several users simultaneously shadow her PC. Setting up a concurrent conference call provides the audio to describe the visual orientation.

Support Personnel   The low administrative requirements of server-based computing combined with features such as shadowing will enable help desk personnel to support many more users once the Corporate ASP migration is complete. During the transition, however, increased staff and training will likely be necessary to handle the demands of the new architecture while supporting users on the old PC-based computing platform.

End Users   Distribution of rainbow documents for general information and at-a-glance documents for frequently asked questions is an expedient way to provide quick user orientation to server-based computing. A *rainbow document* is modeled after the colorful organizational wall charts found in many hospitals for quick reference to services and locations. The rainbow document literally contains a rainbow of colored sheets, each a bit narrower than the other, providing easy reference to the topics on the exposed edge. Some relevant topics might be "Getting Help," "Finding Your Files," "Glossary of Terms," and "Your Thin-Client Desktop."

User Communications Plan

A method for communicating migration plans to users is an often overlooked but nonetheless important component of a successful Corporate ASP implementation. (Strategies for internal marketing are discussed in the last part of this chapter, and you will find still more detail in Chapter 12.)

Project Management

The planning team should incorporate the essentials of project management as part of the plan. Implementation teams must have well-defined tasks, and required resources must be identified. An estimated timeline for the project beta testing and rollout should be included as part of the planning document.

An enterprise server-based computing migration requires project manager authority, stakeholder buy-in, project reporting and tracking, task assignment, project change control, scope creep control, and timeline management. (Project management is discussed in detail in Chapter 12.)

Change Management

The planning document should include the organization's strategy for managing environmental changes in order to enhance management and end-user benefits. Administrator and end-user training, user reference guides, asset tracking, and a frequently asked questions (FAQs) database should all be incorporated as part of the project. The planning team should include survey forms for gathering information prior to implementation and for measuring user satisfaction as the rollout takes place. (These topics are discussed more thoroughly in Chapters 12 and 18.)

Customer Care

The help desk department will be able to handle many more users once the migration to server-based computing is complete. During the transition, however, increased staff may be necessary to handle the glitches of the new architecture while supporting users on the old PC-based computing platform. (Customer care is given further consideration in Chapter 12.)

Migrating to Server-Based Computing

The planning document should include a roadmap for migrating from fat client to thin client. Also clearly documented should be strategies for consolidating data from both PCs and remote office servers, minimizing downtime, and creating a "virtual call center" based upon skill sets. (These topics are discussed more thoroughly in Chapter 18.)

Expanding the Pilot Test to a Beta

The planning team must decide at what point the proof-of-concept pilot test will be expanded to a beta implementation, and they must decide the parameters of the beta. Objectives should be defined and results measured in order to allow adjustments to the team's migration strategy if required. A scope variance process needs to define who has authority to sign off on out-of-scope items, for example, including a new application as part of the beta. (The beta implementation is discussed in more detail in Chapter 18.)

INTERNAL SELLING OF SERVER-BASED COMPUTING

When word of the [server-based computing] project started to spread across the company, a flood of requests for new PCs came in. The requests for new systems were threefold higher than the previous year. Some folks figured we wouldn't ask them to discard a brand new system. A letter from our CFO to all controllers in all divisions reminded them that this project was not optional and that all PC purchases would be subject to heightened scrutiny.

—Anthony Lackey,
VP Electronic Services and CTO, ABM Industries

In most organizations, it is difficult to successfully migrate to a server-based computing environment through mandate alone. While an edict from top management is essential, the planning team needs to supplement it with a strategy for internally selling the project. IT will probably have ultimate project ownership, and an IT member will probably have to take the initiative in promoting server-based computing throughout the organization. For purposes of this chapter, we will assume that the IT person leading the initiative is the CIO.

TIP: IT people often underestimate the resistance that a paradigm shift to a Corporate ASP nearly always generates. Internal selling is likely to be a vital component of project approval and project success.

MIS Marketing

Educating and informing internal IT staff is the first priority, and this can be a challenge in itself. PC fix-it technicians will see the project as a threat. Regional IT staff will also be wary. The CIO must come up with a strategy that presents the project's advantages, including fewer user complaints, elimination of the majority of help desk calls, much more efficient troubleshooting, and more time for IT staff to learn new and challenging technologies to help the organization move forward.

Executive Marketing

The CIO should meet with the division managers either in a group or individually. She should take the time to explain the Corporate ASP philosophy to them along with the financial and other benefits that they can expect. She should also be realistic about the challenges they can expect to face during the project implementation and the results they will see upon its completion. Her team should customize an appropriate excerpt from the project plan to hand out to these executives.

If a subscription model for Corporate ASP billing will be adopted, the CIO should explain to the executives how the program works and how it will impact their departmental budgets. She can emphasize that the IT department will utilize this model to break even but do so in a manner that enables departments to operate far more efficiently and with greater accountability than under a PC-based computing environment. The subscription-billing model for a Corporate ASP is discussed in Appendix B.

PC User and Middle Management Marketing

Videos can be far more effective internal marketing tools than white papers. A video that presents the technology from the user's perspective can be prepared for all PC users in the company. The CEO can add legitimacy by starting the video off with a supportive introduction. The video can help with the orientation process by including footage of the Windows terminal that will be utilized and how the new desktops will look, the applications that will be available from the Corporate ASP, and the process for migrating users' existing data.

Large companies may wish to create a separate video targeted specifically toward middle management. This video can focus on the high-level benefits of server-based computing. It should emphasize how removing the frustrations of PC-based computing leaves employees with more time to concentrate on their business.

Other techniques to help market the concept can include rainbow packets, at-a-glance documents for frequently asked questions, e-mail messages, and phone calls.

NOTE: RYNO Technology has developed a comic book, "RYNOMan and the Thin-Client Adventure," to humorously explain the benefits of thin-client computing. You can order it free from their Web site at http://www.ryno.com.

Creating a Buzz

The ultimate goal of IT should be to create a buzz about the project. This can be accomplished by keeping the pilot program small and controlled, and by making sure that the beta is a resounding success. Including capabilities not possible in the fat-client environment, such as effective logon from home, helps make server-based computing particularly attractive. It is important to limit the size and scope of the beta not only to ensure control, but also to help create an atmosphere of scarcity and exclusivity. The objective is to have users clamoring to be included as part of the Corporate ASP project. Limiting PC purchases before an enterprise rollout also makes users more eager to get on the server-based computing bandwagon.

As mentioned earlier in the chapter, even if your organization has no requirements for new Windows terminals, we still recommend including a few as part of the beta. Windows terminals really drive home the point that users are operating under a different paradigm.

Finally, a key to effectively selling the concept is to constantly solicit and measure user feedback. IT can then make any adjustments necessary in order to ensure user satisfaction. Although some CIOs may be uncomfortable with the selling moniker, this part of the process will add tremendously to the process of building a very successful Corporate ASP.

CHAPTER 5

Data Center Architecture

In this chapter we discuss the importance of building and running your server-based computing environment in a secure, reliable data center facility. The need for this approach may be obvious to IT personnel with a background in host systems, but we will define the data center in the context of building a server-based computing environment. This centralized computing model often entails a new paradigm for network administrators whose IT experience is limited to running distributed networks based on traditional PC technology. We also discuss several key considerations—including environmental, network, and deployment—for the data center architecture.

WHAT IS A DATA CENTER?

A *data center* in this context is a central site or location that houses the server-based computing resources for a company. This site is characterized by limited physical access, superior network and power capacity and quality, and a degree of internal redundancy for these computing resources. Using Windows Terminal Services and Citrix MetaFrame in your data center, you can now provide a familiar PC desktop environment for users, no matter where they are located.

The data center was traditionally the realm of the mainframe, but Terminal Services and MetaFrame are changing this paradigm. The advent of the PC and of networking at the desktop level promised freedom from the "tyranny" of the traditional mainframe environment. Users were supposed to enjoy huge productivity gains upon being granted the power to run whatever applications they needed to do their work. The arrival of client-server computing offered a new promise of access to legacy information while maintaining the friendly user interface of the PC. This desktop freedom came with a huge cost. Distributing computing power and application serving to the desktop has increased total cost of ownership, most notably in the areas of support and obsolescence. The old adage "with power comes responsibility" holds true here. The users have the power, but who has the responsibility to make everything work? That duty still resides with the support staff—the same people who used to be responsible for the mainframe. But now, many more people are required to support the same user base. Personal computers and a sea of software have replaced the once simple environment consisting of dumb terminals and standard applications. Furthermore, users and support staff alike are caught in a never ending spiral of hardware upgrades. Applications continue to get bigger and make less efficient use of the computer and so require a more powerful computer to run them.

Although the centralized mainframe environment is comparatively easy to support, companies will continue migrating to easy-to-use PC applications. Organizations are desperate for a technology that combines the desirable elements of the centralized computing model with the ability to deliver the desired application services to the end user. This is the basis for the server-based computing model utilizing Windows Terminal Services and Citrix MetaFrame presented in this book. In the following sections, we present some important considerations in designing, building, and running a centralized data center environment with server-based computing technology in your company.

DESIGNING A DATA CENTER: OVERALL CONSIDERATIONS

Several seemingly disparate factors come into play when designing a server-based computing data center that, when considered together, give the picture of a secure, reliable, and cost-effective environment. Some of these factors, such as disaster recovery, are traditional concerns of the mainframe world, but they take on additional facets when considered as part of a computing environment using MetaFrame and Terminal Services. In this server-based context, we will examine disaster recovery and other factors in order to provide you with some valuable tools for designing your company's data center.

Disaster Recovery

When initially considering the consolidation of your distributed corporate servers, you may be concerned that you are "putting all your eggs in one basket." In most distributed computing environments, a single failed server probably only affects a small group of people. When everyone is connected to the same server (even a "virtual" one), its failure could be disastrous. Fortunately, through careful planning and diligent execution, you can make your server-based data center even more reliable than your current PC-based architecture.

Disaster recovery (DR) is a broad topic, and complete coverage is certainly beyond the scope of this book, but we will address a number of concerns that present themselves when building a data center for server-based computing. For example: Is one data center enough? Do you need to partner with an off-site disaster recovery services provider? What would be an acceptable level of risk, and which design achieves it? We will discuss these issues one at a time.

Number of Data Centers

At first glance, the idea of multiple data centers is attractive. Conceptually, a degree of fault tolerance is enabled when the centers are configured to fail over to each other. This allows top-priority users to get quickly back online. If your company has geographically dispersed locations, this is especially attractive. Both MetaFrame and Windows 2000 Terminal Services even support load balancing (though different types) over a WAN that would distribute user connections among multiple data centers. In practice, this idea has rarely been implemented well. In our work with one nationwide provider of disaster recovery services, Comdisco, we reviewed case after case of corporations that chose to have multiple data centers and ended up with two disparate centers in which very little was shared. We have found that the limitations outweigh the advantages. First, the advantages:

▼ Multiple links from end users on the WAN provide high availability.

■ Possible reduced cost for vendor disaster recovery services since the mechanisms for moving data would already be in place.

▲ Performance would be higher due to possible load balancing between sites.

The limitations of multiple data centers are as follows:

▼ Very complex solution; issues like data synchronization and system management make it costly to upgrade, as all data centers must be upgraded identically.

■ High network cost.

▲ The temptation to use the excess resources at either site is high, thus reducing the overall effectiveness of the multiple center concept.

Figure 5-1 illustrates an infrastructure with three data centers. If you feel that multiple data centers are justified in your company, you must carefully consider three issues: management resources, data synchronization and network cost, and excess server capacity.

▼ **Management resources**   The question here is simple: do you have adequate staff to handle multiple data centers? Though you will gain some efficiency by centralizing your services in one (or a small number of) data center(s), you still must have enough system administrators to run your services and handle support.

■ **Data synchronization and network cost**   If your data centers will be homogeneous in function, how will you make all data available at all sites to all users? There are plenty of solutions available for file server clustering such as Network-Attached Storage, third-party clustering software, or Microsoft's own Active Directory. But whatever method you choose, the data still has to move across a WAN link. Is your company prepared to incur the cost of this connectivity? Can you find another organization that has done what you want to do and made it work? One option is not to have all data at all sites ready for recovery. Prioritize your users and have critical data replicated to multiple sites but left in a "cold" state until needed. In this way, you could use less frequent batch updates and mitigate the need for online, real-time replication. Chapter 6 provides some guidelines for transporting data between sites.

■ **Excess server capacity**   If you build two data centers and each has the capability of serving 100 percent of your users, that means each center has 50

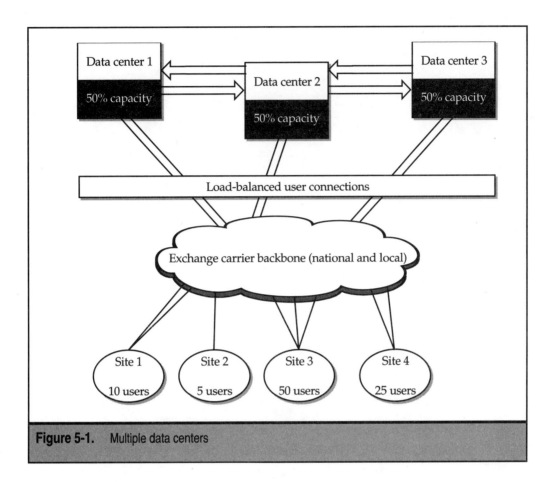

Figure 5-1.   Multiple data centers

percent extra capacity when you are not in failure mode. There is always a temptation to use this excess capacity the first time the support staff at the center runs into a crisis. "Sally ran out of disk space for her financial reports! We have to put more disk space online now!" Have you heard cries like this before? Nature abhors a vacuum, and excess capacity tends to become utilized in daily operations, leaving it unavailable when an emergency strikes. Not only must you resist demands for utilizing the extra capacity, but also when upgrading one data center, you must upgrade all others the same way. Figure 5-2 shows an infrastructure with two data centers and all connections load balanced between them. Figure 5-3 shows how fail-over would work if excess capacity were managed correctly.

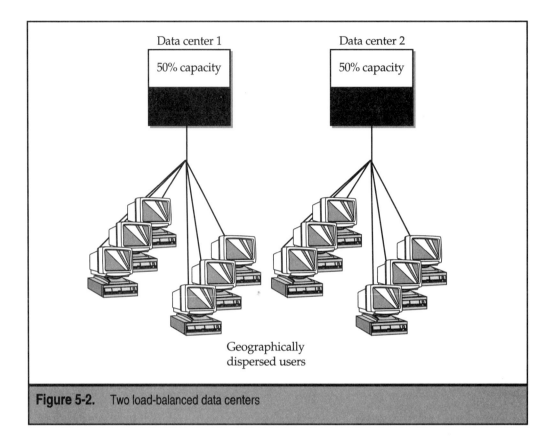

Figure 5-2. Two load-balanced data centers

Regardless of the number of data centers you choose, the following requirements should drive your decision:

▼ Ability to manage the number of sites in a cost-effective manner

■ Optimal price/performance

■ Simplicity of disaster recovery

▲ Reliability of disaster recovery

We have found that, all things considered, one data center (or at least very few) is a more desirable model. Once you've chosen the number of centers to build, you will need help designing a disaster recovery (DR) plan.

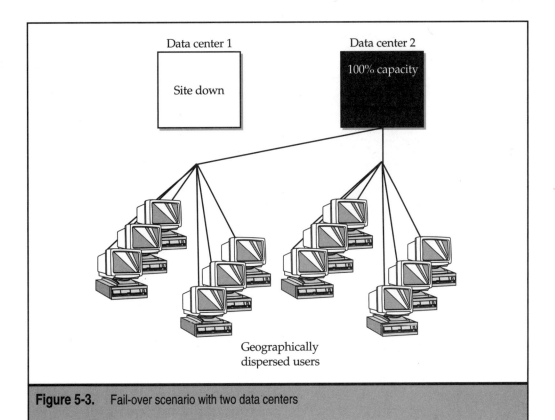

Figure 5-3. Fail-over scenario with two data centers

Recovery Time Objectives

When examining the disaster recovery needs of your company, you will likely find differing service level requirements for the different parts of your system. For example, it may be imperative for your service billing system to come back online within four hours in the event of a disaster. While inconvenient, it may still be acceptable for the e-mail system to recover in 24 hours. A key to a successful DR plan is knowing what your recovery time objectives are for the various pieces of your infrastructure. Short recovery times translate directly into high costs, due to the requirements of technology such as real-time data replication, redundant server farms, and high-bandwidth WAN links. Fortunately, with MetaFrame and Terminal Services, you don't have to hunt down PCs across the enterprise to recover their applications; all of your application servers will be located in the data center. Figure 5-4 shows an example of one company's top recovery time objectives.

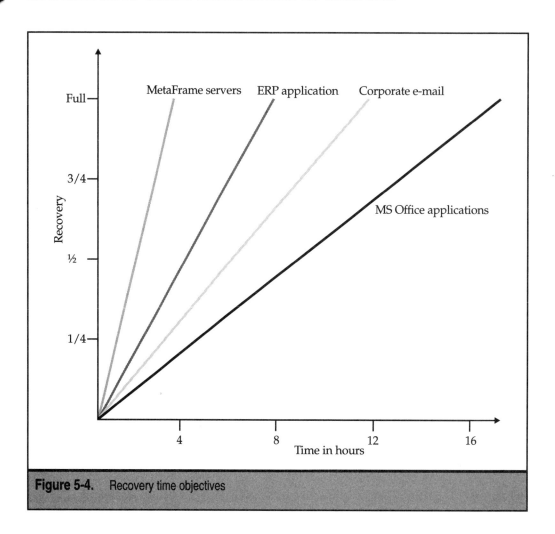

Figure 5-4. Recovery time objectives

The Hot Site

Running multiple data centers with their own fail-over capability is one method for implementing disaster recovery. The alternative is to utilize only one data center and contract with a DR service provider for a fail-over *hot site*. We have found that one robust data center with one hot site is a good model based on the trade-offs between complexity, expense, and the added redundancy of multiple data centers. Figure 5-5 shows a single data center with a hot site. In any case, there are a number of factors to consider:

▼ **Geography** Your hot site should be in an area with different risk elements from those of your main data center or centers. Your impetus for having a hot site in the first place is to mitigate the effect of losing your data center, which is most likely to happen because of a natural disaster. If your data center is in an area prone to earthquakes, for example, it would be wise to choose a hot site that is more tectonically stable and unlikely to be affected by the same disaster.

- ■ **Liability and business continuity**   Corporations, especially public ones, can be exposed to liability if it can be shown that they were negligent in their efforts to restore business operations following a disaster. Many corporations have been driven out of business because they had no DR plan in place and couldn't recover after a disaster. It is important to get your insurance carrier involved and learn both the extent of your company's exposure and what your business continuity insurance covers. Your DR service provider should also be able to advise you on this subject. Knowing the extent of your potential liability will help you gauge the resources needed to implement your disaster recovery architecture.

- ■ **Vendor capacity**   Presuming you have chosen a DR service provider, you need to make sure they have the capacity to respond to a regional disaster. If they have multiple clients in your area and a large disaster strikes, what is their strategy for restoring services? How do they prioritize? Perhaps most importantly, what is their track record? Are they aware of the server-based computing architecture, and are they prepared to customize a plan that will meet your needs in an enterprise Corporate ASP environment?

- ▲ **Hot vs. cold spares**   You've chosen a hot site, but how "hot" is it? Do you have live data being continuously replicated to servers there? Do you have an active network backbone in operation? You need to assess, based on the nature of your recovery strategy, which specific components must be in continuous operation and which can stand by and only be activated in case of a disaster. Standby components can represent significant cost savings, but usually mean a longer recover time. In all likelihood, you will end up with a combination of hot and cold systems.

Disaster Recovery Service Providers

Like network security, disaster recovery planning is one of those duties many managers find distasteful. They rarely plan for disaster recovery as completely as they should. In a centralized server-based computing environment, a thorough DR plan is essential. Fortunately, quite a few reputable firms specialize in helping companies formulate and execute a disaster recovery strategy. Notable DR players include Comdisco, Sunguard, and IBM. You should settle on a company that has the right mix of products and services to match your company's needs.

Outsourcing

Once you perform an assessment of your company's ability to host a data center using some of the criteria presented in this chapter, you may very well find that you do not have adequate facilities or infrastructure in place. It may be too costly to create the proper

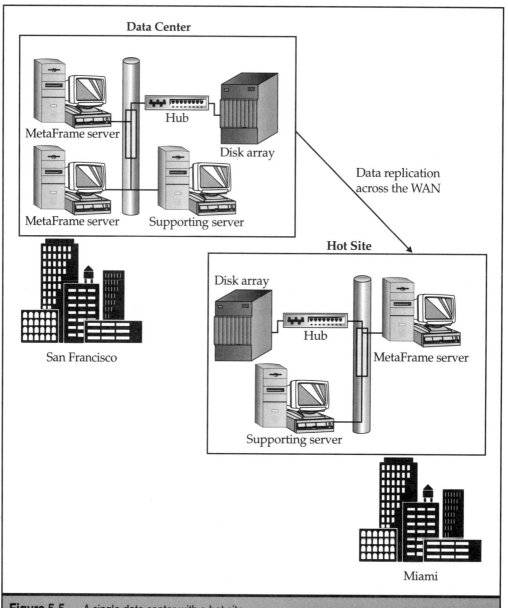

Figure 5-5. A single data center with a hot site

infrastructure, or it may be undesirable to take on the task for a variety of reasons. In this case you should seriously consider taking on a partner in building and running your data center. When you examine this option, you may find that even if your company could build and run a data center internally, outsourcing is attractive due to reasons of cost, staffing, location or built-in resiliency. Let's look at the advantages and limitations of outsourcing your data center more closely.

The advantages of outsourcing include

▼ Facilities built specifically for data center hosting already exist. Extensive new construction is rarely necessary.

■ Redundant power, cooling systems, raised floor, and fire suppression are often already in place.

■ Physical security is usually better than individual companies' internal security. Guards on duty, biometric authentication, escorted access, and other measures are typical.

■ Hosting facilities are often built very close to the points of presence (POP) of a local exchange carrier (LEC). In some cases, they are built into the same location as an LEC, which can dramatically decrease your WAN communication costs. Many national and regional carriers are getting into the hosting business.

■ Managed services that can supplement your own staff are usually available. These services are invariably less expensive than hiring someone to perform routine operations such as exchanging tapes or rebooting frozen servers.

■ Hosting facilities carry their own liability insurance, which could have a significant impact on the cost of business continuity insurance to your company.

▲ Many facilities can customize the service-level agreement they offer you or bundle hosting services with network telecommunication services.

The limitations of outsourcing include

▼ Access to your equipment is usually restricted or monitored. Outsourcing puts further demands on your design to create an operation that can run unattended.

■ WAN connectivity is limited to what the hosting center has available. It can be more difficult to get upgraded bandwidth because the hosting center has to filter such requests through the plans in place for the entire facility.

■ It may be more difficult to get approval internally for the expense because the hosting services appear as a bottom-line cost; whereas many information technology costs are buried in other areas such as facilities and telecommunications.

▲ If unmanaged space is obtained, it may be difficult or impractical to have one of your own staff on-site at the hosting facility for extended periods of time.

CASE STUDY: ABM Chooses AT&T to House Their Main Data Center

Anthony Lackey of ABM on the decision to outsource the data center: "The decision to co-locate the data center was a simple one. First, the single biggest vulnerability point for a thin-client solution is the network portal into the data center. Second, the physical connection from one's office to the network provider's central office is typically the most likely failure point. By co-locating our data center facilities with our network provider, we significantly reduced our vulnerability. Besides eliminating the risk of the last mile, we also eliminate a great deal of expense."

ABM saved approximately $25,000 per month on their ATM circuit by locating their data center inside a POP where AT&T maintained a hosting facility. In this case there was no local exchange carrier (LEC) involved, and the customer could connect directly to the national carrier's backbone on a different floor of the same building. Key features of the AT&T facility that were important to ABM in the evaluation process were the following:

▼ Uninterruptible power: four (expandable to six, 6/30/99) 375kVA UPS systems (N+1), dual (N+1) solar turbine generators 750kW (8000 gallon fuel capacity)

■ Dual power feeds to each cabinet from two different power systems

■ HVAC environmental control from central plant (150 tons of air-conditioning protecting 60 watts/square foot). Six Liebert 20 ton HVACs (another 30 watts/square foot)

■ Switched and diverse paths for WAN links; redundant OC-3/OC-12/OC-48 connections to multiple network access points

■ Fully staffed network operations center with trained systems administrators, data center technicians, and network engineers on duty 24 hours a day, seven days a week

■ Secured cabinets or caged environment with customized space allocation

■ State-of-the-art VESDA fire detection system (100 times more sensitive than conventional fire detection systems) backed up by a cross-zoned conventional system to prevent emergency power-off due to early detection

▲ State-of-the-art Inergen fire suppression system

Outage Mitigation Strategies

Having a good DR plan in place is small comfort to users if they are experiencing regular interruptions in service. Centralizing your computing resources makes it all the more important to incorporate a high degree of resiliency into your design. This goes far beyond just making sure the hard drives in your file server are in a RAID configuration. You must take a global view of the entire infrastructure and assess the following:

▼   *Identify single points of failure.* You may have a RAID-protected or clustered file server, but what about your WAN connection?

■   *Implement redundancy in critical system components.* If one server is good, two are better. If possible, see that they carry balanced loads or, at the very least, have an identical backup server to put online in case one fails.

■   *Establish a regular testing schedule for all redundant systems.* The manufacturer says the system works; does it really? Test it until you are comfortable with it. If it doesn't work as advertised, find out long before you put it into production.

■   *Establish support escalation procedures for all systems* before *you have an outage.* Which number do you call for support? What is your customer account information? What does a user say to get past the first tier of support?

■   *Review your vendor service levels for critical components, and assess where you may need to supplement them or have spare parts on hand.* Is the vendor capable of meeting their established service level? What is your recourse if they fail to perform as promised? Can you get support somewhere else? Can you justify the cost of having an extra, preconfigured unit on hand in case of failure?

■   *Establish a process for management approval of any significant change to your systems.* Two heads are always better than one when it comes to managing change. Make sure both peers and management know about, and approve of, what is happening at the data center.

■   *Document* any *change made to* any *system.* For routine change, approval may not be necessary, but make sure there is a process to capture what happened anyway. The audit trail can be invaluable for troubleshooting.

▲   *Develop a healthy intolerance for error.* Never let yourself say, "Well, it just works that way." Give feedback to your vendors and manufacturers. Keep pushing until things work the way you want them to work.

Chapter 10 has more information on establishing service levels and operational procedures as well as samples for documenting various processes at the data center and throughout your organization.

Organizational Issues

Whether you decide to outsource the data center or run it yourself, it is crucial not to underestimate the organizational impact of moving toward this sort of unattended operation. Unless you are already running such a center you will need to do the following:

▼   Come up with a three-shift staffing plan (or at least three-shift coverage).

■   Decide whether your staff has sufficient training and experience to manage the new environment.

■ Determine whether your staff is culturally ready to deal with the "mainframe mind-set" required to make the server-based computing environment reliable and stable. In other words, can they manage the systems using rigorous change control and testing procedures?

■ Decide which of the existing staff needs to be on-site and when.

■ If outsourcing, determine which services your co-location vendor will be providing and which your company will handle.

▲ If outsourcing, make sure there is a clean division and escalation procedure between internal and external support resources.

ENVIRONMENTAL CONSIDERATIONS

When you set up your network and server farm in the data center, you need to consider environmental factors such as power, cooling, and potential disasters. If outsourcing, your vendor should be able to provide you with details on the physical setup of the facility.

Power

The utilization of an emergency or standby generator is essential when considering power outages that may affect your data center. Outages caused by the local utility that last no longer than 15 minutes will typically be supported by an uninterruptible power supply (UPS). However, a standby emergency generator must be used to support outages that last longer.

Each component has a power rating, usually in watts, that it requires for continuous use. At best, inadequate power will strain the power supply of the component. At worst, it will cause production failure. If the facility has a UPS, make sure it has adequate capacity now and can handle your growth plans. Also, how long can the UPS keep your systems running in the event of a sustained power failure? Is there a generator backup? If so, how many gallons of fuel does it have, and how many hours of operation will that yield? During a power failure, it may be difficult to gracefully shut down all of your servers and equipment. Consider implementing software that will do this for you. American Power Conversion (APC) and other vendors have software that performs this task for a variety of operating systems.

Assessing Your Power Requirements

The first step in assessing your actual power requirements and the resulting UPS need is to estimate the load. This is done in slightly different ways for different equipment, but it comes down to estimating the operating voltage, the load (in watts), and a factor for how often the unit is in operation at this voltage and load—sometimes called a *power factor*. An example for a high-end server might be operating voltage = 120 volts, load = 400 watts, power factor = .75 (since it is in continuous operation at nearly peak utilization). Collect and total this information for all of your equipment. It should be readily available from the manufacturer either in printed form in the documentation or from their Web site. Using this example, 15 servers would require 4500 watts (400 × .75 × 15) plus a "fudge factor" in case multiple servers suddenly run at peak loads—from 5000 to 5200 watts would be wise.

Next, determine what the site voltage is. Data center facilities can often handle multiple voltages, but 230V/400V is common. Also think about how much room for growth you are going to need, and make sure there are adequate connections in the floor space you have planned for your equipment.

NOTE: Facilities at an LEC might also supply –48VDC.

Uninterruptible Power Supply (UPS)

For a UPS you need to determine how long you need your equipment to remain functional after power fails. A UPS vendor will be able to tell you the run time after power failure based on the total number of watts for your equipment. UPS systems are usually rated in volt-amps. To convert from watts to volt-amps, use VA = W / 0.8. Using the example above, 5200 watts would require (5200 / .8) = 6500 volt-amps.

HVAC Units for Cooling and Humidity

Cooling should not only be sufficient for normal operation, but should have adequate backup. The ideal situation is to have a redundant cooling system. The cooling system is often overlooked in data center planning, but its failure can cause serious damage to equipment due to overheating.

The cooling system utilized must not add excess moisture to the environment. Industrial evaporators are available to avoid this potential problem. Many higher-end cooling systems have built-in moisture suppression. Detectors should be installed to provide an alert when moisture exceeds recommended levels. Remember that a dry environment means that people working in the data center should drink adequate amounts of water; so water fountains should be placed at convenient locations.

HVAC Evaluation

When evaluating HVAC units, you should consider

- ▼ Temperature and humidity tolerances of equipment
- ■ Amount of space to be cooled (cubic feet)
- ■ Period of operation (evenings? weekends?)
- ■ Seasonal needs (Are some months much hotter than others?)
- ▲ Whether people will be working for prolonged periods in close proximity to the equipment

Fire Suppression

Fire suppression systems are extremely important in any operational facility. These systems use some type of mechanism to help extinguish fires without damaging hardware or facilities. Today's fire suppression systems must comply with environmental concerns regarding ozone depletion and human safety. This is an important consideration if the data center will be staffed and there is a potential for the fire suppression system to be activated while people are present.

Fire Suppression System Types

Many types of systems are available that comply with environmental requirements and use different agents to suppress fires. We recommend that you compare the qualities of the different types of fire suppression systems to determine which one best meets your needs. Table 5-1 lists the advantages and disadvantages of some of the different systems currently available.

Seismic Activity

If you are in California or another area that is active seismically, adequate facility bracing is a must. Your facility should meet or exceed the earthquake regulations for the area. In addition, your computer hardware, racks and cabinets, and other equipment should have their own bracing and be able to pass inspection.

Physical Security

Since most or all of your company's computing infrastructure will be housed at the data center, it is imperative that physical access be restricted and monitored. Many outsourced hosting facilities have security guards, card-key access, motion sensors, and silent alarms. You can spend tremendous amounts of time and money protecting your network with hardware and software security, but if physical security is not considered, your data can still be in considerable risk. We discuss security in more detail in Chapter 9.

NETWORK CONSIDERATIONS

In the next sections, we discuss some important factors to consider when planning the data network connections into the data center. Chapter 6 is dedicated to network design and provides much more detail on these and other topics.

User Geography and Location of the Data Center

The geographic dispersion of your user community plays a major role in the site selection for your data center. Whether your company has only domestic or domestic and international offices has a profound influence on data center aspects such as availability for WAN bandwidth and hot sites. Ideally, you should choose a site that yields the lowest

Type of System	Chemical Agent	Advantages	Disadvantages
Precharge sprinkler	Water	Provides the best suppression of all fires and protection for structures. No water sits above sensitive equipment.	Extra plumbing is required, including lines and routing of pipes to avoid the data center and sensitive equipment. Major water damage is likely when discharged.
Wet sprinkler	Water	Provides the best suppression of all fires and protection for structures.	Accidental discharge from human or environmental factors can set it off. Major water damage is likely when discharged.
FM-200	Heptafluoro-propane	Doesn't displace oxygen, so it is safe when people are present.	High cost.
Inergen	Argon, nitrogen, and CO_2 (stands for *Iner*t gas and nitro*gen*)	Allows storage or flow over data center room. Inergen leaves enough oxygen for people to breath.	High cost, large storage space.

Table 5-1.   Comparison of Commercial Fire Suppression Systems

overall network cost from the national exchange carriers while meeting all the other requirements mentioned in this chapter. One of the single largest cost items in building your data center will be the data network. If you have ever ordered a data line from a local or national carrier, you know that the distance from your office (demarcation point or *demark*) to the carrier's point of presence (POP) can translate into hundreds or thousands of dollars per month. Your data center is no exception. In fact, it is very likely you will be installing high-bandwidth connections such as ATM. In this case, you could be looking at tens of thousands of dollars in cost for a very short distance to the local POP.

Time Zones

Another issue is time zone support. If your data center is on one coast and most of your users on another, you must have a method to support them as if they were running their servers locally. This may take the form of building your server farms according to time zones (this is examined in Chapter 15), or it may be that your line-of-business applications, such as Lotus Notes, handle time zones internally.

Bandwidth Availability

Another consideration in planning network connections is bandwidth availability in the area where your data center is located. You may be able to order the required circuits now, but what about in six months or a year? Make sure you understand the capacity available, usually from the LEC, and your company's growth plans. We have had Corporate ASP customers experience delays in their entire data center build-outs because there were no additional circuits available from the LEC, and no one thought to check in advance.

TIP: It has been our experience over many years that telecommunication carriers are often overly optimistic when estimating the time required to install a circuit. They are similarly overly optimistic about the time required to make an installed circuit work smoothly. Build extra time into your schedule for getting the circuit in and working. If you change a scheduled installation with a national carrier, make sure you contact the LEC and notify them yourself, as this is often forgotten.

Bandwidth Management

As an example, say you've decided to deploy multiple data centers, and now you need to solve the problem of synchronizing user data between sites. This is possible to do with solutions from many vendors, but you must carefully consider the bandwidth required. A discussion of tools for managing bandwidth is included in Chapter 6.

Reliability

An unreliable network can kill your project. It is crucial to make sure the carrier can provide you with details as to the reliability of the circuits they are selling you. Especially in the case of newer topologies like ATM, assumptions of flawless performance may be tantamount to project failure. Get customer references, and ask those companies how the carrier's product is working for them. Allow adequate time for your own testing to make sure the circuits are reliable enough to meet your needs.

Redundancy

It makes little sense to design all of your data center components with fail-over capability if your network represents a single point of failure. This is especially important with a server-based computing design. Your users will rely on the network to reach one or a few data centers; it must be resistant to production outages. Buying a redundant circuit can be expensive, but carriers are often able to sell access to a circuit to more than one company for far less than the circuit itself would cost. In case the primary circuit fails, they can switch you to this backup, and you can continue operation. Failing that, consider putting a second type of lower-bandwidth circuit in place. If you use ATM, perhaps a few T-3s could act as backup. They wouldn't provide as much bandwidth of course, but some access would at least be available.

Using the Internet as a Redundant Network

Also, there are several technologies available that allow the Internet to be used as a virtual private network (VPN) through the use of encryption. Since it is extremely unlikely the entire Internet will ever fail, your users are guaranteed another route into the data center. Another advantage of using the Internet is bandwidth availability. Availability of a regular telephone line will give the user a modest pipe into your data center when providing that user with a redundant frame relay connection may not be practical or even possible. Chapter 9 contains some examples of using VPN technology in this way.

Cable Management

Just as managing the data center requires more meticulous methods than in a distributed environment, setting up your cabling requires careful organization. Cable management systems with easy-to-understand labeling and adequate capacity for growth should be used. Color coding can contribute significantly to finding the right cable quickly. Red could be used for critical LAN and WAN ports, for example. Green could be used for mission-critical servers, and so on. Cable trays and ties will keep cables out of the way and help to organize them.

Just as important, your power cables should not be a pile of spaghetti. Equipment power cables should plug neatly into racks and cabinets, and the large power cables from the racks should plug into the under-floor power grid with only enough slack to allow for moving the floor panels.

OTHER CONSIDERATIONS IN DATA CENTER DESIGN

There are any number of issues that may apply to your company when considering the centralization of your MetaFrame servers. It is not possible to anticipate everything you may encounter, but the following topics cover some issues we have run into in the past that may help in your planning.

Legacy Hosting

Will you be running applications on your MetaFrame servers that need to access data or programs on legacy systems? Enterprise resource planning (ERP), database query and reporting tools, and terminal emulation are all examples of such applications. If so, you should consider co-locating your legacy systems and your MetaFrame servers to optimize the network bandwidth required between these systems, as shown in Figure 5-6.

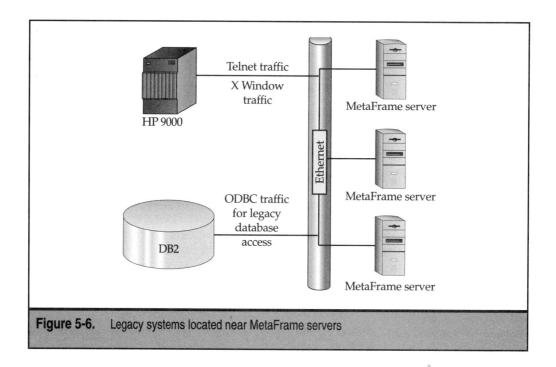

Figure 5-6.   Legacy systems located near MetaFrame servers

Off-Site Data Storage

Even if you have a secure and reliable data center, your data backups should be taken off-site to a *hardened* location. A hardened location is one in which efforts have been taken to have proper fire and moisture protection, as well as physical security for your data storage media. During a production failure or disaster involving a loss of site, such back-ups can mean the difference between a quick recovery and no recovery at all. Many national and regional firms specialize in data storage. We've used Iron Mountain/Arcus many times with good results. Other firms, such as EVault, will use a frame relay connection or the Internet to back up your data to a secure off-site location. If you are outsourcing your data center, make sure you have tape exchange or electronic vaulting as part of the service level agreement (SLA) with your vendor. Otherwise, one of your own people will have to travel to the data center daily to change tapes.

Unusual Connectivity

Do you have systems with network topologies or connection requirements different from those of your MetaFrame servers? Any different topologies, such as SNA, token ring, serial lines, and telephony, will need to be incorporated into the network and facilities design.

Bridging or conversion technologies may be required, and you can't assume they will work the same way in a MetaFrame and Terminal Services environment as they do in a standard Windows NT environment. For example, if you have a Computer Telephony Integration (CTI) application that allows your users to retrieve their voice mail through a PC Windows interface utilizing individual IP addresses, it will probably not work on a MetaFrame server with only one IP address. Another example is running an SNA gateway on a NetWare server to provide PC-to-mainframe connectivity. If, as part of your deployment, you plan to replace your NetWare services with NT servers, you would need to get a new software solution to provide the gateway or possibly look to your router vendor to provide the function.

Nonstandard Systems

Card readers, document scanners, or other automated systems with dependent applications must be taken into account when building your MetaFrame server farm. Depending on the exact nature of these automated systems, you may not be able to incorporate them as part of your server-based computing architecture. Here are some guidelines for making sure these systems will work in your new environment: .

▼   If the system has associated software that runs in DOS or Windows, see whether there is a 32-bit version. Even better, look for a version that has been tested and certified with Terminal Services.

■   If the system has code that already runs on a server (such as NetWare or NT), see whether you can keep the server in place and run the client software on the MetaFrame server.

■   If the system runs at the user's desktop, make sure that any services it needs, such as printing or use of serial ports, will work with MetaFrame's port redirection capabilities.

▲   Test these systems sooner rather than later in the deployment cycle so that you have time to respond if you need to upgrade or completely revise your design to find a new solution.

Rogue Servers and Applications

Is your group or project team in control of all the servers in your enterprise that may be affected by this project? Especially in a large enterprise, it is likely that some servers and applications have been set up regionally without your knowledge. Unless you actively investigate beforehand, the first time you hear of such systems may be when you disable a network circuit or otherwise cut off the regional users from the rest of the network. Develop a plan to have a *sunset period* in which these locations are given a certain amount of time to phase out these systems and begin to access their applications from the new data center.

CHAPTER 6

Designing Your Network for Server-Based Computing

Anetwork optimized for server-based computing has characteristics that don't exist in a traditional distributed, fat-client network. The goal of this chapter is to introduce you to these unique characteristics and give insights on how to apply them to your server-based networking project. Though we will not provide a detailed discussion on a subject as vast as networking, we will define key technologies and concepts to establish a common level of understanding. Experienced network administrators should feel free to skim the sections on the ISO/OSI model and on networking protocols.

In this chapter we cover design goals for the network; some unique features of the client and the server in MetaFrame and Terminal Services; and key considerations for your LAN and WAN topologies, such as bandwidth management. We also include a sample ideal network you can use as a template for your server-based computing project.

HIGH-LEVEL DESIGN GOALS

In starting any technical project we find it useful to begin by setting some high-level design goals. These goals can be used as the litmus test to make sure that the decisions you make on the project conform to one set of criteria or one philosophy. The design goals we have used successfully when thinking of building a server-based network are resiliency, scalability, manageability, auditability, and cost-effectiveness.

Resiliency

The dictionary defines "resiliency" as "an ability to recover from or adjust easily to misfortune or change." This is certainly a desirable end state for an enterprise network. Each component should have its own ability to recover from failure or should be part of a larger system of failure recovery. Network resiliency incorporates concepts of both outage mitigation and disaster recovery.

Outage Mitigation

By "outage mitigation," we mean the ability of a device to reduce or eliminate production failures. A production failure, though not as serious as a full-blown disaster, can nevertheless be devastating to those involved. An example of an outage mitigation technology is RAID for hard drives. By spreading the data across an array of hard drives and tracking the changes and the location of data, the RAID array is resilient to both single and multiple hard drive failures. This concept should be applied to all of the network and data center components. Some common features to look for are redundant power supplies, network cards, backplanes, and clustered CPUs.

Disaster Recovery

A catastrophe or even a serious mishap that could include losing access to the data center calls for disaster recovery. In this case, data moved off-site is prepared and put into production at another site. Engineering this capability into the network design at an early stage can save time and avoid having to ask for a budget increase later. An example of this type of technology is off-site data replication. If the storage system is replicating some or all of your corporate data to a recovery facility, the loss of your main data center is not likely to be catastrophic for the company. You can use this data along with spare hardware and software to get users back online in a timely manner.

Scalability

It is important not to underestimate the growth of the network. If you are in a decentralized environment now, the change to centralized resources alone will increase their usage. Throughout this chapter, we provide estimating guidelines for the various parts of the network, but only you can gauge how much your organization's IT requirements will increase, and how much corresponding capacity should be designed into the network. There are two financially equivalent methods for incorporating expandability into the network. You can either purchase components that are scalable, or you can choose vendors that provide generous trade-in policies on old equipment.

Manageability

The extensive work that network equipment vendors have done during the last few years to simplify their equipment's administration requirements makes this design goal almost a given, but it still bears mentioning. Can your IT staff easily access the component's settings? How does this work—through a Web-enabled GUI or perhaps as a Microsoft Management Console plug-in? Is management of the component self-contained or does it fit into an overall management architecture, such as HP OpenView or CA UniCenter? The component should make it easy to do the following tasks:

▼ Check and back up the current settings to disk.

■ Copy and make changes to the current settings without altering them, then later activate the changes either manually or on a schedule.

■ Provide real-time reporting on important system metrics, for example, bandwidth utilization and port statistics such as error rates, retransmissions, and packet loss. Ideally this information is provided through SNMP, RMON, or some other well-known management protocol.

▲ If using multiple units of the same type, provide a method to create a standard configuration for all of them and a method to address and manage all of them centrally. For example, if you will be using Windows terminals, they should allow the downloading of firmware images and settings from a central location.

Auditability

Even components that are well designed for both resiliency and manageability are not impervious to occasional unexpected crashes. The components should provide enough detailed system and transaction information to make troubleshooting relatively simple.

On many systems, such as routers and switches, troubleshooting is facilitated by detailed logging information. The log should include

▼ Security validations and violations (access denials)

■ Detailed error information

■ Detailed transaction information

▲ Crash dump of the operating system kernel or the equivalent to aid in troubleshooting

Cost-Effectiveness

You may have decided you need the latest, cutting-edge network technology to make your system "really fly." Unless you have unusual or very business-specific needs for this technology, you may find that the added expense of acquiring it is not justified. Just a short while ago, Gigabit Ethernet switches were prohibitively expensive. Could every organization benefit from the extra speed? Possibly, but is the benefit worth the price? The average company that runs word processors and spreadsheets, and accesses data from legacy databases, would not realize the same benefit as a special effects company that needs to move digital film files through the network. In the following sections, we will show you how to gauge the cost of some network components. When comparing components that are similar in nearly every way, it may come down to answering the question, "Which gives me the most bang for the buck?"

THE THIN-CLIENT NETWORK

How is a network that is designed for server-based computing different from one designed for distributed computing? Sun Microsystems' marketing slogan sums it up: "The Network is the Computer." In a network composed of thin clients connected to a data center, every single user has almost constant communication between his or her desktop device and the MetaFrame servers. Both the ICA client with MetaFrame and the RDP client with Terminal Services establish a connection that uses from 20 Kbps to 30 Kbps of bandwidth. This connection links the client to the server that is doing the application serving. In a distributed computing network, on the other hand, the client does its own processing for the most part and makes file requests over the network that are highly variable with regard to the bandwidth used. If a distributed application server is used, the application code resides on the server and is loaded over the network onto the client's resident memory when the program is executed. This is in addition to the file I/O already mentioned. Figure 6-1 shows how these three scenarios compare.

In this chapter we will show you a variety of ways to optimize the flow of traffic over your network for server-based computing. In Chapter 7 we will delve into the intricacies of designing file services and optimizing file I/O for server-based computing.

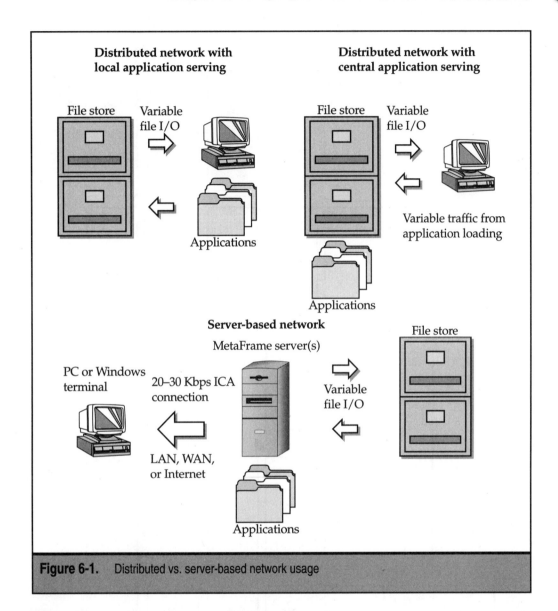

Figure 6-1.   Distributed vs. server-based network usage

The ISO/OSI Seven-Layer Network Model

Understanding how a network designed for server-based computing functions first requires knowledge of how a basic network functions at the protocol level. The International Standards Organization (ISO) created the Open Systems Interconnection (OSI) model in 1983 to define network functionality standards for exchanging information. This model represents how a network communication protocol should be implemented. Figure 6-2 shows the model along with typical network protocols and the layers they occupy.

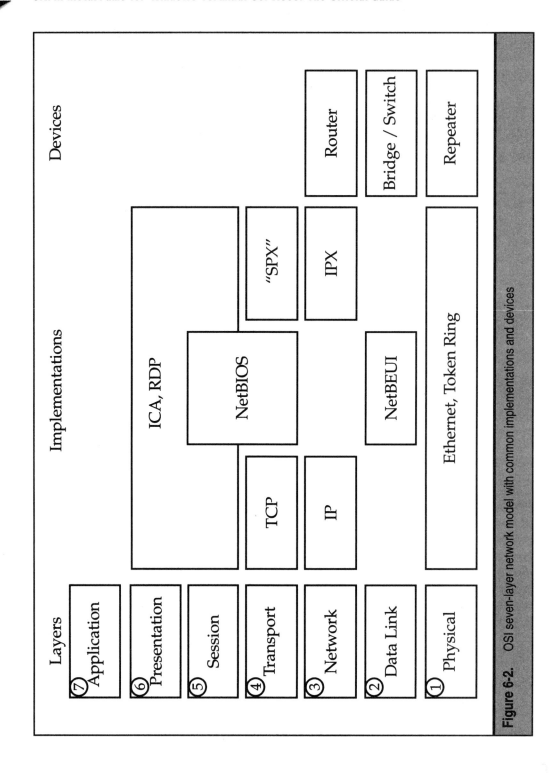

Figure 6-2. OSI seven-layer network model with common implementations and devices

Layer 1: Physical Layer

The physical layer is the point at which the devices on the network actually communicate with each other. This layer defines the electrical and mechanical characteristics of the network. A network signal repeater functions at this layer.

Layer 2: Data Link Layer

The data link layer imposes order on the raw stream of information coming through the physical layer. It makes sure the 0's and 1's conform to the correct format for the network protocol. Appropriately named, this layer is in charge of turning the network "link" on and off and for error correction of the signal. This layer defines the access strategy for sharing the physical layer. All higher layers rely on this for error-free data. A network bridge and most network switches function at this layer. The NetBEUI protocol functions at this layer.

Layer 3: Network Layer

We also think of this as the routing layer. The software that understands the network resides at Layer 3. This layer understands how to use the data link layer to communicate with another device on the network and route packets back and forth. Probably the most common example of a Layer 3 implementation is the Internet Protocol (IP) used to route messages across the Internet. Routers function at this layer. The new class of routing switches also function at this layer, as well as at Layer 2.

Layer 4: Transport Layer

The transport layer optimizes the flow of data and ensures that it is delivered in the correct order. This layer can also handle priority assignments and security. This is the layer where the Transmission Control Protocol (TCP) resides and TCP rate control operates, which is discussed later in this chapter in the "Bandwidth Management" section. The transport layer handles data reliability and integrity so the session layer doesn't have to. The IPX/SPX protocol functions at Layers 3 and 4, respectively.

Layer 5: Session Layer

This layer manages the session or connection between two nodes on the network. It handles establishing and terminating the session based on the requirements of the controlling application at Layer 7. It can also contain logic to restart a session that is dropped unexpectedly.

Layer 6: Presentation Layer

The presentation layer has several jobs. It is primarily responsible for translating the packets between different systems, which enables the data to be understood on each side. This translation can be of protocols, data, encryption, and graphics. Finally, throughput optimization takes place at this layer through compression and decompression. ICA and RDP function at this layer and at Layer 5 because they are session based.

Layer 7: Application Layer

At the top of the stack is where network-aware applications run. FTP, telnet, and IRC programs run here. A network protocol gateway functions at this layer.

Implementations of the ISO/OSI Network Model

You have some choices when implementing a server-based network with MetaFrame and Terminal Services. Though the RDP client still only supports TCP/IP for Terminal Services, the ICA client supports NetBEUI, IPX/SPX, and TCP/IP for MetaFrame. We will take a brief look at each protocol, along with its advantages and limitations.

NetBIOS and NetBEUI   Sytek developed the NetBIOS Extended User Interface for IBM for use in LAN Manager environments, including OS/2. Microsoft later adopted it as a standard. NetBIOS (Network Basic Input/Output System) is a basic protocol that allows communication between nodes on a LAN. NetBIOS can free the application from having to understand the details of the network, including error recovery. A NetBIOS request is provided in the form of a Network Control Block (NCB) that specifies a message location and the name of a destination. NetBIOS provides Layers 4 and 5 of the OSI model, but it does not provide a standard frame or data format. For those, you need NetBEUI.

NetBIOS provides two communication modes: session and datagram. Session mode lets two computers establish a connection, allows larger messages to be handled, and provides error detection and recovery. Datagram mode is "connectionless" (similar to UDP). Messages must be smaller, and the application is responsible for maintaining the session. Datagram mode also supports some broadcast functions. NetBEUI was designed with small networks of fewer than 20 nodes in mind. Because it was implemented at Layer 2, it is not routable. Microsoft and others have overcome this problem by transporting NetBIOS through TCP/IP; the resulting protocol is referred to as NetBT. Novell did something similar by transporting it through IPX. Small networks typically run both NetBEUI and TCP/IP. This enables a computer to communicate using NetBEUI within the LAN and TCP/IP outside the LAN. Local traffic benefits from the resulting performance gains. Some of the advantages of NetBEUI include

▼   Packets are small, and so performance is very good for networks under 20 nodes.

▲   It is supported on legacy Microsoft platforms and quite a few others, such as OS/2.

Some of its disadvantages include

▼   NetBIOS must use a different transport, such as TCP/IP or IPX/SPX to be routable.

■   The protocol is "chatty," requiring many more commands than other protocols to complete a single operation.

▲   It is only appropriate for small networks (under 20 nodes) since the performance gained is rapidly lost as users are added.

IPX/SPX   In the early days of networking, Novell developed IPX/SPX for the NetWare operating system. Based on earlier work by Xerox, IPX (Internetwork Packet Exchange) is a networking protocol that was originally designed to interconnect networks using Novell's clients and servers, but it has since been ported to other operating systems such as UNIX and OS/2. IPX is a datagram protocol similar to NetBIOS in datagram mode, or to UDP. IPX works at the network layer of communication protocols and is connectionless. Packet acknowledgment requires the Sequenced Packet Exchange. In implementing routing functions for IPX/SPX, Novell created three other protocols, RIP, SAP, and then NLSP.

▼ **RIP**   The Routing Information Protocol calls for a LAN gateway such as a router to send its entire routing table to its closest neighbor node every 60 seconds. This routing table is shared node-to-node until all nodes have the same table. For small networks composed of only NetWare servers, RIP provides acceptable performance. In large networks with many routers, or in which there are multiple platforms such as NT and UNIX, RIP can cause significant performance and synchronization problems.

■ **SAP**   The Service Advertising Protocol allows network devices such as file servers, routers, and application servers to advertise their services and addresses. SAP makes the process of adding and removing services on a network dynamic. As servers are booted up, they advertise their services using SAP; when they are brought down, they use SAP to indicate that their services will no longer be available. Similar to RIP, SAP information is loaded into a table shared by routers on a network and made available to nodes requesting a particular service.

▲ **NLSP**   NetWare Link Services Protocol is an enhancement of RIP that provides a more efficient networking solution for larger Novell networks. Routers using NLSP can make incremental updates to their routing tables rather than throwing them out and reloading them from a periodic broadcast.

Some of the advantages of IPX/SPX include

▼ Connection oriented

■ Routable

▲ Well integrated with NetWare environments

Some of the disadvantages include

▼ It is the slowest of the three protocol choices in performance over a WAN due to high overhead imposed by RIP and SAP protocols.

■ Server location address syntax is cumbersome (Network Address and MAC Address combined).

▲ With Novell's stated direction of TCP/IP-based networking, IPX/SPX has a limited life span.

TCP/IP   With the explosive growth of the Internet in this decade, Transmission Control Protocol/Internet Protocol has become the predominant networking protocol in use worldwide. TCP/IP was created by the U.S. Department of Defense as part of the Advanced Research Projects Agency network (ARPAnet) for the purpose of having packetized, routable data in case a large part of the network was destroyed by hostile forces. TCP/IP provided a way to route around the damage and still make delivery highly probable.

TCP/IP is a two-layered protocol. TCP works at Layer 4 of the OSI model and manages the assembling of data into a smaller packet (datagram) that is sent over the network and received by another TCP layer that reassembles the packets into the data. IP works at Layer 3 and handles the addressing of each packet to ensure that it reaches the correct destination. Each router checks the address of the packets and reassembles them in the correct order, even if they were delivered out of sequence.

There are a myriad of protocols related to TCP/IP, but two we want to be sure to mention are the User Datagram Protocol (UDP) and the Internet Control Message Protocol (ICMP). UDP is a smaller alternative to TCP. UDP provides two services not handled by the IP layer. It provides both a checksum to verify that the data arrived intact, and port numbers that help distinguish different user requests. Like TCP, UDP uses the Internet Protocol to actually get a packet from one computer to another. Unlike TCP, however, UDP does not provide the service of dividing a message into packets and reassembling it at the other end. UDP does not provide sequencing of the packets that the data arrives in, but the checksum feature can accept or reject a packet in total. This means that the controlling application has the responsibility of assembling the individual packets correctly. Applications that send very small amounts of data, such as the Trivial File Transfer Protocol (TFTP), sometimes use UDP instead of TCP for performance reasons.

ICMP is a message control and error-reporting protocol between a network node and a router to the Internet. ICMP uses IP packets, but the data is encoded in a way that is not easily recognized by the application layer. ICMP is the "discovery" protocol that networked computers using TCP/IP use to find each other on a LAN, WAN, or the Internet. Some of the advantages of TCP/IP include

▼   Availability of equipment and software support is ubiquitous and pervasive.

■   It is connection oriented and uses ports that are well known and easy to manage.

■   Unique source and destination addressing is contained in each packet, making it robust and not prone to failure.

▲   It supports packet prioritization (TCP rate control).

A few of the minor limitations of TCP/IP include

▼   IP addressing is reaching the point of oversubscription on the Internet, which has spawned IPv6.

■   It has no built-in guaranteed delivery mechanism.

▲   Traffic flow tends to be "bursty" and unpredictable.

We recommend TCP/IP. Aside from its technical advantages, the entire Internet is based on TCP/IP. IPX/SPX or NetBEUI should only be considered as integrating technologies to bring legacy systems into your new network, and then only until they can be migrated to TCP/IP.

ICA vs. RDP

As we discussed in Chapters 2 and 3, both the Independent Computing Architecture (ICA) and Remote Desktop Protocol (RDP) clients can provide a basic remote Windows desktop session. However, when thinking in terms of deploying this technology across an enterprise network, features such as load balancing, non-Windows client support, automatic client update, and local port redirection become very important. With the update to RDP from version 4 to version 5, Microsoft has added some enterprise features such as network-based load balancing. The ICA client still has many unique features that make it a mandatory part of most server-based network implementations. The network-related features unique to ICA include

▼ RSA RC5 128-bit security

■ More robust session shadowing, including one-to-many and many-to-one shadowing

■ Application publishing

■ Cross-domain and cross-subnet management

■ Protocol support other than TCP/IP, such as IPX/SPX and NetBEUI

■ Direct dial-up for remote connections

■ COM port redirection

▲ Automatic update of client software

Networking with ICA

The ICA client was invented to provide Windows desktop services to a client while keeping all of the application processing on the server. The ICA client exists at Layers 5 and 6 of the ISO/OSI model, but requires the underlying protocol of TCP/IP, IPX/SPX, or NetBEUI to function. If TCP/IP is used, ICA uses port 1494 to communicate with the server. ICA is very consistent in the way it utilizes available bandwidth. Since it is only sending screen images, key presses, and mouse movements back and forth to the server, it is optimized to use minimum bandwidth. A typical ICA client providing access to business applications such as Microsoft Office or Lotus Notes without sound or video uses about 20 Kbps. If sound, video, high-density graphics and animation, or ICA printing are run through the same session, this number can grow to 50 Kbps or more. Since most typical business applications do not require video or sound, printing is left as the biggest variable in planning your network for ICA. We recommend avoiding printing through ICA when possible, and using LPR/LPD protocol to send print jobs over the network. This more easily identifies bandwidth and makes it manageable. Printing is such an important topic that we have devoted an entire chapter to it (see Chapter 17).

Although consistent in its bandwidth utilization, ICA is also somewhat sensitive to competing services on the network, especially "bursty" TCP/IP applications such as HTTP or FTP. The graph shown below depicts ICA traffic competing for bandwidth with HTTP. It is important to protect your ICA traffic from "bandwidth starvation," which can result in dropped sessions. We will discuss this more fully later in this chapter in the section on bandwidth management.

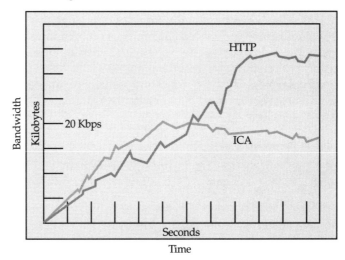

A few ICA and MetaFrame capabilities are of particular interest to us because of the way they utilize the network. A network design is not complete without taking these features into account. We discuss the technical implementation details in Chapter 15.

ICA Browsing

The ICA browser service uses UDP port 1604. The ICA client uses ICA browsing to obtain a list of available Citrix ICA servers. MetaFrame server farms use the ICA browser service to balance ICA client connections among servers. The master browser maintains the browse list and periodically obtains updates from the member browsers (MetaFrame servers) on the same network.

Load Balancing

The Citrix implementation of load balancing allows an application to be published and executed on any MetaFrame server in a server farm. When such an application is selected from an ICA client, load balancing selects which server will run the application or desktop session based on server load. The Load Balancing Administration utility enables tuning of how the load-balancing service calculates server load (see Figure 6-3).

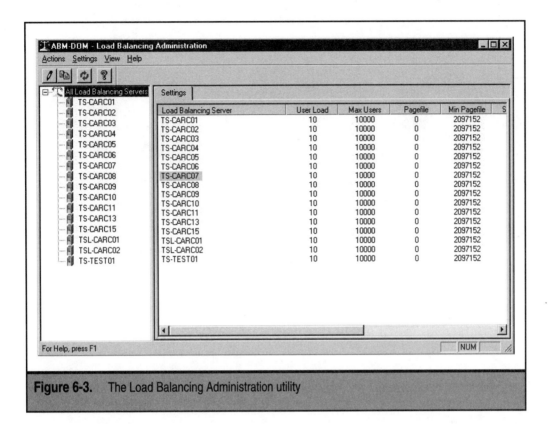

Figure 6-3.   The Load Balancing Administration utility

Microsoft has implemented network load balancing as the Windows Load Balancing Service (WLBS) in Windows 2000. WLBS was engineered to provide a general layer of load balancing for TCP/IP services such as serving Web pages (HTTP). Though it will work with the RDP client, it does not offer the full suite of features specific to server-based computing that can be found in the MetaFrame load-balancing service.

In a load-balanced MetaFrame server farm, every client connection will issue a browse request and will be given the address of the server to connect to by the master browser. Thus, depending on the size of the server farm, there will be many small UDP packets hitting the network at the time most of your users log in and then fewer packets throughout your production hours. The ICA client can find the server by broadcasting these UDP browse requests. If the address of a specific server is given in the client configuration, or in an ICA file, the client can direct the UDP packets to the specified server. Allowing the browse requests to be broadcast provides an advantage in networks with expected changes in the master browser. The direct method can be used for a fixed master browser. ICA browsing is shown in Figure 6-4.

The "query server" command enables discovery of the current master browser. The command will display all servers available from any supported network protocol. In the command's output, an "M" next to the server shows it is the master browser.

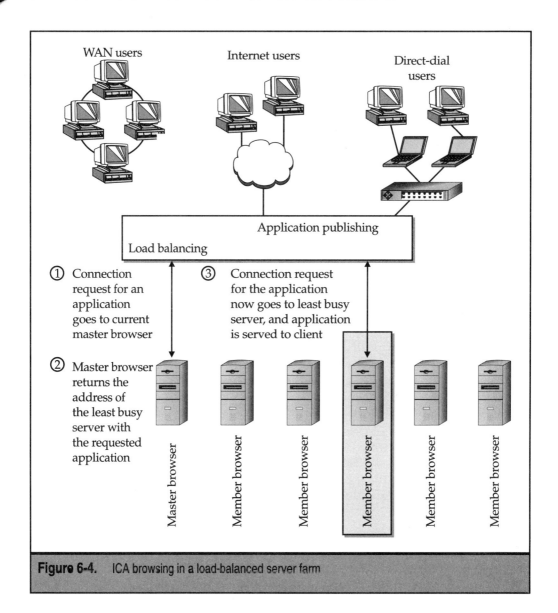

Figure 6-4. ICA browsing in a load-balanced server farm

ICA Pass-Through Connections   It is useful to set up an ICA pass-through connection in cases where you don't want to load an application on all of your MetaFrame servers—usually for reasons of stability—but you do want it to be available to all users. In this case publish the application and create a link to it in the desktop so that it is available to all users via the Seamless Window feature of MetaFrame. The application itself sits on a server apart from the primary server farm, as shown in Figure 6-5. The users execute this application just as they do any other application on their desktop, without realizing it is not running on the server to which they are currently connected. The added advantage of

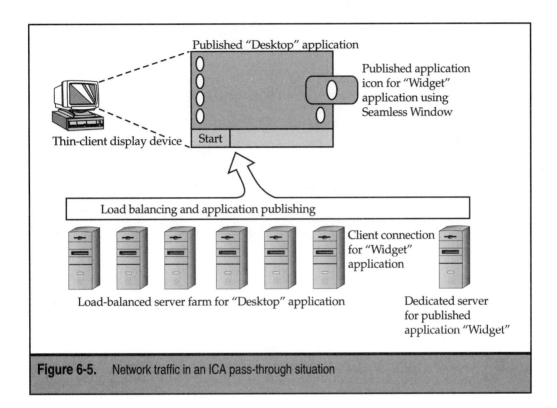

Thin-client display device

Published "Desktop" application

Published application icon for "Widget" application using Seamless Window

Start

Load balancing and application publishing

Client connection for "Widget" application

Load-balanced server farm for "Desktop" application

Dedicated server for published application "Widget"

Figure 6-5.   Network traffic in an ICA pass-through situation

running a Seamless Window setup on the server is for client devices such as Windows terminals. The client devices can use it even though they cannot run Seamless Window themselves like a PC could. This doubled ICA traffic must be taken into account when modeling your bandwidth requirements.

MetaFrame uses a series of tunable algorithms to determine which servers in a load-balanced arrangement are more or less "busy," thereby indicating which server should get the next user connection. Having the connection assignment based on the server's load provides an advantage over strictly network-based load balancing. The MetaFrame server CPU usage may be at a level where resources are better utilized by assigning the next user connection to a different server. In a network load-balancing scheme, only network utilization is considered, not CPU load. The next user connection could very well be assigned to the busy server.

Citrix Web Computing

The ICA Windows Web clients work with any Web browser that supports configurable MIME types. The Citrix ActiveX control for Internet Explorer and plug-in for Netscape Navigator and Netscape Communicator allow these Web browsers to display ICA sessions embedded in Web pages. This is referred to as Application Embedding and is part of the Citrix Application Launching and Embedding (ALE) feature set. When a user clicks a hyperlink to an ICA file or loads an HTML page containing an embedded ICA session, the Web browser passes the ICA file to the ICA Web client, which then initiates a session on the Citrix server using the information contained in the ICA file and in the application definition. The Web client is often used to access a MetaFrame server over the Internet. Communication between a Web server on a public network segment must be established with one (or more) MetaFrame servers on your internal, private segment. Typically, traffic must be allowed to pass through a firewall or proxy server. This topic is discussed in detail in Chapter 9. The traffic used to access this external server would be standard Web traffic or HTTP on TCP port 80. Inside the network, such connections would not look any different from any other ICA connection. Accessing applications in this way is illustrated in Figure 6-6.

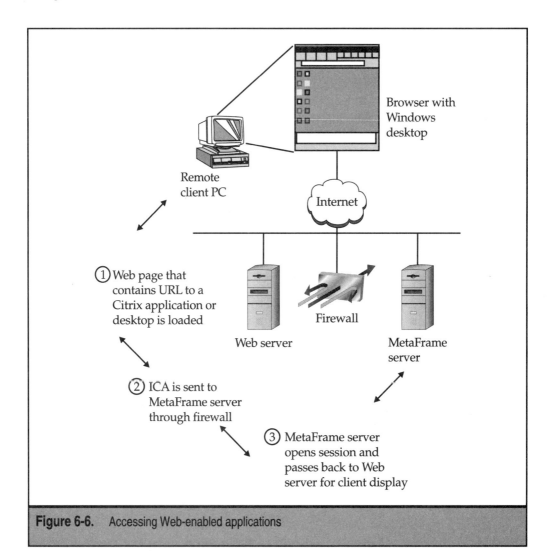

Figure 6-6.   Accessing Web-enabled applications

2

NOTE: Citrix NFuse is the new Web computing technology and works similarly to the ALE model. NFuse adds the full functionality of Program Neighborhood, application publishing, and load balancing to the Web client.

CHOOSING THE RIGHT NETWORK TOPOLOGY

We will keep our original design goals in mind when making the recommendations among the available network topologies and devices. In particular, resiliency and cost-effectiveness will help in choosing the right topology for your server-based computing project. In the following examples, we look at cost-effectiveness in terms of bandwidth per unit of cost. Rather than give specific dollar amounts, since costs can vary widely by region, we compare the topologies with one another.

Wide Area Network

The wide area network (WAN) is the vehicle for transporting data across the enterprise. In a server-based computing environment, the design of the WAN infrastructure is crucial to the IT enterprise. It is essential to create a WAN design that is robust, scalable, and highly reliable in order to protect the value of the data that must flow across the WAN. The WAN refers to an *external* network—that is, the network connecting remote offices to the data center. A WAN is made up of the equipment necessary to terminate carrier lines such as frame relay or ATM, the local loop for that carrier line provided by the Regional Bell Operating Company (RBOC), the national or regional portion of that carrier line, and the services provided by the telecommunication carriers. The next few sections discuss the most appropriate and most available network topologies for building the wide area connectivity portion of a server-based network. Following that, we will describe the necessary components of an *internal* network, or LAN.

Frame Relay

Frame relay is an improvement over older packet-switched network topologies such as X.25. As a packet-switched network, frame relay packages every packet inside a "frame." This frame contains the address for the packet. Unlike X.25, which started out to handle transmission problems on unreliable networks, frame relay assumes every packet arrives in good shape, and it does not strip the frame to read the packet. If the packet is not in good shape, the receiving node can request a retransmission, and any node along the network that has that packet can begin forwarding it even before the entire request is received. This "frame switching" represents a significant performance improvement.

Frame relay is implemented at the first two layers of the OSI model. Though the maximum bandwidth for the line is the same (1.544 Mbps), frame relay is an improvement over traditional T-1/E-1 lines in that it only requires a single end at each site to be connected. A point-to-point T-1 requires data center connection equipment on each line connected to a remote site. Frame relay connects into a "data cloud" in which a Permanent Virtual Circuit (PVC) connects to the remote site. Figure 6-7 illustrates how this works.

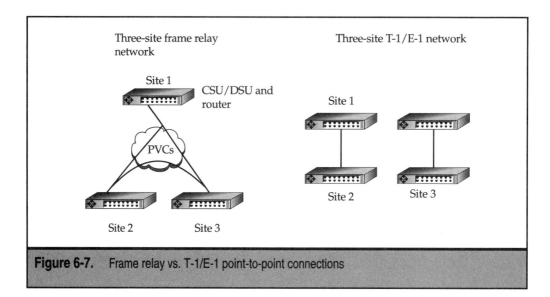

Figure 6-7. Frame relay vs. T-1/E-1 point-to-point connections

Frame relay also operates on the idea of shared bandwidth. Each line has a maximum speed defined by the local Frame port. If you determine that your bandwidth usage will usually be lower than the maximum speed, you can save money by subscribing to a lesser bandwidth. This is called the Committed Information Rate (CIR). Traffic is then allowed to "burst" up to the maximum port speed if needed (and if there is spare bandwidth available from the provider), and you are charged a moderate sum for the privilege.

Installing redundant PVCs for disaster recovery purposes is especially useful in a large regional or national network. If one site's connection to the data center is cut, it can use an alternate PVC and route through another site to get to the data center. Frame relay is ideal for any type of asynchronous data transmission. Historically, frame relay was unable to pass synchronous data such as voice or video because it was prone to transmission delays in groups of packets. Newer implementations have worked to mitigate this problem. It is now more common to see an organization running data, voice, and even video over frame relay. Frame relay is the most flexible and lowest priced topology that we will discuss.

ATM for WANs

Asynchronous Transfer Mode combines the best features of the older packet-switched networks and the newer frame-switched networks. ATM's transport method is called "cell switching." Cells are relatively small—around 50 bytes or so—and do not include large headers and trailers of address information like frame relay. The small cell size makes ATM ideal for transmitting synchronous data like voice and video because the rate at which the cells are transmitted can be easily adjusted. ATM uses a multiplexing method called Asynchronous Time Division that allows it to very quickly assign bandwidth (channels) based on need. Finally, ATM has an "adaptation layer" at Layer 2 that allows it to interoperate with other topologies such as frame relay, or even X.25, as shown in Figure 6-8.

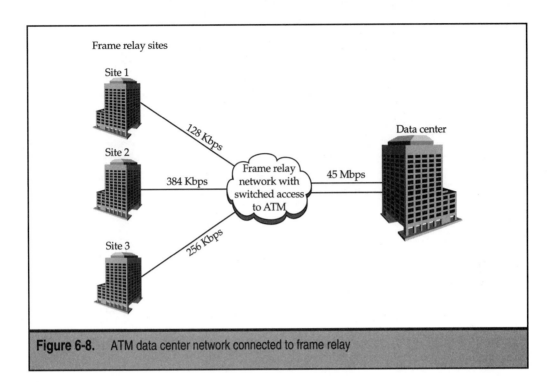

Figure 6-8.   ATM data center network connected to frame relay

ATM is a robust and very fast topology (either 45 Mbps, 155 Mbps, or 622 Mbps, with higher speeds planned), but it is still very expensive, especially at higher port speeds. Placing ATM in the data center of a server-based computing network provides a high-speed port that can accept connections from many lower-speed (and lower-cost) topologies such as frame relay. ATM is an actively developed standard and will form the basis for future technologies such as broadband ISDN.

ISDN

Integrated Services Digital Network was announced in the late 1970s. The original idea was to provide a method for simultaneously transmitting voice and data over the same line. Although it took an extraordinarily long time for ISDN to become widely available, it can be found in most regions of the country today. ISDN uses the same basic copper wiring as Plain Old Telephone Service (POTS). The Basic Rate Interface (BRI) variety of ISDN available to residential and business customers offers two 56 Kbps data channels and one control channel that can operate at 16 Kbps. The control channel is responsible for handshaking and negotiation for the data channels. In a Primary Rate Interface (PRI), usually available only to business customers, there are 23 data channels and 1 control channel, making the bandwidth roughly equivalent to a T-1 or maximum-sized frame relay port. The channels can be used individually or bonded together.

ISDN is a point-to-point technology that requires a network terminator (NT-1) at each end. A single NT-1 can handle multiple ISDN lines. ISDN is also an on-demand link and is usually billed by the minute. Corporate customers can get better deals, but the on-demand nature of this topology makes it appropriate for small remote offices or telecommuters who don't need a full-time connection, or as a backup to another topology. For example, you could purchase a frame relay router with an ISDN backup. If the frame service failed, the ISDN would come up and provide 128 Kbps of bandwidth. You'd only pay for it when you used it. In contrast, it can get quite expensive to use ISDN as a full-time connection. In many cases it is less expensive to buy a 128KB frame relay port than to pay for a full-time ISDN port. Also, many carriers are promoting xDSL over ISDN and providing attractive pricing incentives. Figure 6-9 shows the two types of ISDN in action.

xDSL

Providers use a prefix to specify which of the many variations of Digital Subscriber Line service they are referring to. An "x" prefix (xDSL) means any flavor of DSL. An "A" prefix (ADSL) means asymmetric DSL. An "S" prefix (SDSL) means symmetric or single-line, high-bit-rate DSL. SDSL lines can transmit and receive data at the same rate. ADSL typically receives data faster than it can transmit data. Other varieties include high-bit-rate (HDSL), which provides symmetric, full-duplex speeds up to 1.544 Mbps; very-high-bit-rate (VDSL), which is designed for short local loops and has bandwidth that can exceed 10

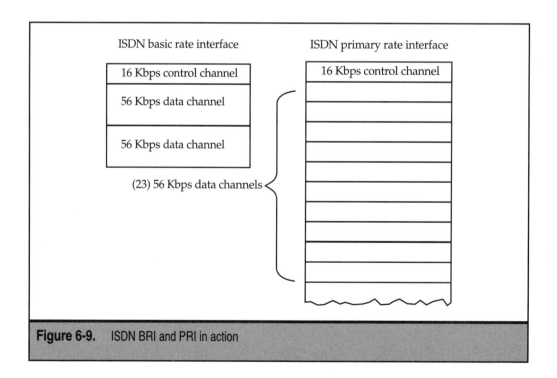

Figure 6-9.   ISDN BRI and PRI in action

Mbps; and ISDN (IDSL), a form of "unswitched" ISDN in which the connection is permanent between two points. Like standard ISDN, xDSL uses the same copper wiring as POTS. By utilizing frequencies above the telephone bandwidth (300Hz to 3200Hz), xDSL can encode more data to achieve higher data rates than would otherwise be possible in the restricted frequency range of a POTS network. Unlike standard ISDN, xDSL is always on, and the maximum bandwidth that can be achieved varies in relation to the distance of the customer from the provider's central office and with the quality of the line. The two most common varieties, ADSL and SDSL, differ in significant ways. SDSL is capable of a maximum of 768 Kbps bidirectional, or half the speed of a T-1. ADSL's most common configuration is to pull data at 1.5 Mbps and push data at only 64 Kbps, but this will vary with the service offering of the provider. For use in a server-based network, SDSL is more appropriate because the sending and receiving of data is likely to be more even.

Similar to frame relay, xDSL providers sell bandwidth in terms of a Committed Information Rate (CIR) but often advertise in terms of the maximum possible throughput. Check providers' offerings thoroughly before you purchase because rating methods vary widely. The primary advantage of xDSL technology is cost. You can achieve T-1 speeds for a fraction of the cost of that topology. The primary limitation is often reliability. This technology is still in the early stages of deployment, and large-scale outages are, unfortunately, not uncommon. You may consider using it as a backup technology or as one where an outage will only affect a few users, but we don't recommend using it as part of your core network infrastructure.

Cable Modems

Cable modems connect to the exiting cable TV (CATV) coaxial network to provide new services such as Internet access to subscribers. Speeds can reach a theoretical 36 Mbps, but end-node technology (such as a network interface card) doesn't yet exist to take advantage of this speed. Speeds of 2 Mbps to 10 Mbps are more common. The service is asymmetrical in its current implementation. Download speeds are far faster than upload speeds. Since the existing coaxial cable network was designed for broadcast, a separate return path is necessary. This is often a standard modem, but some cable plants are capable of running two-way communication over the same connection.

Similar to xDSL, we see cable modems as a good option for small offices or telecommuters only, despite the possibility of huge bandwidth. This recommendation comes for several reasons. Cable companies are new to the data networking business and typically do not have the infrastructure or support capability to ensure a high level of reliability. They also do not offer service guarantees. Finally, due to the hierarchical nature of cable deployment, the amount of bandwidth available at a given end node is highly variable, making bandwidth planning difficult at best.

Internet/VPN

Though this is not a topology in the same sense of the other technologies discussed here, it does provide an alternative connectivity option. A virtual private network (VPN) uses the Internet as a valid network infrastructure option for connecting small offices and telecommuters. The devices available to encrypt and protect networks are very good.

Many Internet Service Providers (ISPs) provide unlimited access deals. This can dramatically reduce connection costs when compared to a standard private, point-to-point connection. We will discuss VPNs and Internet security more fully in Chapter 9.

Remote-Office Issues

Availability and cost of the services described in the previous sections can vary widely if your company spans a large geographical region or the entire country. Below is some advice based on knowledge the authors have gained in rolling out national network projects for server-based computing. We provide a more complete discussion in Chapter 8.

▼ **Premise equipment**   Network access equipment is required at each site. This includes a circuit termination device (which will vary depending on the topology chosen), a router, and an Ethernet hub or switch for connecting local devices. Standardizing on a small set of equipment makes deployment and maintenance much easier. The circuit termination device, such as a Channel Service Unit/Data Service Unit (CSU/DSU) or an NT-1, as well as the router, can be supplied as part of a managed services agreement from a telecommunications provider. This can be an attractive option because the provider, rather than your support staff, must maintain the equipment and respond to problems.

■ **Cold spares and device redundancy**   It is prudent to have spare premise units on hand in case of an outage, regardless of whether they are supplied by the telecom provider. Having an extra CSU/DSU preconfigured and ready to go is likely to be far less expensive than even a few hours of lost work due to downtime. This thinking also applies to router selection. Many routers available from manufacturers such as Cisco and Bay Networks can use one topology as a backup for another. For example, an ISDN option can automatically take over in the event that a primary frame relay main circuit fails. Although the ISDN backup connection might provide reduced bandwidth, it will connect remote office users along an alternate path in seconds. This path could either be a private point-to-point connection into a modem bank at the data center, or it could be a connection to a local ISP. The router would then establish an encrypted channel to the data center through the Internet. We cannot overemphasize the importance of having redundancy in your remote office connections. Centralized computing leaves these users without a local server. They are completely dependent upon the MetaFrame servers and must be able to connect to the data center.

▲ **All-in-one devices**   For small offices with a few users or for telecommuters, this new class of device, costing less than $1000, combines the circuit termination device and router. It can also provide advanced services such as Dynamic Host Control Protocol (DHCP) and Network Address Translation (NAT). These devices are currently available for ISDN and xDSL and will probably be available for other topologies as time goes on. Intel's Instant Internet and the WebRamp from Ramp Networks are examples of all-in-one devices.

Local Area Network

In the context of server-based computing, the LAN resides in two places—inside the data center and inside the remote office. The data center LAN is potentially very complex, while the remote office LAN will be relatively simple, containing little more than a work group hub or switch, printers, PCs, and Windows terminals. Similar to our discussion of the WAN, we must first make sure we have a common understanding of the underlying technology in order to proceed.

Ethernet

As we stated in Chapter 1, Bob Metcalf invented Ethernet for Xerox. Originally it was structured in a daisy-chain design and implemented with coaxial cable. The Institute of Electrical and Electronics Engineers (IEEE) has given it the designation 802.3 to show that it is a member of the set of networking standards that use the same media access method. Its current incarnation is commonly 10BaseT, which is more of a star configuration in which each node connects to a central backplane. Ethernet is implemented at Layers 1 and 2 of the OSI model and has surpassed all other topologies as the most common in use today.

Ethernet uses "contention-based access" to listen to packets flowing on the network and to insert a new packet when the network is not busy. In a busy network, collisions can occur, but Ethernet uses a built-in mechanism called, appropriately, collision detection to drop and retransmit bad packets. Each Ethernet device has a unique address alternatively called the Ethernet Address or the Media Access Control (MAC) address. The MAC address is used at Layer 2 to identify a particular device. Three varieties of Ethernet are available today: 10 Mbps, 100 Mbps (Fast Ethernet), and 1000 Mbps (Gigabit Ethernet).

▼ Fast Ethernet is also referred to as 100BaseT to indicate that it provides for a transmission standard of 100 Mbps across the LAN. The 100BaseT standard is backward compatible with 10 Mbps Ethernet. If such a device is connected to a Fast Ethernet segment, the 100 Mbps data rate becomes a shared data rate for all such devices.

▲ Gigabit Ethernet is a transmission standard that provides for sending one billion bits per second across the LAN. It is carried primarily on optical fiber. It has also been incorporated into the standard Ethernet specification (802.3z) and uses the same Carrier Sense Multiple Access with Collision Detection (CSMA/CD) protocol, same frame format, and same frame size as its predecessors.

For remote office LANs within a server-based computing environment, 10 Mbps is typically adequate because most of the traffic is directed outward across the WAN to the data center. If traffic within an office were high for some reason, such as to facilitate local digital image processing, 100 Mbps could be used. Depending on the number of users accessing a given server simultaneously, 100 Mbps may also be appropriate for individual terminal servers in the data center. Gigabit Ethernet should be used for a device that receives hundreds or even thousands of requests for access per minute, such as a file server or Network-Attached Storage device in the data center. We will discuss some methods for modeling your bandwidth requirements later in the chapter.

Token Bus/Token Ring

Token Bus is similar to Ethernet but uses a different method to avoid contention. Instead of listening to traffic and detection collisions, it attempts to control the sequence of which nodes use the network at what time. The node holds a "token" and passes it on to the next node when it is finished transmitting. Any node can receive a message but cannot transmit unless it holds a token. Token Bus networks are laid out in a serial bus fashion with many nodes daisy-chained together. Token Ring is implemented in a ring topology. The main difference between the two is how the token is handled. In Token Ring, the token becomes part of the packet. With Token Bus, the packet is a separate message that is passed after a node has finished transmitting. Token Ring networks have many of the advantages of Ethernet and even started out with higher possible bandwidth (about 16 Mbps). However, Ethernet is now the unquestioned standard. Token Ring is usually part of a legacy network connecting mainframes, minicomputers, or other IBM equipment.

ATM for LANs

Asynchronous Transfer Mode is often considered as an alternative in the LAN even though it has strong roots in the WAN. When ATM was introduced, many manufacturers touted "ATM to the desktop" as being the panacea of high-bandwidth access. This never materialized in large-scale desktop deployments for many reasons, not the least of which is cost. ATM network cards are still several thousand dollars, and ATM has not been widely implemented in backplane or switching devices. Probably the main contributing factor to its limited adoption is the rising speed of Ethernet. Gigabit Ethernet is common now, and the speed is still increasing while hardware costs continue to decrease. We don't see much value in deploying ATM in the server-based LAN.

FDDI

Fiber Distributed Data Interface is a 100 Mbps LAN topology designed to operate over optical cabling, but efforts have also been made for it to run over standard copper media (CDDI). FDDI uses a media access protocol similar to Token Ring. FDDI employs dual looped rings with traffic flowing in opposite directions (counter-rotating) to improve fault recovery. Different types of fiber-optic cabling are supported—multimode, single mode, and low-cost fiber—which affect the maximum distances possible between nodes. The maximum distances are 2km, 40–60km, and 500m, respectively. If running over category 5 copper wiring, the maximum distance is limited to 100m.

Since its introduction, the cost of FDDI technology has dropped dramatically, and bridging to Ethernet is common. FDDI is a good option for high-access LAN devices such as file servers, though it still tends to be more expensive than Fast Ethernet. When comparing the two, FDDI allows a higher average utilization without congestion and added redundancy of the dual loop topology. However, Intel and other vendors have engineered ways to increase the performance and reliability of their Fast Ethernet implementations. We will discuss these devices in the next section.

Available LAN Technology

In the following sections we discuss some of the technological innovations in network interface cards and network backbone equipment that will make your server-based network more resilient and increase its performance.

Network Interface Cards

Since network interface cards (NICs) have become ubiquitous in modern computing, their implementation may seem like a minor detail to consider. However, the LAN requires a server backbone of sufficient speed to allow the MetaFrame servers to send and receive user environment and application data from the central storage server's array of disks. Users' screen updates must be quick, and the backbone should not be a hindrance, especially in server-based computing. Many vendors have created a server-optimized NIC. These server network cards typically allow up to 1000 megabits of data per second to be sent through attached concentrators or network switching equipment. Most network card vendors have embraced the idea of including a high-speed onboard processor to alleviate the server's central processor(s) from having to spend cycles dealing with traffic generated through the network card. These network cards are usually geared toward file and application servers, which must process far more data than a network-connected workstation. The following requirements should be considered when evaluating NICs:

▼   High-speed access for all servers on the LAN

■   Redundant server and switched links wherever possible

■   Extremely high-speed links to servers that host data or other common services

■   Optimal price/performance

▲   Relatively inexpensive upgrades/expansion

To ensure redundancy, there are several options for allowing a server to have more than one network card to be used at the same time. Several network card vendors support various methods for allowing a server to have multiple redundant links to the network. Technologies available include 10/100 and Gigabit Ethernet, FDDI, and ATM. As of this writing Gigabit Ethernet has been implemented using FDDI as a transport, and some switch and network interface technologies use this type of setup. ATM is still lagging behind with LAN implementations. The following available NIC technologies either fully or partially fulfill our requirements.

Adapter Fault Tolerance   AFT is a software component of network adapters that provides network link recovery with no user or administrator intervention. A server installed with two network cards provides a fault-tolerant, redundant link to the network in the event of a network link failure. The primary network card will work as if it were the only network link to the server. In the event of a link failure, the second redundant network card takes over the identity of the first, including MAC and IP address. Software agents monitor the live link and turn on the redundant link in the event of a failure. Some advantages include

▼ Multiple redundant links from server to network

■ Support for gigabit network cards

■ Transparent recovery from single link failure

■ Automatic alerts sent to NT event log in the event of a link failure

▲ MAC and network addresses switched transparently in the event of a link failure

Some limitations of adapter fault tolerance include

▼ Bandwidth is not aggregated between the two network links.

▲ Network card vendors use their own technology similar to AFT.

Fast EtherChannel   FEC is a port aggregation technology released by Cisco, which combines two or four Fast Ethernet links into a single logical connection. FEC provides fault tolerance and load balancing across multiple adapters. Network switches with FEC technology can allow up to four full-duplex Fast Ethernet connections to form one 800 Mbps channel of bandwidth. If one link in the channel fails, traffic is automatically redirected to the remaining links. Switch vendors such as Hewlett-Packard and Sun, in addition to Cisco, and NIC vendors such as Intel, Compaq, and Adaptec, among others, have embraced this technology. In a data center environment FEC can provide near-gigabit speeds between your MetaFrame servers and the network backbone for far less than gigabit prices. For even higher bandwidth, a gigabit variety of this technology, Gigabit EtherChannel (GEC), has the same characteristics but a base bandwidth of 4 Gbps with four adapters. Some advantages of Fast EtherChannel are

▼ Multiple redundant links from server to network

■ Transparent recovery from single link failure

■ Full-duplex support for 100 Mbps Ethernet cards—200 Mbps for a single NIC, up to 800 Mbps total

■ Compliance with IEEE 802.3 standard

■ Automatic alerts sent to Windows NT event log in the event of a link failure

▲ MAC and network addresses switched transparently in the event of a link failure

Some limitations of Fast EtherChannel include

▼ Ethernet switches must support the FEC or GEC technology.

▲ FEC or GEC NICs in a group must be attached to the same switch.

Adaptive Load Balancing   Intel's Adaptive Load Balancing (ALB), also known as asymmetric port aggregation, works similarly to Cisco's Fast EtherChannel. By using ALB, as many as four Intel server adapters can form an aggregate throughput of up to 400 Mbps with FEC adapters or 8 Gbps with GEC. Some advantages of ALB are

▼ Multiple redundant links from server to network

■ Support for gigabit network cards

■ Transparent recovery from single link failure

■ Compliance with IEEE 802.3 standard

■ Automatic alerts sent to NT event log in the event of a link failure

▲ MAC and network addresses switched transparently in the event of a link failure

A limitation of ALB is that full-duplex support is not included; traffic is faster receiving data from the server.

An example of a NIC that implements ALB is Intel's PRO10/100 and PRO/1000. Intel makes specialized server network adapters in 10/100 and gigabit speeds. AFT, ALB, and FEC are supported on all of their adapters. All of the server-centric NICs are equipped with onboard processors (such as the Intel i960), which help keep server CPU usage to a minimum.

3Com's 10/100 Fast Etherlink and Gigabit Etherlink NICs represent another ALB implementation. 3Com's 10/100 and Gigabit Ethernet network adapters support their own Dynamic Access technology for network link redundancy. Dynamic Access software's load-balancing feature increases the server bandwidth and boosts server throughput by automatically and intelligently distributing packet transfer among multiple NICs that have been aggregated into one virtual NIC.

Aside from the Intel adapters possibly having a more powerful processor to free up the server's CPU(s), the main differentiation between the Intel and 3Com NICs is the adaptive load-balancing technology Intel has included. With this technology, each network card can be linked to separate network switches. Driver support should be completed for Windows NT 4.0 TSE/Windows 2000 by the time this book is published. We used prerelease drivers that were very stable. It should also be noted that many OEM vendors we have encountered (such as Network Appliance and Dell) include Intel NICs as standard equipment because they include a high level of performance and redundancy. Models with 10/100 Ethernet or FDDI/Gigabit Ethernet are available. The only caveat to using the Intel NICs with ALB is that each card in the team sends a "keep alive" packet to the other every 10 seconds, and the other card in turn sends an acknowledgment. You need to account for this activity on your network backbone, but performance is often the first sacrifice for added redundancy.

Switches

Ethernet switching was developed as a way to more efficiently manage bandwidth in shared or routed networks. In a simple routed network, many devices can share the same 10 Mbps or 100 Mbps segment. Since the bandwidth needs of a given device at a given point in time are variable, the performance on a shared segment can be unpredictable. With a switched segment, the bandwidth can be dedicated to a single device. Traffic is only allowed between the source and destination addresses.

> **TIP:** Autonegotiation can cause problems with your switch if you don't pay close attention to the link speed of the connecting device. Autonegotiation is a signaling scheme similar to the one used by modems to advertise their capabilities to the nodes on the connecting network. The problem comes with different implementations of this optional component of the 100BaseT Fast Ethernet standard. We've encountered problems where the port on the device and the port on the switch negotiated to the lowest instead of the highest speed. We've also seen autonegotiation fail and block traffic on a port. The solution is not to have the switch autonegotiate at all but to lock the speed at the appropriate level. This makes management more challenging but may be necessary until different network device manufacturers get their equipment to interoperate correctly.

A central part of the LAN server architecture will be the Ethernet switches used to deploy Fast Ethernet or Gigabit Ethernet to all of the servers on the backbone. Fault tolerance is a major concern in all enterprise network environments, but it is of particular concern for the backbone in a server-based computing environment due to the number of users accessing the centralized resources. Since it is likely that the usage demands of different servers will not be identical, switching becomes even more important to isolate and contain the high-traffic servers. The following features should be considered requirements for switches to be used in a Corporate ASP network:

▼ High-speed access for all servers on the LAN

■ Redundant server and switched links wherever possible

■ Extremely high-speed links to servers that host data or services for all members of the backbone

■ Optimal price/performance

■ Inexpensive upgrades/expansion

▲ Redundant power and cooling

The ability to add switched ports and gigabit uplinks to faster gigabit hardware is very important. Most network switching vendors support several technology enhancements to Ethernet switching equipment. Those enhancements include

▼ **Layer 3 switching**   Layer 3 switching consists of routing functions that are built onto the silicon of a switch. Routing tables are created and automatically adjusted to network changes caused by link failures, device failures, and additions and deletions to the network. Performance can be dramatically improved in a network where Layer 3 switching is added.

■ **Virtual LANs (VLANs)**   A VLAN offers a flexible way of segmenting a corporate network, reducing possible bottlenecks. A VLAN is a group of devices on the network that behave as if they were connected to a single network segment. The servers, or other devices that are part of the VLAN, may be spread throughout the network. The resources that are shared on a VLAN act as if they are a single segment. The resources for the rest of the network, or separate VLANs, can be invisible at the administrator's discretion. By implementing VLANs, network performance can be increased because broadcast and node-to-node traffic can be restricted so that the burden of extraneous traffic is reduced.

▲ **Spanning tree**   Spanning tree is a protocol technology developed originally for use with early bridges to map a redundant topology without causing loops in the network. If you are trying to create redundant network links in an enterprise backbone and are not using spanning tree, you can inadvertently create loops that can cause severe network broadcast storms, crippling performance and overloading switching equipment. Spanning tree helps avoid and eliminate network loops by actively negotiating a loop-free path.

Stackable Ethernet Switches   Stackable or stand-alone network switches can provide excellent performance at a competitive price. Depending on the number of ports needed, stand-alone or stackable switching can also provide a very high speed server backbone with multiple points of redundancy.

Some of the advantages of stackable Ethernet switches include

▼ Link resilience with link aggregation allows multiple connections between switches to act as one large pipe but provide redundancy in case one or more links fail.

▲ It is fairly easy to swap out an existing switch for a newer technology.

Limitations of stackable switches include

▼ Multiple connections between unstacked switches take up more ports.

▲ Overall backplane speed in a stack will generally not match a high-end chassis-based system backplane speed.

An example of a stackable switching product is Intel's Express Gigabit Switch. Intel's gigabit switch features modular upgrades for 10/100 ports and additional gigabit ports. Link aggregation allows multiple switch-to-switch connections to act as a single high-bandwidth pipeline for multi-Gigabit Ethernet throughput and automatic redundant connectivity. The standard Express Gigabit Switch includes seven 1000Base-SX ports and a 32 Gbps switching fabric.

Chassis-Based Ethernet Switches   Chassis-based Ethernet switches provide the highest-end networking solutions available with the fastest possible switching bandwidth. Cisco is the leader in routing and switching technology and offers products that include their standard Internetworking Operating System (IOS), which is found in all of their routing and switching products. Some advantages of chassis-based switches include

▼ High-performance backplane, possible to support more ports per network at a higher performance level than a stackable or stand-alone solution

■ More options to mix and match topologies into a common backplane

▲ Options to include separate devices such as routers and CSU/DSUs into a common backplane

A limitation of chassis-based switches is the fact that upgrading can be more difficult and expensive than in a stand-alone or a stackable environment. As new technology is developed and brought to market, replacement of the chassis and all components becomes a possibility.

An example of a chassis-based switch is in Cisco's Catalyst product line. Cisco's Catalyst 6509 is a chassis-based system with up to nine slots available for a mix of supervisor engines, and interface line cards supporting various port densities and types. As with the breadth of Cisco's product line, the Cisco IOS provides security and management functions that are shared between switching and routing equipment. All system elements are hot swappable without service interruption. The Catalyst 6509 supports up to 384 10/100 Ethernet ports and up to 130 Gigabit Ethernet ports with switching bandwidth of up to 256 Gbps.

With the addition of Cisco's Multi-layer Switch Module, sophisticated Cisco IOS software features support wire-speed multiprotocol routing, enabling aggregate throughput of up to six million packets per second for Layer 3 switching. Port-based VLAN is supported with up to 1000 VLANs simultaneously, as well as Fast EtherChannel for link redundancy to individual nodes.

Cisco offers an attractive alternative for the server-based LAN and has wide industry acceptance. The Catalyst 6509 switch is a good option because it fulfills our network design goals, particularly the resiliency made possible by using redundant NICs with Fast EtherChannel.

PLANNING NETWORK BANDWIDTH

Planning network bandwidth may seem like an obvious need, but it is often skipped because it is difficult to predict the normal bandwidth utilization of a given device or user on the network. In this section, we discuss tried-and-true methods for controlling the usage of your network bandwidth so that the penalty for a false prediction is not a loss of service. Furthermore, you will be able to prioritize your network traffic to give your mission-critical applications a much higher chance of getting through. When planning network bandwidth, keep the following requirements and assumptions in mind:

▼ Thin-client user access has a very high priority.

■ Mission-critical applications should receive a higher priority than personal productivity applications or Web applications such as browsers and FTP.

■ Average utilization of network resources should be high, thus saving money by avoiding unnecessary upgrades.

▲ Rules for bandwidth utilization or bandwidth blocking should be by application, user, and group.

TIP: You will need more bandwidth, not less, when migrating users from your old network. It is likely that you will need to run your old and new network on some of the same network segments while you are moving users from your old network to your new data center network. Tasks such as user data migration, interim file server reassignment, and "backhauling" user data to legacy systems not yet on the new network can all add up to an increased bandwidth need. Some of this is unavoidable, but some of the need can be mitigated with careful planning and staging of which systems will be migrated in which order. Don't underestimate your bandwidth needs and you will enjoy a lower risk of having unhappy users before your project gets started.

Bandwidth Management

As you saw in the previous sections, Ethernet switching was an innovation designed to use existing bandwidth more efficiently. It is a subject that network engineers have been thinking about since the beginning of networking. Until the introduction of ATM, however, there was no protocol designed from scratch to incorporate delivery guarantees or Quality of Service (QoS). ATM was designed to carry high-density digital information such as video. The rate and consistency of delivery is crucial for this type of data. With the introduction of ATM, the limitations of other protocols such as TCP/IP became even more apparent. TCP/IP and the underlying Ethernet fabric have no delivery guarantees, and the traffic tends to be "bursty" and unpredictable. Networking companies had to find a way to help ensure delivery and overall network quality while remaining compatible with the existing network infrastructures. Though many technologies appeared, such as Resource Reservation Protocol (RSVP) and Multiprotocol Over ATM (MPOA), "queuing" has arisen as the de facto standard in gateway devices for QoS over TCP/IP. Be that as it may, a superior method called TCP rate control has particular application to server-based computing. We will discuss the advantages and limitations of these two technologies.

NOTE: RSVP is the bandwidth management method that Microsoft has chosen to implement in Windows 2000. Using RSVP, applications can request session-based, end-to-end QoS, and can indicate requirements and capabilities to other applications. RSVP is a Layer 3 protocol and thus is suited for use with IP. According to Microsoft's white paper on QoS in Windows 2000, their implementation of RSVP will grant the following capabilities to an application that can exploit it:

How the network can identify traffic on a conversation (classification information)

Quantitative parameters describing the traffic on the conversation (data rate, etc.)

The service type required from the network for the conversation's traffic

Policy information (identifying the user requesting resources for the traffic and the application to which it corresponds)

Queuing

The various types of queuing were invented to tell a network device, usually a router, what to do with traffic when congestion begins to appear on a network segment. The first type to appear, *fair queuing* (FQ), simply assigned equal shares of network bandwidth to each application. An application is usually defined by a standard TCP service port (for example, port 80 is HTTP). *Weighted fair queuing* (WFQ) was next and allowed a network administrator to assign levels of priority to a port. After all, not all traffic is created equal. The more important traffic should get through first, while the less important traffic should have to wait. *Class-based queuing* (CBQ) can assign different values to the different attributes of a traffic flow and make adjustments to the queue in real time. TCP/IP queuing has the following advantages:

▼ Queuing works well in a network with only occasional and transitory congestion.

▲ Queuing requires no special software on client devices.

Queuing has the following limitations:

▼ Queuing lacks the ability to manage a fixed amount of bandwidth, making it challenging to manage a real-time bandwidth QoS.

■ Packets delayed beyond a time-out period in queues get dropped and require retransmission, causing more traffic and more queues.

■ Queuing manages only outbound traffic, assuming the inbound traffic has already come in over the congested inbound link.

▲ Queuing has no flow-by-flow quality of service (QoS) mechanism.

TCP Rate Control

TCP rate control provides a method to manage both inbound and outbound traffic to a specific bandwidth. TCP rate control conditions traffic so that it becomes more evenly spaced and less "bursty." By using rate-based flow control instead of queuing, TCP rate control evenly distributes packet transmissions by controlling TCP acknowledgments to the sender. This causes the sender to throttle back, avoiding packet tossing when there is insufficient bandwidth. As packet bursts are eliminated in favor of a smoothed traffic flow, overall network utilization is driven up as high as 80 percent. In a network without rate control, typical utilization is around 40 percent. TCP rate control operates at Layer 4, performing TCP packet and flow analysis, and above Layer 4, analyzing application-specific data. TCP rate control has the following advantages:

▼ Works whether applications are aware of it or not

■ Reduces packet loss and retransmissions

■ Drives network utilization up as high as 80 percent

■ Provides bandwidth management to a specific rate (rate-based QoS)

■ Provides flow-by-flow QoS

■ Provides both inbound and outbound control

▲ Prevents congestion *before* it occurs

TCP rate control has the following limitations:

▼ Not built into any routers yet

■ Only works on TCP/IP; all other protocols get queued

▲ Currently available from very few vendors

Packet prioritization using TCP rate control is a method of ensuring that general WAN traffic does not interfere with critical or preferred data. Using packet prioritization, ICA traffic can be given guaranteed bandwidth, which results in low perceived latency and speedy application performance, and contributes to a high level of user satisfaction in the server-based computing environment.

Packeteer created the category of hardware-based TCP rate control with its PacketShaper product. Although other manufacturers are entering this market (including Sitara, NetReality, and Cisco), we will use the PacketShaper as an example for discussing bandwidth management. PacketShaper is a device that sits behind the router and proactively manages WAN traffic to ensure that critical applications receive the bandwidth they require. PacketShaper does not require any modifications to applications or changes to desktops or servers. Figure 6-10 shows the PacketShaper's place in the network. It is an "edge" device, which means it needs to be deployed at the outer edge of the network. For our purposes that means it resides at the remote sites with large enough bandwidth requirements to justify the expense. A PacketShaper is always placed inside the router so it can manage the traffic flow before routing. In a large network there is also value in placing a PacketShaper at the data center. Though it is not possible to manage individual sessions this way, it is possible to create partitions for particular types of traffic. The flow-by-flow management happens in the PacketShapers at the edge of the network. There are several PacketShaper models available, and they are priced by the amount of bandwidth they need to manage.

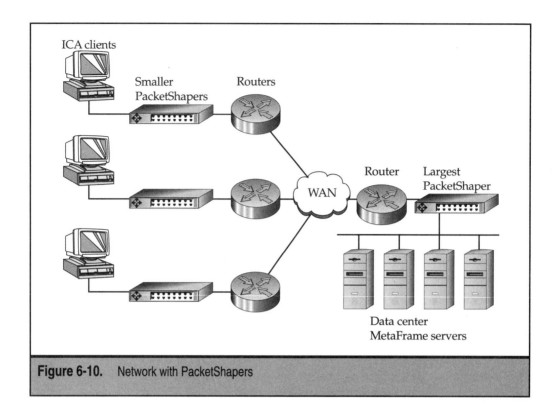

Figure 6-10. Network with PacketShapers

A principal advantage of Packeteer's implementation of TCP rate control is the ability to create rules for bandwidth flows at Layer 7, the application layer. Policies can be created by assigning bandwidth per session, by partitioning the available network "pipe," and by simply assigning priorities. These options are examined more closely below. The PacketShaper provides a Web-based GUI to define these policies and monitor the device.

> *Without the Packeteer PacketShapers, we would not have been able to implement Citrix throughout the company. We used the PacketShapers to minimize our bandwidth requirements to our remote offices, which made the project affordable.*
>
> —Tony Kloeppel,
> Technical Services Manager, ABM Industries

▼ **Bandwidth per session** With the PacketShaper, it is possible, for example, to set a policy that will guarantee 20 Kbps of bandwidth for each ICA session. This has a few important effects. First, each session is protected from every other session. If one user is browsing animated Web pages, she still only gets 20 Kbps, and so her perceived performance decreases. Most other users who are running office applications or e-mail would notice no difference, and their sessions would seem responsive. Second, no user would ever get a session with less than 20 Kbps. In the case where the network was close to full utilization (around 80 percent) and, for example, there was 4 Kbps available to create a user's ICA session, the PacketShaper would stop the session from being created, as shown in Figure 6-11. This ensures that the user isn't connected with insufficient bandwidth and then has a perception that her session is slow. Of course, if your link is at saturation, you have other problems to worry about.

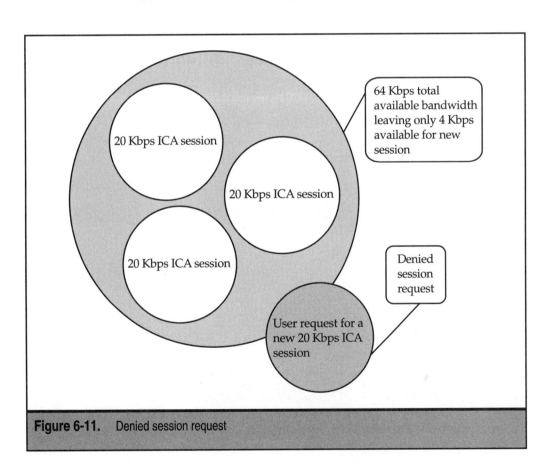

Figure 6-11. Denied session request

- **Partitioning**   Using this type of policy you can "carve up" the available bandwidth and assign portions to each application or type of traffic, as shown in Figure 6-12. For example, in a frame relay circuit with a port speed of 1.544 Mbps, you might assign 80 percent to ICA traffic, 10 percent to HTTP, and 10 percent to LPR/LPD for printing. If any portion is not being fully utilized, the PacketShaper can allow the other partitions to share its available bandwidth.

- **Prioritization**   This is the simplest of the three options. Prioritization allows you to assign a number between 1 and 7 to a traffic flow, 1 being the highest. In this case, as utilization of the available bandwidth increases, the PacketShaper uses its own algorithms to make sure Priority 1 traffic gets more "slices" of bandwidth than Priority 3, as shown in Figure 6-13.

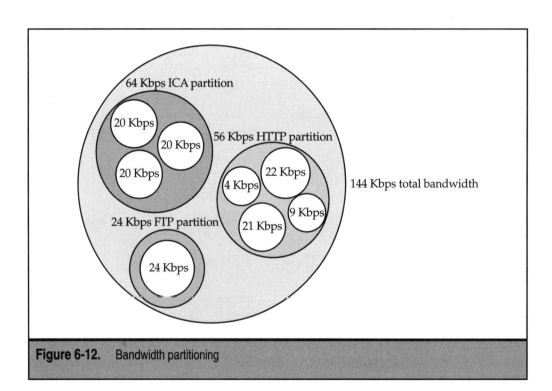

Figure 6-12.   Bandwidth partitioning

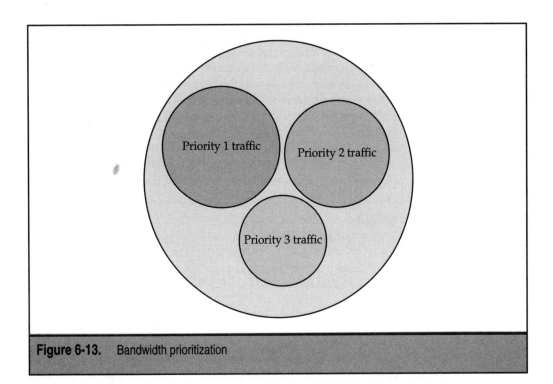

Figure 6-13.   Bandwidth prioritization

TIP: Of the three methods discussed in this section, we recommend session-based policies and partitions for ICA traffic. A session-based policy that guarantees 20 Kbps but allows bursts of up to 30 Kbps is ideal for ICA. However, such a policy can only be implemented when the PacketShaper can control the inbound and outbound traffic, which means you cannot do this over the Internet. In such a case, a partition policy can be used. Depending on the size of the network pipe, you could, for example, guarantee that 50 percent of the bandwidth is available to ICA. You could leave the remaining bandwidth "unmanaged" or define partitions for your most common, known protocols such as HTTP and telnet. We recommend against using priority-based packet shaping with ICA simply because it makes it harder to predict the behavior of a PacketShaper. This is because a priority is not absolute and relies on some fairly complex algorithms to shape the traffic. Partitions and session policies are more rigid, and therefore more predictable and easier to administer.

A limitation of packet prioritization is that print traffic (and resulting print output speed) may be reduced because bandwidth is guaranteed to ICA traffic. Users may find this delay unsatisfactory. If so, you may choose to increase WAN bandwidth to allow more room for print traffic. Printing is a complex issue in this environment and is discussed in more detail in Chapter 17. Another potential problem with packet prioritization is that Internet browsing speed may be reduced because of the guaranteed bandwidth reserved for ICA traffic. Our experience has shown that Internet browsing that includes rapid screen refresh rates appears to substantially increase ICA packet bandwidth requirements—sometimes to as much as 50 Kbps. Disabling Java, ActiveMovie, or other plug-in technology can mitigate this problem that causes the screen to refresh more than a static page. Few companies consider Web browsing to be mission critical (quite the opposite it seems), so this might not be a problem for you. If it is, you can always define a policy by user or group for the users who do need higher-speed access for browsing.

NOTE: Windows 2000 includes the Generic Quality of Service (GQoS) API as a way for network administrators and developers to make applications QoS aware. Applications running at Layer 7 do not keep track of what is going on in the lower layers where QoS mechanisms exist. With this API, Microsoft ensures that future applications will be able to do so. The accompanying QoS service provider responds to the API and provides services based on RSVP, QoS policy support, and invocation of traffic control.

Bandwidth Utilization Modeling

Citrix's ICA client requires 20 Kbps of bandwidth per user. This recommendation is fine as long as you are using applications that do not cause rapid screen refreshes, such as animation, video, or high-density graphics. The other principal variables are printing and Web browsing. If you plan to allow printing within the ICA session and Web browsing with Java enabled, we recommend bandwidth across the enterprise to be 30 Kbps per simultaneous user. This basic measurement will be used in the following sections as we analyze the bandwidth required for the various parts of your network.

Remote Sites

A useful tool for modeling the bandwidth needs of your remote offices is to come up with groupings for the office. The simplest criterion for the grouping is by number of users since the bandwidth need per user is assumed to be 30 Kbps for our model. Thus if we make some arbitrary designations based on the number of users, we could end up with the requirements found in Table 6-1.

Data Center—WAN Backbone

The data center will be providing access to centrally hosted data and applications for all of the users in your enterprise. The connectivity points needed at the central site will be determined by the number of remote users accessing the data center. For the purpose of our example, we assume you have one data center.

The bandwidth needed for each concurrent user in order to receive screen updates and send keyboard and mouse movements to and from the central data center is estimated by

Type of Office	Number of Users	Minimum Bandwidth	Packeteer Model	Redundant WAN
Jumbo	40+	Two T-1 frame relay ports (3.088 Mbps)	4000	Yes, PVC
Large	15–39	One large frame relay port (384 Kbps)	2000	Yes, PVC
Medium	5–14	One smaller frame relay port (256 Kbps)	Optional 2000, depending on office traffic requirements	Yes, ISDN, or xDSL
Small	< 5	VPN or Internet	Optional	Yes, alt. ISP

Table 6-1.   Bandwidth Requirements per Remote Office

Citrix to be up to 20 Kbps. We estimate other traffic, such as file I/O and NT authentication activity, will take approximately 10 Kbps more bandwidth. By utilizing a device that can prioritize bandwidth, such as the Packeteer PacketShaper, any performance problems that might hamper the ICA screen updates should be eliminated. The first task is to estimate the number of users who will be accessing your network and by what route. For our example, we assume that a fairly typical private frame relay network will be used, and a large number of users will be coming over an Internet connection using encrypted traffic.

Assume 4500 total remote users. Of the 4500 users, assume 700 will be coming over the Internet and 3800 will be coming over frame relay. Taking the estimated number of Internet users and assuming that each will be concurrently accessing the MetaFrame servers at the main data center, we can discern the following information:

~30 Kbps of bandwidth needed per user, 700 users = 21,000 kilobits or 21 megabits

Assuming that all users are geographically dispersed, a certain percentage of users will not be connected at all times. East Coast users will have a three-hour lead over the users on the West Coast. This means that at times the bandwidth needed for ICA screen updates and keyboard/mouse movement coordinates may be underutilized, especially since the majority of the Internet-based users will be connecting over analog single-modem connections. However, because the Internet connection will most likely also be used for outgoing e-mail, Web (HTTP) browsing, and other Internet protocols, it is important not to underestimate the bandwidth needs for Internet connectivity at the main data center.

Bandwidth Requirements for Internet Connectivity

A standard T-1 carrier line will provide connectivity capacity of 1.544 Mbps. To support 700 concurrent Internet users running ICA sessions, an Internet connection speed of approximately 14 T-1 carrier lines, or 21.616 Mbps, is needed.

Reduce by 25 percent for nonconcurrent use (assuming an even distribution between East and West Coasts) = 21 Mbps × .75 = 15.75 Mbps.

In large applications, Internet bandwidth is typically sold in increments of 10 Mbps. This example means that you would need to buy a 10 Mbps pipe (probably seven full-size frame relay ports) and four additional frame relay ports, also of 1.544 Mbps each. If rapid growth in this area was expected, you might consider just getting two 10 Mbps pipes. In any case, it is likely that your telecom provider offers a considerably reduced rate for this kind of bandwidth.

For those users who will be accessing the data center's MetaFrame servers concurrently through the frame relay WAN, we can discern the following information:

~30 kilobits bandwidth needed per user × 3800 users = 114,000 kilobits or 114 megabits

Like the Internet-based users, the frame relay sites are also geographically dispersed. Some percentage of users will not be connected at all times. East Coast users will have a three-hour lead over the users on the West Coast. This means that at times the bandwidth needed for ICA screen updates and keyboard/mouse movement coordinates might be underutilized. However, unlike the Internet-based users, the frame relay–based sites will be sharing bandwidth from each site to the frame relay. This means that unlike Internet-based users who must wait for their print job to be sent before continuing work, frame relay–based users may be able to print and work at the same time. Frame relay–based users will be able to utilize a greater amount of bandwidth than a user connected to the data center via an analog modem through the Internet. This means that any extra capacity introduced into the frame relay cloud for the remote sites will likely be used.

Bandwidth Requirements for WAN Users

To support 3800 concurrent frame relay users, you will need a connection speed equivalent to 30 Kbps × 3800 = 114,000 Kbps, or 114 Mbps.

Reduce by 25 percent for nonconcurrent use (assuming an even distribution between East and West Coasts) = 114 Mbps × .75 = 85 Mbps.

This is a huge amount of bandwidth in practical terms, but you need to keep in mind the number of users who will rely on this connection on a daily basis. To achieve this kind of bandwidth, we recommend two 45 Mbps ATM circuits linked into a frame relay cloud with PVCs spanning the country to each remote site.

Let's not forget redundancy for both frame relay and Internet connections—multiple paths to the main data center are critical. For frame relay, redundant PVCs are recommended from the company that provides frame relay access. The second PVC acts as a hot standby for a load-balanced router that waits to connect if the first or main connection is terminated. In normal operation, this router could be sharing the connection point's packet load.

For Internet-based connectivity, a redundant or secondary link to the Internet is recommended. The secondary link could be a lower-speed link, primarily for rerouted transmissions in the event of a failure of the main Internet link. The secondary Internet link should be provided, if possible, by a secondary data carrier.

SAMPLE NETWORK

Figure 6-14 depicts a sample network that includes the recommendations from this chapter. The letters in the diagram indicate the following:

A. The two remote sites shown have frame relay lines larger than ICA traffic alone justifies to allow for other kinds of traffic. Both sites are large enough for PacketShapers to be deployed. The PacketShapers at the edge of the network manage traffic flows for individual sessions.

B. The regional headquarters needs a full-size frame relay port.

C. Home office and traveling users can access the data center using VPN software that establishes an encrypted data channel over the Internet.

D. This small office is using an all-in-one device that includes routing and firewall functions as well as the VPN software needed to access the data center.

E. Employees and customers access the Internet by whatever means they have at hand. Unless users run VPN software, access is limited to Web-enabled applications.

F. Each site has a backup PVC to the regional headquarters in case its primary PVC fails. The regional headquarters has two 1.544 Mbps PVCs to the data center.

G. The data center employs a 45 Mbps ATM circuit to handle the traffic from all the regional offices connected to the frame relay network. There are many more remote offices than are shown in the diagram.

H. The data center employs seven full-size frame relay circuits for an aggregate bandwidth of 10 Mbps in order to handle the traffic coming over the Internet.

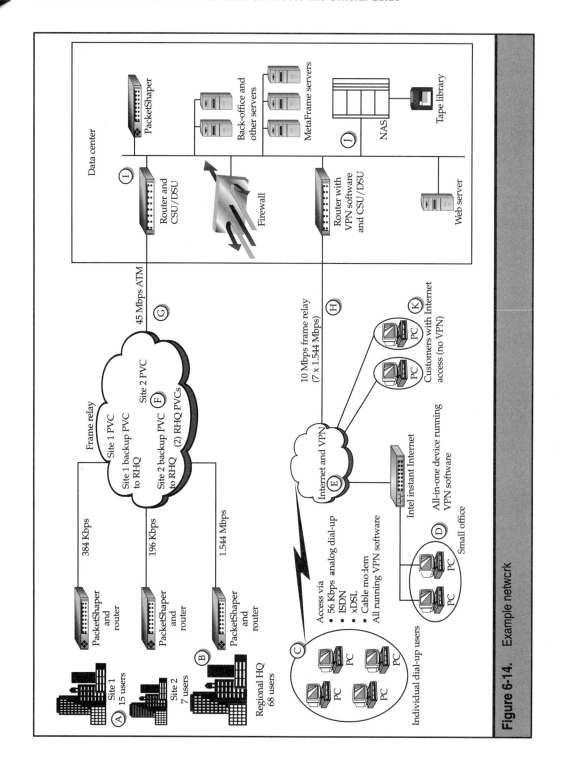

Figure 6-14. Example network

I. The PacketShaper at the data center can use packet prioritization or partitioning to manage traffic of a given type.

J. The Network-Attached Storage device provides file services for all users on the network. This is discussed more fully in Chapter 7.

K. Customers can access Web-enabled applications but cannot access desktop sessions or published applications without the appropriate VPN software.

CHAPTER 7

File Services for Server-Based Computing

Building a file services platform for a server-based computing network is quite different from building one for distributed computing. The centralized nature of the platform demands exceptional reliability, and aspects such as performance and file sharing take on new dimensions. Though it is possible to run file services locally on a MetaFrame server, we recommend against it. We have seen far better reliability and performance when the file services platform is separate and distinct from the platform providing application services. In a server-based computing network, all of the MetaFrame servers access the file services locally over a switched LAN backbone. The largest amount of network traffic occurs between the MetaFrame servers and the file services platform. For this reason we will discuss this platform in detail and determine which of the available technologies will be appropriate for your project.

According to IDC, every year, newly installed server storage capacity doubles. System managers always seem to need to add storage, even if the user's requirements have not changed and no new applications are deployed. The famous line from the Kevin Costner movie *Field of Dreams* seems apropos: "Build it and they will come," or in this case, "Put it online and they will use it." With a distributed network, this unchecked growth can be particularly miserable to manage when many servers at many sites need to be upgraded. The problem is simplified in a server-based computing environment, since all of the file servers are in one or very few sites; but new problems, such as managing a very large amount of storage in one place, are introduced. In this chapter we will discuss the underlying technology for storage in a MetaFrame and Terminal Services environment and the hardware and software options for large-scale storage and backup.

FILE SERVICE PROTOCOLS AND APPLICATIONS

In order to understand how to optimize file services for server-based computing, you must first have a solid grasp of the underlying protocols employed by Microsoft to provide these services. In this part of the chapter, we discuss the Windows NT file systems, the file sharing protocols, related protocols, and how they work together to provide network file services.

NT File System (NTFS)

NTFS represented a marked improvement in file system technology over the older File Allocation Table (FAT) file system. NTFS was included with the first versions of Windows NT to provide performance, scalability, and security. NTFS supports very large files—up to 16 terabytes—and has an integrated compression scheme to minimize the amount of space the file takes on disk. It supports long filenames as well as the older "8.3" format for backward compatibility with DOS-based systems. NTFS supports different cluster sizes to optimize the space allocation of different-sized hard drives. The administrator can choose to increase performance at the expense of some amount of space efficiency by varying the cluster size, based on application requirements. Finally, the security features provide an access control list of files and directories so that administrators can assign access rights by user or group.

NTFS attempts to locate contiguous space when storing a file. When a file is stored, a record is created in the Master File Table (MFT) with a map to all of the clusters used by that file. In addition to the MFT record and the actual data content, each file contains a description of its attributes or "metadata." This approach aids in recovering the data in case the physical media is damaged.

File Allocation Table (FAT)

Similar to the Master File Table in NTFS, the File Allocation Table contains pointers to the clusters that contain the file's information on disk. Unlike NTFS, however, the files themselves contain no attribute information. If the FAT is damaged, the file may be unrecoverable. FAT-based systems typically support cluster sizes of 2048, 4096, or 8192 bytes. Until Windows 95 (OEM Release 2), FAT entries were 16 bits in length, which limited the hard disk size to 512 megabytes, assuming an 8192-byte cluster size. This cluster size makes inefficient use of the disk space. DOS 5.0 and later versions allowed up to 2 gigabytes of hard disk space to be addressed by partitioning the disk into four areas. VFAT is an additional driver-level service that supports long filenames in Windows 95 and later. With the introduction of FAT32 in Windows 95, up to 2 terabytes can be addressed. Windows NT 4.0 and Windows 2000 can read and write to FAT and FAT32 partitions, but it is not possible to implement NT security or some file attributes unless the partition is formatted with NTFS.

Common Internet File System (CIFS)

CIFS is the protocol for file services across all Microsoft operating systems, and versions of it have been created for many non-Microsoft platforms as well. CIFS runs over TCP/IP and can use either the standard Domain Name Service (DNS) or NetBIOS to locate resources, though the default is DNS. It is especially suited for use in large internetworks or even over the Internet because it has a built-in mechanism for using different "dialects" that can contain different character sets, such as Unicode. It also incorporates functions for server name determination, server name resolution, opportunistic locking, and distributed file system (DFS) support. The CIFS security model handles authentication of the user before any file services are granted. Since CIFS has now been submitted to the Internet Engineering Task Force (IETF) as a draft for approval, a separate working group is responsible for defining the specification. The group's Web site can be found at www.cifs.com. CIFS is already an Open Group standard (X/Open CAE Specification C209).

CIFS allows multiple clients to access the same file by means of some sophisticated file sharing and locking semantics. These mechanisms also permit aggressive caching without loss of cache consistency.

> **NOTE:** The most important feature of a file service protocol is how it maintains cache consistency in the case of failure or inconsistent network performance. For example, what if a client machine dies while holding locks on some files? This is the point between the time a user initiates the update from a client and the time that the file is actually updated on disk on the server. Both CIFS and NFS (the network file system common on UNIX systems) have built-in mechanisms to ensure that the chance of this occurring is very low. Nevertheless, it is crucial to design the network so that the path between the file server(s) and MetaFrame servers is stable and has not only plenty of available bandwidth but also predictable bandwidth usage.

CIFS operates by providing named areas on disk, called "shares," to users across the network. CIFS shares are referred to directly and accessed when needed. For a given file request, CIFS assumes that the client can determine the name of the server, share, and location of the file within the server. CIFS supports the concept of opportunistic file locking, or "oplocks," as a way to increase network performance. The idea is to allow a client to dynamically alter its buffering strategy. For example, if the client determines that no other client has a particular file open, it can buffer all the update information for that file and send it when all operations are completed. There are three different types of oplocks. An "exclusive oplock" allows a client to open a file for exclusive access and perform arbitrary buffering, as in our example. A "batch oplock" allows a client to keep a file open on the server even though the local user on the client has closed the file. A "level II oplock" indicates that there are multiple readers of a file and no writers.

Samba

An acronym based on the name of the original CIFS implementation, SMB, Samba is an open-source version of CIFS that was available even before CIFS was submitted to the IETF. Today, it is the most common implementation of CIFS on non-Microsoft platforms, such as LINUX. Samba is compatible with native CIFS and can be used, for example, to integrate UNIX or LINUX into NT networks. Samba lacks any generally accepted graphical configuration tool (though there are many candidates), so it can be a challenge to configure. Since it is a free implementation, many network administrators take the time to work out its intricacies. Once configured, a Samba server can be an inexpensive and reliable addition to your network. Several storage network vendors incorporate Samba as a core part of their products. Samba consists of the following major components:

- ▼ **smbd** The smbd server process provides CIFS services to clients. It reads its configuration parameters from the smb.conf file when it is started.
- ■ **nmbd** The nmbd server process provides NetBIOS name services.
- ■ **smb.conf** The smb.conf file contains configuration data for smbd and nmbd and is read when those services are started.

- ■ **smbclient** The smbclient client program allows file and print services on CIFS servers. For example, a LINUX client running smbclient could send a print job to a Windows 2000 print server.
- ▲ **Other utilities** Several utility programs are included for testing various aspects of the CIFS network.

Distributed File System (DFS)

DFS provides a way for administrators to build a single, hierarchical file system that contains shares on many different servers throughout a network. For example, a user could request the "Marketing" share, not knowing or caring that the server containing that information is in a different office (as shown in Figure 7-1). The administrative benefit is a central "tree" to administer, which is shared throughout an organization. File searches, virus scanning, and backups can be done centrally using DFS. With the release of Windows 2000, DFS became part of Active Directory (AD) services. DFS in AD supports the creation of fault-tolerant shares. These shares use replication to transfer file and directory information between participating servers. In practice this can cause a tremendous amount of traffic if the servers are distributed across a WAN. In the case of a server-based network where all of this replication traffic would be on the LAN with a switched backbone, this isn't as much of a problem. In fact, DFS can provide your users with a convenient single point of access to your entire file system.

CAUTION: If you plan to use Microsoft Cluster Services (MSCS), you cannot use fault-tolerant shares with DFS. MSCS has its own method for creating fault-tolerant shares.

Anatomy of a CIFS Operation

CIFS functions by exchanging System Message Blocks (SMBs) between client and server. A series of predefined messages for various operations are exchanged to carry out a file request. Table 7-1 details a typical CIFS SMB conversation.

Network File System (NFS)

NFS is not a Microsoft file service protocol, but it has become so ubiquitous on other types of platforms that we mention it here. If you are in an organization with legacy systems or UNIX platforms, it is likely that you already use NFS. We will suggest strategies for integrating your server-based network with these systems. The Network File System protocol was originally created by Sun Microsystems so that large networks of UNIX workstations could easily access each other's storage resources. Over the years, it has been ported to many different operating systems, including all the variations of Windows. NFS is characterized by strong security and a robust implementation of remote file

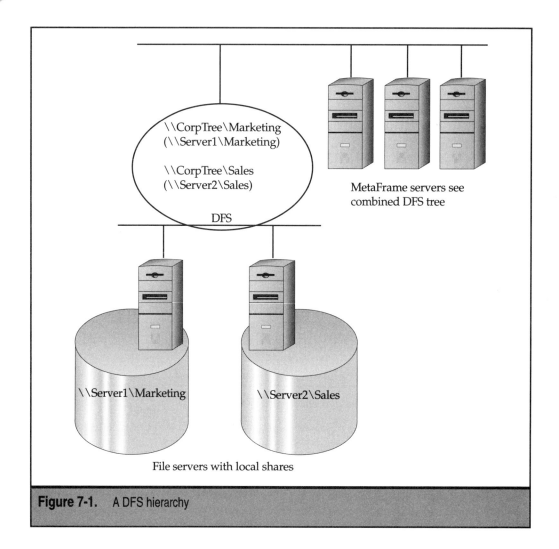

Figure 7-1.   A DFS hierarchy

system locking (in version 3). NFS versions 2 and 3 are both still in common use. Version 2 generally uses UDP and IP as a transport, while version 3 uses the standard TCP/IP protocol suite.

NOTE: Actually, NFS version 3 can fall back to UDP if necessary, and some NFS version 2 implementations use TCP instead of UDP. Check with your system vendor on the behavior of your specific implementation if necessary.

SMB Message from Client	Server Response
SMB_COM_NEGOTIATE	The client publishes all of the SMB dialects it will support, including flags for optional elements such as Unicode. The server responds with the dialect to be used. By default this is the most recently published dialect in an attempt to make the connection as secure as possible.
SMB_COM_SESSION_SETUP_ANDX	The client now sends the username and password encrypted by the method agreed upon in the previous step. The server then accepts or denies the login. If the login is successful, a user identifier (UID), which will uniquely identify the session, is returned.
SMB_COM_TREE_CONNECT	The client specifies which share it wants to use, and the server returns a tree identifier (TID) to uniquely identify the connection throughout the session.
SMB_COM_OPEN	The client sends the name of the file relative to the TID. The server responds with a file identifier (FID).
SMB_COM_READ	The client supplies the FID, TID, starting position, and the number of bytes to read. The server then sends back the requested data.
SMB_COM_CLOSE	The client closes the file represented by the FID and TID. The server responds with a code indicating success or failure.
SMB_COM_TREE_DISCONNECT	The client disconnects to the TID session. The server responds with a code indicating success or failure.

Table 7-1.   A Typical CIFS SMB Conversation

NFS functions by publishing a list of available volumes that represent mount points in a directory hierarchy on the hard disk of the publishing computer. Another computer on the network can then request to "mount" that volume. In NFS terminology the server is the machine exporting the file system, and the client is the machine mounting the file system. A machine can function as an NFS server while simultaneously functioning as a client mounting file systems from other machines. A PC running NFS can publish a volume just as easily as a large UNIX server can. Fortunately, this paradigm translates well into the world of CIFS. All that is necessary to integrate NFS into a CIFS network is to translate the NFS protocol and security. It is possible to set up an NFS client on all the computers that need access to an NFS volume, but we recommend setting up a gateway between NFS and CIFS servers, as shown in Figure 7-2. This allows both clients and server to use native CIFS operations, and the overall network complexity is reduced. This paradigm fits well in a server-based computing network since the gateway can be located centrally. Figure 7-2 shows DFS being employed to provide a further level of abstraction, but this is not necessary to the function of the NFS gateway.

FILE SERVICES DRIVE TECHNOLOGIES

The technology that goes into building disk drives and arrays is in a state of constant innovation. If Moore's Law determines the rate and capacity at which processors are introduced, it might also suggest the same for drive capacity. As you read this, the price of a 9GB IDE hard drive might be around the same as a few boxes of floppy disks. You wouldn't necessarily want to build your server farm's storage on such a platform, but the downward trend in drive prices affects higher-capacity drives as well. In the following sections, we define the drive technologies you will most likely encounter in your search for a storage solution for your enterprise.

Integrated Drive Electronics (IDE)

IDE and its newest implementation Enhanced IDE (EIDE) require the simplest controller technology because the drive's intelligence is built into the drive itself. The original IDE implementation was limited to two drives per controller—one master and one slave. EIDE allows up to four drives. Speed has also been a limitation of this type of drive, as it has traditionally lagged behind SCSI in this area. Even with the latest Direct Memory Access (DMA) technology (UltraDMA/66), EIDE drives are slower than corresponding SCSI drives in terms of total throughput. The biggest advantage of EIDE is cost. Prices of EIDE drives are usually at least 30 percent less expensive than comparable SCSI drives, which is probably why EIDE drives are found in most manufacturers' prepackaged desktop computers.

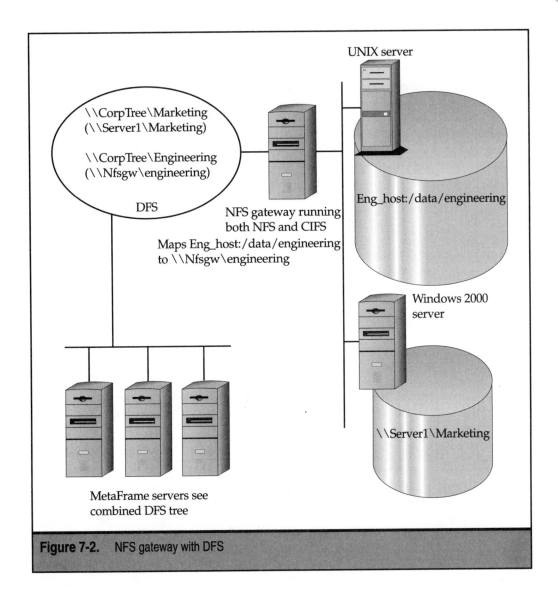

Figure 7-2.   NFS gateway with DFS

Small Computer Storage Interface (SCSI)

SCSI was introduced by NCR to provide an inexpensive way to add storage to an existing computer. The original SCSI (SCSI-1 and SCSI-2) allows up to 7 drives to be connected on a common cable. The latest SCSI standard, Ultra-3 SCSI for a 32-bit bus, can transfer data at up to 160 MBps (that's megabytes per second as opposed to megabits per second). As illustrated below, SCSI allows up to 7 or 15 devices (depending on the bus width) to be connected. SCSI-3 provides an extensible command set to handle not only SCSI drives but also new topologies such as Serial Bus Protocol, Fiber Channel, and the Serial Storage Protocol (SSP).

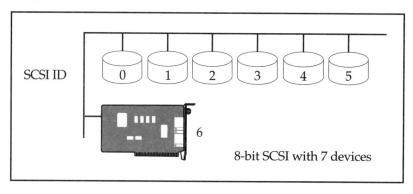

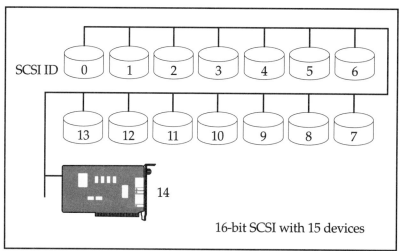

Fiber Channel Asymmetric Loop (FC-AL)

Fiber Channel combines aspects of network technology with channel-based information access technology such as SCSI. Like SCSI, Fiber Channel provides a robust connection between storage devices and servers or clients, as in the sample loop shown below. Like Ethernet, Fiber Channel supports many devices on one network and can support different topologies. It was designed with Storage Area Networks (SANs) in mind to bridge the gap between traditional host controller technology and high-speed networking. Fiber Channel supports rates over 800 Mbps, with a 4 Gbps standard proposed. Several types of cabling, including coaxial and twisted pair, are supported, but optical cable is required to reach the maximum distance of about 10 kilometers. Fiber Channel supports switched, loop, and point-to-point interfaces and can be bridged to interoperate with IP networks.

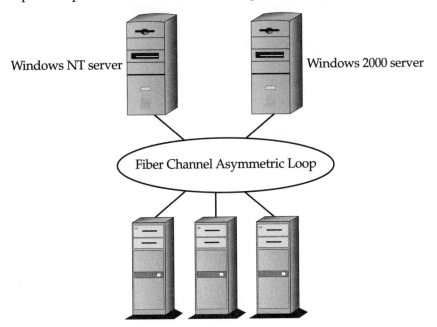

Windows NT server

Windows 2000 server

Fiber Channel Asymmetric Loop

FC-AL RAID arrays

Redundant Array of Independent Disks (RAID)

RAID provides a method for storing a single piece of information on multiple physical drives to provide redundancy. Since multiple drive heads can seek for the data simultaneously, separating or "striping" the data also provides a performance advantage. Using multiple disks in parallel allows recovery in case of failure of any one disk. RAID can be implemented through hardware or software. It is generally better to use hardware-based RAID that is transparent to the operating system. In this way the RAID controller, which is already processing all I/O requests to disk, can coordinate splitting the data to the various disks in the array. If software RAID is used, a separate layer of coordination is involved between the operating system and the disk controller to synchronize this file I/O, which will hinder performance. RAID disk arrays are sometimes called "just a bunch of disks" (JBOD). There are at least nine types of RAID plus a nonredundant array (RAID-0), but RAID-1 and RAID-5 are the most common.

▼ **Striped disk array without fault tolerance: RAID-0**   This technique has striping but no redundancy of data. It offers the best performance but no fault tolerance.

■ **Mirroring and duplexing: RAID-1**   This type is also known as disk mirroring and consists of at least two drives that duplicate the storage of data. In the illustration below, the original disks A1 and B1 are duplicated on A2 and B2, respectively. There is no striping. Read performance is improved because either disk can be read at the same time. Write performance is the same as for single disk storage.

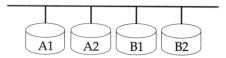

- **Hamming Code ECC: RAID-2** This type uses striping across disks, with some disks storing error checking and correcting (ECC) information. Each data word has its Hamming Code ECC word recorded on the ECC disks. On read, the ECC code verifies correct data or corrects single disk errors. It has no advantage over RAID-3.

- **Parallel transfer with parity: RAID-3** This type uses striping and dedicates one drive to storing parity information. The embedded error checking (ECC) information is used to detect errors. Since an I/O operation addresses all drives at the same time, RAID-3 cannot overlap I/O.

- **Independent data disks with shared parity disk: RAID-4** This type uses large stripes, which means you can read records from any single drive. This allows you to take advantage of overlapped I/O for read operations. Parity information is stored on a single drive, and since all write operations have to update the parity drive, no I/O overlapping is possible. RAID-4 offers no advantage over RAID-5.

- **Independent data disks with distributed parity blocks: RAID-5** This type includes a rotating parity array, thus addressing the write limitation in RAID-4 and enabling read and write operations to be overlapped. RAID-5 stores parity information but not redundant data. RAID-5 requires at least three and usually five disks for the array, as shown below, where each cylinder represents a disk and each section represents a data or parity block.

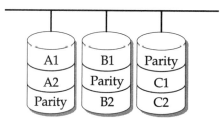

- **Independent data and parity disks: RAID-6** This type is similar to RAID-5 but includes a second parity scheme that is distributed across different drives and thus offers extremely high fault and drive-failure tolerance. This RAID type is not commonly used.

■ **Optimized asynchrony: RAID-7**   This type includes a real-time embedded operating system as a controller, caching via a high-speed bus, and other characteristics of a stand-alone computer. All I/O transfers, including host interface transfers, are asynchronous, independently controlled, and cached. This RAID type is not commonly used.

■ **High reliability combined with high performance: RAID-10**   This type offers an array of stripes in which each stripe is a RAID-1 array of drives. This offers higher performance than RAID-1 but at much higher financial cost.

▲ **High I/O rates and data transfer performance: RAID-53**   This type offers an array of stripes in which each stripe is a RAID-3 array of disks. This offers higher performance than RAID-3 but at much higher cost.

FILE SERVICES SOLUTIONS

In this part of the chapter, we examine several different approaches to providing file services to the server-based network, from the traditional to the cutting edge. These solutions are not mutually exclusive, and the reader should keep the application requirements of the project in mind when reviewing the material. Several solutions may be necessary to fulfill all of these requirements in a large network. Storage networks are an area of rapid development and advancement, with new solutions and approaches appearing almost constantly. It is important to sift through the confusion this causes and choose solutions that provide rock-solid reliability regardless of other features. No matter what solution is chosen, there are some requirements that apply to all of them:

▼ Redundancy within each server for critical subsystems such as power supplies, memory, and disk

■ Redundant power source—ideally a UPS with separate power sources, (possibly one from the local grid and one from a generator)

■ A shared bus with Fiber Channel rather than traditional SCSI if an external RAID is shared between nodes

▲ Redundant network interface cards (NICs) and network routes from the MetaFrame servers to the cluster server, which we discussed in Chapter 6

General-Purpose File Servers

A general-purpose file server (GPFS) is what is traditionally thought of when referring to a network file server. It is a nonclustered computer running an operating system such as Windows 2000, NetWare, or LINUX with a number of disks that provide file services to users (as in a RAID array), as shown below. Though it is the simplest of the solutions we will discuss, it also has some significant limitations when considering its deployment in an enterprise setting.

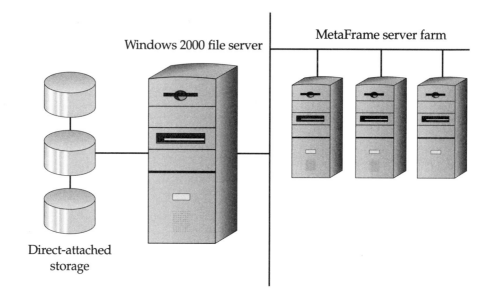

Windows 2000 file server

MetaFrame server farm

Direct-attached
storage

The advantages of a GPFS include

▼   Relatively low cost

■   Inexpensive hardware

■   Inexpensive or even free software (included in OS)

▲   Ideal solution for small work group storage

The limitations include

▼   Lack of flexibility; it is limited to the number of disks in internal drive bays or
    accessible in external direct-attached RAID storage

■   Monolithic operating system, which is not optimized for file input or output

■   Limited network bandwidth available on file server(s) for a potentially large
    number of users

▲   Lack of server based fault tolerance or load balancing

Clustered File Servers

A clustered file server (CFS) is a grouping of GPFSs that together provide fault-tolerant
and possibly load-balanced file services to users. Microsoft Cluster Services (MSCS) and
Microsoft Load Balancing Services (MSLBS) are the applications that provide these capabilities in Windows NT–based platforms. There are also several third-party solutions,
such as Legato's Co-Standby Server and Octopus, that can provide capabilities different
from the standard Microsoft offerings.

What is it exactly that we are clustering? In order to effectively plan the file services implementation, this question must be answered. A typical CFS would cluster the services listed in Table 7-2. It is possible for "cluster-aware" applications to be written to access the cluster software's capabilities directly, providing an even higher level of fault tolerance.

NOTE: CFS does not prevent user interruption during a failure. If the user is running a typical client-server application on the MetaFrame server, such as Lotus Notes or an ERP package such as PeopleSoft, the session will be interrupted when a cluster node goes down, and the user will need to reconnect. If the user is running a stateless application, such as a Web browser, he or she will experience a connection delay while the cluster resynchronizes. Access can then continue.

Whatever services or applications are chosen, several different configuration options are possible when configuring a CFS, including Active/Active, Active/Passive, Mirrored Disk, Shared RAID, and Shared Nothing.

Service or Application	Description
Physical disk	Disks in a shared RAID device accessible by all nodes.
File shares	Shares accessible to users on the network.
IP address	The node's Internet Protocol address.
Network name	The DNS host name and the NetBIOS server name.
Non-cluster-aware application	Many generic applications can be clustered that do not have specific support for clustered services. Examples are desktop applications such as Microsoft Office or database programs such as Microsoft Access. The cluster software will mirror the application binaries and Registry keys alike.
Non-cluster-aware service	As with non-cluster-aware applications, the same is true of services such as print spooling and Web servers.
Cluster-aware application	Applications that can utilize clustered services directly include databases such as Microsoft SQL Server.
Cluster-aware service	This includes services such as Microsoft Distributed Transaction Coordinator (DTC).

Table 7-2. Typical Clustered Services and Applications

Active/Active

In this configuration, shown below, all nodes in the cluster are available to run applications. Work can be load balanced manually or automatically depending on the specific clustering software's capabilities. MSCS supports this model with configurable load balancing. The Windows 2000 version, when shipping, will have more automatic load-balancing features.

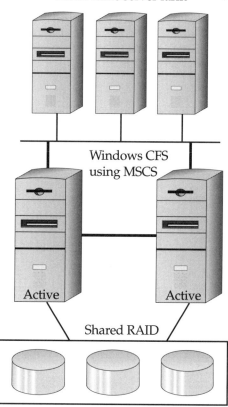

Active/Passive

This configuration, shown next, can be thought of as a hot standby. One or more servers are idle awaiting the primary server to fail. Upon failure, the standby server will assume the primary server's identity and take over its disk resources.

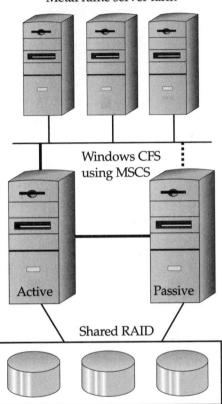

Mirrored Disk

In addition to the different methods for implementing a CFS, there are different approaches to achieving fault tolerance. In the mirrored disk model, shown below, each server in the cluster maintains its own disks, and software replicates data between servers. The software must take great care to track updates so that all servers in the cluster stay synchronized in case of failure. MSCS and Legato Octopus can provide this functionality.

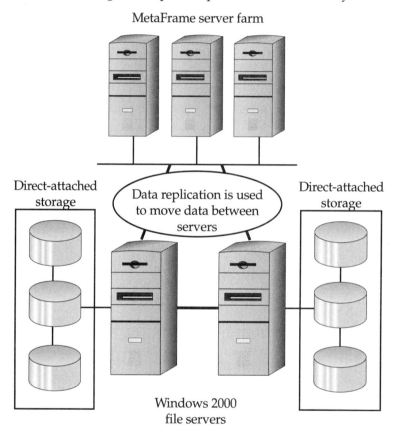

Shared RAID

This model allows any node in the cluster to access any disk device. The disk devices are directly attached to the servers in the cluster. This is more efficient than the mirrored disk method because each node has the duty to write its own data to disk. However, synchronization is particularly challenging in this case, so the software must filter and queue all writes. The Distributed Lock Manager (DLM) performs this task in MSCS (see the following illustration), and it requires that the applications accessing the shared device supply DLM instructions.

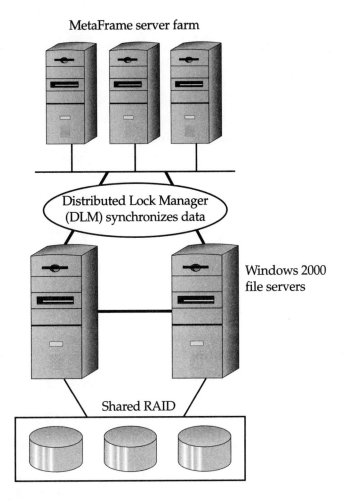

MetaFrame server farm

Distributed Lock Manager
(DLM) synchronizes data

Windows 2000
file servers

Shared RAID

Shared Nothing

This method of fail-over is similar to mirroring in that each node maintains its own disks. A synchronization manager (such as DLM) is then used to transfer control of the disks from one server to another. The main difference is the presence of a standard API (in this case DLM) to maintain data consistency.

Advantages and Limitations of a CFS

We will emphasize again the importance of matching your application requirements when choosing any of the configuration options. For example, if you are running an Oracle database, some clustering software or storage arrays may not be compatible with the database software. In any case, a CFS offers some advantages and disadvantages when comparing it to other storage options for server-based networks. The advantages include

▼ It is made up of relatively low-cost GPFSs.

■ It is based on standard, well-known operating system platforms.

■ It has configurable clustering options.

▲ Relatively inexpensive disks can be used.

Limitations of the CFS include

▼ It doesn't scale well; it is limited to the number of servers supported by clustering software and the number of disks supported by servers.

■ It is a monolithic operating system, which is not optimized for file input or output.

■ It has limited network bandwidth available on file server(s) for a potentially large number of users.

▲ Complex layers of hardware and software could compromise reliability and performance.

Storage Area Networks

A Storage Area Network (SAN) can include clustered file servers, RAID arrays connected through a controlling server, or any storage scheme that relies on a host to pass data and control traffic. Servers connect to storage devices either directly through a Fiber Channel Host Bus Adapter (HBA) or via SCSI or Ethernet through a bridge device over the SAN's shared bus. Many storage vendors offer native Fiber Channel disk arrays, but legacy SCSI disks can be incorporated through the same bridge devices.

With most SAN implementations, disk space must be dedicated to a specific server. In a server-based computing network, the ideal is to have users connect transparently to any server that contains the data for the application they are using. Achieving this transparency with a SAN requires an extra layer of software such as DFS or MSCS. Remote access to data on a SAN must pass through a host server providing remote access and file services (RAS and CIFS), which can complicate the design in an enterprise network. SAN solutions are available from all major storage network vendors, including IBM, Hewlett-Packard, Compaq, and Sun. Figure 7-3 shows a typical SAN implementation.

The advantages of a SAN include

▼ Creation of a shared bus using Fiber Channel for all connected devices provides a degree of fault tolerance and increased performance over accessing the data through a traditional network.

■ Centralized management helps when storage space requirements, sharing, security, or other key factors are in constant flux.

- It is useful when a large number of file servers need to be consolidated.
- The centralized scheme allows IT staff to regain control of enterprise storage and more efficiently grow over time.

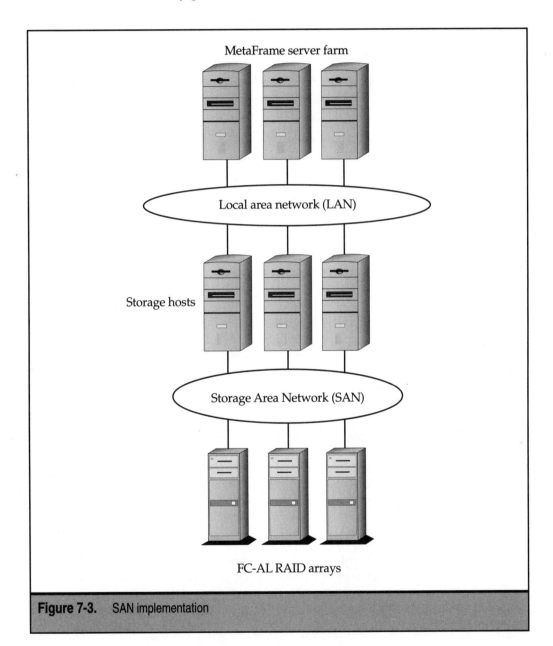

Figure 7-3.   SAN implementation

- Disk arrays and tape devices can be accessed over the shared bus by many hosts on the SAN.

▲ Devices on the SAN can be disbursed in a campus environment because Fiber Channel supports distances up to 10 kilometers with optical cabling.

SAN has the following limitations:

▼ Operating systems require partitions on the disk arrays, making implementation of a "virtual file server" for your MetaFrame server farm difficult.

- Backup data from host to tape device must travel over the SAN.

- Hardware and software support for SAN is relatively immature, making interoperability between SAN devices problematic.

- Training in the technology is required in order to support SAN.

▲ Dedicated servers are required to move data through a SAN optimally, making the solution more expensive.

Network-Attached Storage

A Network-Attached Storage (NAS) device is disk storage that connects directly to a network backbone via a LAN interface—for example, Gigabit Ethernet, ATM, or FDDI. A NAS server typically runs an operating system highly tuned for file I/O and runs NFS, CIFS, or other network protocols to serve file-oriented content to users. Popular NAS vendors include EMC, Network Appliance, and MetaStor. A NAS differs from a SAN in that it does not require a traditional file server running an operating system such as Windows 2000 or UNIX. Also unlike a SAN, it does not require any special software running on the storage host. A NAS device is essentially a "data appliance" that is placed on a network and provides file services to users.

A NAS approach to file storage is especially appropriate with a MetaFrame server farm. In this scenario, a NAS server appears as one large virtual file server and provides transparent access over the LAN from each MetaFrame server. Remote access is also simplified in this scenario. A user simply has to connect to the network to get access to the NAS server. This can be accomplished through a variety of methods, including the Internet, direct dial-up to a communication server, or VPN. Figure 7-4 shows a typical NAS implementation.

Advantages of NAS include

▼ Centralized management helps when storage space requirements, sharing, security, or other key factors are in constant flux.

- It is useful when a large number of file servers need to be consolidated.

- It provides heterogeneous file sharing between CIFS and NFS (and perhaps even AppleShare) without requiring a gateway host or third-party software.

■ Remote access to the NAS server does not complicate support of remote users.

■ It is better at enabling large amounts of data to be backed up. Backups based on the Network Data Management Protocol (NDMP) provide the speed of direct-attached devices and the manageability of network-based backup.

■ A NAS data appliance typically requires less training than SAN or other large-scale storage solutions.

▲ Native file service protocols are used, and no special software is typically needed on the client.

Limitations of NAS include

▼ Hardware and software support for NAS is relatively immature, making interoperability between NAS devices problematic.

■ High-speed, switched networking is required between MetaFrame servers and NAS devices.

▲ Clustering and fault-tolerant features are usually proprietary and must be provided by the manufacturer.

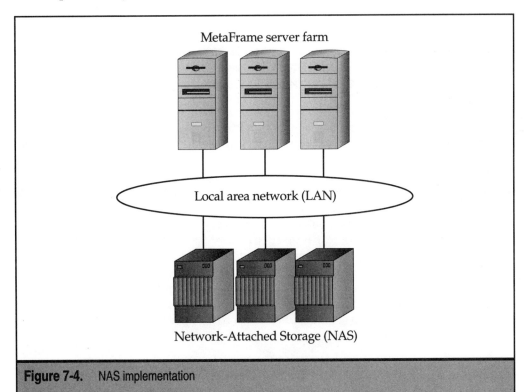

Figure 7-4. NAS implementation

NAS Implementations

The following companies offer NAS implementations that we have worked with and know to be compatible with MetaFrame and Terminal Services. We feel that NAS technology provides the best fit in the enterprise for server-based computing. It offers all of the advantages of SAN with few of its limitations. Fiber Channel bridging and switching technology is advancing, allowing a SAN and a NAS to occupy the same network. Large and small manufacturers alike are embracing it, despite the fact that it is relatively new on the market.

Network Appliance   The Network Appliance F760 filer works well in a MetaFrame environment. Supporting up to 1.4TB of data, the F760 provides high-performance, mission-critical data access, redundant components, and clustered fail-over to help ensure nonstop data availability. The F760 uses RAID-4 to protect data, and it features native Fiber Channel drives that can automatically rebuild from spares.

> **NOTE:**   We find it interesting that Network Appliance has chosen RAID-4. The typical disadvantages of this type of RAID include an inefficient data rebuild in the event of failure; a slow write transaction rate, both single file and aggregate; and the block read transfer rate of a single disk. The advantages are a very high read rate, both single file and aggregate; and a low ratio of parity disks to data disks, meaning high efficiency and low cost. Network Appliance has worked to overcome the disadvantages with an optimized controller and operating system design. We can only presume they chose RAID-4 due to the low ratio of parity to data disks, which keeps the cost down and allows users the flexibility to create separate RAID arrays and assign parity disks as needed.

The NetApp filer uses a proprietary file system, called WAFL, which maintains a consistent disk image and features fast repair on reboots in one to two minutes. It supports both CIFS and NFS and will allow either UNIX or NT authentication. For CIFS, it supports file-level Access Control Lists and appears to the NT network as another NT file server, allowing standard NT tools such as User Manager and Server Manager to administer it. One of the more interesting features of the NetApp filer is the snapshot. Up to 20 images of a share can be saved at specific points in time. The file system uses an ingenious method of saving only changed bits and adding very little overhead to the amount of storage required. The snapshots can be used to restore the data image to a specific point in time (SnapRestore) in just a few minutes, and to mirror the data to another filer (SnapMirror) even if that filer is off-site. Traditional tape backups are also simplified, and the snapshot feature enhances their performance. A backup is run during production hours directly from the snapshot and does not require access to the production data image. The OnTap operating system is optimized for this operation, and the performance impact from such a backup is minimal.

> *We originally tried clustering our NT file servers, but found that the clustering software it-self added an element of instability and complexity. We actually suffered data corruption, as the clustering software failed to properly manage the locks. Using the Network Appliance Filer NAS solution enables us to enjoy a much more reliable and scalable architecture.*
> —Andrew Zollars,
> Systems Engineering Group Manager, Westaff

EMC   The EMC Celerra also supports CIFS and NFS and represents an evolution from EMC's popular direct-attach and SAN storage solutions. Celerra incorporates a standard Symmetrix file system, several Data Movers, and a real-time operating system (RTOS) tuned for file input and output. The Data Movers can fail over to a hot standby Data Mover in a manner that is transparent to the user. The Celerra also features disk mirroring, RAID-S (basically, RAID-5 with some proprietary modifications to enhance performance and reliability), Symmetrix Remote Data Facility (SRDF), and TimeFinder/FS business continuance volumes. SRDF is the EMC facility to replicate data to another Symmetrix array.

ENTERPRISE BACKUPS

Whether you choose NAS, SAN, GPFS, or CFS, backing up terabytes of data every day presents some unique problems. In distributed networks, we typically see a server running a standard network operating system such as NT with a direct-attached tape device acting as a backup server. This configuration causes all the data to flow over the network as it is backed up. The conventional logic is that if the backup is run at night, it will not contend with production network traffic. In many Corporate ASPs, very little time or bandwidth is available to do backups because business-related traffic is flowing around the clock. "What to do?" In this part of the chapter, we discuss some of the available backup options and technology and recommend a solution for your archive strategy. In order to choose the right solution, you must first decide what the most important requirements for your backup are. The following are options we have found to be important in most Corporate ASPs:

- ▼ Ability to do full, incremental, and differential backups.
- ■ Direct connection to the storage array as opposed to a LAN connection for performance
- ■ Ability to back up an entire array in less than eight hours
- ■ Ability to restore an entire array in less than eight hours

- Optimal price/performance
- Relatively inexpensive to expand for growth
- Ability to do image backups for disaster recovery
- Hot-swap capability for tape drives
- Proven, industry-standard drive technology
- ▲ Industry-leading company solution with adequate financial and support resources

Backup Hardware Standards

There are two tape technologies we feel are likely to continue into the future and become de facto standards. Other technologies, such as 8mm digital tape, are available but either do not offer the capacity we require or are nearing the end of their practical life cycle. Digital Linear Tape (DLT) has been around for a while and continues to be improved. Advanced Intelligent Tape (AIT) and now AIT-2 are relatively new to the archive storage arena but are receiving broad industry support and have some compelling implementations.

Digital Linear Tape (DLT)

DLT was pioneered and patented by Conner, which was later purchased by Quantum. All drives and loaders are made with their agreement. The advantage of DLT technology is that multiple parallel channels allow the products to deliver higher and higher levels of performance. DLT tape drives utilize a stationary head with multiple read/write channels. While other tape products such as 8mm helical scan use a limited single-channel technology that can read or write only one track at a time, Quantum's multiple-channel architecture can read or write multiple channels simultaneously. The result is that more data is passed through the head for significantly higher throughput. For example, the DLT 7000 utilizes four parallel channels to provide the fastest transfer rates in the midrange tape marketplace. With a sustained native data transfer rate of 5 Mbps, the four-channel DLT 7000 is 65 percent faster than the closest competitive tape drive in its class. DLT tapes offer five times more surface area than traditional 8mm technologies—over 10,000 square inches. The cartridge capacity for DLT is 35GB native and up to 70GB compressed.

Advanced Intelligent Tape (AIT)

AIT was pioneered and patented by Sony. All drives and loaders are made with their agreement. The AIT format was designed to set new performance (6.0 Mbps) and capacity (50GB native) standards. Unlike many conventional tape drives, there is no need for periodic cleaning of AIT drives. The drive itself constantly monitors head output to check for possible contamination and will then invoke the built-in Active Head Cleaner. Under extreme environmental conditions, a cleaning cartridge may be required. This self-cleaning feature tends to extend the life of the media considerably. AIT drives typically get higher data compression rates than other drives—up to 2:1. In addition, access speed is considerably faster than competing technologies. This is due to a 16KB nonvolatile memory chip stored in the spine of the tape. All backup set headers are stored on the chip. When an appended backup or restore request is received, the drive can go directly to the right spot on the tape without searching or *retentioning*. Retentioning spins the tape to tighten up the loops inside the cartridge. Tighter loops inside the tape translate into improved reliability. Individual AIT tape drives tend to cost around half that of DLT drives in typical street prices. AIT-2 is now widely available and further increases the storage capacity of the tape to over 100GB compressed. AIT-2 drives can read and write AIT tapes.

Backup Hardware

The following examples of tape drive hardware represent products we have deployed with success in a variety of customer networks. We feel that AIT has a price/performance advantage over DLT and a longer obsolescence life cycle. The new AIT drives (AIT-2) are fast, efficient, and backward compatible with older AIT tapes. Figure 7-5 shows how a tape library is implemented in the storage networks we have discussed thus far.

Exabyte 230D DLT Tape Library

This 2.1TB-capacity tape library accommodates up to two drives and 30 cartridges and is loaded using 5-cartridge magazines. It features a throughput of up to 72GB per hour. The 230D incorporates a laser bar code scanner to improve file management and reduce inventory time. Both DLT 4000 and DLT 7000 drives are supported with SCSI-2 Fast Narrow and SCSI-2 Fast Wide Interfaces, respectively. The 230D can be incorporated into a SAN with the use of a Fiber Channel bridge.

Spectra Logic "Bullfrog" 10000S AIT Tape Library

This unit is a four-drive library unit with 40-tape capacity. Native throughput for this unit is 12 Mbps or 31.2 Mbps compressed. This allows up to 112.4GB per hour, which would back up the F760 filer with 500GB in less than five hours. The 20-tape capacity would allow three weeks of backup tapes to be kept online. The maximum capacity of this solution is 3.6TB compressed. Bar code–based management is also included to ease tape administration. A bright LCD display adorns the front of the unit for controlling all functions.

Backup Software Standards

There are so many enterprise-class backup software packages that it is beyond the scope of this chapter to do an exhaustive evaluation of them all. However, we will concentrate on some of the most popular and most appropriate for server-based computing. First we will discuss three emerging standards for enterprise backups that we feel have particular application to the server-based network.

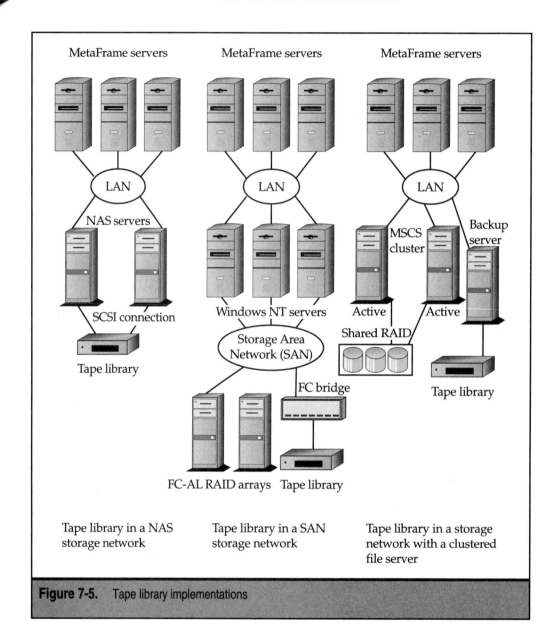

Figure 7-5. Tape library implementations

Network Data Management Protocol (NDMP)

NDMP is an open standard protocol for network-based backup for Network-Attached Storage. The objective is to help address the problem of backing up networks of heterogeneous file servers, including dedicated file servers, with any of several backup applications.

This new network-based backup protocol enables the creation of a "universal agent" for the file servers to be used by any of the centralized backup administration applications. With NDMP, the administrator can manage backups from a central console without requiring the data being backed up to flow across the production network. The console sends instructions to the backup device, which is directly connected to the storage array, as shown in Figure 7-6. The file storage vendors need only be concerned with maintaining compatibility with one well-defined protocol. The backup vendors can place their primary focus on the sophisticated central backup administration software.

Hierarchical Storage Management (HSM)

HSM is the mechanism whereby files can be marked as inactive and moved to semi-online storage media such as optical disks. The pointer to the file remains on the production media so that when a user attempts to access it, the HSM system retrieves the file from the other storage media transparently, as illustrated in Figure 7-7. This serves to keep only active files on relatively expensive production media while making the entire operation

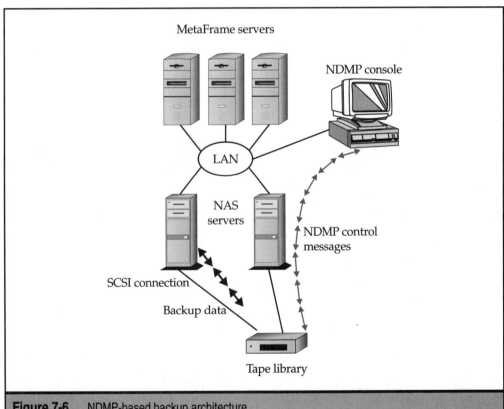

Figure 7-6.   NDMP-based backup architecture

invisible to the end user. HSM solutions have been available for years for UNIX and legacy platforms. Unfortunately, the third-party HSM market is relatively immature in terms of what is available for Windows NT. However, HSM capabilities are built into Windows 2000 in the Remote Storage service.

RAIT/RAIL

Redundant Array of Inexpensive Tapes or Libraries applies some of the technologies developed for hard drive arrays to tapes. By using RAIT, a "virtual tape" composed of several individual tape drives is created. Parity information as well as the actual data is stored to the tape array. This not only increases write performance, which is critical for large backups, but it decreases the chances an entire backup image will be lost if one tape is damaged. The entire image can be rebuilt using the parity information, as in RAID. RAIL applies the concept to tape library devices. With RAIL, performance and resiliency are further increased by striping the data across several libraries, each composed of several individual tape drives.

Backup Software

A recent flurry of mergers has consolidated the backup software market somewhat. The remaining companies are positioning themselves to offer a "soup to nuts" archive solu-

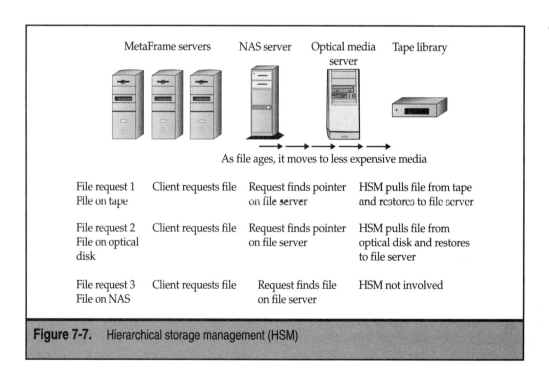

Figure 7-7. Hierarchical storage management (HSM)

tion with support for SAN, NAS, a large number or servers, multiple operating systems, and more integrated HSM and disaster recovery options. The backup software chosen should fulfill the following key requirements:

▼   Provide optimized performance (data compression)

■   Support a variety of single-tape drives and multitape libraries

■   Ease administration and allow flexible backup and restore policies

■   Use Windows NT or a browser for the control console and fit well into the overall system architecture

■   Provide the flexibility to support a variety of storage network topologies, including NAS, SAN, or direct attached

■   Support NDMP

▲   Support HSM

Computer Associates ArcServ*IT*

We include this package for comparison because it is popular in distributed network backup architectures. Originally called ArcServe, this product has provided a flexible, stable backup solution on multiple operating systems for some time. With its recently released SAN modules, the Enterprise and Network Library options, it promises to continue as a solid backup solution. It provides support for image backups for disaster recovery, open files, multiple operating system platforms, HSM, RAIT/RAIL 1, and a variety of tape drives and libraries. Unfortunately, it does not support NDMP. Computer Associates also offers a data replication module and fail-over support for a variety of databases.

Veritas Backup Exec

Recently purchased by Veritas from Seagate Software, this is also a popular package in the distributed network arena. Veritas is no stranger to large-scale storage and backup, having supplied solutions to the UNIX community for years. They seem committed to creating just as strong a presence in NT backup solutions. Also like ArcServIT, Backup Exec has recently added SAN backup capability with its Shared Storage option. Backup Exec provides support for open files, multiple operating systems, backup of MSCS, reading tapes created with other programs, RAIT/RAIL (0, 1, 3), and agent support for databases and disaster recovery. The disaster recovery feature is interesting in that it provides for the creation of bootable floppies, rewritable CDs (CD-RWs), and bootable tapes to restore a server.

Veritas NetBackup

This backup solution's two major advantages are its distributed architecture and its tight integration with third-party applications. The distributed architecture allows clusters of backup servers to be set up to share the load of backing up large amounts of data. NetBackup's agents for many popular databases allow data to be backed up "live" without shutting down the database. It has a nonproprietary tape format (TAR) and provides for data encryption. Key features include integrated SAN support, HSM, dynamic tape device sharing, snapshot backup, server-free backup, disaster recovery support, and both NT and Java administrative consoles. NetBackup also provides a variety of agents for leading databases such as Oracle and MS SQL Server. NetBackup has about the largest base of supported tape devices and libraries in the industry. Perhaps most importantly, NetBackup supports NDMP through an extension, and Veritas seems committed to supporting that protocol across its product line.

Legato BudTool

Intelliguard was purchased by Legato to fill out their enterprise storage product suite. BudTool began as a UNIX-only backup solution but due to its efficient design has become the leading backup solution for network-attached storage. A native NT version should be available as this book is published. The backup status monitor is Web enabled, so you can use a browser to monitor the backups from any operating system. Some of the major advantages include efficient management of multi-terabyte backup images, native support of NTFS, a fast file history database, full implementation of NDMPv3, a log browser for analysis to isolate problems, and direct support of tape robotics. It uses nonproprietary data formats that allow native commands to restore data reliably (UNIX "dump" and "load" format).

Legato Networker

Like NetBackup, Networker from Legato gears many features toward the enterprise and has its roots in the UNIX backup market. It provides support for multiple operating systems, databases, encryption, HSM, disaster recovery, and media server fail-over. A "Power Edition" provides support for 32 backup devices in concurrent operation and backup of very large files.

SAMPLE STORAGE NETWORK

The network shown in Figure 7-8 incorporates the concepts and recommendations covered in this chapter. It provides detail on the different types of file service platforms if placed in the same network.

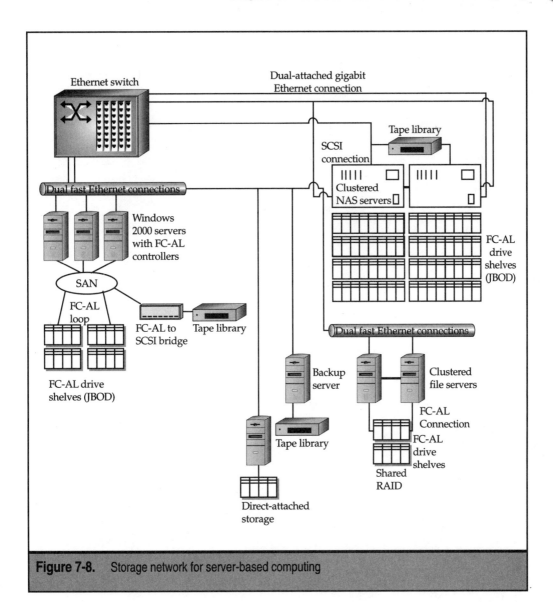

Figure 7-8.   Storage network for server-based computing

CHAPTER 8

Remote Access Strategies

In the world of server-based computing, the concept of remote access takes on new meaning. In a traditional, distributed network, the capabilities afforded by remote access are for the fringe users who typically do not make up the majority of the user population. They connect from outside the main network and might be traveling salespeople, telecommuters, contract workers, or even customers. By contrast, in a server-based network where all of the computing resources are centralized, anyone not working in a data center will need remote access. The majority of users fit into this category. For the purposes of this discussion, we will limit the group of remote users to those in small offices, those working at home, or those accessing computing resources via the Internet. This includes the "small" and "medium" categories we defined in Chapter 6, Table 6-1. Those in larger offices have equipment and requirements more similar to a data center than to a home office. In other words, instead of dialing in, they will utilize leased lines and permanent premise equipment such as routers and CSU/DSUs.

> *As a property management company, we have scores of small remote offices across several western states. MetaFrame enabled us to save a great deal of money on the equipment and PC administration of both our remote-office and headquarters users. We consequently felt no qualms about the relatively small cost of implementing world-class equipment and support for our data center.*
>
> —Jeff Doan, Vice President,
> IT Operations, Pacific Gulf Properties

In this chapter we will discuss strategies for getting remote users connected and keeping them connected. To do this we will first define the overall requirements for remote access, fit users into different categories for access, discuss the underlying hardware and software technology, and then provide solutions for the different types of users.

REQUIREMENTS FOR REMOTE ACCESS

Before your users can be divided into groups with similar access needs, the requirements for all users must be established. The following requirements have provided a useful guide for us in large, server-based network projects. Your network may have special needs, so feel free to add to this list as you deem appropriate.

▼ **Low cost**   The remote connections should not be subject to usage fees, and the devices and software used should not be expensive to purchase or operate.

■ **Security**   Established connections should not be subject to access by unauthorized users. Passwords and encryption should be used.

■ **Resilience**   Each user should have multiple network paths to the MetaFrame servers.

▲ **Support for user applications**   The chosen technology should support ICA, PPP, and any other services that will be used.

CATEGORIES OF REMOTE USERS

It is important to assess the remote access needs of the user population as early in the project as possible. Invariably, special needs are uncovered, especially in a large organization. It is not uncommon to find divisions running servers and applications that the corporate IT staff knows nothing about. Server-based computing is about centralizing your resources, controlling costs, and providing a consistent computing experience for all users. Before this can be done, all of the methods used to connect to the current corporate computing resources must be assessed. This is one of the most challenging exercises in this type of large-scale project, but the payoff is worth the effort. Not only will you end up with fewer, more reliable and secure methods to access the data center, you will be able to control access costs and know who is accessing the network, when, and from where.

In the drive to quantify and classify these remote access users, every effort should be made to be as "thin" as possible. This simply means that the client device does as little as possible while still fulfilling the application requirements of the user. The reasons for this thinking were made clear in Chapter 4 in the discussions of total cost of ownership (TCO) and return on investment (ROI). In practical terms, the fewer client platforms and access methods there are, the less time and resources are required to support them. That being said, we fully realize that not all clients can be thin. Sometimes a user will need to run an application that does not fit well in a server-based computing environment but is still required for that user to get his or her work done. Such an application might be a high-end graphics program, video editing, or simply a legacy program that will not run well on a MetaFrame server. Every effort should be made to provide a functional equivalent for this application that does run well on a MetaFrame server, but if no alternative is available, the application must be run locally (though it might still reside on a network-attached disk).

It is possible to run local applications and still realize some of the benefits of server-based computing. Any common applications such as office suites (for example, Microsoft Office), e-mail, Internet browsing, or groupware can be run on the MetaFrame server. Specialty applications can be run locally. Using the Seamless Window capability of the Citrix ICA client, users won't necessarily notice they are running applications from a server. They experience one integrated desktop. We refer to such a desktop as a "hybrid," meaning it incorporates applications for both distributed and server-based computing. When the use of such a platform is necessary, we recommend the following steps to avoid the chaos that is common when a PC with an operating system is part of the equation. The goal is to create a "managed PC," in which the control over its function rests with the IT staff and not with the user.

▼ Standardize on one operating system platform for all users or, if you must, only a few. We recommend Windows NT 4.0 Workstation or Windows 2000 Professional due to the security and reliability features.

■ Make every effort to remove control of the operating system from the user. With NT-based platforms, the ability to do this is built in.

- ■ Do not enable access to local devices from the ICA session unless there is a legitimate need. For example, it is possible to allow users to access the local drive on their PCs from an ICA session. This feature is convenient for the user but can pose security risks. If this feature must be enabled, we will discuss some options in Chapter 15.

- ▲ Have a method for central management of any administration activities on the local system. Such activities include backups and software updates (including operating systems, virus programs, and local applications). Most backup vendors provide agents that will allow clients to be backed up centrally. Similarly, many network management software (NMS) vendors provide the ability to update software and even help lock down the desktop centrally. Microsoft System Management Service, HP OpenView, and CA UniCenter are examples of such NMS systems. NMS will be discussed in detail in Chapter 10.

We have used the following user categories in our own projects. We provide the characteristics of each to make it clear whether or not they will be appropriate for your project. It may be necessary to add categories of your own or modify these. We discuss our reasoning for each choice in detail in Chapter 11. Table 8-1 lists the four types of clients and describes their unique requirements.

Client Type	Remote Applications	Local Applications	Use VPN	Local Peripherals	Local File Sharing
Thin client only	✓		*		
Mobile user	✓	✓	✓	**	**
Simple hybrid	✓	✓	✓		
Complex hybrid	✓	✓	✓	✓	✓

*A thin-client-only device such as a Windows terminal could use a VPN through a special access router with built-in VPN software. To date, no terminal vendor has made VPN software a standard feature of their terminal devices.

**A mobile user could theoretically use local peripherals or share files, but we recommend restricting this to users who have an absolute requirement to do so.

Table 8-1. Remote Access Client Categories

▼ **Thin client only**   These users require access only to the applications running on the MetaFrame server farm. They have no need for local peripherals (network printers are not considered local). This could be a mobile user, but it is most likely a stationary office worker or a telecommuter with a Windows terminal (see the following illustration). This is the most locked down of all options and therefore the hardest for a user to change. Remote access parameters are stored securely—either in the Windows terminal or the Remote Access Device (RAD)—and protected by a password. All applications must be run on the MetaFrame server farm. Windows terminals provide limited access to direct-attached peripherals, with no local file sharing since there is no local disk.

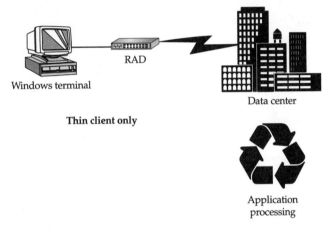

RAD

Windows terminal

Thin client only

Data center

Application processing

■ **Mobile user**   This category (illustrated below) describes a "road warrior"— a mobile executive or salesperson with a laptop who needs to run local applications as well as access corporate computing resources. The laptop is a managed PC. The user gains access to the Corporate ASP through a VPN over the Internet or by dialing in directly. Use of direct-attached peripherals is possible as is file sharing from the local hard disk.

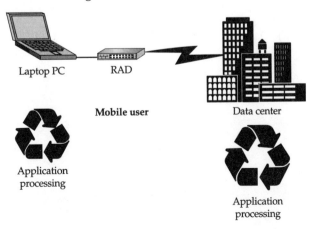

Laptop PC   RAD

Mobile user

Data center

Application processing

Application processing

■ **Simple hybrid**   This category describes a managed PC with one or two special-purpose applications that must be run locally. The remaining applications are run from the data center. The user is presented with a unified desktop using the ICA client's Seamless Window feature. The user can be a single user dialing in directly, as with the mobile user, or part of a work group sharing an access router. This category has no requirement for local file storage or direct-attached peripherals.

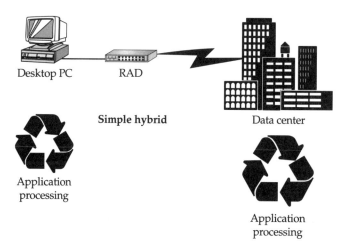

■ **Complex hybrid**   This category is similar to a simple hybrid in that common applications are run from the Corporate ASP using Seamless Window. It differs in that multiple applications must be run locally, local file sharing is needed, or local peripherals such as digital cameras, scanners, or drawing tablets are needed. This is the least thin of all the options and therefore the least desirable.

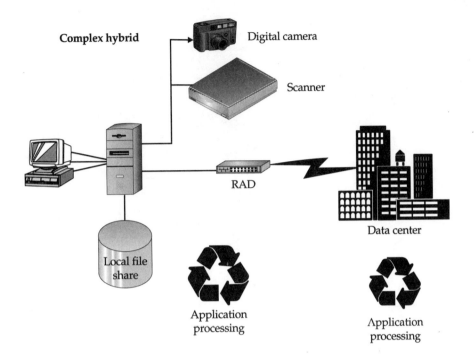

In a large organization, many users may need to share files in the local office. These users run either simple or complex hybrids, and their specialty applications require them to share files with another user on their local network. As desirable as it is to have all the applications and data residing in the data center, it is not always possible. One way we have found to enable this type of file sharing is by using TCP/IP for the WAN connection to the data center but NetBEUI for the local connection, as shown next. Since NetBEUI is not routable, it will not clog the RAD or add much overhead to a small network. This software is included in any recent version of Windows. All that is needed is a SOHO device with network hub ports or a dedicated hub between the client devices and the RAD.

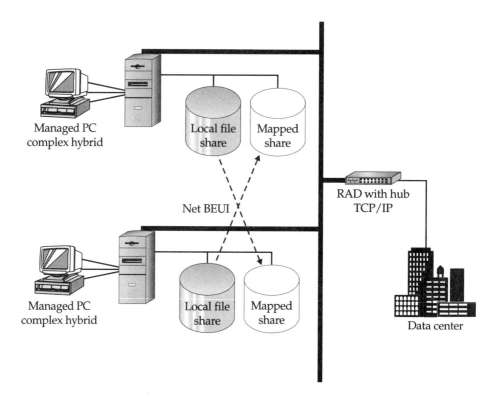

CONNECTION STRATEGIES

Now we'll take a close look at the software and hardware technology that can be used to establish remote connections to the MetaFrame server farm at the data center. In the last few years, U.S. companies have been experimenting with the "alternative workforce." Job sharing between individuals and a willingness to allow certain employees to work from home are trends that characterize this experimentation. We believe that this trend will continue, particularly telecommuting. Now that the "genie is out of the bottle," telecommuting workers are unwilling to move back into the office. Furthermore, companies are extending this work metaphor to other aspects of the business, connecting customers and job sites, and setting up kiosks to interact with the public. MetaFrame and server-based computing are poised to allow companies to exploit this trend. We have some recommendations for companies that wish to take advantage of it.

TCP/IP Protocol Suite

The explosive growth of the Internet has spurred an unprecedented level of research and development in the networking hardware and software industries. Since the Internet is made up of computers running TCP/IP, the fruits of this labor are devices and utilities that interact with or support this protocol. Though efforts have been made to tie in legacy protocols such as X.25, SAA, and the like, your company should plan on deploying a TCP/IP-based infrastructure for remote access. The low-cost, high-reliability devices and software available provide substantial benefits.

Software vs. Hardware

The flexibility provided by TCP/IP-based hardware and software, and the myriad of available solutions and approaches, may leave you confused about the right approach to implementing a remote access infrastructure. For example, why would you buy an expensive Cisco router when you can build a router out of an old PC running LINUX and a few extra network cards? Similarly, why would you buy a dial-up communications server when you can use the Remote Access Service (RAS) built into Windows NT? Though these scenarios are certainly possible, and perhaps even desirable in a limited number of cases, we recommend using hardware for both the client and the server in your remote access infrastructure for the following reasons:

▼ **Speed**   In nearly every case, hardware engineered to do a specific task will be faster than software running on top of a general-purpose operating system. In the case of remote access, this translates into more user connections and less load on the CPU at the client and server ends of the connection.

■ **Reliability**   A desktop PC or server running an operating system like NT or LINUX has more moving parts and far more complexity than, for example, an access router. The router may have one integrated board full of components and not even require a fan. Fewer parts, running cooler, translate into a much higher mean time between failure (MTBF) than a typical PC.

▲ **Total cost of ownership**   This can be a tricky concept to quantify. What we mean here is that the ease of remote administration and upgrades, the ability to swap equipment in case of failure, and no need for daily intervention tend to drive down the price of operating hardware devices such as routers, modems, Windows terminals, and network print servers.

Roaming Profiles

The principal method for allowing users to log in anywhere in a MetaFrame network, to be properly authenticated, and to have their own desktop is through the use of roaming profiles. In a distributed NT network, the users' desktop settings can follow them to any computer on the network, but the applications cannot; they have to be installed and executed on the computer that the user is currently operating. In a MetaFrame network, the users' desktop settings and server-based applications can follow them anywhere they may roam within the network. There are three types of user profiles:

▼ **Local profiles**   These reside on a given MetaFrame server and do not move from server to server as users move in a load-balanced configuration.

- **Roaming profiles** As the name suggests, these profiles follow users no matter which server they happen to connect to. By default, users can modify roaming profiles. The profiles are stored in a central location, such as a file server, which can easily be accessed by any MetaFrame server.

▲ **Mandatory profiles** These profiles function as roaming profiles but cannot be modified by the user.

Using roaming profiles ensures that users get their own desktop and applications settings no matter which server they happen to log onto (as shown below), but it can cause an administrative burden since the user can modify these settings at will. For this reason we use policies to lock down areas of the system we don't want users to change. This can also be done with mandatory profiles, but these prove much too restrictive in practice. Not only all the system settings are locked down but also all the user preference settings. For example, the path to which users save documents cannot be altered if mandatory profiles are used. For this reason we recommend using roaming profiles with specific policy settings. We will discuss strategies for effectively managing profiles in Chapter 16.

User connects

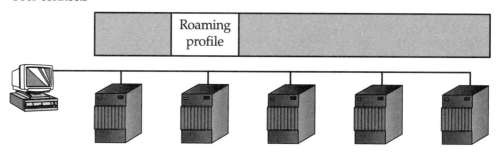

Same user
connects later

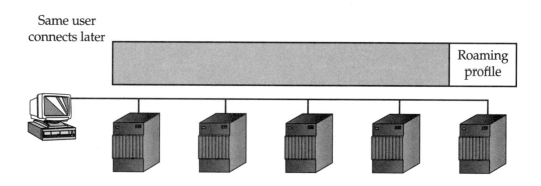

NOTE: Though desktop and application settings follow the user with a roaming profile, what about printer settings? Unfortunately, they do not. A user from Dallas who logs into a Windows terminal in Des Moines will still get her printer assignments from Dallas. The standard solution from Citrix and Microsoft is to use the capability of MetaFrame and Terminal Services to create a new, temporary printer assignment. Though this works, it places a burden on users, who must know how to do it, and on the help desk if they don't. We will discuss how to overcome this problem in Chapter 17.

Software Technology

In the following sections, we examine the standard offerings from Microsoft and Citrix in the context of building a remote access infrastructure. Though we recommend using hardware-based solutions, the software discussed here is often part of those solutions and is therefore important to understand. You may also have legacy PC platforms you wish to reuse as remote access clients or servers, and we will discuss the software you will likely be using for that purpose.

Point-to-Point Protocol (PPP)

PPP was created to encapsulate datagrams over a serial line. When PPP was being formulated, the only standard encapsulation methods were for LANs and not serial communication. PPP uses the Internet Protocol (IP) and provides Layer 2 (data-link layer) services relative to the OSI model. PPP is a full-duplex protocol that can be used on various physical media, including copper, fiber-optic lines, or even satellite communication media. PPP is an improvement over Serial Line Internet Protocol (SLIP). SLIP was the first attempt to standardize networking over serial lines, but it had no error correction feature, which makes it difficult to use over noisy phone lines. PPP is the standard for serial networking over the Internet. It represents the core protocol for Microsoft's Remote Access Service and virtually all commercial dial-on-demand services in use today.

Microsoft Routing and Remote Access Service (RRAS)

During beta testing, RRAS was known as "Steelhead." It represents an expansion of the original RAS released with NT. RRAS is a standard service in Windows 2000 but can also be added to Windows NT 4.0 Server with Service Pack 3 or higher. The original Windows NT distribution included RAS, which is a decent remote access service that allows PPP connections using NetBEUI, TCP/IP and IPX, and MPR. MPR is a very simple multiprotocol routing service that supports IP and IPX. RAS supports dial-up connections over a modem, ISDN, or X.25 and provides multilink capability that aggregates bandwidth across connections to the same server. RRAS expands the capabilities of the RAS and MPR components significantly and includes

▼ **Regular LAN routing**   This capability enables an NT server to be configured as a router that can route network traffic between as many as 16 interfaces. It supports both LAN and WAN network interface cards.

- ■ **Dial-up routing** Similar to LAN routing, this function allows the automatic creation of routes over serial lines (dial on demand). It supports any dial-up interface that NT recognizes, such as ISDN and X.25. Up to 48 such routes can be managed simultaneously.

- ▲ **RAS** Like the original Remote Access Service, the new RAS can handle up to 256 simultaneous connections. The suite of protocols supported has been expanded to include OSPF, RIPv2, Novell RIP and SAP, DHCP Relay Agent, static routing, and MPPC (Microsoft's data compression feature). It also now includes Point-to-Point Tunneling Protocol (PPTP), Remote Authentication Dial-in User Service (RADIUS), packet filtering, and integration with MS Proxy Server for enhanced security. Security protocols are discussed fully in Chapter 9.

TIP: Though RRAS is very functional, it can also be rather slow. If you plan to implement RRAS as a remote access method in your network, the server component should be run on a dedicated server to avoid affecting the performance of your MetaFrame application servers.

Microsoft Internet Connector Service (ICS) for RAS

Originally code-named "Base Camp," ICS is a set of tools that expand the capabilities of RAS and enable it to be used over the Internet. ICS uses the RADIUS feature of RAS, which enables a user to be authenticated and establish a secure connection to a RAS server over the Internet. Presuming the RAS server has a route to the MetaFrame server, an ICA or RDP session can then be established. ICS includes the following components:

NOTE: The term ICS is sometimes also applied to the Internet Connection Sharing feature of Windows 98 and Windows 2000. We realize this is confusing. In this book ICS denotes the more generic Internet Connection Service.

- ▼ **Internet Authentication Service** An implementation of RADIUS that works seamlessly with the NT authentication model.

- ■ **Microsoft Connection Manager** A tool that allows PPP connections to be customized. It also includes the Connection Manager Administration Kit, which contains wizards to help the administrator configure customized connections for common applications, such as dialing an ISP or corporate VPN.

- ▲ **Connection Point Services** A tool to keep connecting clients updated on the latest connection information, such as ISP phone number updates.

In a server-based network, ICS running on a managed PC could be used as the remote access router for connecting to the data center over the Internet or over direct dial, as illustrated in Figure 8-1. In this scenario, the managed PC is on the same LAN as the remote

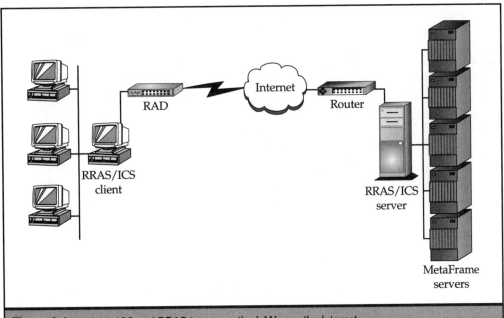

Figure 8-1. Using ICS and RRAS to access the LAN over the Internet

clients. The need for a PC running Windows NT makes this solution appropriate only for larger groups of remote access users.

Citrix ICA

As we discussed in Chapter 2, the Citrix ICA client and server components serve to transport an entire desktop or application to the user while processing the application on the MetaFrame server. This simplifies the implementation of remote access in that it only has to support ICA to support every application remotely. ICA has a number of beneficial features specific to remote access.

NOTE: Though a typical ICA session uses around 20 Kbps of bandwidth, it can take significantly more unless care is taken to limit elements such as high-resolution background graphics, animations, Web browsing with Java animation, or video. ICA will faithfully transport all screen updates, mouse movements, and keystrokes no matter how much bandwidth it takes!

ICA Gateway Routing   Gateway routing is a feature of the MetaFrame server that allows a user on one network to reach a server on another network. For example, say a company has two data centers. All of the administration expertise for the ERP application is at one data center, but the application needs to be published at both data centers. Using the gateway routing feature, a server is configured to reach both networks, as in Figure 8-2. The server doesn't have to be a master browser, it just enables communication between the master browser on each network. We recommend configuring more than one gateway for redundancy.

SecureICA   The secure version of ICA works over all protocols and connections supported by MetaFrame. As such, it does not require special consideration when integrating it into a remote access infrastructure, with one exception: SecureICA can take the place of specialized VPN software and provide security from the client, through the pub-

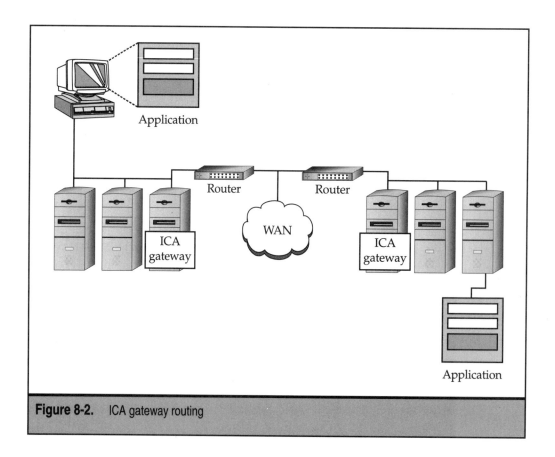

Figure 8-2.   ICA gateway routing

lic Internet, and into the data center (see the following illustration). SecureICA comes in varying levels of strength, including 40-, 56-, and 128-bit encryption.

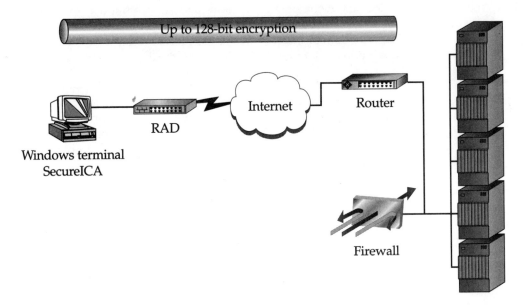

Windows terminal
SecureICA

RAD

Internet

Router

Firewall

MetaFrame
servers running
SecureICA

 NOTE: Forty-bit encryption is now considered trivial to break by brute force attack. The U.S. government now allows unregulated export of up to 128-bit encryption for commercial software, and there is little reason not to use at least 56-bit encryption.

Since the ICA protocol is composed of screen prints, mouse movements, and keystrokes, further encryption serves to make it very secure. A principal advantage of SecureICA is that it is built into many devices that have ICA clients, such as the Wyse WinTerm. Using such a low-cost device can provide a secure connection through the Internet and full MetaFrame functionality to the client. We will examine this use of SecureICA in more detail in the next chapter.

ICA Web Client (NFuse)   When referring to the Web client, we are really referring to two things: the browser plug-in and the Java applet. Both support application linking and embedding. As we discussed in Chapter 6, a browser can be used from the client to connect to a Web server that is located at the data center and loaded with the ICA Web client server-side components. In this situation, remote access can be through any method that uses the Internet, such as a modem or ISDN connection. PPP is invariably utilized, and if an extra layer of security is desired, either SecureICA or a third-party software (VPN) product can be used.

Java Client   The ICA Java client is functionally equivalent to the Java applet, but it runs on the client device in a Java Virtual Machine (JVM) environment, either stand-alone or in a Web browser (see the following illustration). The Java client only supports TCP/IP. Other than where the Java client is being executed, the characteristics for remote access are the same as the ICA Web client.

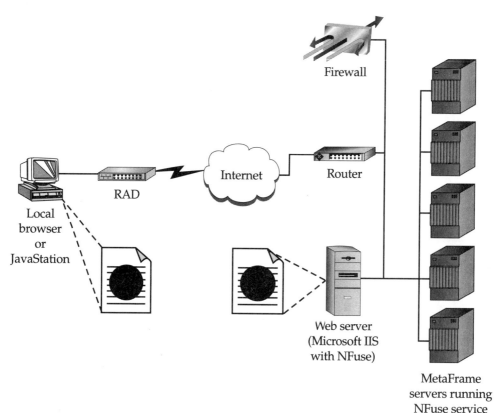

DirectICA   This variant of the ICA client was engineered to support multiconsole devices from vendors such as Maxspeed and Stone Microsystems. Such devices incorporate a VGA display card, a mouse, and supporting hardware, as shown below. Some also include parallel and serial ports. Since each console station is a direct extension of the server hardware, very few benefits of ICA can be realized. DirectICA does not include remapping of hard drives, COM ports, or parallel ports, for instance. It also does not support session shadowing, load balancing, encryption, or the reconnection of disconnected sessions. The single advantage seems to be in having multiple consoles. Though the majority of administrative tasks for MetaFrame and Terminal Services can be done from an ICA client using standard tools like User Manager and Connection Manager, some things can only be done on the console. For example, some error messages will only appear on the console and need user interaction to be cleared. We recommend against using DirectICA unless you have a legitimate need for multiple consoles.

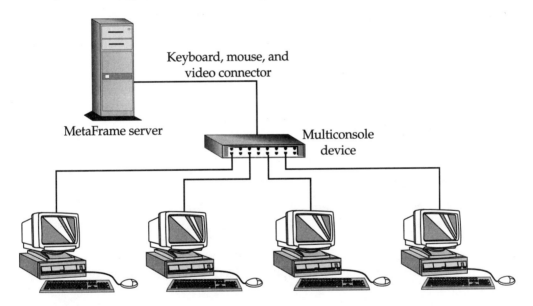

Hardware Technology

Next we examine the hardware options for building a remote access infrastructure. Earlier in the chapter we mentioned the need for keeping things as thin as possible. This applies not only to the client but to all equipment and software. The less complexity there is in the field, the easier it is to maintain and the lower the total cost of ownership. It is also of critical importance to standardize the equipment chosen. For each functional area, try to have one primary solution and one or two backup solutions in case your first choice becomes difficult to purchase. For example, there may be four different ISDN routers that meet your criteria for features, cost, and reliability. One should be chosen and preferred above the others. Sticking with mainstream vendors such as Cisco, Intel, and Nortel (Bay Networks) will help to make this task easier.

Modems

Not much needs to be said about the basic modem. For the purposes of our discussion, the modem should be given serious consideration for one- or two-user sites. Though the simplicity of the typical modem can be somewhat limiting, it should be suitable for most purposes in connecting to the data center either directly or over the Internet. Some high-end modems have limited security features, such as dial-back (the receiving modem hangs up and dials the caller back at a predefined number) and password protection. For further security, it should be possible to implement PAP or CHAP authentication through PPP regardless of the modem used.

Advantages of modems include

▼   They cost relatively little.

■   They are readily available.

■   They work with virtually any client device for server-based computing.

▲   They require only a Plain Old Telephone Service (POTS) line to function.

Limitations include

▼   Low speed limits the number of simultaneous users.

▲   Low functionality limits how they can be deployed.

A number of modem-based remote access configurations are possible through the use of the RAS and PPP capabilities of Windows NT/2000 and the asynchronous dial-up capability of MetaFrame.

Direct Dial-up ICA   MetaFrame has its own capability for enabling dial-up connections that is independent of RAS. A direct asynchronous connection is established between the client and the server with no associated network protocol, as shown next. A RAS connection establishes the client as a node on the network. Since a pool of modems is required on the server end, and the number of modems is limited by the server hardware, we don't recommend this as a general-purpose solution unless the network is very small. However, it can be a useful way to connect a few privileged users in an enterprise network.

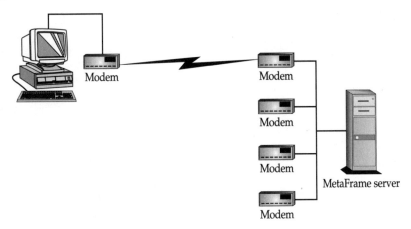

Advantages of MetaFrame's dial-up capability are

▼   No additional software required

▲   Performance overhead not as great as with RAS

It has one limitation:

▼   Supporting hardware required at the data center can be expensive and limits the number of simultaneous sessions.

Direct Dial-up PPP/RAS   Establishing a PPP connection with RAS makes the client a node on the server's TCP/IP network. Unlike establishing a direct, asynchronous connection, a PPP connection can be routed. This means that it is unnecessary to dial directly into a modem connected to the server. The client can dial into a high-density communications server that is on the same network segment as the server, as illustrated next. Such units are available from Cisco and Lucent (Livingston) and can typically terminate dozens of dial-in lines using high-capacity trunks such as T-1 or Primary rate ISDN. PPP has become ubiquitous and is not only included in desktop operating systems like Windows 98 and Windows 2000 Professional, but is also built into dedicated thin-client devices such as the Wyse WinTerm and the Sun JavaStation. Where a private dial-up network connection is desired, this is the recommended method.

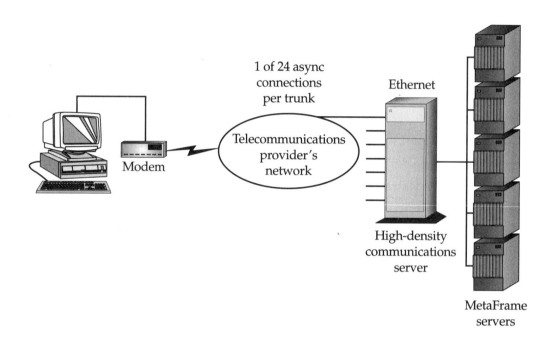

The advantage of this solution is

▼   No additional software required

Its limitations include

▼   Supporting hardware required at the data center can be expensive and limits the number of simultaneous sessions.

▲   RAS can introduce a significant performance overhead for a server.

Internet Dial-up PPP/RAS   Establishing a PPP connection to the Internet is something many of us do every day. The Internet is ubiquitous, and offers for unlimited usage with a very low monthly cost are common. There are a few ways to exploit the public network for use as a remote access infrastructure for server-based computing:

▼ From a PC running Windows NT/2000, use ICS/RRAS or third-party VPN software to establish an encrypted tunnel to a server at the data center; then run ICA through that tunnel.

■ From a PC running Windows or a Windows terminal, use PPP to establish a connection to the Internet. Use SecureICA to encrypt traffic to a MetaFrame server at the data center that is connected to the Internet.

▲ From a PC, run a local browser and establish a PPP connection to the Internet. Run applications at the data center through a Web server using MetaFrame's ALE capability.

Advantages of a PPP connection to the Internet include

▼ Access to the Internet is inexpensive and readily available.

■ The Internet itself is very robust. It can't really go down like a private network can.

▲ Multiple Internet Service Providers (ISPs) can be used for redundancy.

Limitations include

▼ An external security mechanism for safe travel over the public network, such as SecureICA, ICS/RRAS, or IPSec (see Chapter 9), is required.

▲ Widespread support of security protocols on dedicated thin-client devices is limited.

Small Office/Home Office (SOHO) Devices

This class of device is essentially a low-cost network router designed for use by telecommuters or small work groups to reach the corporate office. Devices can be purchased for use with a variety of network topologies, including asynchronous dial-up, ISDN, xDSL, or cable modem. Such devices are much less complex than routers designed for frame relay or ATM and can typically be configured by the motivated consumer. This class of device is an excellent choice for a work group that needs access to the MetaFrame servers at the data center. Like modems, these devices can connect privately or through the Internet to the Corporate ASP, as shown below:

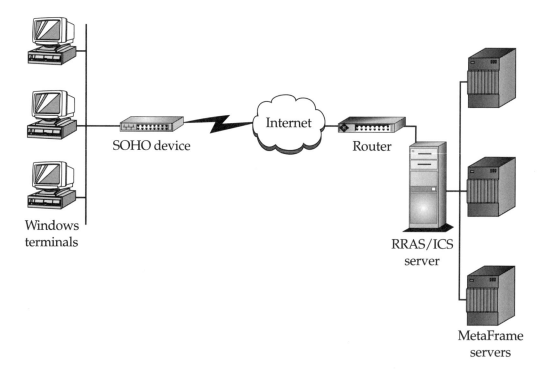

They are typically priced well under $1000, making it economical to have an extra preconfigured unit on hand for redundancy. Like larger routers, most of these devices support the Simple Network Management Protocol (SNMP) for sending status and alert messages to a network management console. Most provide either a Windows-based GUI or a Web-based administration tool, and some even provide a command-line interface for configuration. We recommend that your SOHO device meet the following minimum requirements:

▼   Support for multiple WAN topologies such as dial-up, ISDN, DSL, and cable modem from the same manufacturer. This will aid a national deployment greatly because different services are available in different areas of the country.

■   Support for end-to-end security with the data center, using a standard protocol such as IPSec.

▲   Remote management through a Windows GUI or Web browser.

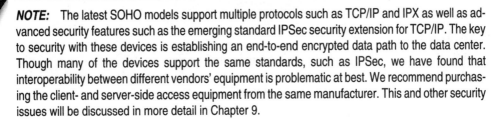

NOTE: The latest SOHO models support multiple protocols such as TCP/IP and IPX as well as advanced security features such as the emerging standard IPSec security extension for TCP/IP. The key to security with these devices is establishing an end-to-end encrypted data path to the data center. Though many of the devices support the same standards, such as IPSec, we have found that interoperability between different vendors' equipment is problematic at best. We recommend purchasing the client- and server-side access equipment from the same manufacturer. This and other security issues will be discussed in more detail in Chapter 9.

SOHO Examples   The following companies have good SOHO solutions for a variety of applications. They also provide end-to-end solutions, including both client- and server-side components that support the latest security standards and differing network topologies.

▼   **Cisco**   Cisco estimates that over 80 percent of the Internet utilizes their router technology. They are the market leader in access technology and IP routing, and are here to stay. Cisco offers a complete line of SOHO solutions. The 800 and 700 series are for DSL and ISDN, respectively. These product lines are geared toward telecommuters and very small offices. They offer basic security but not IPSec. The 900 series is for cable modems. It offers greater speed and user capacity as well as a full copy of the Cisco Internetwork Operating System (IOS), which includes advanced configuration and security. A Cisco router at the data center is required for full functionality between the client and the server.

■   **Nortel (Bay Networks)**   Nortel's acquisition of market leader Bay Networks demonstrates their commitment to the network equipment market. Bay was a pioneer in the area of VPN technology with their Contivity line of data center extranet switches. For the remote office, Nortel offers the BayStack Instant Internet 100 and 400 access routers. The BayStacks support encrypted tunneling with IPSec. Versions for DSL, ISDN, dial-up, and leased lines are available. The 400 unit includes Web caching, or storing commonly accessed pages locally, which decreases the perceived access time to those pages. A Contivity switch at the data center is required for full functionality between the client and server.

▲ **3Com**   3Com offers both a software-only VPN client and a full line of SOHO devices for remote access. They are also the only solution currently supporting Microsoft Point-to-Point Encryption (MPPE) for establishing a secure, encrypted network link to a Microsoft server. The OfficeConnect NETBuilder routers support as few as 5 ports and as many as 28. The WAN topologies currently supported are ISDN, fractional T-1, dial-up, and full T-1. Either the VPN software or a small OfficeConnect device is required on the client end, and a larger OfficeConnect device is required on the server end.

SOLUTIONS

In the following sections we make recommendations on remote access configurations for each category of user discussed in this chapter. The recommendations are based on current technology. Contacting the manufacturer will provide the latest pricing and options.

Thin Client Only

For a single user, we recommend a Windows terminal with SecureICA loaded on it, an analog modem (either internal PCMCIA or external), and two local ISP access numbers—one for production and one for redundancy. It is even safer to have two different ISPs in case the first one becomes unavailable, but this is so unlikely that it is a questionable use of money. Most national ISPs have a local number and an 800 number that costs more to use. The goal is always to have more than one way to get on the Internet. A typical Windows terminal configuration is shown below:

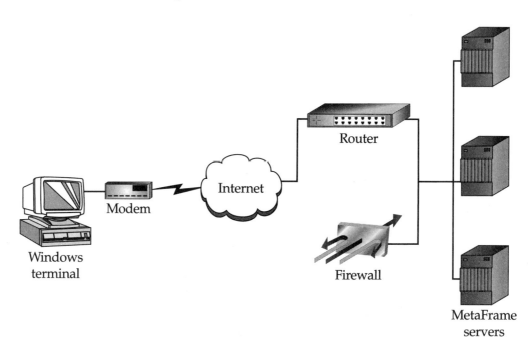

For a small work group, we recommend Windows terminals or PCs, with an Ethernet connection to a SOHO device that supports a WAN connection to the Internet with adequate bandwidth (20KB per user) for handling all users. In this case SecureICA is not needed if the SOHO device handles the connection security to the data center through the Internet. If possible, the SOHO device should be configured to reach the Internet through a primary and an alternate route. For example, if the primary DSL line becomes unavailable, the device uses an analog modem to dial the Internet.

NOTE: It is, of course, possible to use Citrix NFuse to run applications at the data center with nothing more than a local browser, but this introduces a possible problem for Windows terminal users. The ICA Web client runs as either a browser plug-in or a stand-alone Java application with a local Java Virtual Machine (JVM). Most Windows terminals do not support dynamic loading of a plug-in, but there are several that will run a local Java application if it is first loaded into the terminal's firmware. Though SecureICA is supported in the Java version of the Web client, it must also be supported by the firmware of the Windows terminal. Some Windows terminal manufacturers, such as Wyse, plan to implement IPSec directly in firmware at some time in the near future.

Mobile User

For laptop users, we recommend establishing a standard configuration, or managed PC, with as few local applications running as possible. Using ICS/RRAS or other VPN software, a connection can be established through the Internet to the data center. As with the thin-client-only configurations, we recommend having two different access numbers for the ISP.

Simple and Complex Hybrid

For one user, we recommend the same configuration as the mobile user. Load VPN software on a managed PC and run as few applications as possible locally. For multiple users in a small work group, we recommend a SOHO device with two different ways to reach the data center and with built-in security.

CHAPTER 9

Security

To use a broad definition of the term, *security* means protection against unauthorized use of, or access to, any computer resource or data on your network. This definition is too broad to be practical, but it does lead to some important questions. Where is the critical data that needs protection? From whom are you trying to protect the data? Do you care about unauthorized use of your resources or only about unauthorized access to your data? Finally, are the major threats to security likely to originate inside or outside the company? The answers to these and related questions will provide the foundation for the most useful weapon your company has against unauthorized use—a comprehensive security policy.

Your company's security policy will define threatened areas and assign values to the various components of your computing infrastructure. It will also define how you respond to breaches of security. The formulation of such a security policy is more than adequate subject matter for its own book. RFC 2196, available from the IETF, provides an excellent approach to general network security. The purpose of this chapter is to focus on the unique characteristics of security for server-based computing. Citrix and Microsoft have provided features and tools to enhance security for MetaFrame and Terminal Services, but these do not mitigate the need for a global perspective on security for your enterprise. We will integrate the offerings from these companies into our discussion and shed light on other areas of the network with particular security needs. Once we have painted a global picture of the security requirements for a typical server-based network, we will make recommendations about securing your network and choosing some useful tools for that purpose.

SECURITY FOR SERVER-BASED COMPUTING

In a typical distributed network, computing resources are dispersed throughout the enterprise, as shown in Figure 9-1. This means that sensitive information resides on the hard drives of employees' personal computers and on work group servers at several locations. If physical access to data is one area of concern for securing that data, it can be said that such a distributed model is less secure than a centralized model.

In the centralized model, shown in Figure 9-2, the bulk of computing resources are concentrated in one or just a few data centers. As a result, physical access to that data is much more restricted. Does this mean that server-based computing is inherently more secure than distributed computing? It may seem so, but there are numerous areas of concern in server-based computing that can make such a blanket assertion shortsighted.

As a government entity, we have to be particularly cautious with matters of security. We gradually expanded the external reach of our server-based computing environment only as internal planning and testing indicated that the associated risks would be both acceptable and managed. It is extremely important to constantly weigh your corporate strategy, the technological and human risk factors, as well as return on investment.

—Steve Steinbrecher, CIO, Contra Costa County

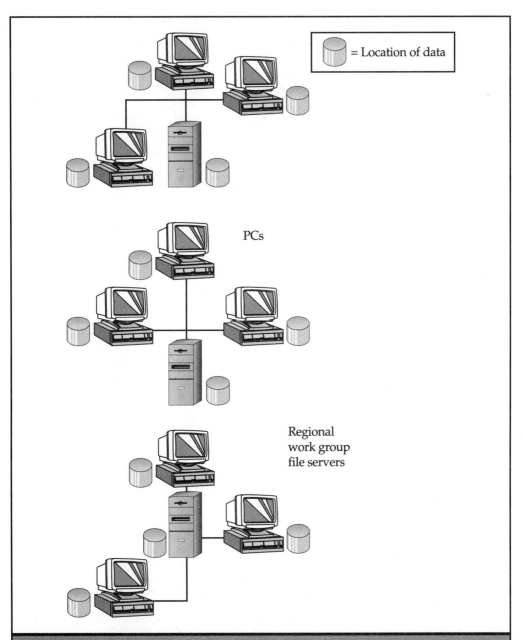

Figure 9-1.   A distributed network in which each regional work site has its own resident file server

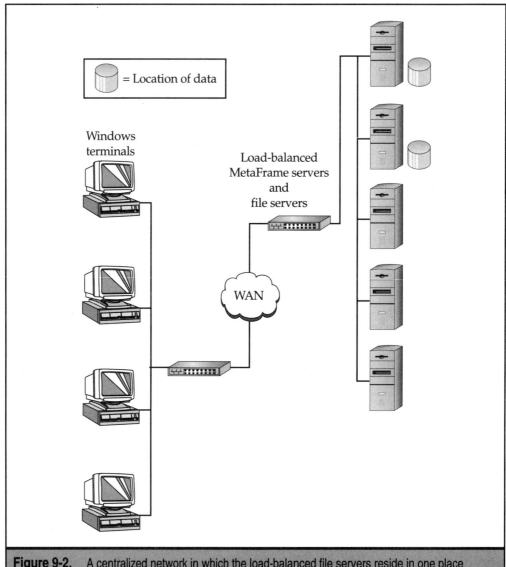

Figure 9-2.   A centralized network in which the load-balanced file servers reside in one place

THE NATURE OF SECURITY

As in a chain, the security of the whole computer system is only as strong as the weakest link. A global or systemic model is critical to the formulation of an effective approach to security in the enterprise. We have seen large companies decide, almost arbitrarily, that a particular area of their network is open to attack and invest tens of thousands of dollars to "patch the fence" without realizing that someone could walk right through the front gate. In one case, a company invested $50,000 in an Internet firewall without setting up a system to enforce strong passwords. With the firewall in place, no one could enter the system from the Internet—that is, unless the intruder could guess that the system administrator's password was his daughter's first name and birthday.

Taking a global view of security for the enterprise can be intimidating, which may account for the woefully inadequate attention paid to the subject in many companies. It is important to realize that the effects of securing your infrastructure are *cumulative*. Even a few simple changes to secure certain access points to the network can make a huge difference. For example, installing an effective Internet firewall can be a strong deterrent to the casual hacker. Before deciding to install such a system, however, you need to assess the overall computing infrastructure. Without such an assessment, you could be securing part of your network while leaving another part open to attack. A useful question to ask to get started is "What are you trying to protect?"

What Are You Trying to Protect?

Few would deny that the most critical component of a company's computing infrastructure is the data, but the story doesn't end there. Exactly what do we mean when we say we want to protect the company data? We further define data protection as addressing the following areas:

▼ **Access**   We want to prevent unauthorized access while ensuring that access is not overly restricted for those with a legitimate claim to the data.

■ **Integrity**   We do not want the data to be added to, modified, or deleted except by authorized individuals. Furthermore, we may need to establish rules concerning which individuals have the right to perform these operations on the data.

■ **Processing resources**   We need to reserve adequate processing capability to run the applications necessary to manipulate the data. Put another way, we need to prevent "denial of service" attacks. Furthermore, we do not want an unauthorized individual posing as an internal employee to use the resources to perform malicious acts.

▲ **Liability/reputation**   We include this because some companies may actually have to close their doors if certain data becomes public. Engineering designs, business merger and acquisition plans, or other data that constitutes a competitive advantage, if exposed, could have a crippling effect on operations in certain companies. Not only that, but if it can be proven that a company's officers knew about the lack of security and were negligent in correcting it, they could be liable for damages to the stockholders.

In addition to the data, the company's infrastructure usually constitutes a substantial investment. The switches, routers, servers, gateways, and even desktop PCs should be protected in a manner that addresses the above points as well.

Areas of Exposure

If data and computing resources are at risk, are there any areas more exposed than others? The following are areas of potential exposure in a server-based network. These are the areas, as shown in Figure 9-3, that require particular attention when formulating and implementing a security policy.

▼   Since data and computing resources are centralized, the security at the data center or centers is critical. This means the computers have to be secure electronically as well as physically.

■   All users in a server-based network will share a common pool of server and network resources. These resources need to be secured from *internal* breaches of security, either intentional or unintentional.

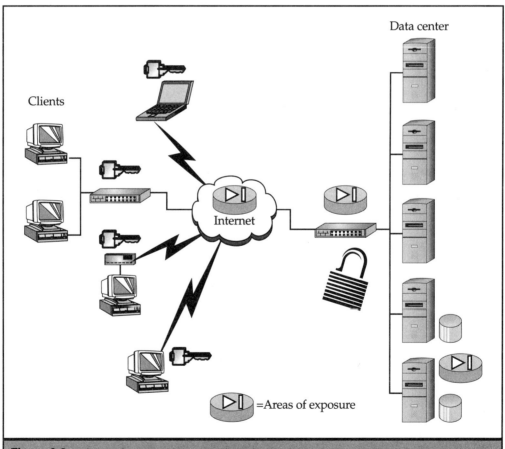

Figure 9-3.   Areas of exposure in a server-based network

▲ In this book we have recommended using the Internet as the infrastructure for access to the data center. The Internet is a public network, and all access points in the corporate private network must be protected.

A SECURITY MODEL FOR SERVER-BASED COMPUTING

A good security model should incorporate the ideas of scope and of posture. *Scope* refers to the degree to which your model will apply to the enterprise. Is this model just for the data center or for the entire company across divisions and countries? Scope also refers to the degree to which your infrastructure is to be secured. For example, a popular scope in the world of Internet firewalls is "That which is not explicitly allowed is denied." This might be fine for the Internet gateway, but can it apply to the MetaFrame servers as well? It may be difficult because of the different ways security is handled in NT. Nevertheless, this question should be answered for each major area of the computing infrastructure.

Posture refers to the company's attitude about security breaches. Will the breaches simply be logged and corrective efforts made to prevent the occurrence in the future? Perhaps your company will take a more aggressive stance and make efforts to track down the source of the breach and report it to the appropriate authorities. The decision on the posture your company will take affects the choice of policies, procedures, and tools chosen to secure the infrastructure and, more specifically, the network.

Finally, the security model should break down your infrastructure into zones and gateways. Some zones, like the data center, may need a very high degree of security, while other zones, like the home network of a telecommuter, need less security. A gateway is a transition point between zones of security. The gateway, often a router or firewall system, is responsible for ensuring that the transition between zones does not introduce a security risk. For example, consider Figure 9-4. A computer in Zone A trusts a computer in Zone B. The gateway between Zone A and Zone B contains rules about what services are allowed between the two computers, in what direction, and by which users. The computer in Zone B now wants to extend trust to a computer in Zone C, which is an unsecured public network. How can this be done without compromising the security of the entire network? Ideally, the gateway between Zones B and C would communicate with the gateway between Zones A and B and not allow the trust to be created.

NOTE: With Kerberos 5 security under Windows 2000, each host would contain information about its own level of security. When extending a trust, as described above, the hosts themselves would limit the information that could pass between them.

Security Zones

In our server-based computing model, we can be specific about the security zones and their requirements. The data centers hold the "company jewels" and need a high degree of protection. The regional offices may have local computing resources and file sharing and need a moderate degree of protection. Last is the small office or individual users that need a lesser degree of security. Figure 9-5 shows the three security zones.

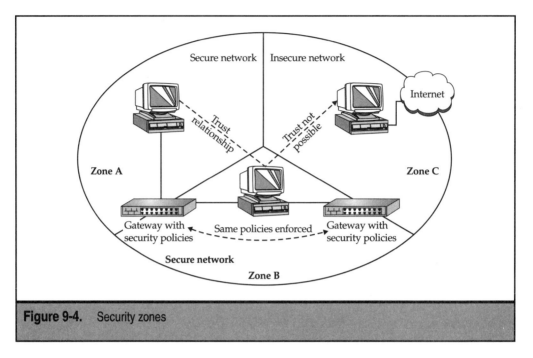

Figure 9-4. Security zones

Data Center—Internal Security

The data center zone needs the most protection. In server-based computing, the company's business-critical data is stored in large disk arrays in the data center. Losing this data through malice, theft, or failure could be catastrophic. To help enhance internal security, we have the following recommendations:

▼ Do not extend trusts from data center hosts to other hosts across the WAN unless the hosts are at another data center and the link between them can be trusted.

■ If the data center network backbone is also connected to the Internet, an Internet firewall should be used with the scope "Whatever is not explicitly allowed is denied."

■ All administrative activity done by employees at the data center should be logged.

■ Physical access to the data center should be monitored, logged, and restricted to prenamed individuals. If possible, the individual's activities should be witnessed.

▲ Electronically validate an individual's identity. This can be as simple as imposing passwords, through traditional methods such as using card readers, or more modern biometric methods such as thumbprint or retina scanners.

Regional Office—External Security

The network security needed for the regional office will depend somewhat on the exact configuration of the office. If very little computing resources are present, other than client devices for accessing the data center, then the need is similar to the small office category,

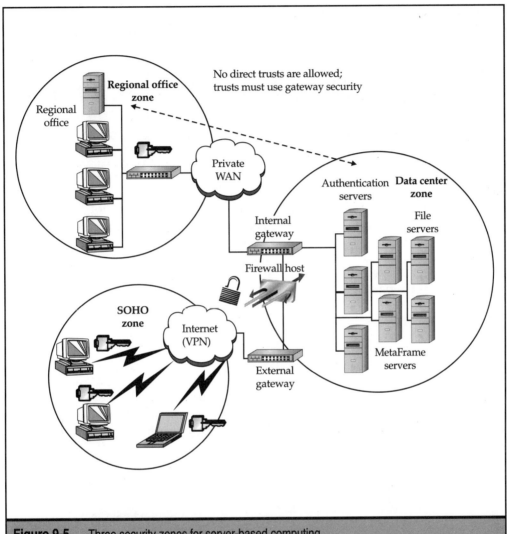

Figure 9-5.   Three security zones for server-based computing

discussed next. If local file servers or local shares are present, the same care in extending trusts between hosts should be taken. We have the following recommendation regarding external security for a regional office:

▼   If it is necessary to allow hosts outside the data center to use resources inside the data center, as would be the case with a regional work group server, a firewall should be used on the internal link between the two servers. The firewall should be defined to enforce the exact services to be used, by which users, and in which direction.

Small Office/Home User—External Security

For a small office or home user, security is no less of an issue. We have the following recommendations:

▼ Disable local drive mapping if at all possible. Many users may be opposed to this policy, but allowing local drive mapping allows the data protected at the data center to be distributed to local hard drives where its physical security cannot be guaranteed.

▲ If the Internet is to be used to access the data center, use a virtual private network with strong user authentication and encrypted data streams.

SECURITY CONCEPTS

Of particular interest in discussing security are those concepts that provide protection for the server-based network from both within and outside the organization in several key areas. Outside threats are countered by authenticating users over the WAN or Internet, encrypting the data stream, and hiding internal resources by using proxy technology. Inside dangers are mitigated by verifying user identities, logging suspicious activity, and alerting the appropriate people if a concern is flagged.

Firewalls

A discussion of modern security would hardly be complete without mentioning the network firewall. It is the piece of security equipment on the network most strongly identified with protection. Unfortunately, many organizations mistakenly view it as a panacea of network security. A firewall is a system or group of systems that enforce a boundary between two or more networks. It is typically implemented as a group of hosts and routers, as shown here:

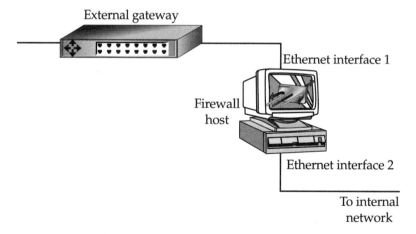

A firewall can perform a number of different functions, but the following are common:

▼   **Protection of internal resources**   Hides internal addressing schemes and hosts from external detection.

■   **Authentication**   Uses strong authentication techniques to verify a user's identity before granting access to corporate information.

■   **Privacy**   Protects sessions and data streams over trusted and untrusted networks alike.

▲   **Auditing**   Provides detailed logging and accounting of communication attempts and other relevant metrics.

In addition to these common features, we also recommend that any firewall solution perform the following:

▼   **Attack and intrusion detection**   If an attack gets through the firewall's security policy agents, the network equivalent of flashing red lights and loud claxons should go off. No automatic countermeasures can ever be as good as a well-trained security administrator. The sooner that person's attention is on the problem, the sooner the attack can be stopped.

■   **Content security**   A firewall should be "aware" of certain applications and provide application-level gateway functionality. It should be possible to define access rules based on the application that is attempting to pass the firewall.

■   **High availability**   The firewall systems themselves should be hardened enough to protect themselves from being brought down by an attack or simple mishap.

■   **Distributed security**   It should be possible to apply one set of security policies to all points of exposure on the network.

▲   **Electronic countermeasures**   This is really a wish more than a requirement since it is a goal rarely attained by purveyors of firewall systems. Ideally, a firewall should perform certain defensive actions if certain types of attacks are detected.

Though firewalls can be placed between any two networks, the most common placement by far is an Internet firewall—a firewall between an internal, corporate network and the untrusted, public Internet. The boundary enforced by a firewall is also called a "DMZ" or demilitarized zone. Public resources, such as Web servers and e-mail gateways, are commonly placed in the DMZ because they contain transitive information that has limited exposure to attack and could be replaced or rebuilt relatively easily. The host running the firewall software is often called a *bastion* host, as illustrated below:

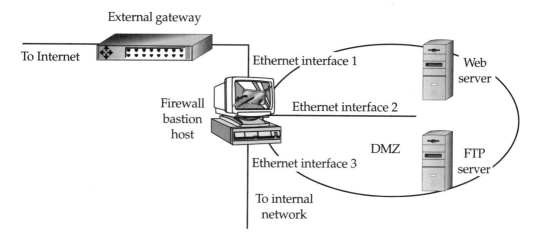

Several types of firewalls are available that roughly correspond to the layers of the OSI network model. A circuit gateway and a packet filter operate at the network layer. An application gateway, sometimes also called a trusted gateway or proxy, operates at the application layer.

Circuit-Level Gateway

A circuit-level gateway ensures that an external, trusted client has no direct contact with an internal, untrusted host. The gateway takes a connection from the client, establishes a separate connection to the host, and then transfers packets between them.

Packet Filter

A packet filter is set up to block certain types of incoming and outgoing packets as they pass through the firewall. A packet filter examines the TCP and IP headers and screens for certain information that can include source or destination address, source port number, and destination port number as follows:

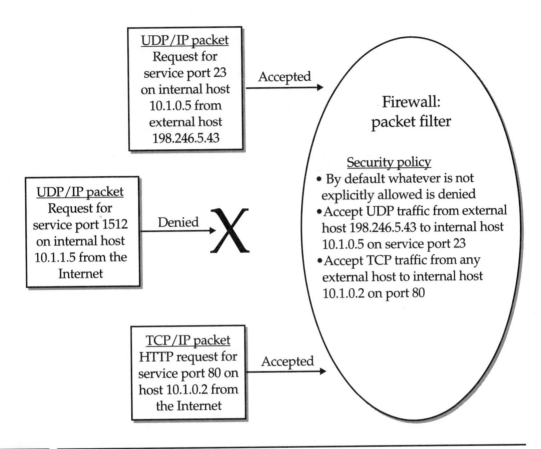

TIP: To configure a firewall so that it allows ICA connections, you need to allow TCP destination port 1494 to pass through with a source port range of 1024 to 65535. You also must define UDP port 1604 to pass through.

Application-Level Gateway

Application-level gateways obfuscate the source of traffic by readdressing the packets as they pass through the firewall. To an application such as HTTP or FTP, this activity is transparent. The effect is that from either side of the firewall, the traffic cannot be traced to the other side because it appears to have originated at the firewall. Implementations of this translation include Network Address Translation (NAT) and IP Masquerading.

Proxy Server

A proxy server is a type of application-level gateway. In addition to the functions attributed to an application-level gateway above, a proxy server can also maintain a pool of addresses for use by a much larger number of users. In this way, a large number of users can access a temporary pool of addresses only when they need them and then release them to the pool when they are finished. Modern proxy servers, such as Microsoft Proxy Server, also provide a performance advantage by caching commonly accessed Web pages. The page can then be loaded from the proxy server itself instead of over the Internet. Proxy servers typically provide a mechanism for blocking access to undesirable Web sites as well.

NOTE: Though the PacketShaper from Packeteer was designed as a tool for bandwidth management, it can also be used as a kind of application-level firewall. By creating a policy that assigns no bandwidth to a particular application, the application is effectively blocked from passing through the PacketShaper.

Virtual Private Network

Using the Internet as part of the corporate WAN infrastructure has obvious security implications. The Internet is a public network and as such exposes the company's private information to unauthorized individuals by its very nature. So if it is not secure, why use it? You should seriously consider using the Internet to access your server-based computing resources for the following reasons:

▼ **Accessibility** The Internet is everywhere. There are so many points of access that it is likely every satellite office, telecommuter, or mobile worker has ready access. This ubiquity would be nearly impossible for a private network to match. When you factor in international access, the Internet is an even more compelling alternative.

■ **Resiliency** Though some industry pundits have predicted the Internet would collapse under its own weight, it hasn't happened yet. A line may be cut or a major exchange carrier may go down, but business continues as usual on the rest of the Internet. Through the judicious use of backup ISPs and connection methods, corporate users can take advantage of this resiliency.

▲ **Cost** The cost of unlimited dial-up Internet use for the average user is currently around $20 per month. It would be challenging to find a private solution this inexpensive.

Most major vendors, including Microsoft and Citrix, realize the benefit of using the Internet and have developed technologies to make using it less risky. Standards-based initiatives have spawned technologies that have been incorporated into all manner of network equipment, such as routers and switches, as well as operating systems.

TIP: Instead of building your own VPN using encryption tools over the Internet, consider outsourcing the VPN to a third party. Many telecom providers, such as AT&T and Qwest, provide private networks for far less cost than was common just a few years ago. The advantage is that the provider supplies a service level agreement with the contract along with many related "managed" services such as automatic fail-over, Internet gateways, and data center operations.

Encryption Standards

At the heart of any VPN is a method to strongly encrypt the data traveling over the network. Encryption is the conversion of data into a form called a cipher that obscures the true meaning of a message such that only the intended recipient can understand it. So-called strong encryption refers to ciphers that are so obscure that the data can only be read with the decryption key. Though not strictly true, for practical purposes, this is true. For example, a 128-bit key would take 10,000,000,000,000,000 (that's 10 quadrillion) years to break using conventional cracking methods on a computer capable of 100 MIPS (millions of instructions per second).

There are two basic types of encryption algorithms: symmetric, or *private key*, and *public key*. Private key encryption requires that the same key used to encrypt the data be used to decrypt the data. The advantage is speed, since less computation is involved than in other methods. The main disadvantage is that the key must be distributed to the intended recipient through some secure mechanism; the symmetric algorithm itself provides no way to distribute the key. The second type of algorithm, the public key, calculates a list of keys, some of which can only encrypt the data and some of which can only decrypt the data. The encryption key is the public key. The decryption key is the private key. A message encrypted with the former can only be decrypted by the latter. A major advantage of this scheme is that the encryption key can travel in the open without compromising security. Having the public key will not allow someone to decrypt the data.

NOTE: In some applications, such as Secure Sockets Layer (SSL), the public key is made freely available to any client requesting it. The client machine uses the public key to encrypt the data before sending it over the unprotected network. Only the possessor of the private key will be able to decrypt it. This is how e-commerce sites can function: any customer who comes to the site can obtain the public key without any special arrangement or mechanism.

Several encryption algorithm and transport standards have arisen that have been adopted by Microsoft, Citrix, and others. Understanding them will help you to judge whether they are appropriate for your server-based computing project. By implementing an encryption algorithm and transport method in the network backbone, the task of authenticating and securing the network session is made further transparent to the end user. Cisco, Lucent, Nortel, and other vendors facilitate this seamless authentication by their adoption of one or more security standards.

Microsoft Point-to-Point Encryption (MPPE)   As we discussed in Chapter 8, the RRAS remote access suite from Microsoft includes Microsoft Point-to-Point Encryption. MPPE uses preshared keys for authentication. This method uses a shared, secret key that is previously agreed upon by two systems. MPPE can be used as the authentication method for PPTP or L2TP. Both are supported in Windows 2000.

Internet Protocol Security (IPSec)   IPSec is another proposed standard for encryption. It is an optional feature for the current version of TCP/IP, but it is mandatory in the next version, IPv6. IPSec is unique in that it handles encryption at the network layer, while other methodologies handle it at the application layer. This provides a degree of transparency in that security arrangements can be made without requiring changes to individual applications. IPSec can be used with PPTP or L2TP. The great advantage of IPSec is that it is end-to-end at the network layer. Application security protocols like SSL require the application to change, while data link protocols like PPTP only protect you on that specific link; the packets travel over other links in the clear.

IPSec provides two choices of security service: Authentication Header (AH), which essentially allows authentication of the sender of data, and Encapsulating Security Payload (ESP), which supports both authentication of the sender and encryption of data. The specific information associated with each of these services is inserted into the packet in a header that follows the IP packet header. Separate key protocols can be selected, such as the ISAKMP/Oakley protocol. Since it is implemented at the protocol layer, IPSec is an excellent choice for server-based computing. It does not interfere with higher-level protocols like ICA and is therefore nearly transparent to the end user.

Point-to-Point-Tunneling Protocol (PPTP)   PPTP is an extension of the Point-to-Point Protocol (PPP) and has two functions. First, it establishes a control channel between the client and the server. Second, it builds a "tunnel" for passing data between the client and the server. The tunnel is constructed using an encryption algorithm (PPTP can support many) so that the client and server exchange keys. PPTP supports multiple tunnels with a single control channel and can multiplex between them. PPTP currently enjoys the widest support in network backbone equipment such as routers and switches.

Layer 2 Tunneling Protocol (L2TP)   L2TP is an alternative to PPTP proposed by Cisco Systems. Like PPTP, L2TP is an extension of PPP and attempts to include the best features of PPTP. Like PPTP, it can encapsulate other protocols besides TCP/IP. L2TP provides flexibility in the assignment of IP addresses when TCP/IP is used. Dynamic, static, and privately managed IP addresses are supported. It uses a similar keyed encryption scheme to establish a tunnel. Both L2TP and PPTP are proposed IETF standards. Both are also supported as standards in all Cisco routers.

MICROSOFT SECURITY

At the heart of Microsoft security are the authentication methods used to validate users and hosts. MS authentication works differently in the Windows NT 4.0 family than it does in Windows 2000. It is important to understand the basics of both in order to design your network now and be ready for the future. Both have slightly different methods for handling the logon process to the local machine and to work groups. Since this book has an enterprise orientation, we will use the example of domain authentication to illustrate how Microsoft security works.

Windows NT LAN Manager (NTLM) Domain Authentication

NTLM-based authentication works as follows:

1. After entering the userid and password, and selecting the domain from the login window, the password is "hashed" and sent to the Local Security Authority (LSA).

2. The LSA is responsible for creating unique access tokens during the logon process and logging audit messages to the event log, among other things. The LSA makes a call to the NT authentication package, and because the login request is not local, the NETLOGON service on the domain controller is called. NETLOGON is responsible for communicating with the domain controller and authenticating the session.

3. In response to NETLOGON's request, the server does a number of things, including generating a random number and encrypting that with the password, then storing the result.

4. The server then compares the encrypted key with the one stored in the Security Account Manager (SAM) database.

5. If the keys are the same, the NETLOGON service returns the user's system identifier (SID) and global SID to the client that is requesting authentication.

6. The LSA process on the client looks in the local SAM database to get the local group SID. Finally, the user SID, global SID, and local SID are combined to generate a unique access token. The user application process—by default the Explorer shell—is then opened with that access token. Figure 9-6 illustrates this process.

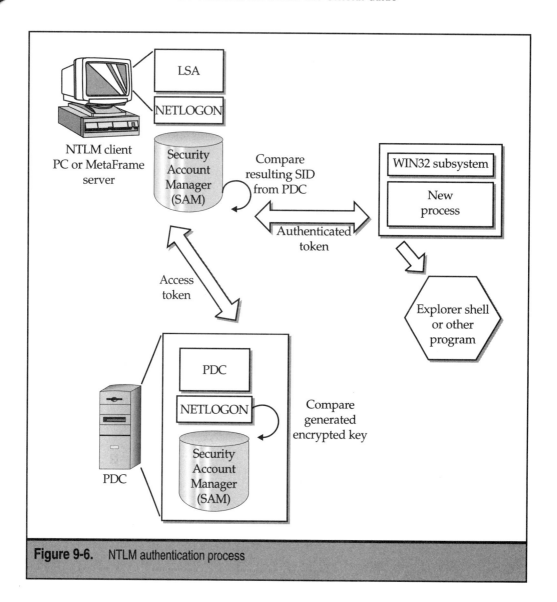

Figure 9-6.   NTLM authentication process

Windows 2000 Domain Authentication with Kerberos 5

Windows 2000 maintains backward compatibility with NTLM authentication, but provides a new authentication scheme based on Kerberos version 5. Kerberos is a security system invented at MIT in the 1980s for UNIX-based computers. Microsoft has mostly adhered to the IETF standards for Kerberos authentication, and as a result, a Windows 2000 computer can exchange authentication information with a UNIX system or any other standards-based system using the same protocol. However, Microsoft has added some extensions to the Kerberos 5 protocol. The Microsoft Kerberos server running on Windows 2000 will allow both NT and UNIX clients to log in, but a UNIX machine running the standard Kerberos server cannot serve as an NT domain authenticator due to the missing extensions only found in the Microsoft protocol.

The database used for authentication is distributed so that a client no longer has to find a domain controller to authenticate. A key can be generated once and reused. This scheme also enables two-way authentication and a simpler system of creating trusted hosts than that of NTLM. Kerberos functionality varies slightly by implementation, but Kerberos 5 on Windows 2000 functions basically as follows:

1. Any resource on any server on the network requires a "ticket" for access. In order for a user to get a ticket, an exchange of information is made between the local Kerberos client and the Authentication Server (AS) on the Kerberos Domain Controller (KDC).

2. The Authentication Server creates a session key based on the user's password and a random value that represents the requested service. The session key is effectively a "ticket-granting ticket" (TGT).

3. The TGT is then sent to a "ticket-granting server" (TGS). The result is a ticket that can be presented when requesting services or access to resources on a particular computer.

4. The TGS returns the session ticket that is then sent to the LSA. The service either rejects the ticket or accepts it and performs the service.

The session ticket is time stamped and can be reused without causing the requestor to go through the authentication process again, while limiting the amount of time a compromised key can be used to access the network resources. Figure 9-7 illustrates this process.

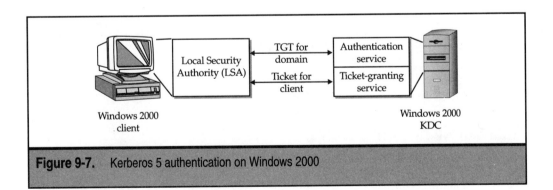

Figure 9-7.   Kerberos 5 authentication on Windows 2000

Terminal Services and the Registry

As shown in Chapters 2 and 3, the Registry contains a wealth of settings for both the Terminal Services and MetaFrame environment. As such, it can be a particular source of risk. Whatever version of Windows is involved, incorrect Registry information can lead to system instability. It is critical to protect the Registry from intentional, as well as unintentional, attempts to damage it. For example, many installation programs use system calls to access the Registry directly without checking system policies on whether this action should be allowed. Unless the Registry key itself is locked, this change may be allowed and may cause damage to other installed applications. The Registry keys of most importance in locking down the MetaFrame server are

    HKEY_LOCAL_MACHINE\HARDWARE
    HKEY_LOCAL_MACHINE\SAM
    HKEY_LOCAL_MACHINE\SOFTWARE
    HKEY_LOCAL_MACHINE\SOFTWARE\HKEY_CLASSES_ROOT
    HKEY_LOCAL_MACHINE\SYSTEM
    HKEY_LOCAL_MACHINE\SYSTEM\HKEY_CURRENT_CONFIG

Of these keys, only the SOFTWARE key and subkeys are not marked read-only to non-administrators by default. Many of the subkeys under SOFTWARE have "special access" permissions. Though it is desirable to change as many of these keys as possible from special access to read-only for users, you must take great care in doing so. We've found that the majority of programs will not function correctly if the SOFTWARE key is changed to read-only for users. This is because many applications store temporary and preference-type information in this key. If you intend to run only a small number of applications on the server, it may be worth your while to try changing the permissions of each SOFTWARE subkey. For a server running 10 applications, this is not practical. As applications certified to run under Windows 2000, and thereby certified to run multiuser, begin to appear, this will become less of a problem.

TIP: We've found that HKEY_LOCAL_MACHINE\SOFTWARE\ODBC should have its permissions changed to read-only for users. It's proven to be safe to change, and it prevents the intentional or accidental deletion of system data sources.

There are other ways to secure a user's environment using the login scripts and the HKEY_USERS subkey, which we will discuss in Chapter 16.

Terminal Services Connections

By default, an installation of Terminal Services and MetaFrame will set up three connections: ica-ipx, ica-tcp, and rdp-tcp. Unless you are using Novell NetWare, we recommend deleting the ica-ipx connection. Similarly, unless you are using the RDP client, we recommend deleting it as well. Once the list of connections to be supported is complete, launch the Terminal Server Connection Configuration tool (or Citrix Connection Configuration tool if MetaFrame is installed), which is found under Administrative Tools on the Start menu of the MetaFrame server. The Citrix dialog box looks like this:

```
\\RYNO-TSE2 - Citrix Connection Configuration                           _ □ ×
Connection  Options  Security  Help
        Connection Name    Transport    Type              Comment
        ica-tcp            tcp          Citrix ICA 3.0
        rdp-tcp            tcp          Microsoft RDP 4.0
        ica-dialin001      async        Citrix ICA 3.0    COM1 - Courier V.Everything External:
        ica-dialin002      async        Citrix ICA 3.0    COM2 - Courier V.Everything External #2:
```

Again, by default, five users and groups are created with associated permissions. Though managing connection security with group accounts is a good method, these defaults are not appropriate for a production environment. Table 9-1 shows the accounts and associated default permissions.

We recommend removing all of the accounts except SYSTEM and adding the local groups shown in Table 9-2. You can use the ADDUSERS command from the NT Resource Kit, or the User Manager for Domains tool, to add users. The ADDUSERS command can be particularly useful in scripting repetitive functions. If you do use it, however, you must use the Terminal Services TSPROF command to alter any account information that is part of MetaFrame and not part of Terminal Services.

Local User or Group	Default Permissions
Everyone	Guest
\\Server Name\Administrators	Full Control
\\Server Name\Guests	Guest
\\Server Name\Users	User
SYSTEM	Full Control

Table 9-1.   Default Users, Groups, and Permissions for MetaFrame Server Connections

Local User or Group	Function	Permissions
Admins	This group will have access to all administrative functions on the MetaFrame server, including control of other sessions.	Full Control
Shadow_Admins	This group will have permission to shadow other users. Otherwise, it is the same as the Users group. We've found this helpful in peer support situations.	User + Shadow privilege
Operators	This group is typically composed of help desk workers. Members can perform routine administrative tasks such as adding users, changing file permissions, adding printers (with existing drivers), and shadowing other users.	Shadow + associated permissions
Users	Members of this group are the rank and file of the company. They have permission to run applications, manage their own and shared files, and print.	User

Table 9-2. Recommended Users, Groups, and Permissions for MetaFrame Server Connections

TIP: We have found that removing the standard NT Administrator account and replacing it with an "Admin" account can help achieve "security by obscurity." The Administrator account is so common that even the casual hacker will attempt to log in and guess the password. We, of course, also recommend using strong passwords, but obfuscating the main administration account can be surprisingly helpful. If you choose to make this change, remember to change the local and global groups, such as Domain Admins, that contain the Administrator account.

Once the new local groups are created, you will need to add the appropriate global groups to them. These changes will need to be made on all of the MetaFrame servers you intend to use; however, we don't recommend making the changes manually or with scripts. It should be part of the imaging and automation process you adopt to create your servers. (Details on this process are given in Chapter 14.)

NOTE: In Windows 2000, the User Manager for Domains tool has different default locations depending on which version of the operating system you use (Enterprise, Workgroup, or Professional). It is either in the customary place under Start > Programs > Administrative tools or in the Control Panel under Users and Passwords.

Other Connection Settings

Several other connection properties should be changed from their default values for each connection. Table 9-3 lists the settings and indicates how each should be adjusted in the Citrix Connection Configuration (CCC) program. Most of the settings have the default value, "inherit user config." For the most part, however, this isn't practical. In an enterprise setting, you will not be managing settings at this level of detail on a per-user basis. Where there are exceptions, we note the reason in the Comments column. (IUC stands for inherit user config.)

There are two reasons why you will always want to force users to connect to a server via published applications rather than a direct connection to the server. First, published applications make use of load balancing. By forcing users to connect to the published application "desktop," for example, the ICA master browser will route each user to the server with the lightest load at the time of connection. If a user connected directly to the

Setting	Purpose	Default Value	Desired Value	Comments
Timeout: Connect (values in minutes)	Limits the time a user can be connected.	IUC	No change	Some users may require a "hard-coded" limit for this setting.
Timeout: Disconnect	Limits the time a user session can remain in a disconnected state before being terminated.	IUC	10	This should be a short enough window to allow users to reconnect if they wish, but release server resources quickly if they don't.

Table 9-3.   Security Settings for Connection Properties

Setting	Purpose	Default Value	Desired Value	Comments
Timeout: Idle	Limits the amount of time a user session can be idle, that is, not sending any information to the server.	IUC	180	Though an idle session will chew up resources just like a disconnected session will, we recommend against setting a short interval here since it tends to annoy users who may not be at their desks continuously.
Security: Required Encryption	The levels of encryption available will be different if SecureICA is installed. There is no functional difference between the settings.	Low, Med, High	Varies	The recommended choice will depend on whether you have SecureICA installed.
Security: Use default NT Authentication	Controls whether or not to participate in the NT Domain Authentication.	None	Yes	Third-party GINAs are supported, such as Novell's client. Use NT unless you have a good reason not to.

Table 9-3.   Security Settings for Connection Properties *(continued)*

Setting	Purpose	Default Value	Desired Value	Comments
On a broken or timed-out connection	Action to perform when a connection is broken, as in a network problem or time-out.	IUC	Disconnect	Set it to disconnect so that your Timeout: Disconnect setting takes effect.
Reconnect sessions disconnected	Controls whether the session can be reconnected to, from a particular client or any client.	IUC	From any Client	In a load-balanced server farm, this setting is nearly meaningless. Use it to ensure that users can retrieve their session if at all possible.
Shadowing	Controls how the MetaFrame session's shadowing feature works. Input controls whether the shadower can input information into the session or just view it. Notify controls whether the users are explicitly notified that they are being shadowed.	IUC	Enabled, Input ON, Notify ON	Shadowing is an invaluable support tool and so should be enabled. Input is needed to fully troubleshoot application problems. Notify set to ON is the "politically correct" setting since it allows the users to know they are being shadowed.

Table 9-3. Security Settings for Connection Properties *(continued)*

Setting	Purpose	Default Value	Desired Value	Comments
AutoLogon	Default settings to make the connection automatically log onto the domain.	IUC	Disabled	Unless this connection is going to be used to control a kiosk, autologon should not be used.
Initial Program	Allows the setting of a program to run upon connection.	IUC	None	Again, unless this is a kiosk, the setting should be blank. Published applications are the preferred method for running an application.
User Profile Override: Disable Wallpaper	Controls whether users can set their own wallpaper.	None	None	We will cover this and many other settings in our policy file. (Refer to Chapter 16.)

Table 9-3.   Security Settings for Connection Properties *(continued)*

server of his choice, load balancing would be bypassed. Second, some servers will undoubtedly exist not to provide a user's desktop but to provide second-tier applications that are accessed via the ICA passthrough client in the user's desktop session. To force users to connect via a published application, select the check box "Only run published applications" in the Advanced tab of the CCC utility for each connection that you have enabled.

TIP: You can create certain published applications with security set so that only administrators connect to them. For example, as an administrator, you will want to be able to establish a desktop session on every server in the farm. To accomplish this, publish an application called "desktop_1" on server 1 and grant administrators exclusive access to it; then repeat this process for every server in the farm.

Account Management

The policy settings for the user accounts on the MetaFrame server are another source of security risk that needs to be addressed.

Password Management

According to the Computer Emergency Response Team (CERT), hackers use three common methods to get passwords:

▼   Using known or assumed user names and guessing the password. Many routers and other network equipment come with default passwords that a surprising number of companies never change. Many administrators also pick passwords, such as "Administrator," that are very easy to guess.

■   Running dictionary attacks against stolen password files. There are numerous utilities that will extract a password file from an NT system (such as Exporter from System Tools). With that file in hand, a dedicated hacker can automate the process of "guessing" the password against every common word in the dictionary, even if it is encrypted.

▲   Accessing a compromised workstation and "sniffing" the password out of the network data stream. Though this is not as easy with the ICA client, it is still theoretically possible. This possibility is an argument not only for strong password policies, but also for network-level encryption, as discussed earlier in this chapter.

CERT maintains "security improvement modules" for many operating systems, including Windows NT, on its Web site (www.cert.org). We recommend reviewing the site and deciding which modules might be appropriate for your organization. CERT is also a good source for information from both the vendor and user community on new security threats.

Password management can be strengthened in a server-based computing environment in several ways. First, protect the password file. In case an unauthorized individual obtains the file, it is smart to make sure it is as scrambled as possible. Microsoft provides a tool for this called SYSKEY.EXE. It applies a 128-bit encryption scheme to the password file. SYSKEY.EXE is included with most versions of NT. It has no other effect on password functionality, but it is not run by default.

Second, enforce strong passwords. The practice of allowing users to select their own password according to whatever format they choose is so pervasive that it is almost an epidemic of carelessness. The default password entry field in User Manager for Domains does not help this problem, but there are external utilities that can.

One useful utility provided by Microsoft is called PASSFILT.DLL. It implements the following password restrictions:

▼   Passwords must be at least six characters long.

- Passwords must contain characters from at least three of the following four classes:

  English uppercase letters (A, B, C, ... Z)
  English lowercase letters (a, b, c, ... z)
  Westernized Arabic numerals (0, 1, 2, ... 9)
  Nonalphanumeric characters such as punctuation symbols

▲ Passwords may not contain the user name or any part of the user's full name.

TIP: If you plan to use Windows NT 4.0, PASSFILT.DLL needs to be installed on all PDCs in the domain. The following changes are needed on each PDC. You should make this change part of the image you create for the PDC servers (see Chapter 14).

1. Install the latest Windows NT 4.0 service pack.

2. Copy PASSFILT.DLL to the %SystemRoot%\System32 folder.

3. Use regedt32.exe to add the value "Notification Packages" of type REG_MULT_SZ under the LSA key.

4. If the following key exists,

   HKEY_LOCAL_MACHINE\SYSTEM\CurrentControlSet\Control\Lsa
   double-click the "Notification Packages" key and add the following value: PASSFILT.

5. Save changes, exit, and reboot.

Although PASSFILT.DLL will properly enforce the required password characteristics, there are a few caveats to using it. First, an administrator is still allowed to change a password with the User Manager tool and assign a password that no longer meets the criteria. This is due to the way password filtering occurs with users as opposed to administrators. When a password change request is sent over the network, filtering is activated. When an administrator changes a password, the change is written directly through the Security Account Manager (SAM), and filtering is bypassed. The second limitation is that the error messages and dialog boxes regarding passwords do not match PASSFILT.DLL because it did not exist when that part of User Manager was created. As a result, if users try to enter an erroneous password, they will receive an error message that does not make sense. This is unfortunate, but you can mitigate this limitation by covering it in the user orientation session of the deployment and by making sure your help desk is aware of the problem.

The functionality of PASSFILT.DLL is already included in the Windows 2000 environment and simply needs to be enabled.

TIP: To enable strong password support in Windows 2000 do the following:

1. Start the Local Security Policy application.

2. Locate the setting under Configuration\Software Settings\Account Policy\Password Policy.

3. Enable Passwords must meet complexity requirements.

Additional Account Settings

In addition to taking the measures described so far, we recommend making the policy settings shown in Table 9-4 in the Account Policy section of User Manager.

File System Security

As we discussed in Chapter 7, every MetaFrame server and NT server should be built using the NTFS file system because the FAT file system does not support any of the security features provided by these operating systems. In Chapter 13, we will discuss the recommended

Policy Setting	Recommended Value	Comments
Maximum Password Age	60 days or less	The more often the password changes, the better—but you don't want to change it so often that it is disruptive to users.
Minimum Password Age	2 days	The minimum should stop frivolous changes of passwords.
Password Length	6 or higher	The higher the value, the more difficult the password will be to crack via statistical measures.
Password Uniqueness	Remember 10 passwords	The more passwords that are remembered, the less likely a user is to use the same password again. If a password file is stolen, having a high number here will help ensure that the current password is different from the stolen one.

Table 9-4.   Recommended Account Policy Changes

Policy Setting	Recommended Value	Comments
Lockout after	3 bad logon attempts	Giving users more than a few opportunities to enter their password is an invitation to dictionary-based attacks.
Reset count after	180 minutes	Let some time pass before allowing users to attempt to log on again without administrative intervention.
Lockout duration	Forever	If an account locks for a legitimate user, forcing the user to call the help desk to get it unlocked is better than providing free access for a hacker to attempt to penetrate the system repeatedly.
Forcibly disconnect remote users from the server when logon hours expire	Checked	If you intend to establish logon time windows, this option needs to be enabled.
Users must log on in order to change password	Checked	Users should be authenticated before being allowed to change their password.

Table 9-4. Recommended Account Policy Changes *(continued)*

layout for the MetaFrame server and other supporting servers. We will defer the discussion of recommended file system security until then in order to provide a richer context for that discussion. What we will discuss here are the tools and methods for altering file system security.

▼ **ACLSET/ACLCHECK**   These utilities are provided by Citrix to change or display file system attributes in a predefined way. If ACLSET is run with no arguments, it proceeds to change permissions on the file system of all local hard drives. It sets all file and directory permissions to Full Control for Administrators and SYSTEM and No Access for users. ACLCHECK is designed to provide a "quick and dirty" audit of system security. It displays file access allowed by accounts other than Administrators and SYSTEM, key Registry information on access or ownership assigned to accounts other than Administrators and SYSTEM, the list of applications created by the Application Security utility and which accounts can run them, and the system security level (Low, Medium, or High).

- **CACLS**   This command provided with Terminal Server and Windows 2000 allows you to display or modify Access Control Lists (ACLs) from the command line. The command can be useful in script files for automating mass changes to the file system.

NOTE: You can replace permissions on directories, but if the user account is set up correctly (see Chapter 16), users will normally never see these directories. The exception is that some applications, such as Word, will allow browsing up and down the directory hierarchy from the File menu to places where Explorer or the command line would not. This is why it is important to change the permissions on system directories so that critical files cannot be modified or deleted.

- **Zero Administration Kit (ZAK) Utilities**   In addition to the ZAK provided for NT workstation and server, Microsoft provides an extension for Terminal Server called ZAK4WTS. The Terminal Services ZAK will perform an automatic lockdown of system directories and implement a predefined set of policies designed to limit what users can do on their desktops. We have found that neither group of settings is terribly useful in a production environment. The file system settings are so restrictive that problems will occur with most applications when writing to specific directories. The user policies are not specific enough about which settings they lock down, and the result is a desktop that allows undesirable changes and restricts some things that should be allowed. (We will provide more production-hardened recommendations for file system settings in Chapter 13, and for usable but restricted user policy settings in Chapter 16.)

- **NTSec**   This is actually a group of commands available as a suite from System Tools. The set of tools allows a wide variety of security operations to be performed on the file system, Registry, users and groups, and shares. We've found these commands to be stable and highly useful. One of the more useful features is the ability to save and restore ACL or Registry settings. The commands can also easily be used in scripts. System Tools has another product, Security Explorer, that allows an administrator a unified, graphical view of security on a given system.

Application Security

Microsoft provides a policy setting to restrict which executables can be run on the server. In the Policy Editor, under Default User > System > Restrictions, the option is called "Run only allowed Windows applications." The Show button opens a window where each individual EXE file can be specified, as shown here:

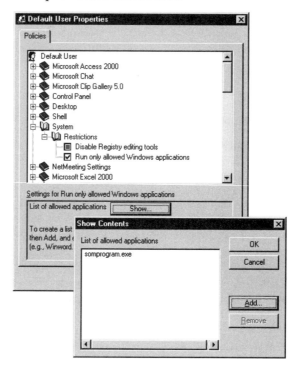

Though this can be useful for a small number of applications, we've found that it can cause more problems than it solves on a server that must run many applications simultaneously. The problem occurs when one executable must call another. The second EXE file tries to run and fails because it is not in the list. Ironically, programs from Microsoft, such as the Office suite, are the worst offenders here. If you take the time to map out all the possible executables that will be called, this tool can provide a useful measure of security by virtually eliminating rogue applications. Be prepared to spend some time, however. We recently examined one client's server that was running about 20 applications and found over 1000 executables!

CITRIX SECURITY

By default, the ICA protocol adds little to the security already existing in Terminal Services. ICA uses a very basic method to encrypt, or more accurately scramble, the data stream by using a key. It is really meant to help ensure that clear text is not visible in the data stream.

SecureICA

SecureICA adds strong encryption to the ICA in 40-bit and 56-bit international flavors, as well as a 128-bit version available in the United States. It uses the RC5 encryption algorithm from RSA Data Security. RC5 uses a combination of symmetric and public-private key algorithms. The MetaFrame client and server use the Diffie-Hellman key agreement algorithm with a 1024-bit key to generate RC5 keys. Citrix bills this client as being safe enough to run sessions over the Internet, and indeed, many companies use or base their products on the RC5 encryption algorithm. SecureICA contains both client and server components and is configurable with the CCC.

AUDITING

We've saved the discussion of auditing until now because the same general guidelines can be applied to all the subjects we've addressed so far. Auditing in this context is simply the process by which certain system events are captured to a persistent data store so that they can be reviewed at a later time. All versions of Windows NT and Windows 2000 provide copious amounts of log settings for virtually all system activity. Enabling all of them is not useful because the resulting logs would be so cluttered as to be nearly unreadable, especially with a simple tool such as the Event Viewer. The trick is to find the right level of logging for the kind of activity you are undertaking. For example, normal daily operations need a much less granular level of logging than does troubleshooting. In addition to deciding what level of granularity is desirable, you must decide which areas of the system you want to audit.

NOTE: Auditing is a passive activity. The missing component is alerting or notification. Most firewall products and even some networking equipment have the ability to send e-mail or pages if security policies are successfully bypassed or broken. No less should be required for the servers. (We will discuss this more fully in Chapter 10.)

The Registry

Registry auditing is enabled in the REGEDT32 tool by selecting the key to audit and then selecting Audit from the Security menu. Since we are very concerned with any changes made to the Registry, the group Everyone should be assigned in the Audit window for the keys HKEY_LOCAL_MACHINE and HKEY_CURRENT_USERS. Of particular interest in the HKEY_LOCAL_MACHINE key are the subkeys that deal with authentication enforcement and other security settings. They are

    SYSTEM\CurrentControlSet\Control\Lsa
    SYSTEM\CurrentControlSet\Control\Security\Providers
    SOFTWARE\Microsoft\Windows NT\CurrentVersion\Winlogon

Nine types of access can be audited for Registry keys. For each type, you can choose to audit success or failure events. The possible types are Query Value, Set Value, Create Subkey, Enumerate Subkeys, Notify, Create Link, Delete, Write DAC (change to security), and Read Control. In general, attempts to add or delete a key or modify security information are of the most concern and should be audited. The events that should be audited for these keys are Set Value, Create Subkey, Create Link, Delete, and Write DAC.

User Accounts

User Account auditing is defined in the User Manager tool by selecting Audit from the Policies menu. Table 9-5 lists the events that can be audited, our recommended settings, and comments.

Policy	Production Setting	Troubleshooting Setting	Comments
Logon and Logoff	Failure	Success and Failure	Failures may point to unauthorized attempts to log on. Successes can show user activity. In production there are better ways to track user activity, such as with the Citrix RMS tool.
File and Object Access	Failure	Failure	The same is true for failures here as the previous category. Take care if logging successes because users have access to a huge number of objects. Define auditing as narrowly as possible to avoid large logs.

Table 9-5.   User Account Audit Settings

Policy	Production Setting	Troubleshooting Setting	Comments
Use of User Rights	Failure	Failure	Again, be careful of logging successes here.
User and Group Management	Success and Failure	Success and Failure	Even in a large organization, the amount of activity generated by adding, deleting, and changing user accounts should be moderate. Enabling logging here provides a good audit trail for this activity.
Security Policy Changes	Success and Failure	Success and Failure	Changes to the security policy should be deliberate and only done by a very small number of people. The activity generated by these settings should be correspondingly small.
Restart, Shutdown, and System	Success and Failure	Success and Failure	Only administrators will have the ability to do this in a production environment, so full logging will not generate a lot of activity.

Table 9-5.   User Account Audit Settings *(continued)*

The File System

Auditing the file system can quickly fill megabytes of disk space with logs. Setting too many files, directories, and groups to be audited can also significantly degrade overall performance on the server. We recommend limiting audits to sensitive areas of the server, such as the \WTSRV or \WINNT directory on the System volume. Also limit auditing to users or groups who should not normally be allowed to read or write information to these areas. For example, the Users and Operators groups should not have write access to the \WTSRV or \WINNT directory and so should be audited. Administrators do have access, so auditing is unnecessary unless there is a troubleshooting situation. Your auditing definition can be made even more granular by specifying the actual file operations for each group. You can audit Read, Write, Execute, Delete, Change Permissions, and Take ownership. There are some specific settings we recommend for certain sensitive subdirectories on the server. (We will discuss those, along with file system security settings, in Chapter 13.)

Auditing Tools

We recommend defining a set of auditing policies and then making it part of the standard server image. This way, the policies do not need to be set on every server, only on the original. (Other automation techniques are discussed in Chapter 14.) The following tools can be used in auditing:

▼ **Event Viewer**   This is mentioned for completeness, but it is really only useful for small logs or logs with a very high level of granularity. It can be used to export log files for examination by other tools (such as AUDITLOG).

■ **AUDITPOL**   This tool comes from the NT 4 Server Resource Kit Supplement 2 and can be used to set policies on a particular computer or on an entire domain if the PDC is used as an argument. Since it can be used on the command line, it is a useful tool for writing scripts that set policies.

▲ **AUDITLOG**   This command is provided with MetaFrame and allows the extraction and formatting of data from the Security portion of the Event Log, provided that Logon/Logoff auditing is enabled. It can be a useful troubleshooting tool to isolate the events or time frames of particular interest in a verbose log.

SECURITY PRODUCTS

In this section we discuss specific implementations of the security concepts presented in this chapter. We've already covered the recommended settings for the servers, so we will focus on some of the other equipment necessary for a server-based computing solution. In Chapter 8 we presented options for remote-office equipment, including desirable security features. For the data center, we will concentrate on two areas: the firewall and other premise equipment. The remaining network security measures are related to the servers.

Firewall Products

The firewall is the primary line of defense against intrusion-related attacks originating outside the data center network. However, a firewall can also provide security measures between networks within the data center, if they exist, or between segments of a private WAN. Some firewall products we have experience with in a Corporate ASP include

▼ **Cisco PIX**   Cisco's firewall offering runs on a dedicated hardware box and also provides VPN features. The latest version supports IPSec natively and has options for 56-bit encryption (DES) or 168-bit encryption (3DES, or triple-DES). Cisco provides software for a variety of Windows clients in case the encrypted tunnel request comes from a PC and not another PIX box or router. Though the PIX firewall runs on a dedicated box, many individual software components, including IPSec, also run on Cisco's routers. Using these software modules for Cisco IOS (Internetwork Operating System), it is possible to encrypt the entire enterprise network. The advantage of this solution is that it is transparent to higher-level protocols, such as ICA client and ICA browsing, provided it is implemented correctly.

■ **Checkpoint Firewall-1**   We have found Firewall-1 to be an excellent and highly adaptable firewall for the enterprise. It contains "stateful inspection" technology that installs itself at the kernel level of the operating system and checks all packets before they are processed by the operating system. The packets are not allowed to pass unless they comply with the defined security policy. The packet filtering and application gateway functionality also analyzes all seven layers of the OSI network model and supports the definition of security policies at each level. The firewall can also enforce policies on third-party network equipment from vendors such as Cisco.

Firewall-1 features a GUI management tool, and the various inspection modules can be distributed to different machines on the network while maintaining one database of security policies. Checkpoint software also has plug-in modules available that integrate with both standard and third-party security products. For example, IPSec is supported through the VPN-1 add-on, and the SecurID suite of products from Security Dynamics is supported if hardware token-based security is desired. Firewall-1 addresses all of the requirements we put forth for firewalls earlier in the chapter, including some ability to respond to threats with countermeasures.

▲ **MS Proxy Server**   Though not strictly a firewall, MS Proxy Server has come a long way since its early days of just providing Web proxy services. Its capabilities have been extended into the general-purpose firewall arena by adding functions for packet filtering and application gateway. Though its suite of features is not nearly as extensive as that of Firewall-1, it has a lot of value as a cache server for Web access. With MS Proxy Server 2.0, it is possible to configure a cluster of load-balanced Web cache servers that both store commonly accessed Web pages locally and serve to even out network traffic traveling to and from the Internet. Rules can also be established regarding unacceptable Web sites. We've seen Web-based bandwidth utilization drop sharply in sites using Proxy Server. In situations where the functionality demanded of a firewall is not extensive, MS Proxy Server can serve well.

Other Premise Equipment

As we mentioned in Chapter 8, it is important to match the security capabilities of the network access equipment at the data center and at the remote office. For example, if IPSec is chosen as the encryption technology of choice, a high-capacity IPSec-capable router or switch will be necessary at the data center, along with a network access device at the regional or remote office that supports it. This way, an encrypted tunnel can be created to transport ICA traffic in a manner that is transparent to the users.

CHAPTER 10

Network Management

In the old days of small work group LANs, it was relatively easy for a system administrator to keep tabs on the status of desktop PCs, servers, and the network simply by looking at the lights on the front of the equipment. As these networks grew in complexity and scope, it became more than any person, or group of people, could do to know the status of all parts of the network at all times. This problem provided the challenge for the first network management system (NMS). The early NMS software was little more than a log reader, similar to the Event Viewer in Windows NT and Windows 2000 today. Next, the ability to read status and alert messages in a standard format was added. This standard format became the Simple Network Management Protocol (SNMP). Manufacturers quickly added the ability to format and send SNMP messages to all of their equipment. Today, virtually all pieces of network hardware, such as routers, switches, bridges, and CSU/DSUs, as well as servers and operating systems, can report status using SNMP. It is this capability that makes modern NMS packages like Microsoft SMS, Citrix RMS, and HP OpenView possible. The ability to receive and collate SNMP messages is only the tip of the iceberg of what an NMS can do and what your company should use it for.

Although server-based computing is by nature more centralized and architecturally simpler than distributed computing, this does not mitigate the need for a strong system management environment (SME). It is even more critical to establish service level agreements for services delivered and to use tools, such as an NMS, to manage them. In this chapter we define some of the standards for messaging in an SME; discuss some of the unique characteristics of creating an SME for server-based computing, including monitoring and reporting; and take a look at implementations of the SME concept in available tools from Microsoft, Citrix, Hewlett-Packard, and others, and examine how they might fit into an SME for your company.

PEOPLE, PROCESSES, AND PRODUCT

Utilizing an NMS is only part of an organization's overall SME. An SME consists of the people, processes, and product ("three Ps") within an organization that effectively manage the computing resources of that organization. "Product" is more accurately "technology," but "two Ps and a T" doesn't have the same punch as "three Ps." We find the simplest way to think of the interrelationship between the three Ps is in terms of service level agreements (SLAs).

SERVICE LEVEL AGREEMENTS

An SLA in this context is an agreement between the IT staff and the user community about the services being provided, the manner in which they are delivered, the responsibilities of the IT support staff, and the responsibilities of the users. An SLA serves many important functions, including setting the expectations of the users about the scope of services being delivered and providing accountability and a baseline of measurement for the IT staff. The established SLAs in your organization also provide the framework for the SME. After all, if you don't first figure out what you are managing and how you will manage it, what good will a tool do you? In addition to incorporating the three Ps, a service level agreement should address the following three areas of responsibility:

▼ **Availability**   This section should explain when the services are provided, the frequency (if appropriate), and the nature of the services.

■ **Performance**   This section describes how the service is to be performed and any underlying processes relating to the delivery of the service.

▲ **Usability**   This section should show how to measure whether the service is being used effectively. For example, a measure of success could be infrequent help desk calls.

Table 10-1 shows a sample SLA for an enterprise backup service.

Ideally, the SLA is an extension of the overall business goals. Defining a group of SLAs for an organization that has never used them can be a daunting task. The following tips will help you with the effort:

▼ Start by deciding which parts of your infrastructure go directly to supporting your business goals, and define exactly how that happens.

■ Do not define an SLA in terms of your current support capability. Think "outside the box" regarding how a particular service *should* be delivered. The result will be your goal for the SLA. Now work backward and figure out what has to be done to reach the ideal SLA.

▲ Rather than starting at the ground level with individual SLAs for individual services, try laying down some universal rules for a so-called Master SLA. After all, some things will apply to nearly every service you deliver. A good place to start is with the help desk, where all user calls are taken. Decide how the help desk will handle, prioritize, and assign calls. The problem response time, for example, will be a standard time for all nonpriority calls. Once that is established, you can think about whether different services may need different handling for priority calls. Decide what the mission and goals are of the IT staff overall and how they support the business. Work backward from that to how the service management function must be defined to align with those goals.

The subject of defining and working with SLAs is adequate material for a book all its own. Our intention here is to get you started in framing your network management services in terms of SLAs. You will find them to be not only a great help in sorting through the "noise" of information collected but also an invaluable communication tool for users, IT staff, and management alike.

Volumes to Be Backed Up	Availability	Performance	Usability
Palo Alto Data Center Network appliance filer cluster (400GB) HP 9000 Oracle database (120GB) Denver Data Center Network appliance filer cluster (800GB) HP 9000 Oracle database (220GB) Backup device is a Spectra Logic tape library with eight drives using AIT tapes at each data center.	Daily incremental backups of all volumes. Weekly full backups. Monthly full backups. Quarterly full backups. Three months of daily tapes are used, then rotated.Online backups: a snapshot is taken every 4 hours for the NetApp. The last 12 snapshots are available, covering 48 hours. Archive/grooming backup every two weeks.	Backups are scheduled and designed not to affect production system performance. Five weeks of tapes per month are used. Daily log report is generated noting which tapes are in what backup set. Full backups are taken off-site the following Wednesday and returned according to three-month cycle. Sample files are restored and verified three times per week. Archive/grooming backup: files not touched in 14 months are written to tape every two weeks and after three backups are deleted from production storage.	Problem response according to standard help desk SLA. Nonpriority requests for restorations and archive turnaround is three days. Service performance reports are published weekly to users via intranet site.

Table 10-1.   SLA for Enterprise Backup

MESSAGING STANDARDS

You will need to be familiar with current messaging standards for network management and understand the basics of how they work in order to effectively plan an SME.

TCP/IP and UDP

We defined TCP/IP and UDP in Chapter 6, but we mention them again here in the context of network management in order to show the different philosophies under which some of the standards were created. As you know, UDP uses a "best effort" delivery mechanism. There is no guarantee the packet will ever arrive at its destination. The advantage is that UDP packets are small and of a similar size, lacking the complexity of a TCP/IP packet.

NOTE: UDP packets are not of fixed size; they are variable up to 65,536 bytes—the largest datagram IP can support. Generally, UDP frames will be 576 bytes or less, because IP requires all network links to support an MTU of 576 bytes. Sending a UDP datagram larger than this risks fragmentation.

Given the limitations of UDP, it may seem that TCP is more appropriate for delivery of management information. This is not necessarily true; it depends on the application. All TCP really does is automatically retransmit if it doesn't receive an acknowledgment (ACK). When running with UDP, the SNMP manager is responsible for detecting the lack of response and retransmitting. Consider the case in which a response packet is lost, and the network remains down for five seconds. With a TCP-based SNMP, TCP will retransmit several times and will eventually deliver the response. The response it delivers will be at least five seconds out of date. With UDP, the management console will reissue the request, and when the network is finally operational again, the response will be the most up-to-date possible.

TCP/IP also lacks a guaranteed delivery mechanism, but it at least supports packet resequencing and destination routing, making it less prone to delivery failure. This is important when considering which protocol would provide a better transport option for system status and alert messages.

Simple Network Management Protocol (SNMP)

SNMP is an application layer protocol that uses the underlying transport services of the protocol stack. SNMP version 1 (SNMPv1) uses UDP and IP. The inclusion of SNMPv1 in networking equipment is widespread, and you are likely to encounter it. SNMPv2 has been enhanced in a number of ways to make it more robust than its predecessor and is the most common implementation today. Ironically SNMPv2 fell far short of the vision set forth in its specification, particularly in the area of security. SNMPv3 is the implementation designed to address the security issue as well as the other shortcomings of its predecessors. The current specifications, RFCs, and a supported hardware list can be found at www.snmp.org.

SNMP operates on the concept of a manager-agent relationship. The manager is a centrally situated application that can obtain information from agents distributed throughout the network. Information is obtained through polling, or the agent can send unsolicited event messages, called *traps*, to the manager, as shown here:

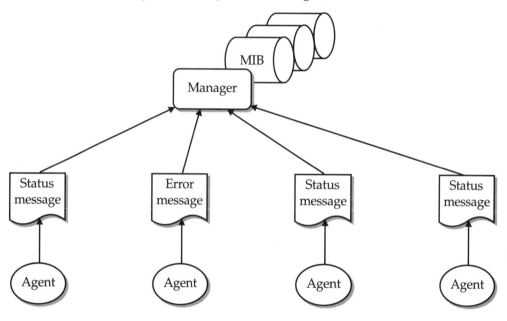

NOTE: A trap, however, can be lost. Generally, administrators don't depend on SNMP traps as the only notification of failures because traps work poorly in a lot of NMS implementations. Instead, the management console periodically polls for status.

The data exchanged between managers and agents follows a standard hierarchical format described as the management information base (MIB). The manager is responsible for taking the MIB data sent by the agents, interpreting the format, aggregating, collating, and correlating it to higher-level events. The manager's task is also to make this information available for queries or reports. The structure of the MIBs is defined by the IETF in several requests for comments (RFCs), and new MIBs are being created all the time. MIBs for various categories of devices store their information in a standard place on the tree hierarchy. Thus, all routers are in the same branch of the tree, all hubs are in the same branch, and all CSU/DSU devices are in the same branch, as shown in Figure 10-1—a simplified view of a network equipment MIB.

SNMP's *community* is similar to a domain in NT networking. An SNMP community defines a set of agents that are related in some way. A community could define a com-

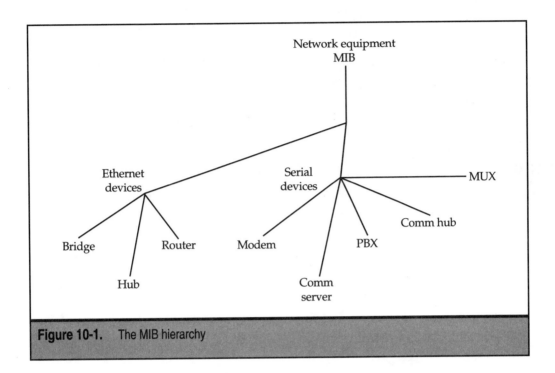

Figure 10-1.   The MIB hierarchy

pany division, a geographic location (such as a data center), or even a similar class of equipment, such as all routers. A manager can typically receive and process messages from multiple communities and provide views into the messages separated by those communities, as shown in Figure 10-2.

SNMP is being improved and extended continuously, but the current widespread standard is SNMPv2. Though any implementation must provide the basic features of the manager and agent, vendors are free to add functionality as they see fit based on the needs of the platform. SNMP has the following advantages and limitations.

Advantages of SNMP include

▼   It works well in its limited scope and is easy to extend.

■   Agents are ubiquitous on network equipment and operating systems.

■   The specifications are simple and easy to implement.

■   The performance overhead of an agent is minimal.

▲   A polling approach to collecting data is good for managed objects on a LAN.

Limitations of SNMP include

▼ It is very limited in scope and does not scale well in large implementations.

■ Its unique messaging structure makes it hard to integrate with other management tools.

■ Polling can cause a large bandwidth overhead in large networks.

▲ It has many vendor-specific extensions to each standard MIB.

NOTE: SNMPv1 and SNMPv2 can coexist by implementing a so-called SNMP Proxy to convert message formats. Many manufacturers of monitoring tools, such as Hewlett-Packard, include such a proxy with their standard offerings.

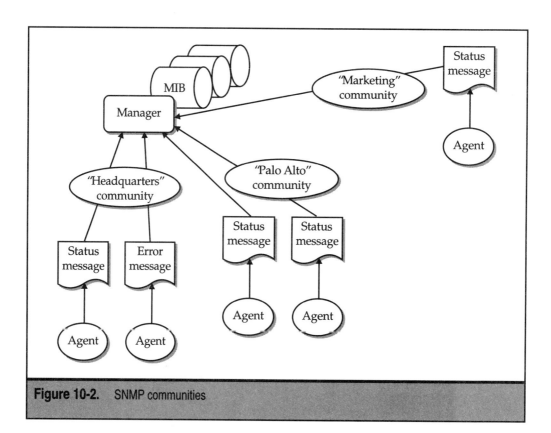

Figure 10-2. SNMP communities

Remote Monitoring Agent (RMON)

Defined in RFC 1757, RMON is an extension of the most current SNMP MIB structure (MIB II) and attempts to address many of its limitations. RMON collects nine types of information:

▼ Host table of all addresses

■ Host statistics

■ Historical data

■ Alarm thresholds

■ Configurable statistics

■ Traffic matrix with all nodes

■ "Host top N" tables

■ Packet capture/protocol analysis

▲ Distributed logging of events

RMON represents the next generation in network monitoring and addresses the need for network planning, fault troubleshooting, and performance tuning better than any other current monitoring implementation. The additional capabilities of RMON change the agent-manager paradigm somewhat. Since sending richer data packets over the network would increase the SNMP demand for bandwidth significantly, implementations of RMON agents are typically "smarter" than their SNMP counterparts. That is, more processing is done on the agent platform, and only aggregated information is sent over the network. The trade-off is that more processing power is needed on the agent platform.

Telecommunication Management Network (TMN)

TMN is mentioned here because it is the "shape of things to come." The OSI standardization process has yielded TMN to address the functional integration issues of network management systems. TMN is described by three architectures: functional, informational, and physical. Each architecture describes how network management systems should function in that area. For example, the physical architecture describes functions for the management of

▼ Configuration

■ Performance

■ Security

■ Accounting

▲ Faults

The primary management protocol used within TMN is the Common Management Information Protocol (CMIP).

CMIP

Similar to RMON, the complexity required of a CMIP agent and the potential amount of information the agent sends over the network are high. It is a common feature in telecommunications equipment specifications, but it is rarely used in practice. It was probably included due to the fact that messages can be sent over an alternate channel from data.

> **NOTE:** SNMP is common in telecommunications equipment, even though the ISO standards say it shouldn't be. For example, the Sonet D1+D2+D3 bytes are an out-of-band communications channel used to communicate control and management information between Sonet equipment. According to the Sonet specifications, CMIP is used over this channel. If you look at actual Sonet networks, the D1+D2+D3 channel is actually carrying either Bellcore's old ASCII command language, or SNMP.

CMIP functions similarly to SNMP, in that it sends an alert if certain thresholds are reached or a fault is detected.

Advantages of CMIP are

▼ Its object-oriented approach is very ordered, making extensions relatively easy to accomplish and to manage.

■ It supports communication between managers as well as managers and agents.

▲ It supplies a standard framework for automation.

Limitations include

▼ It is not widely supported in the data networking world.

■ It is the most complex protocol and puts high demands on the agent platform.

■ Its sheer complexity also means that CMIP implementations from different vendors frequently cannot communicate.

▲ Its extensible messaging architecture can cause high network bandwidth utilization.

SYSTEM MANAGEMENT ENVIRONMENT FOR THE CORPORATE ASP

In a Corporate ASP, where information resources are centralized, the need for tools and procedures that serve to decrease the frequency of unscheduled downtime is more important than ever. The operations necessary to support a Corporate ASP have more in common with the Network Operation Center (NOC) of an Internet Service Provider (ISP) or commercial hosting service than with a traditional, distributed corporate network. It is no longer acceptable for IT staff to discover problems after they occur, as an audit function. They must have tools and procedures in place to perform predictive analysis on potential problems and to isolate and contain problems during the troubleshooting process. An effective SME will address these needs through measurement of the various systems and through the enforcement of service level agreements. The data collected during measurement can be used in troubleshooting and making corrections. For example, if a MetaFrame server crashes due to an application fault, the Citrix RMS package will have recorded which applications were running at the time of the crash. Without this information, it would be challenging to find the exact cause of the crash. An effective SME has the following objectives:

▼ Improving the availability and performance of the Corporate ASP resources.

■ Lowering the cost of IT maintenance and support services.

▲ Providing a service-level view of Corporate ASP resources.

The "people" part of the three Ps are not only the IT staff and the users, but also any group affected by the services being delivered. For many organizations, this means external customers, business partners, and even competitors. The SLAs associated with the services being delivered, and the associated reports, are the "process" part of the three Ps and are collectively the tool that shows whether the above objectives are being met. The "product" consists of all the hardware and software necessary to deliver the information needed to measure the SLAs. Any technology utilized in the SME should meet the following basic requirements:

▼ *Provide a central point of control for managing heterogeneous systems.* A "central point" refers to one tool or collection mechanism used to gather information from all sources. The actual data repository could be distributed to multiple locations where administrative activity takes place.

■ *Allow event management across heterogeneous systems and network devices.* The toolset should support all the common operating system and network hardware platforms and provide enough extensibility for custom interfaces to be configured if necessary.

▲ *Provide service level views of any portion of the infrastructure.* A "service level view" is an aggregation of lower-level events that correlate to show the impact of various failures in terms of an established SLA. A message stating "Server 110 has crashed with an unknown error" has far less meaning than "Application service capacity has decreased by 10 percent" and "Application services for users in the San Antonio region have been interrupted."

To further refine these requirements, more detail on the exact duties to be incorporated in the SME is needed. Defining in specific terms what will be measured and how it will be measured will greatly aid in the selection of the proper technology. We will discuss SME tools later in the chapter.

Configuration Management

Arguably the most common problem in managing distributed computer systems is configuration management. Even companies with very organized IT staffs can have complete chaos on the desktop with regard to which application or application versions are installed and which changes to the operating system are allowed. In a Corporate ASP, the chaos, so to speak, is limited to the data centers, but the need for configuration management is even greater. If a user changes a setting on his PC that causes it to crash, that user experiences unscheduled downtime. If an administrator makes a change to a MetaFrame server that causes it to crash, every user currently logged onto that server experiences unscheduled downtime. An effective SME must have in place controls to restrict and audit changes within the Corporate ASP. A configuration management system should have the following characteristics:

▼   Have in place a system to submit proposed changes for approval.

■   Provide an audit trail for system changes that can be detected (such as changes to the registry or the installation of a new application) and a facility to manually enter information about a change (such as the installation of new hardware).

▲   Provide guidelines for making a change, such as how to save the current state before a change, how to decide if a change is not working, how to back out of a change, and how to use collected information to modify the original change request and resubmit it.

Modern computing environments are far too complex for an automated tool to check and restrict any change. A combination of an effective automated tool and "best practice" procedures for change management are the key to a successful configuration management function.

Security Management

Security management serves to ensure that users only have access to the applications, servers, and other computing resources they are authorized to use. Again, a combination of automated tools and employee policies are called for. The implementation of an Internet firewall to prevent unauthorized external access will do nothing to prevent a disgruntled employee from accessing and publishing confidential information. Only the combination of automated internal system limitations, effective monitoring, published "acceptable use" policies, and committed enforcement of those policies can serve to deter such unforeseen incidents.

Alerting

As we discussed in Chapter 9, it is not enough simply to log attempts to bypass security within the Corporate ASP. An effective SME should include a network management tool that will actively alert the appropriate personnel if a security breach of sufficient severity is detected. For example, say an employee figures out where in the registry his group information is stored and figures out how to change that value to Admin without using User Manager. First of all, the registry should not allow the change to be made by that user because it has been locked against changes by anyone not currently in the Admin group. If the change is somehow made, the system should log an event in the event log. The management agent program on that system should be watching the event log, and it should detect the event and send a "911 page" to the security administrator. Alternatively, the offending user's account could be locked, as shown in Figure 10-3.

IP Address and Host Name Management

In a large enterprise network, managing the identity of each node on the network can be a daunting task. Many network management tools will "autodiscover" nodes on the network, but this task can be laborious and chew up processing and network bandwidth

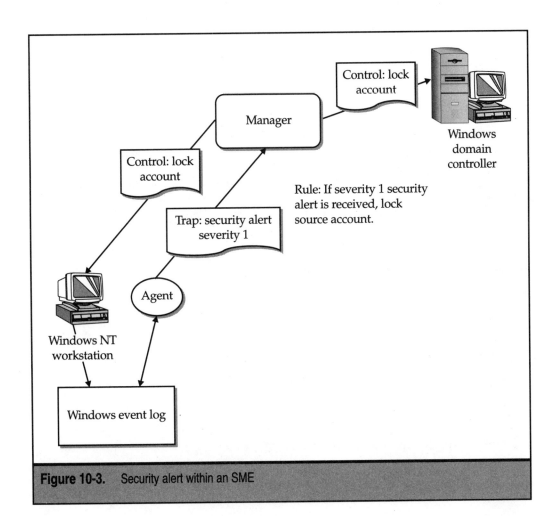

Figure 10-3.   Security alert within an SME

unless the addressing and naming schemes are well ordered. An effective SME will include policies for standard naming practices as well as an efficient IP addressing scheme. Some ideas we have seen effectively used are

▼ Create host names based on department and geographic location, then numerical. (For example, a user's Windows terminal in the Seattle accounting division might have SEA_ACC_16 as a host name.)

■ Create host names incorporating the type of device. (To extend the above example, an LPR printer might be named SEA_ACC_LPR_4, and the above referenced user might be named SEA_ACC_WTM_16.)

▲ Use the second octet of the IP address specific to a division and geographic location, and the third octet specific to the type of device. The final octet would be sequential. (For example, if 50 is the accounting division and 10 represents Windows terminals, a user might have an IP address of 10.50.10.16.) This presumes that there is network address translation (NAT) in place between the internal corporate network and the Internet. It also presumes that division and geographic location are the same; otherwise, routing would become overly complex.

NOTE: Many large organizations use Dynamic Host Control Protocol (DHCP) and Dynamic Domain Name Service (DDNS) to dynamically assign IP addresses and host names, respectively, to network nodes. These services have several advantages, including automated host name standardization and reduction of the number of IP addresses in use at one time by assigning temporary ones from a pool. If you utilize these services in your organization, be aware that it may complicate the SME if the NMS you choose is not compatible with or not aware of these services. An NMS must be able to discover and manage dynamically assigned hosts, or you will have the problem of all of these nodes going unmanaged.

Using Service Level Agreements

As we mentioned earlier, a service level agreement defines the policies and procedures that will be used within the SME. The execution of those policies and procedures will rely in equal parts on automated tools and "acceptable use" policies that the employees within the organization must abide by. Employing SLAs within the SME will have the following effects:

▼ *User expectations will be much closer to the reality of how a particular service is delivered.* Many users see the network as a public utility that has 100 percent uptime. This is a good goal but often is not realistic. Publishing an SLA will show the users what *is* realistic and what their options are if the service delivery doesn't conform to the SLA. After all, very few public utilities can show a track record of sustained 100 percent uptime.

- *IT staff growth will slow.* IT organizations without SLAs tend to spend an inordinate amount of time "fighting fires" because the service personnel don't know where the boundaries are for the service that they are providing. Users don't know where those boundaries are either. The cumulative effect is that users will inevitably try to get as much service as they can, and the service staff will try and satisfy the users by delivering as much as they can. This serves to increase the number of service personnel needed.

▲ *IT service quality will increase.* When the service is well defined and understood by both users and service personnel, the delivery of that service will be more consistently good. This happens for a couple of reasons. First, the people trained to administer the systems have more time to pay attention to their effective management since they spend less time fighting fires. Second, the users' expectations of the service will be more in line with its delivery, which will reduce the number of complaints. A relatively new concept, Application Quality of Service (Application QoS), is a measure of how effectively applications are delivered to the user and thus can be one measure of IT service quality in a Corporate ASP. Application QoS service level views can be found in some of the network management tools we will discuss later in the chapter.

SME Architecture

With what has been defined so far, we can now look in detail at some specific duties covered by an effective SME for the Corporate ASP. The overall architecture should include, at a minimum, the functions described in the following sections for the entire Corporate ASP infrastructure.

Network Discovery

It would be incredibly tedious if you had to enter information about each node before it could be managed. Fortunately, nearly every modern NMS tool provides the ability to actively discover information about nodes on the network. Though most polling is TCP/IP-based, an effective NMS uses a variety of other methods to discover nodes, including NetBIOS and SAP broadcasts. The basic philosophy is "anything that will work." The majority of nodes will respond *somehow*, and those that don't can be handled as an exception and entered manually. Network discovery is a function shared by both the agent and the manager, and is shown in Figure 10-4.

Hardware and Software Inventory

This function is similar to node discovery in design but is much more detailed. Once a node is discovered and is identified as a desktop computer, the discovery process will interrogate the computer to find out about the software and hardware configuration. If fat clients must be used, this can be an invaluable tool to "meter" software—that is, to find

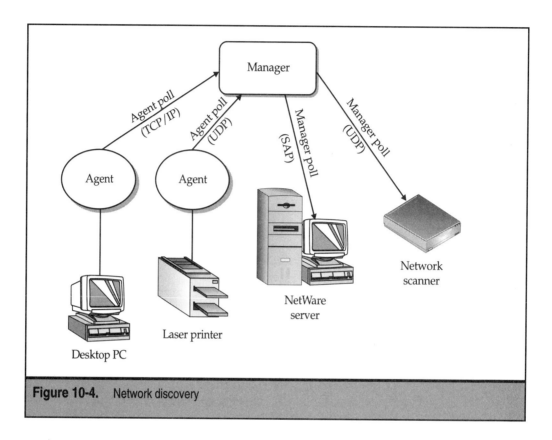

Figure 10-4. Network discovery

out if the number of licenses purchased matches the number of licenses in use. It can also aid in creating inventories of hardware that need to be upgraded for a particular project.

Monitoring and Messaging

The most common agent function is to "watch" the system and look for problems as defined in a rule base. Ideally, this rule base is administered centrally and shared by all similar agents. The agent's job is to send an appropriate message whenever an item in the rule base is triggered, as illustrated in Figure 10-5. These items can consist of both errors, or traps, and collections of information such as traffic thresholds, disk utilization, and log sizes.

With SNMP-based systems, the agent processes events and sends messages with little to no filtering or processing on the local system. This is acceptable because SNMP messages are typically small and not likely to flood the network. In systems with more intelligent agents, where much more detailed information can be collected, the agent has the added task of collating or summarizing the data before sending it to the manager. Otherwise, the added traffic caused by unsummarized messages could cause a bandwidth utilization problem.

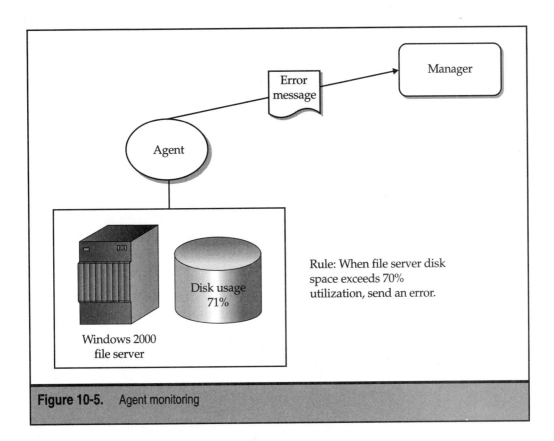

Figure 10-5. Agent monitoring

NOTE: SNMP uses standard UDP ports 161 and 162. Port 162 is reserved for traps only. As a result, it can be made subject to bandwidth utilization rules in a router (queuing) or in a device such as the Packeteer PacketShaper. Similarly, CMIP reserves UDP and TCP ports 163 for the agent and 164 for the manager. These ports are common, but your platform may use different ones.

Management by Exception or Negative Monitoring   This can be a function of an agent or a manager. Sometimes *not* receiving a piece of information from a system is just as critical as receiving one. A system may become nonresponsive without ever sending a trap. In cases like this, it is useful to have a periodic "heartbeat"—a small message that says nothing more than, "I'm here." If the agent or manager does not receive this heartbeat, an alert is generated for follow-up. We have found this type of monitoring to be a crucial part of the SME since not all platforms send alerts when they are supposed to.

Network Monitoring and Tracing   The NETMON program, which ships with versions of NT, can track network traffic at a very detailed level, but its scope is limited to the data streams coming into and going out of the server it is running on or the similar nodes it can recognize. An SME must measure network traffic and problems between any two arbitrary points. It should follow established rules to do detailed monitoring on critical paths, such as between data centers, an Internet router, or between MetaFrame servers and back-end database servers. Thresholds can be established that serve to guarantee acceptable performance and send alerts if those thresholds are reached. In many ways, a Corporate ASP's heavy reliance on network performance makes this one of the most crucial monitoring functions. Effective monitoring in the SME can provide critical data for predictive analysis about when the network is approaching saturation before it ever happens. Figure 10-6 shows how agents at multiple sites can feed data to a centralized manager.

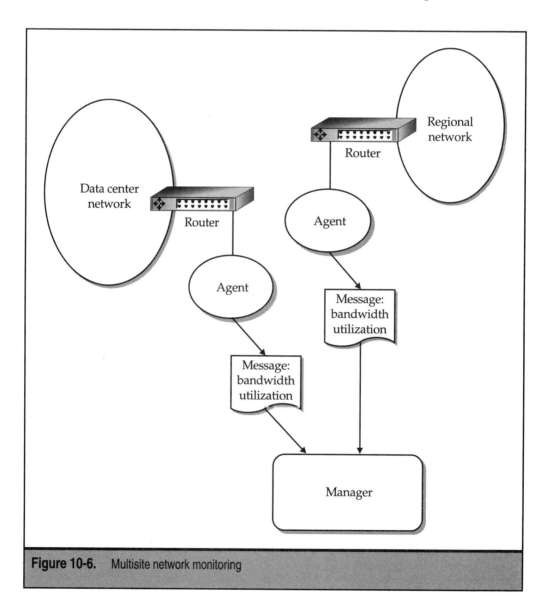

Figure 10-6.   Multisite network monitoring

Remote Diagnostics   By using the MetaFrame shadowing function, administrators can attach to and run a user's session anywhere on the network from a central location. Similarly, an SME should provide the ability to attach to network equipment and perform basic operations, such as uploading and downloading configurations and rebooting. If a particular node cannot be reached, the SME should provide enough data from surrounding nodes to determine what is wrong with the unresponsive equipment.

Data Collection

While monitoring is the primary duty of the agent, data collection is the primary responsibility of the manager. The manager must record all incoming information without filtering, or auditing could be compromised. Relevant information can be easily extracted from the manager's database using query and reporting tools.

Data Collation and Event Correlation

There should be a function above the level of the manager or managers (see Figure 10-7) that collates data from all sources and compares this data with established patterns and rules. This type of collation is called *event correlation*. When the events have been correlated, the result can be expressed in terms of an SLA.

For example, a large enterprise network has a router failure between a large regional office and the main data center. The router sends a trap saying that the memory stack has been corrupted. Immediately after the router goes down, several other traps indicating that the regional office cannot be reached are sent from surrounding nodes at the data center. The manager in the data center collects several hundred messages in only a few minutes. At the point the first critical message is received by the manager, an automatic page is sent to the system administrator on duty. When the system administrator logs on and begins investigating the problem, he sees the hundreds of messages in the database. Fortunately, the event correlation function has categorized the different messages for him. He checks the display of service level views and sees that the SLAs for network connectivity and application services to the regional office are not being met. His reaction to these issues is defined in the SLA for the associated service. Now he can use filtered queries to examine the detailed messages from across the network in order to solve the problem.

> **NOTE:**   Though having service level views into problems is extremely useful, sometimes getting the information as soon as it is sent by an agent is more desirable. It is perfectly acceptable to define certain key events from key agents so that they travel the entire escalation path directly to an administrator for follow-up. It is even possible to define some agents so that they send a page at the same time that a trap is sent across the network. (Sometimes bad news needs to travel faster than good news for an SLA to be met.)

Other SME Functions

A few additional functions common to an SME take on a slightly different role when applied to the Corporate ASP. We discuss these next.

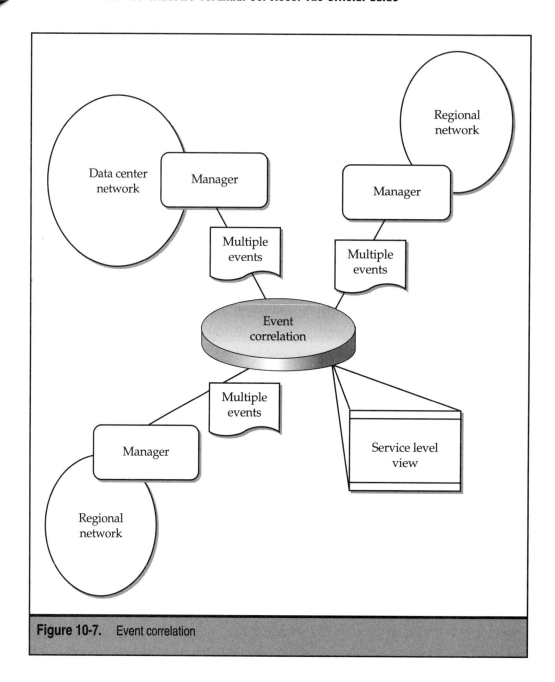

Figure 10-7. Event correlation

Software Distribution/Unattended Install When thinking in terms of a thin client, MetaFrame performs the function of software distribution. There is no reason to distribute an application any further than the server farm when nothing is running on the desktop except the

ICA client. Thus, the need for unattended installation of desktop software loses its importance. Even with a server farm containing 50 servers, it is not that difficult to install applications manually if necessary. This would be a far different proposition with 5000 desktops.

NOTE: Fortunately, it is not necessary to install applications manually on your server farm. We will discuss methods for streamlining this process in Chapter 14.

If you don't have the luxury of taking the entire enterprise to thin-client devices, software distribution and installation is more important and should be considered a critical part of the SME. We will discuss this function as part of the tools discussion later in the chapter. Figure 10-8 shows software distribution in a thin-client network, or Corporate ASP, while Figure 10-9 shows the same function in a traditional distributed, or fat-client, network.

Software Metering   Similarly, software metering becomes far simpler in a Corporate ASP. All the applications are running on the server farm, and administrators can use Citrix RMS to determine which users are running which applications. Furthermore, scripting techniques can be used to assign application access to user groups and to lock down the desktop to the point where users cannot run unauthorized applications. We will show these methods in Chapter 16.

In a distributed client network, software metering becomes much more complex and difficult to manage. Typically, an agent running locally on the desktop takes on the task of conversing with a manager and determining whether a user is authorized to run a particular application. It also takes any punitive measures that are necessary.

Desktop Lockdown   A common function of SME tools is to lock down the desktop so that users cannot install unauthorized applications or make changes to the local operating system that would make it unstable or affect performance. Within the server farm of a Corporate ASP, this restriction happens through appropriate scripting of the user login process, and extra software is not necessary. In a distributed environment, the major SME tools from Microsoft, HP, and other third parties such as Softblox provide this functionality.

Desktop Remote Diagnostics   In the past, remote control tools such as PCAnywhere from Symantec were used to connect to a user's desktop and allow an administrator to see what the user sees. With MetaFrame, the session shadowing feature built into the ICA session protocol provides this functionality from a central location in an efficient manner.

Management Reporting

The parts of the SME architecture presented so far have dealt mainly with collecting information and controlling the environment. Publishing and sharing the collected information and the results of those efforts for control are just as important. The value of management information increases the more it is shared. The IT staff should adopt a policy of "no secrets" and share information in terms of measured SLAs with users and management. That being

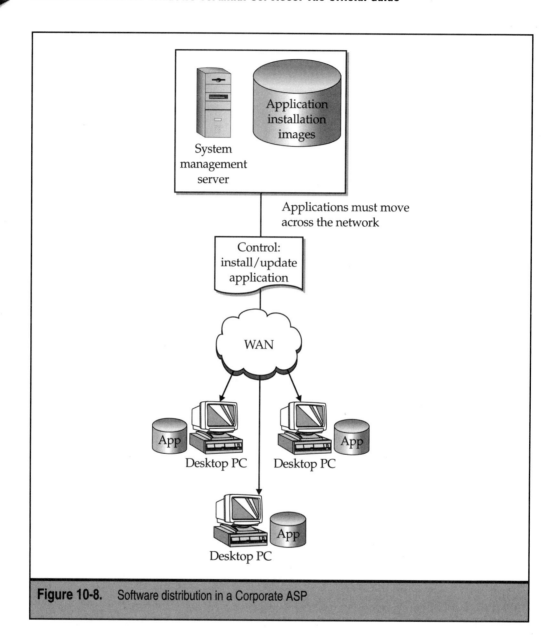

Figure 10-8. Software distribution in a Corporate ASP

said, it is also important to present the information formatted appropriately for the audience. Management typically is most interested in bottom-line information and would not find a detailed network performance graph very useful. A one- or two-page report listing each service level and the key metrics used to show whether that service level is being met would likely be more appropriate. Users make up a diverse group in most large organiza-

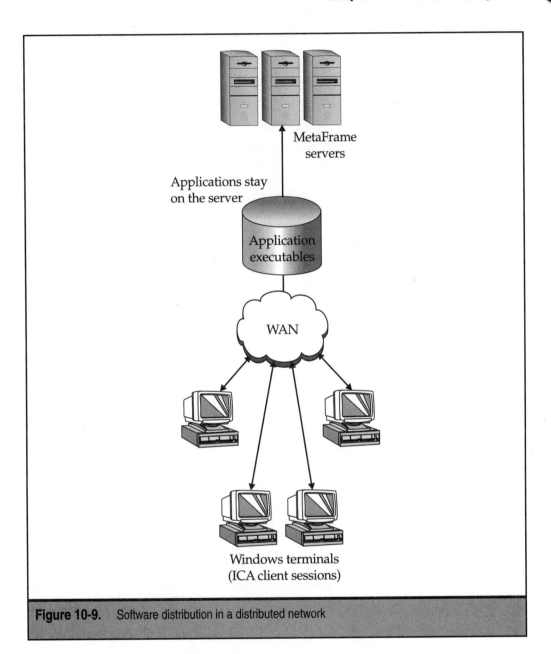

MetaFrame
servers

Applications stay
on the server

Application
executables

WAN

Windows terminals
(ICA client sessions)

Figure 10-9.   Software distribution in a distributed network

tions, making it prudent to err on the side of showing too much information. We have found that publishing the user SLA reports on a corporate intranet is a convenient method since it provides a central location for the information. If a more proactive method for distributing the information is desired, the URL for the intranet page can be e-mailed to the users.

NOTE: The format of your reports should *not* be determined by the capabilities of the measurement and reporting tools. The report should reflect the results of business-driven service level agreements in order to be useful to their recipients. If your SME tools can produce the reports using this format, so much the better. If they cannot, don't be afraid to process some of the reporting data manually until an automated system can be worked out.

Communication Plan   Part of effectively reporting results is to establish a communication plan. A communication plan can also be thought of in this context as a "reporting SLA." You must decide who is to receive the reports, at what frequency, and at what level of detail. If interaction between individuals or groups for review or approval is needed, define how this is going to happen and document it as part of the plan.

On the subject of what to publish, we have found the following reports to be very useful.

Daily Reports   The idea behind a daily report is to provide users and management with a concise view of performance against SLAs. The report should show only key indicators for each SLA. Sometimes also called a *hot sheet*, this report should only be one or two pages in length. Figure 10-10 shows an example of such a report. The ideal delivery mechanism for such a report is on an intranet site or through e-mail.

Periodic Reporting   Periodic reports should have more detail than daily reports. At whatever interval is defined in the communication plan, detailed performance information should be published to users and management. This type of report should show *all* indicators used to measure SLA performance. The data used to generate this type of report is also used for predictive analysis or *trending*. For example, periodic views of disk space utilization will show how fast new disk space is consumed and when new storage should be put online. Trend reports allow you to stay ahead of demand and avoid resource-based outages.

ENTERPRISE SME TOOLS

We consider two classifications of tools in this discussion: system management tools and framework tools. Framework tools are designed to manage virtually all components in the enterprise, including servers, routers, backplanes, and anything with a local management agent. Framework tools can integrate with other tools such as those for help desk call tracking. They are designed to be extensible and often come with built-in scripting capability to allow them to manage equipment that would otherwise go unmanaged. Examples of such tools include HP OpenView, IBM Tivoli, Computer Associates UniCenter TNG, and Cabletron Spectrum. Framework tools can include targeted component programs for doing specific functions, and they often overlap with system management tools. However, they are really intended for large enterprise networks.

System management tools are far more targeted in scope and typically focus on only part of the infrastructure. Examples of such tools are Citrix Resource Management System (RMS) and Microsoft System Management Server (SMS). System management tools can fit

Daily Report									
Network Connectivity	**Target**	**Mon**	**Tues**	**Wed**	**Thurs**	**Fri**	**WTD**	**MTD**	**YTD**
* **Availability**		Fri-Sun	Mon	Tues	Wed	Thurs	WTD	MTD	YTD
Lost User Hours	.5hrs per yr.								
Core Hours (9AM - 8PM)	per user	0	3				3	23	23
All Hours (except maint.)		0	3				3	23	23
Servers - Lost User Hours	15 min/week								
Core Hours (9AM - 8PM)	in hours	0	0				0	0	5
All Other Hours (except maint.)		0	0				0	0	5
Perfect Days (0 Lost Hours)		1	0				1	29	135
* **Usability**									
Total 911 Calls	1 per week	0	0				0	0	45
* **Performance**									
# User sessions monitored	564								
Hours 'Slow'	0	0	0				0	3	7

Figure 10-10. A daily report, or hot sheet

well within a large management framework. Since framework tools often sacrifice deep functionality for broad coverage, the combination of the two is often required. This paradigm of cooperative management tools is covered in depth in the white paper entitled "Complementing Enterprise Management Platforms with Microsoft SMS," available from D. H. Brown Associates (check their Web site). Since this book's focus is on MetaFrame and Terminal Services, we will provide a detailed look at RMS and SMS and leave the evaluation of framework tools to the reader.

Citrix Resource Management Services

RMS is the only management product specifically designed for MetaFrame and Terminal Services. It is an invaluable tool for collecting information in a session-based format on applications in use and system resources consumed. Its key features include audit trail capability, system monitoring, and billing reports.

CAUTION: The installation of RMS replaces several DLLs in the %SystemRoot%\System32 directory and does not reassign the appropriate permissions to the replacement files, leaving users without "read" permissions to them. This will cause problems with other applications that use these DLLs. Therefore, it's necessary to manually reset permissions to the %SystemRoot%\System32 directory.

RMS can be used with most ODBC-compliant databases such as Microsoft SQL Server and Oracle. A wide range of data is captured, including applications used and the time they are in use, as well as logs of connections, disconnections, and duration.

TIP: We recommend creating a file Data Source Name (DSN) (as opposed to a system DSN) because it saves time when setting up multiple servers. The DSN definition file can be placed on a file server and loaded on each MetaFrame server as needed. We also recommend setting the database to purge data automatically every few weeks or so if billing is not being used. If billing is being used, it will purge the data as part of its process.

Many graphs can be created from various system metrics, such as application ranking and system utilization over time. The following is an example:

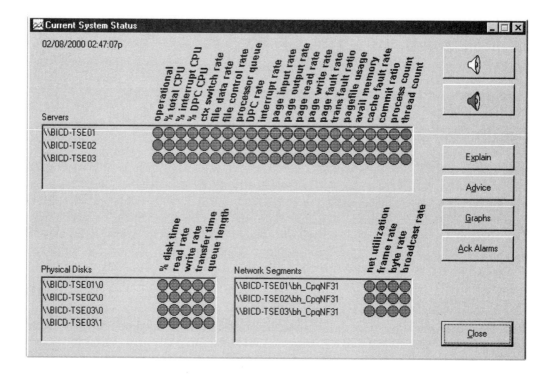

RMS tracks over 30 real-time performance metrics and displays them with green, yellow, or red status indicators. One or multiple servers can be monitored from the same screen. Event thresholds can be defined, and when reached, RMS can send out an SNMP message, page, or e-mail.

CAUTION: The default alarm profile was designed for a small server with a light load. A new profile needs to be created after collecting a baseline of information for a few days or weeks. The period should be long enough to get a representative sample of usage. The problem is that certain counters fluctuate wildly, and unless the alarm profile thresholds are set high enough, RMS will generate alarms too frequently.

If your organization wishes to use a charge-back model, the RMS billing services can be used. Fees can be tracked for connection time and various types of system utilization. Users can be grouped into cost centers for reporting.

When RMS is used in a server farm, the data collection service runs in the background of each MetaFrame server, as shown in Figure 10-11.

Microsoft System Management Server

SMS 2.0, the current version of System Management Server, provides its services through interaction with the underlying Windows Management Instrumentation (WMI), though it does have limited ability to receive and read SNMP and CMIP messages.

Windows Management Instrumentation

WMI is an implementation of the Desktop Management Task Force's (DMTF) Web-Based Enterprise Management (WBEM) initiative. It utilizes the Common Information Model (CIM), also defined by the DMTF, to represent network nodes in an object-oriented fashion.

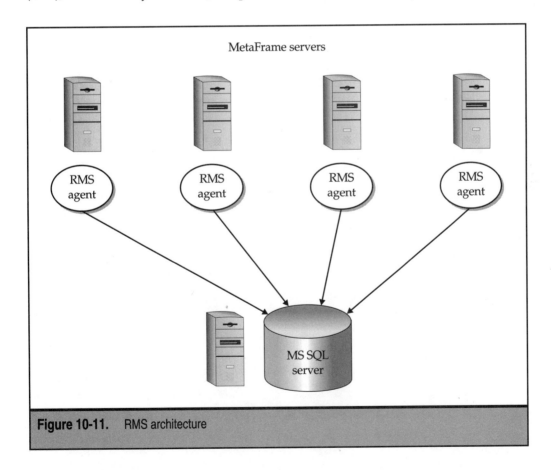

Figure 10-11.   RMS architecture

SMS creates a global view of information resources using information gleaned from the network. It works very well for status reporting and does provide some downstream management in the form of remote control and diagnostics, software inventory, distribution and metering, and hardware inventory.

SMS is part of the Microsoft BackOffice suite of products. It can provide detailed monitoring functions for other members of the BackOffice family and store its accumulated information in a SQL Server database. A small client program acts as the SMS agent and provides the server with relevant statistical and error information.

SMS version 2.0 has been enhanced to support thousands of client nodes on a single server instance, though for purposes of practical deployment, you would at least want to run a cluster of two servers.

Windows 2000 Management

With the advent of Windows 2000, the WMI programs are built into the operating system. Active Directory provides a global view of resources and abstracts the resources available from one server to be equally available to all users in a domain, or across domains. So much of the functionality of SMS is built in, it is unclear to us what role SMS will play as a product in the future. Windows 2000 systems would fit very well into a management framework tool "as is." Until Terminal Services and MetaFrame are able to send session-based statistics to such a framework, however, a tool like RMS will still be necessary.

CHAPTER 11

Choosing the Right Thin Client

In Chapter 8 we discussed remote access strategies and introduced four categories of clients: thin client only, mobile, simple hybrid, and complex hybrid. In this chapter we will delve into more detail on devices and configuration options for each type of client. We will also discuss deployment strategies and installation tips not covered by the standard documentation from the manufacturers. Finally, we will introduce the concept of the *client decision matrix* to help you establish standards for determining the appropriate client for a given user or group.

As we've said before, the thinner the client the better—"better" is defined as the lowest TCO, the easiest management, and the most control. We fully realize that in any given organization, it is not possible to give every user a Windows terminal. A mix of clients is much more typical. As such, it is necessary to explore complementary technologies to make hybrid and mobile users take on as many of the desirable characteristics of the Windows terminal as possible. The idea is to allow the IT staff to mandate a standard image and not allow users to load unauthorized software or to make local configuration changes that can cause the PCs to become unstable. In the context of the discussion on these types of hybrids, we will describe some available technology and techniques to accomplish this.

Much of the information in this chapter is based on our work with ABM Industries. ABM is committed to making all desktops in the company as thin as possible. They allow PCs to be used only if there is a clear business need, based on a specific application requirement. Otherwise, the user is issued a standard Windows terminal.

CLIENT CLASSIFICATIONS

You will recall the table from Chapter 8 in which we classify four categories of clients, shown here as Table 11-1.

We described these client categories in Chapter 8, but we did not go into detail on how to classify a user into a given category. The process of changing a user's desktop environment can be a traumatic experience for the IT staff and the user alike. Unless it is handled correctly, users will feel that something is being taken away from them. They will not see how it benefits themselves or the company. What is needed is a client decision matrix. Defining such a matrix will provide the following benefits:

▼ By applying the same set of criteria to the classification of each user, you will avoid making decisions based on political or nontechnical reasons.

■ When the decision-making process is communicated to the users, they will feel that they are not being singled out, but rather are subject to the same rules as everyone else.

▲ Users can be classified *en masse*, relatively quickly, and decisions about the number of clients of each type, necessary upgrades, or disposition plans can then be made.

Client Category	Remote Applications	Local Applications	Use VPN	Local Peripherals	Local File Sharing
Thin client only	×		−		
Mobile user	×	×	×	−	−
Simple hybrid	×	×	×		
Complex hybrid	×	×	×	×	×

Table 11-1.   Client Categories[1]

CLIENT DECISION MATRIX

Start out with two basic evaluation questions, as described here.

Does the user require access to only ASP-approved applications?

In other words, does the user only need access to the applications already planned for hosting by the Corporate ASP? If so, the categorization of that user can be easily made.

Is the user's existing computer an ASP-compatible PC?

The factors determining whether a user's PC is ASP-compatible are the following:

▼ *The PC is network capable.* The PC has a network interface card (NIC) and the operating system and network client capable of connecting it to the data center.

■ *The PC meets the minimum ASP speed requirement.* The PC is capable of running the ICA client and any required networking or security (VPN) software at an acceptable level of performance.

■ *The PC meets the minimum ASP memory requirements.* As above, the PC contains adequate memory for the job. The mitigating factor here is the price of memory. It is often more economical to put larger amounts of memory in the PC even if all of it won't be used.

---

1   × Indicates that the client has the requirement
     − Indicates that the client *could* have the requirement

▲   *The PC is Y2K capable.* This will be determined by a test to be completed by the deployment teams. Several tools and utilities are available from Microsoft and third parties to test a PC's BIOS for Y2K compatibility.

NOTE: Although it may seem unnecessary to check for Y2K compliance since the deadline is long past, many large companies still have a number of older PCs on the books. If they are to be used, they should be compliant.

Based on the above listed factors, all users fall into four basic categories:

▼   A user who will be a Windows terminal user and whose PC meets the ASP requirements (thin client only).

■   A user who will be a Windows terminal user and whose PC does *not* meet the ASP requirements (thin client only).

■   A user who will *not* be a Windows terminal user and whose PC meets the minimum ASP requirements (hybrid, all types).

▲   A user who will *not* be a Windows terminal user and whose PC does *not* meet the minimum ASP requirements (hybrid, all types).

NOTE: According to Citrix, version 4.21.779 of the ICA client for Windows (32-bit) requires a minimum of

▼   Windows 95, Windows 98, or Windows NT 3.5 or greater

▲   8MB RAM or greater for Windows 95, 16MB RAM or greater for Windows NT 3.51 or 4.0, and an 80386 or higher PC processor

If you intend to run additional applications, you will need to add these resources as well as the necessary resources for whatever base operating system you will be running.

Table 11-2 shows the resulting decision matrix, with deployment plans for each category of user.

NOTE: All users will run an application from the Corporate ASP, and not locally, if it is available. The exception to this rule is the mobile user who must be able to run applications locally.

The client decision matrix can also be expressed graphically, as shown in Figure 11-1.

> *While we still use many hybrids, most of our new PC purchases are in fact Windows terminals. We find that our users actually prefer them to PCs because there is almost nothing that can go wrong with them.*
>
>   —Tom Boyle, Accounting Manager, Researchers

Category	Deployment
Windows terminal user Non-ASP PC	User gets standard Windows terminal. Existing PC goes through disposition (disposal, donation).
Windows terminal user ASP-capable PC	User gets standard Windows terminal. PC goes into pool to be reassigned.
Non-Windows terminal user Non-ASP PC	User gets ASP-capable PC from reassignment pool or new purchase. ICA client is loaded on PC.
Non-Windows terminal user ASP-capable PC	Deployment team loads ICA client on PC. IT staff disables or uninstalls applications from PC that exist in the Corporate ASP environment.

Table 11-2.   User Categories and Deployment of Equipment

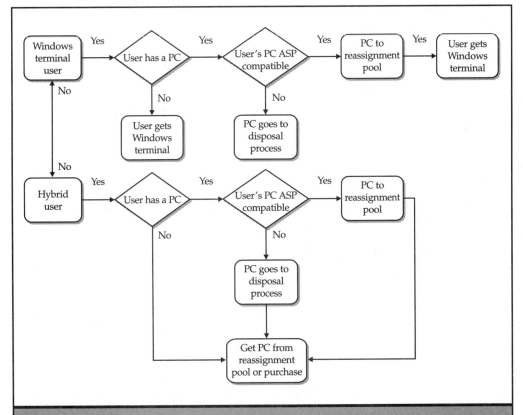

Figure 11-1.   Client decision matrix

PC Disposition

The problem that arises when updating so many desktops is what to do with all the PCs. This can be a significant problem for an organization that is committed to being as thin as possible. PCs that are no longer appropriate for a given user may still have book value, and the company will need to see some kind of return on them. Below are some ideas for dealing with this, based on what we have seen at other companies.

Reassignment Pool

As the client decision matrix above indicates, even if a PC is considered ASP capable, it may be removed from a user's desktop strictly based on the user's need. Why do this? When you examine the total cost of ownership for any desktop PC versus any Windows terminal, the reason becomes clear. Even a new PC with plenty of book value costs far more to support than a Windows terminal. We examined the reasons for this in detail in Chapter 4, but the gist is that a PC is far more prone to spawn a call to the help desk due to an application or operating system problem. Very little can go wrong on a Windows terminal.

The idea behind a reassignment pool is to create a standard for PCs to be used in your organization and assign the PCs to those users with a legitimate need. As PCs come in, they can be evaluated for reuse, rebuilt to the proper specifications, and loaded with a standard image of the operating system and the ICA client. The standard image contains the base operating system in as locked down a state as possible, the ICA client, and whatever other minimal applications are needed. The user's specific application can then be loaded. This sounds like a lot of work, and it is. But it is far less work in the long run to deliver a PC in a known state than to deal with one in an unknown state later in the field. The reassignment pool process is illustrated below:

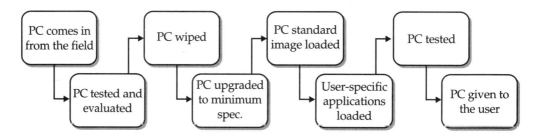

PC Disposal

So far in this chapter we have talked a lot about getting rid of the PCs in your organization. This may or may not be an acceptable approach for your particular situation, but it is an optimal one in terms of TCO. If you are leaning toward keeping your PCs and just running your applications in a Corporate ASP, you should be very clear about your reasons for this since it can have a big impact on the overall value returned by the project. The following are some advantages and limitations for you to consider if you plan to keep most of the PCs in your organization.

The advantages of keeping PCs include

▼   PCs are ubiquitous. It is likely that your organization already has a large number of PCs with residual book value and would like to use them if possible.

■   The skills necessary to support PCs are already available. Supporting other types of devices may take additional training.

▲   PCs are multipurpose platforms that can perform many functions outside those required for the Corporate ASP.

The limitations of using PCs include

▼   Every available public study shows that PCs are significantly more expensive to administer than Windows terminals.

■   PCs have many moving parts that are far more prone to failure than a mostly solid state device.

■   PCs are prone to obsolescence, which also contributes to the high TCO. This problem is somewhat mitigated by using the PC as a thin client, but if you plan to run *any* applications locally, you still must deal with the constant hardware upgrades required when upgrading software.

▲   PCs require additional configuration and possibly additional software to approach the level of security and stability of a Windows terminal. The only way you should consider delivering PCs in your organization is locked down in a manner that prevents users from making detrimental changes to the registry or loading unauthorized software.

HYBRID CLIENTS

Regardless of whether you plan to use PCs in a limited or widespread manner, you will have a certain number of hybrid clients in your network. In Chapter 8 we provided details on the categories of clients, three of which were hybrids. We will summarize them here for purposes of this discussion.

▼   **Simple**   A simple hybrid is a PC running just enough software to interact with the Corporate ASP. This usually means the ICA client and possibly a client for the management software or framework in use at your company. Minimal or even no data is stored locally.

■   **Complex**   The complex hybrid is a PC that not only runs the ICA and management clients, but also local applications. It may also do local file sharing and have local peripherals.

▲ **Mobile** A mobile hybrid is similar to the complex hybrid, but usually has an even greater number of local applications. This is somewhat unavoidable since laptop users need to do work while not connected to the network.

Desktop Lockdown

If you plan to use PCs as clients in your Corporate ASP, you should consider preventing user access to the operating system settings in order to ensure the project's success. According to several studies, including one by the Gartner Group cited in Chapter 4, the PC operating system is the source of most of the support requests from users. Even though the ICA client runs on a variety of operating systems, including MacOS and Linux, we will focus our discussion on Windows clients since they are by far the most common.

Registry Settings

The various Zero Administration Kits (ZAK) published by Microsoft for Windows 95, 98, NT Workstation, NT 4.0 TSE, and Windows 2000 Professional, contain a wealth of information on beneficial changes to the system registry. The strategy is to make changes to *prevent* the following:

▼ **Installing applications** Since the PC should come to users with the necessary local applications installed and the ICA client for running applications from the Corporate ASP, there should be no reason for them to install additional applications. Upgrades or requests for new applications should go through the help desk.

■ **Changing system settings** Even more so than with applications, users should have no reason to change system settings. Setting appearance or screen savers seems innocuous at first, but simple changes like this can generate calls to the help desk when they conflict with the use of a given application. We recommend preventing *any* change to the system settings.

▲ **Recognizing installed hardware** If the client operating system has the ability to recognize new hardware, it can prompt the user to install drivers. The drivers may conflict with other drivers or system libraries and, again, generate calls to the help desk. Even if users know how to install hardware, the standard operating system image should prevent them from doing it. Even plug-and-play devices have no place in the corporate desktop. It may seem simple to plug in a USB device, for example, since it will be automatically recognized, but what guarantee do you have that it will not cause a conflict?

Our impression is that the scripts provided in the ZAKs for client operating systems work well after being customized for the environment. For example, the ZAK for NT Workstation contains command files to install NT in an unattended fashion (cmdlines.txt), make custom registry changes for applications (appcmds.cmd), and set restricted access to the file system (acls.cmd). Be warned, the settings chosen tend to be *very* restricted and may cause problems with specific or custom applications. This is especially true of the ZAK for NT 4.0 TSE. We found the resulting registry and file system settings were so restrictive that very few applications worked well. In some cases the application couldn't even be installed because the installer tried to access protected directories or registry settings. The various client ZAKs are supplied free of charge from Microsoft's Web site and should be evaluated as a way to restrict user activities on the desktop. At the very least they can provide you with a platform from which to build your own custom set of scripts.

Third-Party Software

Providers of software for restricting user activities present a friendlier interface than REGEDT32 and can even track and roll back changes. One such tool with which we are familiar is AppScape/Manage from SoftBlox. One of a suite of AppScape applications, AppScape/Manage can make user profile, policy, or direct registry changes to a workstation based on a centralized rules database. The rules can be assigned by user, group, application, or even time schedule. Though the result of the application's activity is to change the registry on the client—something you can do manually—it does it in a way that is easy to manage and scales across a large organization. It also does it without the overhead of a full-blown system management server or management framework application, as presented in Chapter 10. Perhaps most importantly, the application is compatible with both distributed and centralized application hosting. It can impose the same restrictions on an application hosted from a MetaFrame server farm as it can on one running on a local desktop. Figure 11-2 provides a simplified view of how AppScape/Manage functions.

Software Distribution and MetaFrame

One question we are asked quite often in planning sessions for large Corporate ASP projects is this: "Server-based computing is great, but how are we going to distribute software?" The question usually comes from a company that already has an infrastructure in place to distribute and install application binaries to the desktop. We discussed the difference between server-based and distributed application hosting in Chapter 10. We bring it up again here to emphasize the fact that running MetaFrame largely mitigates the need for an automated software distribution system. Applications can be made a part of the standard image that is used to build a server. New applications are made part of a new image, after testing, and that image is then loaded on the server. Using this method, application conflicts are nearly eliminated in the production environment. We will go into more detail on the tools and methodologies to accomplish this in Chapter 14.

The ICA Client for Hybrids

In Chapter 2 we presented the details of the ICA client, including Program Neighborhood. In this section we will focus on the differences between the various hybrid clients you might consider.

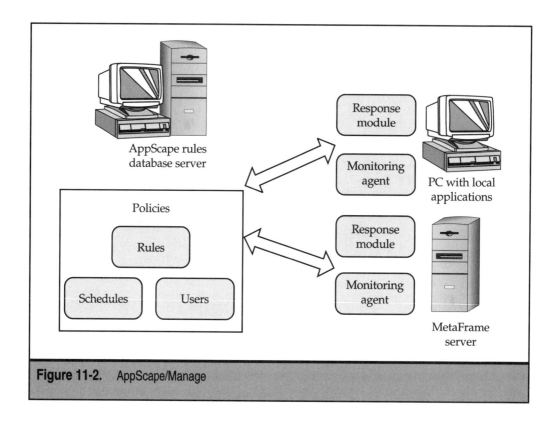

Figure 11-2.   AppScape/Manage

Significant Platform Differences

For purposes of this discussion, the 32-bit ICA client for Windows will be considered the functional base for all other client versions. Other clients typically contain fewer features or work slightly differently. If you intend to allow mixed desktops or standardize on a client operating system other than Windows, this section will aid in your planning.

▼ **Macintosh**   The ICA client for the MacOS does not offer the functionality of Program Neighborhood but does allow you to connect to a server or to a published application using the Client Editor. The Mac client supports local printers but has no support for other peripherals or remapping of local ports. It also does not support audio. Like all non-Windows ICA clients, the Mac client provides access to Windows key sequences through local key combinations.

■ **LINUX/UNIX**   This client offers the most complete functionality for any non-Windows ICA client, but not all features are supported on all flavors of UNIX. Check your platform against the feature list on the Citrix Web site for specific support. The Program Neighborhood is not supported, but virtually all other functions are present, with the following exceptions: COM port remapping currently only works on LINUX. Printer remapping works, but note that the local printer should be set up as a "binary pass-through" printer. This means that the local system should not attempt to format or filter the contents of the print job, only pass it through to the printer; otherwise, conflicts could arise between the formatting done by the MetaFrame server or NT print server and the local UNIX or LINUX system. Windows key sequences are provided through local key combinations that are designed not to conflict with the ALT key sequences normally reserved for the X Window System, though these can be reprogrammed if desired.

- ■ **Java** The Java client features are difficult to generalize because different platforms support different features. Java on Windows, for example, is very similar to the normal Windows client.

- ▲ **Web client (NFuse)** NFuse is the latest Web-based client from Citrix. Formerly project "Charlotte," this client represents a quantum leap in functionality over the older Web client. We will address NFuse in its own section later in this chapter.

Local Peripherals

The thing to keep in mind about local peripherals is that the data stream used by the device must travel over the network from the server farm to the client device. This can cause excessive bandwidth utilization unless measures are taken to control it. We discuss methods for accomplishing this with printers in Chapter 17.

NOTE: The ICA COM and LPT port redirection allows a variety of local peripherals to be used, but many require tweaking because the ports do not work exactly as they would if they were local ports. For example, we have found that excessive latency is an issue that can crop up when there is a long-distance WAN between the client and the server. In Chapter 15 we will provide some deployment tips for the Palm Pilot HotSync feature that will illustrate how to work around some of the limitations of port redirection.

WINDOWS TERMINALS (THIN CLIENT ONLY)

Windows terminals are available from a variety of manufacturers, and they are variations on the same theme. Most Windows terminals have no moving parts, except perhaps for a fan, and all the operating system and client software is stored in hardware. They typically run Windows CE, Embedded Windows CE, or LINUX as the operating system, and implementations of other software, such as the network protocol stack, are proprietary to the device. This and the fact that they have different CPUs and graphics capabilities contribute to the performance differences between the devices. In no particular order, some of the devices we've tested and used in production are the Maxspeed Maxterm, Wyse WinTerm, Boundless Capio, and IBM NetStation. We've tested other brands from HP, IBM, and other major companies, but they are actually OEM versions of one of these other terminals. Here is what a basic Windows terminal setup looks like:

Models are available that offer clients in addition to the ICA or RDP client necessary to connect to the MetaFrame server or Terminal Services. Many also contain X Window System software or legacy terminal emulation clients, such as IBM 3270 and telnet. Local browsing is also available with either proprietary browsers or OEM versions of Netscape Navigator or Microsoft Internet Explorer. There can be a significant advantage in cost and ease of use in having multiple clients in the device when integrating the terminal into an environment where legacy functions as well as the new features of the Corporate ASP must be supported. This is a key differentiator among products. Figure 11-3 shows a Windows terminal with a variety of local, embedded software.

NOTE: Windows terminals with local LPR/LPD software are beginning to appear on the market. This software enables a server to act as a network print server, just as an HP JetDirect or Intel NetPort does. If you intend to implement network printing, as we discuss in Chapter 17, this feature can save the complexity and expense of deploying a separate network print server device.

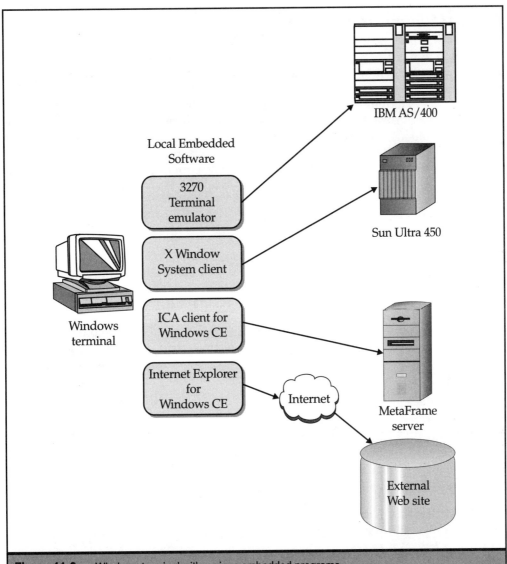

Local Embedded
Software

3270
Terminal
emulator

X Window
System client

ICA client for
Windows CE

Internet Explorer
for
Windows CE

Windows
terminal

IBM AS/400

Sun Ultra 450

Internet

MetaFrame
server

External
Web site

Figure 11-3. Windows terminal with various embedded programs

Windows Terminal Management

Another key differentiator that is not always clear when evaluating different Windows terminals is in how they are managed. Windows terminal management falls into two general categories: self-booting, as shown in Figure 11-4, and remote booting, as shown in Figure 11-5.

One group of terminals are self-booting and have the ability to receive partial downloads of software. The other group requires an external boot and can only receive a complete software image. The external boot can be from a flash card, another terminal on the LAN with a flash card, or a local management server with the boot image. Table 11-3 summarizes these differences. We recommend self-booting terminals for the following reasons:

▼ They are generally less expensive to deploy because they do not require an external boot device.

■ They are easier to manage because the software can be updated incrementally.

▲ They utilize less network bandwidth because they do not require the download of the boot image every time they reboot, and they do not require the entire firmware image to be downloaded every time they are upgraded.

Another area of difference in management is in how the terminals are monitored. Some manufacturers supply their own management software that can monitor the terminals and report errors as well as provide software download functions. Other manufacturers supply tools or scripts to integrate the terminals into a management framework, such as HP OpenView. Still others provide almost nothing in the way of monitoring. Manufacturer-supplied software can work as long as it is scalable enough to handle the

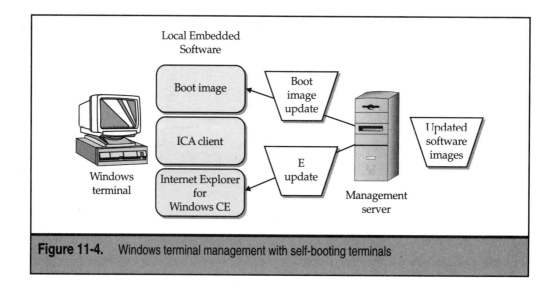

Figure 11-4. Windows terminal management with self-booting terminals

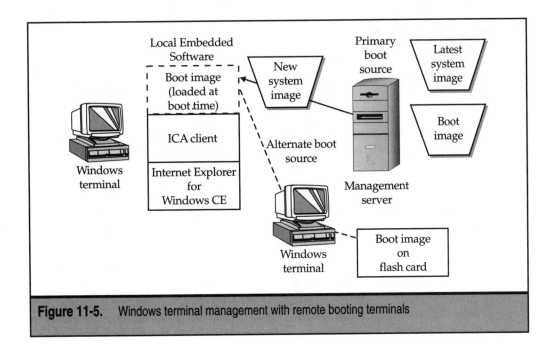

Figure 11-5. Windows terminal management with remote booting terminals

network infrastructure in your company. If it can't, you should consider a solution that integrates into a management framework. At the very least the terminal should send SNMP messages and supply a MIB for your management software.

Feature	Self-Booting	Remote Booting
Update a single application	×	
Update entire firmware image	×	−
Boot from local firmware	×	
Boot from remote boot image	×	−

Table 11-3. Windows Terminal Management Differences[2]

---

2 × Indicates that the feature is present
 − Indicates that the feature *may* be present, depending on the exact model

Functional Differences

The ICA client for Windows CE supports all of the functions of the client for Windows, as does the client for LINUX on Windows terminals. The differences are due to the fact that one runs on a PC and one runs on an embedded device, or Windows terminal. Keep the following differences in mind when planning your deployment:

▼ **Client software updates** Upgrading the embedded software can be a challenge since it is in firmware, depending on the particular brand. Some manufacturers offer tools to make this relatively easy, and with others you are on your own. Upgrades are typically done via a download or by loading a flash card through a PC card slot. Some terminals support the MetaFrame Auto Update feature, which can be a big time saver when a new version of the ICA client needs to be deployed. At the very least, the terminal should support a centralized method for downloading software, either operating system images or applications, and rebooting the terminal without user intervention.

■ **Local browsing** Embedded browsers are limited with regard to storing local data. They can allow a limited bookmark list and, of course, do not allow downloads.

■ **Java** Stand-alone Java applications (those that do not require a browser to run) require a Java Virtual Machine (JVM) to be installed on the Windows terminal firmware. The JVM must be the correct version, and the Java application must also be loaded into firmware in order to execute.

■ **Autologin** Similar to the Task Station function in the ZAK for Windows 95 and 98, Autologin can be used when you want to present a limited number of choices to the user when logging in. When Autologin is enabled, the user is limited to one terminal session, either a desktop or a specific, published application. If you want the user to have access to multiple published applications at login, Autologin should be disabled.

■ **Connection security** Some terminals have SecureICA built in to provide connection security, and some have IPSec or other more generic VPN security protocols. Pay attention to which security method is supplied in the terminal so you can effectively integrate it into the overall network architecture.

▲ **Configuration security lockout** Whatever configuration settings the terminal offers, it is very important that it also provide the ability to prevent users from changing them once established. If the configuration cannot be protected, you run the risk of configuration-related support calls driving up the TCO.

CITRIX NFUSE

NFuse evolved from the Citrix ALE technology used to deploy applications to Web browser clients. NFuse combines the Web-publishing features of the ALE client with many of the management features of Program Neighborhood, including the ability to dynamically publish a new application to a logged-on user. Users just click the Refresh button on their browser, and the new application icon appears on the desktop within the browser. An example of an NFuse session from the Citrix Web site is shown below:

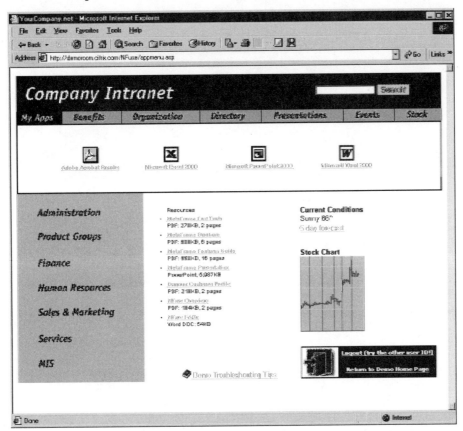

NFuse is a three-tier solution that includes a Citrix server component, a Web server component, and an ICA client component with the Web browser. NFuse doesn't replace the ICA client; rather, it interoperates with it to provide the capabilities native to the operating system platform. NFuse extends the publishing capabilities of the ALE client by providing a means to integrate applications from other sources, such as MetaFrame for UNIX, and by allowing applications and access to be customized by users. Figure 11-6 shows the NFuse application publishing architecture.

NFuse supports the features of Program Neighborhood within the context of the browser. Instead of pushing an application icon to a PC's desktop using the Seamless Windows feature, the icon would appear on the desktop within the browser.

A subtle but important advance offered by NFuse is that the Web components can be configured to resolve application names to IP addresses, eliminating the need for the ICA client to use the UDP-based ICA browser. UDP access can then be eliminated from the

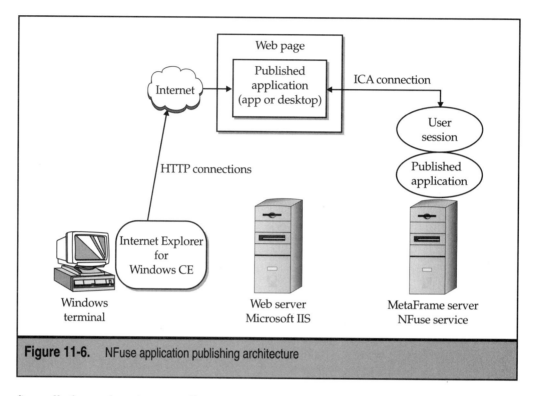

Figure 11-6. NFuse application publishing architecture

firewall, thus enhancing overall security. NFuse is also compatible with Secure Sockets Layer (SSL) and other industry-standard encryption and authentication mechanisms.

Finally, NFuse offers both client and server scripting capabilities to run external programs, customize the user session, or integrate with other Web technologies such as COM, Java Server Pages (JSP), or Active Server Pages (ASP).

Three components are required to run NFuse: a MetaFrame server running the NFuse Service, a supported Web server (Microsoft IIS, Apache, or Netscape Server), and an ICA client with a supported Web browser.

OTHER CLIENTS

Thus far we have discussed PCs and Windows terminals as the most common devices used to access the MetaFrame server farm. Since the ICA protocol has been ported to Windows CE, LINUX, and other platforms in progress like PalmOS, the server farm can be accessed from a variety of client devices, as shown in Figure 11-7. Though it is clearly not practical to run a Windows desktop on the tiny 320×260 screens of some of these de-

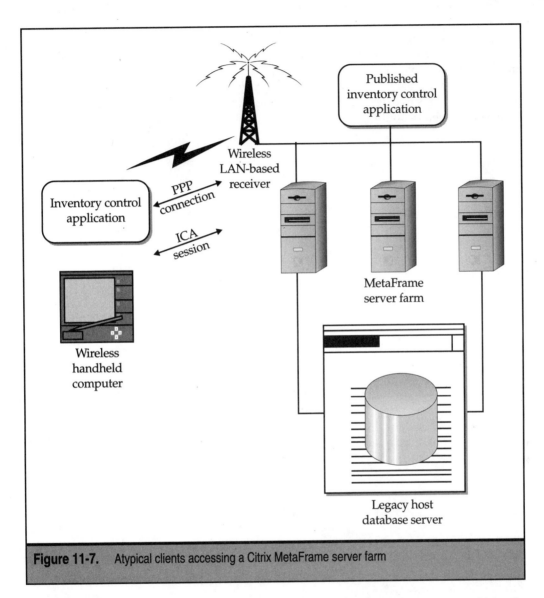

Published
inventory control
application

Wireless
LAN-based
receiver

PPP
connection

Inventory control
application

ICA
session

Wireless
handheld
computer

MetaFrame
server farm

Legacy host
database server

Figure 11-7. Atypical clients accessing a Citrix MetaFrame server farm

vices, it can be very useful to run a small, published application. Imagine a warehouse in which each stockperson had a Palm Pilot with wireless networking and a physical inventory application that fed directly into the corporate inventory database. Perhaps your company employs a large number of hourly employees who could use a Windows terminal touch screen to punch in and out of a virtual time-clock application. Using an example of sales force automation, perhaps a field salesperson could use his handheld computer to wirelessly connect to the home office and check stock before filling an order, or check and approve special bulk pricing for a special customer.

Once your company has committed to deploying server-based computing, there are innumerable ways to extend your information infrastructure to remote employees, customers, and even the public.

PART III

Implementing a Corporate ASP Solution

CHAPTER 12

Project Managing the Corporate ASP Implementation

A fter the project plan design is complete, the implementation begins. Project management is a key element in successful execution. This chapter, while not attempting an in-depth discussion of such a large topic, covers certain elements crucial to a Corporate ASP implementation, including executive sponsorship, project manager authority, stakeholder buy-in, project reporting and tracking, task assignment, project change control, scope creep, and timeline management. We also show examples of how tools such as service level agreements and help desk software help manage changes to the environment to enhance benefits to management and end users. Finally, we talk about the needs for the support environment both during and after the implementation.

STEPS IN PROJECT MANAGEMENT

We continue to emphasize that the process of converting to a Corporate ASP is a huge undertaking. When implemented properly, the results can be spectacular. But changing a major paradigm involves technical challenges on a large scale, along with the inevitable cultural and political issues. As with project planning, a major Corporate ASP conversion should utilize a detailed implementation plan with clearly defined roles and responsibilities for participants. Here are the major steps in in project managing a Corporate ASP implementation:

- ▼ Identify a project manager
- ■ Put together a project management team
- ■ Assess your organization
- ■ Create a project implementation plan
- ■ Prepare for implementation
- ■ Start the project
- ■ Provide user support
- ▲ Measure success

Identify a Project Manager

A dedicated and competent project manager is essential to a successful implementation. There should be only one manager for the overall project, and that person should have both the responsibility and the authority to keep it on track. Communication is key. The project manager needs to make sure that both good and bad news travel fast.

CAUTION: According to a four-year study by The Standish Group International of 23,000 IT projects, only 24 percent of projects are successful (ComputerWorld: Online News, 06/18/98). The larger the project, the less chance it has for success. Migrating to a server-based computing environment is a major IT project. Give this project the full attention of your IT staff, and do not run it in parallel with other IT projects.

Put Together a Project Management Team

Although one project manager should have overall authority, it is often a good idea to appoint a team to assist with the project implementation plan. An IT manager and business manager are two key roles to help resolve problems and keep the project on track. Someone from procurement should be on the team along with experts in the various technologies that will be utilized. The executive sponsor should at least be associated with the team in order to lend his or her authority. It is important to include employees who are involved in the areas of the company that will be affected by the project. This provides two benefits: First, the team benefits from their expertise in the area in question. Second, the employees get to be involved in the change, and the hope is that they will be less resistant to it.

Assess Your Organization

The feasibility committee should have discussed organizational issues such as culture and politics. The project management team must take a hard look at the organization's status in order to make any required changes before the implementation.

IT Staff Assessment

Is your IT staff ready for server-based computing? They should be early users of the technology during the pilot phase and be convinced enough about the benefits so that they are advocates themselves.

   If your staff is used to operating in the ad hoc manner normally associated with network administration, they need to understand that server-based computing requires the rigors of mainframe shop methodology, including limited access, change control, and planning and procedures. Put the controls into place to ensure that your IT staff will help, and not hinder, your Corporate ASP implementation. If certain staff members are unwilling or unable to support the project, reassign them to another support area.

Skill Levels   Does your IT staff have the necessary skills to install and manage a Corporate ASP environment? They must have NT expertise and experience, including the ability to do registry edits. Scripting capabilities are also a requirement for large implementations. A router expert must be available to manage large wide area networks. Make sure a skills assessment is part of the initial project planning, and plan to obtain training or additional personnel to cover the skill areas that are lacking.

IT Training   What training is appropriate for your staff prior to implementation? A Windows Terminal Services class and MetaFrame class are strongly recommended. If most of the work will eventually be done internally, an advanced MetaFrame course is recommended as well.

Cultural Assessment

How will server-based computing be received in your organization? The project manager should modify the design plan, where necessary, in order to ensure that the organization's cultural norms will not be a roadblock to success.

Working Environment   In an environment where users commonly run similar applications and work as part of a unit, such as a bank, a Corporate ASP is likely to be very well accepted. Users will immediately appreciate the higher reliability and increased flexibility that a Corporate ASP enables. An engineering firm, on the other hand, with independent users accustomed to purchasing and loading their own software, will likely run into severe resistance if they try to force employees to operate only in the thin-client mode.

Remote Users   Remote users tend to be more accepting of a Corporate ASP in general because they receive access to the corporate databases and networking services they need in order to do their jobs more productively. It is crucial to provide both adequate and redundant bandwidth to prevent problems with reliability and performance that can quickly turn remote users hostile toward server-based computing.

Managers   Managers, in general, tend to resist the idea of a Corporate ASP until they actually use one; then they quickly become converts. They are usually impressed by the increased productivity they witness among their employees, as well as the capability for their employees to work from home. The project management team can help foster enthusiasm among the managers for the Corporate ASP by showing them when the reduced corporate IT costs should be reflected on departmental bottom lines.

Political Assessment

Politics usually comes down to allocation of resources, money, power, or all three. How will the Corporate ASP project impact the profit-and-loss statements of the different departments involved? What happens to a regional IT division when the computing model switches to a centralized Corporate ASP? An astute project manager should be aware of these issues in order to take actions to minimize potential disruption to the project. Some scenarios and resolutions are described later in this chapter under the section "Stakeholder Buy-In."

Controlling Project Change

Scope creep is highly likely in a large Corporate ASP deployment. Users will often insist on accessing applications that were never included in the plan. They may insist that the project's viability in terms of meeting established performance and uptime SLAs as well as projected ROI targets hinges on these additions. The ability to rapidly deploy an application in a server-based computing environment is one of its strongest selling features, yet the application implementation is a detailed process requiring extensive preliminary testing. A change control process is essential for keeping the Corporate ASP project on track.

Change Control Process

Change requests in server-based computing range from minor, such as a user's request to continue accessing his local C: drive, to major, such as a demand to host a DOS application that is known to have problems running under NT. Because you are implementing a central processing environment, all changes to the design plan should be approved by the project manager and recorded. Changes that will affect the project budget or schedule may require additional approval.

Consider, for example, a request to add an application to the Corporate ASP during the server farm rollout phase. This requires that the rollout be postponed while the new application is thoroughly tested in conjunction with the other hosted applications. All affected parties and stakeholders require notification of the rollout postponement. Once the new configuration proves stable, a new server image disk needs to be created, and the server rollout begins again. Since this seemingly innocuous change can have broad implications, not only for the project time and budget but also for many users, it is probably appropriate to have the business manager and IT manager sign off on the change along with the project manager.

Change Control Guidelines

Changes should only be made when required by stakeholders or when circumstances cause a significant deviation from the project design plan. The reasons for all changes should be documented along with any changes to the schedule or budget that result. We provide suggestions for testing procedures and change control in Chapter 15.

Conflict Resolution

Conflicts are inevitable in a large project. A Corporate ASP will demand IT resources that are already likely to be in short supply. Some users will be frustrated at a perceived loss of personal flexibility. Many users consider themselves IT experts and will disagree with the technology or the way it is deployed. Conflicts should be quickly referred to the project manager for resolution. Approaches to solving the problem include

- ▼ **Ignoring the conflict**   Sometimes it is better for the project manager to simply ignore the conflict if it is not likely to have a big impact on the project or is likely to resolve itself.

- ■ **Breaking up the fight**   This approach is useful if both parties are stuck in an argument. The project manager can interfere in order to take the energy out of the argument.

- ■ **Compromising**   Compromise may be required at times, such as allowing a user who was scheduled to be entirely thin client to run in hybrid mode. Keep in mind, though, that any nonstandard implementations detract from overall project efficiency and organizational computing effectiveness.

- ■ **Confronting**   This approach involves getting all parties together to work out their problem in an environment promoting conflict resolution.

- ▲ **Forcing a resolution**   Sometimes the project manager must use his or her authority or the authority of the IT manager or the business manager to mandate a resolution. This method should be used as a last resort.

CREATE A PROJECT IMPLEMENTATION PLAN

A Corporate ASP project starts with a project definition document that states the goals, scope, roles, risks, success criteria, and project milestones. The project design plan then lays out the specifics of the major Corporate ASP components. A project implementation plan is the third step in this process. While the project planning document provides a roadmap for implementation, the project implementation document covers the project management aspects of migrating to a Corporate ASP.

Project Constraints

The project implementation plan must be created with regard to time, money, and people resources. Identifying these constraints will help determine how to apply corporate resources to the project. The following table indicates that management has decreed the Corporate ASP implementation be done quickly:

	Most Constrained	Moderately Constrained	Least Constrained
Time	X		
Budget		X	
People			X

Time is the most important element, while human resources are less constrained. Since time has the least flexibility, internal resources need to be diverted to the Corporate ASP project, while funds also should be used to bring in outside consultants and perhaps implementers.

Another constraint, often inevitable in a server-based computing implementation, is user satisfaction. Users can make or break a Corporate ASP implementation, and they are likely to resist the change if no preparatory work is done. It is therefore essential for the project manager to keep the users in mind when designing the project plan. The objective should be both to minimize disruption in user operations and to generate enthusiasm among users for the new server-based computing paradigm.

Defining Your Plan

Your plan will take shape as you define the major elements of implementation. Consider timing, key milestones, and budget, and communicate the plan to everyone involved.

Project Timing

Time is invariably the most constrained resource, and it is often not the most visible to participants. Clearly communicating the timing of the project's phases will help to convey the appropriate level of urgency.

Key Milestones

Identifying key milestones enables participants to easily measure progress. Stakeholders should be involved in defining milestones. The milestones can provide a chance for the team to pause and ask, "Where are we and how far do we have to go?" They can also provide an opportunity for positive communication to the stakeholders and the company at large when they are reached on time and on budget.

Estimated Project Costs and Cash Flows

Defining the broad budget for the project conveys the significance of the resources being expended. It also enables appropriate stakeholders to measure expenditures against it.

Implementation Strategy

There are certainly many different ways to implement a Corporate ASP. Providing a summary of your strategic approach will help eliminate confusion and uncertainty.

Upside and Downside Potentials

Any new IT project has risks as well as potential rewards that should be identified. Upside potential in this environment can include many unexpected results such as increased sharing of best practices among previously isolated corporate divisions.

Likely Points of Resistance with Strategies for Overcoming Them

Potential technical, financial, and political roadblocks should be listed along with approaches for resolving them. For instance, if employees in a particular remote office are determined to keep their own file server and LAN, a strategy for a phased implementation might be appropriate in their case.

Technical Challenges

Terminal Services is an evolving technology. Technical challenges will be present in every large enterprise rollout. Identify any problem areas that could jeopardize customer satisfaction with the project. Set action plans for resolving technical challenges. For instance, if a 16-bit application is quirky on NT, it should either not be hosted, or it should be isolated on a separate server or server farm and accessed from the main production farm via pass-through.

Identify Unresolved Design Issues

Some design parameters will remain vague prior to the project implementation. These questionable areas should be referred to experts to help eliminate any confusion or uncertainty. For instance, when designing a Network-Attached Storage solution, we bring in the manufacturer in order to size the unit appropriately.

Define Project Roles

Define the roles and responsibilities of staff members during the project implementation. Some of the roles you might need to define include project management assistance, teams for implementing server-based computing migration, procurement, wide area network implementation, bandwidth management facilitation, and storage consolidation. If using an integrator or consultants, define their roles, responsibilities, and tasks as well. These may be limited to consulting, or they may include project management or hands-on implementation.

Manage the Tasks

Projects are broken down by tasks that can be defined as a unit of work that is important to the project completion. Tasks can also include related subtasks. Assign managers to each task and set performance SLAs. For instance, one task may be to order an ATM link to the data center by a certain date. The SLA may be to order all data lines and equipment on or before the due date.

Develop a Work Breakdown Structure (WBS)

Tasks need to be organized into logical milestones, sequenced, assigned, associated with necessary resources for their completion, and communicated to team members. The WBS is a standard method of organizing project tasks in one of two formats: either an organizational chart with each box listing tasks, as shown in Figure 12-1, or an outline WBS, as shown in Figure 12-2. The outline form tends to work better for projects with many layers of tasks. Both techniques show the different levels that are required and include subprojects or milestones, major tasks, subtasks, and minor tasks.

Develop a Project Schedule

The key is to find ways to schedule parallel activities in order to complete the project within the allotted time frame. Building a Corporate ASP is somewhat akin to a construction project. The most common scheduling technique in this case is the critical path method (CPM), which uses historical data to estimate task durations.

Coordinate Tasks

In a large enterprise project, different elements of the organization will require coordination between them. Assign specific managers, as necessary, to ensure this coordination takes place. For each task it should be clear who has ultimate responsibility for its completion. Though several people may contribute, only one person can be responsible. This is the person the project manager will rely on for communication on the status of that task.

Define Project Documentation

Detail how the project will be documented for IT staff, managers, and end users. This documentation should conform to the communication plan described later in this chapter. It

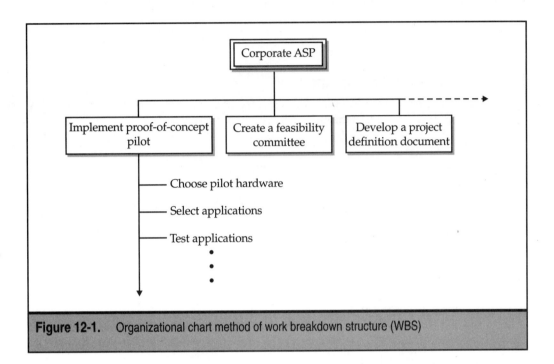

Figure 12-1. Organizational chart method of work breakdown structure (WBS)

Implement a proof-of-concept pilot

1. Choose pilot platform
    1.1 Configure MetaFrame server
    1.2 Identify back-end file server and network backbone
    1.3 Configure MetaFrame server on network backbone
    1.4 Set up Windows terminal

2. Select applications
    2.1 Select representative samples
    2.2 Eliminate duplications
    2.3 Develop selection criteria

3. Test applications
    3.1 Create test lists
    3.2 Test components
    3.3 Test functions
        3.3.1 Test specific functions
        3.3.2 Test generic functions

Figure 12-2. Outline method of work breakdown structure (WBS)

should include documentation about the data center configuration as well as about equipment and data lines at each remote office.

Establish an Internal Marketing Plan

Formulate an internal marketing plan, as described in Chapter 1. Identify points of resistance in the organization and establish action plans for overcoming them.

PREPARING FOR IMPLEMENTATION

Organizational preparation for the project implementation should start with a word from the executive sponsor. Surveys can then be distributed in order to more precisely define the project tasks. Ordering lines and equipment is the next step in preparing for deployment of implementation teams.

Executive Sponsorship

In Chapter 4 we discussed the importance of obtaining executive sponsorship for the project. Inevitably, conflicts will arise in terms of resource availability, and even outright opposition to the project can surface. The executive sponsor must be able to step in and resolve these issues in order to keep the project on track.

Stakeholder Buy-In

Users and department heads must buy into the goals of the Corporate ASP project and understand its powerful positive implications for the organization. Chapter 4 discussed some of the internal marketing techniques that should be an ongoing part of the project implementation preparation. In addition, steps can be taken during this phase to smooth the way for implementation.

Management Meetings

Hold group meetings with managers from different departments or divisions. Give them a chance to air their concerns and perspectives. Emphasize the benefits to the entire organization of implementing a Corporate ASP. Stress that, although they may perceive that their employees have less control over their environment within a Corporate ASP, managers actually can now devote their time to their business rather than to managing their computing infrastructure.

While the goal for these meetings should be to provide a forum for managers to ask questions and air concerns, it should be clear that the project is going to take place. It is important to emphasize the positive benefits and to develop a spirit of cooperation and enthusiasm.

Entitlement Issues

Department staff may feel that because the money for the new system is coming out of their budget, they are entitled to their own servers. Employees may feel that they are entitled to their own PCs to run in fat-client mode. These perceptions need to be changed. Users need to understand the benefits that server-based computing provides to the organization as a whole. Some former capabilities, such as the ability to operate CD-ROMs, might be limited if they run in pure thin-client mode. On the other hand, users will gain computing advantages such as the ability to see their desktop from any PC or Windows terminal. Another powerful user incentive is the potential for telecommuting. Many users discover that they prefer a server-based computing environment because they experience increased reliability and performance. They also do not have to worry about causing problems by inadvertently changing their desktop. A properly configured Corporate ASP will limit their ability to delete icons or INI files or create other mischief.

Problems with Perception of Central IT

If the corporate network has a history of performance or reliability problems, department managers are going to be very reluctant to put all of their eggs in the corporate data center basket. To reassure them, explain the elaborate steps that are being taken to upgrade the network infrastructure and describe the policies and procedures that will result in a far more reliable network environment. Explaining the redundancy and disaster recovery capabilities of the Corporate ASP can help further mitigate any fears.

It is often productive to define an SLA in cooperation with the department managers in order to clarify expectations. If IT fails to meet the SLAs, the managers should have recourse, such as credits in a bill-back situation.

Budgetary Concerns

A Corporate ASP, by nature, means centralized computing. Individual computing fiefdoms will disappear. You may wish to implement a billing model that charges departments for actual system usage in order to alleviate fears of arbitrary budgetary impacts. An example of a Corporate ASP subscription-billing model is presented in Appendix B.

Disposition Issues

If the project design plan calls for replacing certain PCs with Windows terminals, department heads may not be happy about the impact on their budgets. During this preliminary stage, discuss disposition issues and how they will impact book value. If possible, incorporate charitable deductions in order to lower the burden. Chapter 18 covers disposition of old equipment in more detail.

Announce the Project to the Organization

Announcement of the project should incorporate sponsorship statements from key corporate executives and give all employees a clear vision of what is coming, what it will look like, what to expect, how it will benefit them and the organization, and how it will affect their daily work. At ABM Industries, the vice president of Electronic Services created a "Back to Business" video that emphasized the Corporate ASP's ability to eliminate much of the futzing that PCs tend to foster. By mixing humor with a description of benefits, ABM created an extremely effective marketing tool.

Executive Mandate

Although we put a lot of emphasis on selling the project to users, an executive mandate is still required. A formal letter should go out from a high-ranking executive, preferably the CEO, telling all managers and users that a Corporate ASP will be taking place. It should emphasize that this is an organizational initiative and that everyone is expected to make it work.

Surveys

The distributed nature of a PC-based computing environment means that many organizations, particularly larger ones, do not have a good grasp of the exact equipment and applications run by users. This is especially the case with remote offices or where managers have had the authority to purchase their own hardware and software. Creating surveys for both users and remote offices will enable the project manager to assess the true environmental condition and make appropriate ordering decisions. Even organizations with an existing network management system (NMS) in place often find that the inventory capabilities are not accurate enough to rely upon. In such cases, the inventory report from the NMS can be used as a basis for the survey, and then the user representative for the site can be asked to correct the report.

WAN Survey   If the existing WAN infrastructure does not provide adequate connectivity to all remote offices under Terminal Services, a site survey should be completed at least 60 days before the installation in order to allow for bandwidth upgrades. This timing is crucial due to the inevitable delays caused by the local and national exchange carriers. A user count and printer count (including types of printers) will help determine the type and size of bandwidth connection to each site. Including the address and zip code helps the WAN team decide whether certain technologies, such as a DSL connection, are viable options.

LAN Survey   Make sure the LANs in the selected remote offices are ready for a transition to server-based computing. For example, daisy-chained hubs that might have worked in a PC-based computing environment can kill server-based computing sessions. This is because users often have at least one more Ethernet hop to the data center server backbone that may be enough to exceed the IEEE Ethernet standard. Another example is a poorly performing server that may have problems when the implementation team tries to copy data from it. Such problems can also give the field deployment teams a "heads up" for what equipment they might need in order to migrate local desktops and servers. For example, if the LAN backbone has problems, the field technician might plan on bringing his own hub to connect the server to the deployment PC with a Jaz drive to pull the data from the server.

Application Survey   Despite the best efforts of the planning committee and despite any company policies that are created regarding the Corporate ASP, some users in remote offices will nearly always have local applications that they insist are required for them to do their job. It is far better to learn about these applications ahead of time in order to make appropriate accommodations for them as part of the implementation design process.

> *NOTE:*   In the infrastructure assessment phase described in Chapter 4, we discussed the importance of learning everything about an application before hosting it via server-based computing. This rule must still be followed even in the sometimes-unwieldy arena of remote office migration. We learned this the hard way. In one implementation, we came across many custom-written applications utilized in remote offices. Most were written in Microsoft Access and easily migrated to server-based computing. At one site, however, we migrated an application to the corporate data center and were told it no longer worked. After extensive debugging, we asked the user for more information. The user confessed, "The application never really worked, but I thought that it might work once you moved it."

Printer Survey   An accurate count of the number and type of printers and print servers will help determine the type and size of connection required to each remote site. It is also important to identify any printers required apart from users' default printers. Printers that are not going to be supported as part of the Corporate ASP should be eliminated. Otherwise, they are bound to cause problems and may even lead to Terminal Server blue screens. The implementation team can bring new printers with them to replace the nonsupported units.

IP Address Survey   It is important that the IP addresses are managed across the enterprise. Whether this is done manually or by using management software, the point is that the lack of a workable scheme can cause a lot of system administration overhead and confusion. If such a system is not in place before the Corporate ASP project, consider using the project as an excuse to put one in place. This is covered in more detail in Chapter 18.

PC Survey   Determining the condition of each user's PC may aid a decision about whether to replace it with a Windows terminal. The decision matrix for this analysis was presented in Chapter 11. Create criteria for determining whether a PC is compatible with the Corporate ASP. This might include having an existing network interface card, having an existing desired local operating system, or being within a certain number of years old.

User Survey   Complete a user survey at least two weeks before installation to allow enough time to order and ship required equipment as well as to set up the user accounts. This survey should cover all relevant information about each user, including whether the user requires access to only Corporate ASP–approved applications and whether the user's existing machine meets Corporate ASP standards. The survey should also measure users' satisfaction with the existing computing environment in order to establish a baseline for judging the success of the Corporate ASP once implemented.

Order Equipment

Equipment must be ordered for the Corporate ASP implementation as well as for any upgrades to the existing infrastructure.

Equipment Purchase Lead Time

The surveys will show the existing type and condition of the equipment at headquarters and at remote offices. Order new equipment required for the installation a minimum of two weeks beforehand. This is necessary in order to stage the equipment prior to a large rollout. If you are rolling out 2500 Windows terminals to remote offices, for example, the logistics become daunting in terms of delivery confirmation, asset tracking, and shipping.

Asset Tracking System

It is important to have some type of asset tracking system in place in order to record the equipment ordered and where it is deployed. If your organization does not yet utilize one, the Corporate ASP project is a good time to start. Ideally, the system would be accessible by the field deployment technicians so that as they deploy each user, they can enter that user's equipment information directly into the system.

Remote Office LANs

Remote offices may have inadequate hubs, or even lack a network altogether. Order any hubs, switches, network interface cards, print servers, and cabling to be put in place ahead of the migration team. If you are ordering for many remote offices, order four weeks ahead of time to allow for staging and shipping.

Personnel Resources

Necessary personnel must be identified for both the upgrades and for the actual project implementation. For instance, in Chapter 18 we describe the composition of the implementation teams. Decisions need to be made about the number of technicians required to migrate users at headquarters and at all remote offices. While the actual migration time for a user in a remote office can often be kept down to about an hour, travel and logistics make a four-hour average estimate more realistic. The time, money, and resource constraints will determine how many technicians are assigned to the project.

Infrastructure Upgrades

In Chapter 4, we discussed the importance of doing an in-depth infrastructure assessment. The project management team needs to review that assessment again, factoring in the results from the surveys. Deficiencies in the network infrastructure that were tolerated in a PC-based computing environment are likely to be disastrous once users depend upon the corporate data center for all of their processing. Any infrastructure deficiencies must be resolved prior to the Corporate ASP migration. Both equipment and human resources must be secured for the upgrades and for the project implementation.

Data Center Upgrade

The data center often requires upgrades such as implementing a gigabit switching solution or a new firewall to enable secure Internet access. These projects require planning and implementation before the enterprise rollout.

Network Backbone Upgrade

One way to think of the MetaFrame server farm is as if it were actually hundreds or thousands of PCs. The backbone infrastructure, therefore, needs to be both very fast and reliable. Examine the existing backbone carefully using a network analysis tool, if necessary, in order to spot any deficiencies. Any problems must be fixed before the beta implementation.

Network Operating System Upgrades

Some organizations take the opportunity during a Corporate ASP upgrade to either upgrade or migrate their network operating systems. This should be treated as a separate subproject, and the migration or upgrade should be completed before the server-based computing enterprise rollout—ideally, before the beta. Attempting to do this project concurrently with a Corporate ASP implementation leaves far too many variables to troubleshoot in the event of problems. It can have another undesirable side effect: users who experience problems related to the change in operating system or infrastructure may think that the Terminal Services or MetaFrame software is responsible.

> We found that Citrix can easily become a lightning rod for blame. If, during a thin-client migration, users suffer from infrastructure or other problems completely unrelated to Citrix, they still are likely to think it is the cause. Perhaps this is just a case of transference, but the remedy is clearly to minimize potential problems by not trying to do other IT projects concurrent with a Citrix implementation.
>
> —Sean Finley,
> Assistant VP and Deputy Director of Electronic Services,
> ABM Industries

Data Center Storage

The project design planning document will include the selected storage medium at the data center, whether NAS, SAN, or general-purpose file servers. The surveys will show the amount of hard drive storage currently required by users and by remote office servers, enabling ordering of the appropriate storage for the data center. Of course, user and remote office storage requirements for Corporate ASP–hosted applications can be ignored. Significant economies of scale are obtained by centralizing all data storage instead of requiring a surplus for each user. As a result, the requirement for central storage will be less than the cumulative totals of existing distributed hard drives.

Wide Area Network Upgrades

The surveys will show the number of users per remote office, enabling decisions about how much bandwidth to supply. Some organizations will install their first WAN as part of the Corporate ASP. Others will upgrade their existing system, while still other organizations will add redundancy. In an ideal world, this implementation should be completed well before the Corporate ASP rollout, but in practice it is often not possible. Allow 60 days for ordering and installing data connectivity lines or upgrades whether using a frame relay connection, a leased line, DSL, cable, or ISDN. Do not rely on your telecommunications company; follow up to make sure they are staying on schedule. Test the lines once they are in place before sending an implementation team to a remote office. Also test redundancy, even if this is just a dial-up to the data center.

STARTING THE PROJECT

Establish a regular meeting schedule to review milestones and budgets. Work on the exception principle. Focus on what is not going according to plan. Fix it fast. Be prepared to add resources in order to meet the schedule. Issue a weekly list of targets and key troubleshooting assignments.

Maintain Quality and Accountability

Make careful and informed decisions about key equipment purchases or leases. System reliability should be a prime consideration in any ASP project. Unreliable system elements can jeopardize overall system performance. Monitor all subcontractors and vendors to ensure that they are staying on target with their assigned tasks. Move quickly to correct targets that aren't being met.

Project Budget

It will be difficult to accurately estimate the budget required for a large Corporate ASP deployment because of the tremendous number of variables involved. Fortunately, server-based computing tends to save organizations so much money that even significant budget overruns would compare favorably with the PC-based computing alternative. Appendix A shows how to prepare a financial analysis of server-based computing versus PC-based computing.

Budget Contingencies

Management will want to see a budget and expect the project manager to hold to it. This is why it is important to build in contingencies for travel, cost overruns, and unexpected problems. It will sometimes be necessary to spend more than planned in order to achieve the desired results. It is also wiser to deviate from the budget in order to circumvent a problem before it becomes a crisis. Again, the vast savings enabled by the overall project should make this the wise alternative.

Budget Monitoring

Tying the budget to the project milestones is a good method for monitoring progress and keeping expenditures on track. It also can provide stakeholders with a clearer example of benefits. For instance, a project milestone might be replacing 500 old PCs with new Windows terminals. The Windows terminals cost $500 each, while purchasing 500 new PCs would cost $1000 each (including the extra installation PCs require). Offset the project budget at this point against the cost of purchasing new PCs and the cost of upgrading those new PCs in two or three years.

Communication Plan

It is essential to communicate about the project with users. We recommend over-communicating about the project migration parameters and expectations. Regular e-mails are certainly valuable. Prepare a list of frequently asked questions (FAQs) to help inform users about their new environment.

Issue Regular Project Updates

Relay the key achievements since the last update. Talk about the project status and where the project is going in the next period. Discuss what is required to ensure success. Part of the established communication plan should be to report on the project's progress to key stakeholders.

Handling Complaints

Enhance the help desk department as explained later in the chapter. Enlist the aid of regional managers, if necessary, to help set user expectations during the implementation. Managing user expectations is something that should be done continuously during the process. This will decrease the number of calls to the help desk.

Publish Deployment News

Use e-mail or an intranet to publish ongoing news about the migration. Let users know of potential bottlenecks or other problems before they take place. Share the wins as well. Publish user testimonials about the migration.

Success Metrics

Establish success metrics ahead of time and measure results against them. For instance, an SLA might be to enable users in remote offices to access their data within 24 hours of migrating to server-based computing. Measure and report the actual results of how long it takes users to gain access.

Deployment Guide

Creating a deployment guide for implementation teams is discussed in Chapter 18. In some organizations, users will be doing their own client setup. In these cases, the deployment guide can be of great assistance to them as well.

Use Measurement Tools at Milestones

Survey users at project milestones to measure their perceptions versus expectations. For instance, a project milestone might be to have all small remote offices online as Corporate ASP users. Surveying users can reveal any problems with performance or reliability, which will enable adjustments to the design plan before proceeding to the next milestone.

CUSTOMER CARE

Providing adequate user support is essential to a successful Corporate ASP implementation. Even though users may experience initial problems, they will have much better attitudes if they can receive prompt and competent help.

Enhance the Current Support Structure

Part of the infrastructure assessment described in Chapter 4 is an analysis of the organization's help desk methodology and escalation procedures. Once the Corporate ASP is in place and stabilized, help desk requirements will fall. Not only does Citrix MetaFrame enable superior troubleshooting through shadowing capabilities, but also the number of problems will fall because the processing takes place centrally. During the implementation phase, however, the frequency of support requests will increase. In addition to the confusion and problems of implementing a new computing infrastructure, the help desk will, in effect, be supporting two environments during the transition. Be prepared to supplement the help desk with additional personnel during this period.

Establish Service Level Agreements (SLAs)

Establish and manage SLAs for the help desk during project implementation. Ensure that users receive the help they need to get them through the transition without frustration. Refer to Chapter 10 for tips on formulating SLAs.

Support Processes

Cover every shift and every time zone. A process should be in place, and the appropriate personnel identified, for escalating problems that are not resolved by the first-line support people in an acceptable time frame.

Virtual Call Center   Create a virtual call center whereby any member of the implementation team can assist if required. Use help desk software to enable this collaboration among different individuals from different areas working on the same user problem. ABM Industries, for instance, wrote custom software in Lotus Notes that tracks every help desk request from initiation of the call to ticket closing. Any implementation team member can sort by user or by problem in order to more quickly troubleshoot and resolve the issue.

Triage Process   Have a swat team available to go on-site to handle particularly tricky problems that surface during the implementation. Consider using outside experts for the swat team that have a high level of experience with MetaFrame, Windows, and networking.

Status Reporting

The help desk should work in conjunction with the purchasing department and the project management team to give continuous status updates. These updates can take place through phone calls, e-mail, and an intranet. They should reflect user attitudes about the migration process in order for adjustments to be made.

POSTDEPLOYMENT MANAGEMENT

The last stage of the Corporate ASP rollout is to measure its success. Performance should be compared with both expectations and established success metrics. The results should be reported to both management and users.

Measure User Satisfaction

One method for measuring user satisfaction is to send out surveys asking users to grade the project on various criteria, including performance, reliability, how well it meets expectations, ease of use, training, and implementation. Compare the user satisfaction results with those obtained in surveys taken before the Corporate ASP deployment. You can also use the surveys to find out what other attributes users would like.

Rate Project Milestones

Were project milestones reached on time? For instance, one milestone may have been to migrate all headquarters users within 60 days of the project start. Record and publish the results.

Update the Budget

Measure actual expenditures against the budget. Update the financial feasibility model with the project costs as well as with costs as they accrue going forward. This will enable a return on investment (ROI) to be calculated for the project over a three-to-five-year period.

Measure Corporate ASP Benefits

Everyone in an organization has something to sell. The champions of the Corporate ASP concept had to sell management and users on their vision. It doesn't hurt to periodically publish a list of Corporate ASP–enabled benefits. For instance, IT could point out the ability of the company to assimilate an acquired company much more quickly than would have been possible with a PC-based computing architecture.

CAUSES OF PROJECT FAILURE

Examples of server-based computing failures are, unfortunately, not in short supply. They often occur when an organization implements a server-based computing pilot or beta with a goal toward enterprise expansion, but then forgoes the rollout. Many organizations approach a Terminal Services implementation from a PC networking perspective. Although it is sometimes possible to deploy a successful NT or Novell network without extensive planning and piloting, this will rarely work in an enterprise server-based computing deployment. Think of installing a Corporate ASP as replacing employees' PCs with a mainframe. Both cultural and political aspects are added to the technical challenges to make unplanned deployment nearly a guarantee of failure.

Skipping Project Planning Steps

Many organizations skip the pilot, project definition, and infrastructure assessment steps and go straight to project planning, or even a beta. This is bound to be troublesome if not an outright failure.

Lack of a Proof-of-Concept Pilot Program

The proof-of-concept pilot is essential for testing all applications under server-based computing before implementation. Proceeding immediately to a production pilot or beta can leave users frustrated with application performance or reliability or both. Even a small number of frustrated users can provide the type of negative feedback that will quell any further server-based computing expansion.

Lack of a Project Definition Document

Some internal evangelists might be sold on the idea of a Corporate ASP and persuade management to implement one without enough thought to the objectives, scope, roles, risks, and success criteria. Without a project definition document, the planning, project management, and implementation teams have no touchstone with which to keep the project on track.

Lack of an Infrastructure Assessment

Project design committees often like to skip the infrastructure assessment step and jump straight to planning. This tends to be the most enjoyable part of the project, when participants contribute their knowledge to build a solution. Unfortunately, it is virtually impossible to create an optimally effective plan without a detailed infrastructure assessment. Additionally, infrastructure flaws that are tolerated under distributed computing are likely to be amplified in a server-based computing environment. When users become completely dependent upon a central server farm for executing their applications, the infrastructure has to be extremely solid.

Inadequate Planning

Sometimes, even large server-based computing implementations are performed without knowledge of basic tools and methodologies that can dramatically facilitate deployment. We once had lunch with the architects of a 5000-seat MetaFrame project who were complaining about bandwidth issues. It turned out that they had never even heard of the bandwidth management tools discussed in Chapter 6. Using bandwidth management from the start would have prevented their problems.

EXECUTING THE PROJECT DESIGN PLAN

Good project management enables proper execution of the project design plan. The remainder of Part III covers the other aspects necessary to successful deployment of a Corporate ASP.

In Chapter 13, we discuss installation and configuration of server-based computing. The chapter contains hands-on installation checklists, as well as tips and tricks related to creating a stable installation. We include information on major known problems and work-arounds as of the time of writing. Also included are details on installation options that users need to consider and their ramifications on the resulting server function.

In Chapter 14, we cover automation using scripting technology, such as WSH, ADAI, and Kixtart, and its application to user scripts, system administrator scripts, and server and application installation automation. We cover Citrix Installation Management Services (IMS), the server imaging utilities Ghost and ImageCast, along with ways to automate the distribution and installation of the images.

Chapter 15 covers the building of the Corporate ASP platform. Topics include application and desktop publishing and building a server farm.

In Chapter 16, we discuss user profiles, policies, and procedures. This chapter covers the differences between the NT mandatory and roaming profiles and the pros and cons of each. You learn the general methodology for creating scripts to lock down desktops while still enabling user flexibility in selecting default drives and printers. Discussion of policies and procedures includes local drive access, application selection, support policies, and recommendations for migrating to a standard application suite.

Chapter 17 covers one of the most challenging parts of a Corporate ASP architecture—printing. You learn how to centralize all printing on a central print server and how to use scripting to automate the configuration for specific remote offices. Topics include different printing alternatives (including UNIX, LINUX, and NT), redundancy, disaster recovery, remote office printing, and local PC or Windows terminal printing.

In Chapter 18, we discuss the methodologies to help ensure a successful migration from a PC-based computing environment to a server-based computing environment. Topics include techniques for data consolidation from both PCs and remote office servers, replacement of older PCs with Windows terminals, strategies for minimizing downtime, and creation of a virtual call center to handle incoming support requests. We include strategies for implementing pilots, betas, rollouts, and postproduction practices.

CHAPTER 13

Installation and Configuration of MetaFrame and Terminal Services

As we've established thus far in this book, it takes far more to make a Corporate ASP succeed than just following the installation manuals for the software. In this chapter we will discuss the installation and configuration tips, tricks, and techniques we have learned in our years of working with the server-based computing products from Citrix and Microsoft. We recommend that you thoroughly familiarize yourself with the installation and administration books for those products. It is not our intention to reprint those works, but to augment them. We will provide installation steps in the form of checklists. Our checklists will include not only the steps to get the software installed and configured, but also explanations of pertinent options and their effect, indications where additional configuration may be required, information on hot fixes and service packs, and general information we think you will need in order to deploy the technology effectively.

We will cover the deployment of MetaFrame using both Windows NT 4.0 Server, Terminal Server Edition, and Windows 2000 Advanced Server as the base operating system. Client configuration is discussed in Chapter 15 as it relates to options for publishing applications and optimizing Program Neighborhood. We will assume, for this chapter, that you are familiar with the basics of installing and configuring, and with administering Windows NT.

Although we give you detailed, step-by-step instructions, we are not advocating that you build every server from scratch. Rather, we expect you to use this information to create a standard image, as described in Chapter 14. This standard image will be accessed from an application deployment server or CD-ROM to automatically build a server in your server farm.

CAUTION: Many of the suggestions and recommendations in this chapter involve making changes directly to the Registry. We recommend you adhere to the following safety guidelines before making any of these changes:

▼ Become familiar with REGEDT32.

■ *Always* make backups to the key you are changing with the REGEDT32 "save key" feature. This will allow you to go back to a previous state and possibly save hours of rebuilding as you create your first "gold image."

▲ Never change the Registry on a production server or on a server you can't otherwise afford to lose.

We have tested these changes on several production systems, but it isn't possible to test them on all hardware platforms and configuration settings. Also, the settings may work slightly differently on Windows 2000 since much of the operating system kernel has changed. As such, we recommend strongly that you follow the pilot and beta methodology and thoroughly test these changes before relying on them in a production Corporate ASP.

CONFIGURATION STANDARDS

In addition to reviewing the hardware compatibility list (HCL) from Microsoft, we have found that certain hardware features are desirable if you are to get the most from your Corporate ASP.

Server Hardware

We strongly recommend against running your Corporate ASP on clone, or no-name, servers. Even if you are thoroughly familiar with the internal components of the clone server, you will only be asking for trouble. Choose a hardware manufacturer that offers priority on-site service or at least overnight parts shipment and has a competent technical support staff. Ideally, that support staff is familiar with Terminal Services and MetaFrame. The extra cost of buying brand-name hardware will be more than offset by the savings in time and headaches in dealing with failures.

NOTE: It is important to keep each server in the farm as similar as possible, because variations in hardware can lead to the need for additional images or scripting work. (This process is discussed in Chapter 14.)

Central Processing Units

The number of processors in a server, along with memory, will most influence the number of users that can run applications on that server. It might be tempting to use 4-, 16-, or even 32-processor servers. Since these servers will be running in a load-balanced farm, the number of users per server must be balanced against the number of servers in the farm. It is better for fault tolerance, but may be more expensive, to have more servers with fewer users per server. This way if a server crashes, the least number of users are affected. We have found a good compromise to be a two-processor server with 2–4GB of RAM (depending on the version of Windows). You will get good performance with 30–50 users, depending on the application suite, and still not have "too many" users per server.

Memory

Using error correcting, parity memory will reduce the number of page faults and the resulting server crashes. If you intend to use Windows NT, Terminal Server Edition, keep in mind that only about 2GB of memory will be used no matter how much you have in the server. We have tested this and attempted to optimize memory utilization on a wide variety of server hardware. Windows 2000 does not have this restriction.

Network Interface Cards

We recommend only using the "server" type—that is, those NICs that have their own processor and can off-load the job of handling network traffic from the CPU. We also recommend using two NICs that can take over for each other in the event of failure. This feature is often called *teaming* and can reduce the amount of downtime due to link loss or

NIC failure. Many NICs have the ability to autonegotiate between full- and half-duplex settings. We have seen problems with this in production, especially when mixing NICs and network backbone equipment from different vendors. This is why we recommend picking a setting, preferably full duplex, and standardizing it on all equipment.

Server Hard Drives

Though a RAID setup for your Corporate ASP servers is desirable, there is no need to go overboard. Remember, you will not be storing data on these servers, only programs. You will also have a standard image of the server on a CD-ROM or deployment host, making rebuilding very simple. As such, it is not necessary to build an array optimized for data protection. A simple mirrored drive pair (RAID-1) is more than sufficient and will yield good read performance for loading programs.

CAUTION: Imaging products, such as Ghost and ImageCast, have limited support for hardware-based RAID systems. If you intend to use a product of this type, check with the manufacturer for support of your hardware before proceeding. This will be discussed in more detail in Chapter 14.

Disk Partitioning and Swap Files   As we mentioned in Chapter 7, you should only use NTFS on your MetaFrame servers. We also recommend the following guidelines for building your disk partitions and swap files:

▼ **Windows NT Server 4.0, Terminal Server Edition (TSE)**   Windows NT only supports a system drive of 4GB. On the first physical drive, we recommend a 4GB partition for the C: drive and the rest of the space for the D: drive since it can be larger. We also recommend a second physical drive for the swap file, called Y: in Figure 13-1. Windows NT also limits the swap file to 4GB. This works out fine since you can only use a little over 2GB of RAM and we recommend making the swap file twice the size of the RAM. With our recommendation of using disk mirroring, this configuration calls for four physical drives.

NOTE: Unless the swap file is on the C: drive, it is not possible to capture a dump file resulting from a server crash. This is often a problem since the C: drive can only be 4GB in size. One work-around is to temporarily locate a 1GB or 2GB swap file on the C: drive of a server that is having problems and allow it to run in this degraded state in order to capture the dump file. Of course, this will only work if there is enough space for the applications, the swap file, and the dump file.

▲ **Windows 2000 Advanced Server**   Windows 2000 does not have any of the partitioning limitations of Windows NT as stated above; thus a simpler partitioning scheme is possible, as shown in Figure 13-2. As of this writing, most Intel-based servers have a limit of 4GB of RAM and four processors. Your decision as to the optimal partition structure and swap file size can be more easily made based on system and application requirements than on operating system limitations.

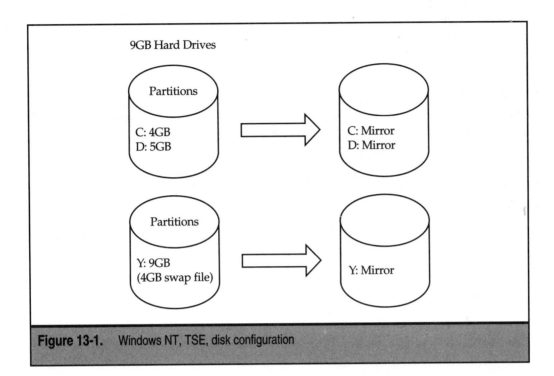

Figure 13-1.   Windows NT, TSE, disk configuration

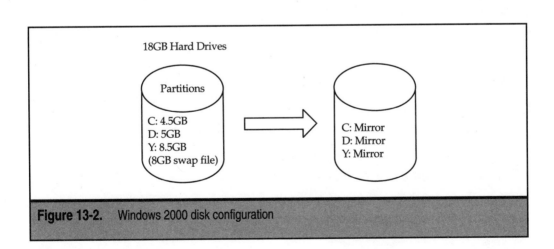

Figure 13-2.   Windows 2000 disk configuration

Other Hardware Factors

The following are related recommendations for your Corporate ASP hardware environment:

▼ **Power supplies** Server power supplies should be redundant and fail over automatically if the primary unit fails. You should also make sure the voltage is adequate to feed the power supplies.

■ **Racking** Your server farm should be racked for safety and ease of access. The rack system should be compatible with the brand of servers you choose. Only use generic racks if adapters are available to bolt down your servers. Never put your servers on unsecured shelves within a rack.

■ **Cable management** Clearly label or color code (or both) all cables traveling between your servers and the network patch panel or network backbone. We cannot emphasize this enough. It will save a tremendous amount of time later if you need to troubleshoot a connection.

■ **Multiconsole** Use a multiconsole switch instead of installing a monitor or keyboard for each server. It saves space and usually only requires you to push one button to access a server.

▲ **Console remote access** Consider installing a dial-up or network-accessible console remote access card. Such a card will allow you to access the server's console display in the event the server is unavailable. This way you can see any error display when the server attempts to boot and load the operating system.

Service Packs and Hot Fixes

The Golden Rule for loading postrelease service packs and hot fixes is "Don't Unless You Have To." Unfortunately, you often have to. Microsoft periodically releases service packs that are the culmination of fixes to problems discovered by customers and Microsoft technical support. Customers with an urgent need for a fix that was created after a service pack can often receive it in the form of a hot fix from Microsoft technical support. Citrix also releases a periodic service pack in order to reduce the number of interim hot fixes.

The following list shows the current recommended service packs as of this writing:

▼ MetaFrame 1.8 for Windows NT 4.0 Server, TSE: Service Pack 1

■ MetaFrame 1.8a for Windows 2000 (includes fixes in SP1)

■ Windows NT Server 4.0, Terminal Server Edition: Service Pack 6

▲ Windows 2000 Advanced Server: no service packs yet, only postrelease hot fixes

We strongly recommend checking the Citrix and Microsoft Web sites for the current level of service packs and related issues to evaluate whether they apply to your Corporate ASP project.

NOTE: Windows 2000 uses a "Windows Update" feature similar to Windows 98 that allows hot fixes to be automatically downloaded from the Internet. We strongly recommend against allowing this on production servers. It does not provide the level of testing rigor that is required to maintain a stable and robust server farm.

PREINSTALLATION CONSIDERATIONS

Before you get started loading and configuring MetaFrame and Terminal Services, there are some important considerations to think about.

▼ *Review the Microsoft hardware compatibility list.* Microsoft publishes this list for your benefit, so take advantage of it. Microsoft does not guarantee that the hardware listed will work flawlessly with Terminal Services, nor that hardware not listed will not work. It does certify that the hardware listed has been tested and provides a good starting point for evaluation. Only consider hardware not on the list for your project if you know it is going to work with Terminal Services and MetaFrame.

■ *Check your existing NT domain and see that it is functioning properly.* If your current domain has problems with performance or structure, the problems will not get better with Terminal Services.

■ *Make sure your existing NT file server is installed and functioning properly.* You will be storing scripts, policies, and templates centrally, not on each MetaFrame server. You will need a file server to be installed and accessible when your servers go online. We will describe this process in Chapter 16.

■ *Make sure all required drivers and startup disks are available.* Invariably, special drivers are required for RAID controllers, NICs, the BIOS, or other server components when loading Windows NT or Windows 2000. Make sure these are available and on the appropriate media before you begin.

■ *Review information on platform-specific issues.* The respective Web-based knowledge bases from Citrix and Microsoft have a wealth of information on different server hardware. It is prudent to review this information and circumvent potential problems before they occur. This review may even serve to change your mind about which hardware to purchase.

- *Prepare hardware.* Thoroughly prepare and test your hardware before attempting to load any software. Make sure all shipping protection has been removed. Open the case and make sure all components are securely seated and installed correctly. Power-on the server and run the vendor's diagnostics on the entire system. If your vendor hasn't "burned in" the server, let the diagnostics run at least overnight, if not for a few days, to eliminate any "lemons" before you begin to rely on the system.

▲ *Double-check data center environment.* Don't assume power, cooling, or moisture levels are adequate. Check them out with the data center staff and compare them to published tolerances from the hardware manufacturer.

Installation Checklists

The following checklists are meant to provide a quick reference for installing the given software. For detailed installation instructions and options, refer to the appropriate documentation from Citrix and Microsoft. Following each checklist are the postinstallation changes we recommend to address limitations in the operating system or MetaFrame itself. These limitations are often due to insufficient default values, but they can also be settings to work around bugs, or simply changes we think are necessary to the "health and well-being" of a Corporate ASP. After each recommended change, we provide the setting value or instructions, as well as the reason. Where possible, we have also provided a URL reference to Citrix, Microsoft, or other organization with more information on why that change may be necessary.

Windows NT 4.0 Server, Terminal Server Edition

The installation checklist for Windows NT 4.0 Server, TSE, has 33 steps.

1. Insert the Terminal Server CD into the computer's CD-ROM drive and power-up the system.

> **TIP:** Most current servers support bootable CDs through the "El Torito - No Emulation" standard. Make sure the computer's BIOS has a boot sequence set that has the CD-ROM drive as the first boot drive.

2. After the computer finishes initializing the hardware (POST checks), the CD should begin the boot process and display the familiar blue-and-gray Windows NT Setup screen indicating "Setup is inspecting your computer's hardware configuration."

> **TIP:** Pressing F6 at this point is necessary on some systems containing RAID controllers. Doing this stops the detection process and allows you to insert the proper drivers from the hardware manufacturers. Not pressing F6 and forcing the prompt to load these drivers could lead to a blue crash screen and an aborted install.

3. In a few minutes, you'll see a Welcome to Setup screen with options to repair an existing install or set up a fresh copy of Terminal Server. Naturally, you'll want to press ENTER to proceed with a new install.

4. On the next screen, you are prompted to specify the type of mass storage or disk controller(s) installed in the machine. Windows NT Setup will attempt to automatically detect your disk controllers. If you haven't already loaded drivers from the hardware manufacturer and need to, press S and then ENTER to select "Other (Requires disk provided by a hardware manufacturer."

5. The next screen should display Microsoft's Software License Agreement. You must press the F8 key to agree to the terms in order for the installation to continue.

6. If Terminal Server is being installed on a clean drive, the next screen will offer partitioning options. But if an existing installation of NT, Winframe, or Terminal Server is detected, you'll be given the option to upgrade. We recommend strongly against an upgrade. Some systems include a utility partition containing software from the manufacturer. Leave this partition alone and just delete any Windows NT partitions or those from any other operating system. Delete any partitions by selecting Delete and then pressing L on the following screen.

7. Press C to create a new partition. We recommend separate boot and data partitions. (Refer to the section "Configuration Standards" at the beginning of the chapter.) Once each partition is created, you'll select Install to proceed to the formatting options.

NOTE: Windows NT Setup will only format the partition that is being used for the operating system. Any other partitions will remain unformatted until after the install. You can format these partitions from the command prompt or by using the Disk Administrator utility.

8. After formatting completes, you'll be prompted to name the directory where Terminal Server will reside. We recommend that you use the default \WTSRV directory.

9. Next, the Setup program will ask you to press ENTER to allow an examination of the hard disk. Setup will then proceed to copy necessary files from the Terminal Server CD-ROM.

10. You'll be prompted to press ENTER to restart once the copying is complete. Make sure the system doesn't boot to the CD-ROM this time around by removing it.

11. Setup should boot the system and enter graphical mode for the first time. At the next screen, you'll have the option of either using the mouse to click Next or just pressing the ENTER key.

12. You'll be prompted to enter your name and organization before clicking Next to continue.

13. Setup will also prompt for the CD Key to be entered. Enter the key and click Next.

14. At this point, select Per Server or Per Seat licensing mode. Also, enter the number of concurrent connections if you select Per Server. Click Next to continue.

15. Input the number of Terminal Server desktops that will connect to your server and click Next.

16. Enter a name for your Terminal Server. Click Next.

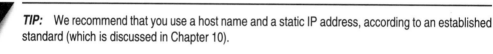

TIP: We recommend that you use a host name and a static IP address, according to an established standard (which is discussed in Chapter 10).

17. Select the type of server for this computer. We strongly recommend Stand-Alone Server. You should already have a Primary and Backup Domain Controller. You do not want your Terminal Server applications competing for resources with authentication requests from users. Click Next.

18. Enter the password that will be used to lock the Administrator Account and click Next.

19. Choose No to create an Emergency Repair Disk. When you finish configuring the server you will create an image of the disk for rebuilding purposes. Click Next.

20. Select which Windows components to install. Deselect any games or multimedia components. Click Next.

21. Select No to skip installing Internet Explorer 4.0. All applications will be installed after the base operating system is configured. Click Next.

22. Click Next again to allow Setup to proceed. Select "wired to the network" as the type of network connection your Terminal Server will use. Click Next.

23. Select No to skip installing Microsoft Internet Information Server. Click Next.

24. Setup will now set up the network interface card (NIC). We recommend obtaining the latest drivers from the card manufacturer and creating a driver disk. Click the Have Disk button. Select A:, or the drive letter of your floppy. Click OK and Next when prompted. You may be asked to verify the resource settings of your NIC.

25. Next, select the TCP/IP protocol to install and click Next.

26. Accept the default services to install. Click Next.

27. Click Next again and configure TCP/IP. Enter the static IP address as well as the host name, domain, domain name server, and gateway. Click Next.

28. After the services are installed and bound, click Next to continue.

29. Select the domain for your Terminal Server and click Next. The computer account must already exist on the PDC, or you will be prompted for the Administrator password to add it now.

30. Click Finish to continue. More files will be copied and configured by the system.

31. Select the appropriate time zone, date, and time for your Terminal Server. Click Close.

32. Accept the standard video display settings for now. Click OK.

33. Click Next as prompted, and eventually, a screen should display showing that "Windows Terminal Server 4.00 has been installed successfully." Press ENTER to restart the computer and boot the Terminal Server OS. Allow the computer to reboot.

TIP: In order to shut down Terminal Server, you'll need to press CTRL+ALT+DELETE and choose Shutdown from the resulting window. To prevent unauthorized use of the feature, Shutdown is not on the Start menu.

Windows 2000 Advanced Server

The installation checklist for Windows 2000 Advanced Server has 26 steps.

1. Insert the Terminal Server CD into the computer's CD-ROM drive and power-up the system. After the computer finishes initializing the hardware (POST checks), the CD-ROM should begin the boot process. You will see a prompt to "Press any key to boot from the CD…" Press the SPACEBAR.

2. If there is a previous version of Windows NT or Windows 2000 on the system, you will be prompted to upgrade. We recommend against upgrading. Choose No Upgrade.

3. Press F6 at this point if you have any third-party drivers to install. The screen will now change to the Inspecting Hardware screen similar to Windows NT.

4. The next screen, entitled Windows 2000 Server Setup, will prompt you to press R to Repair, F3 to Quit, or ENTER to continue. Press ENTER.

5. The next screen prompts you to press F8 to accept the license agreement. Press F8 to agree.

6. A screen will allow you to create partitions. Refer to the section "Configuration Standards" earlier in this chapter. Unlike Windows NT, Windows 2000 will check and format any partitions you create in this step.

7. At this point, Windows 2000 Setup switches to graphical mode and begins to copy files. Wait while this happens, and allow the system to reboot when prompted.

8. After the system begins to boot, you will again be prompted to "Press any key to boot from the CD…" Do not press a key. Wait for the timer to expire. This will make the system boot from the hard drive.

9. You will now be taken to the Windows 2000 Setup Wizard. Click Next.

10. Setup will now attempt to detect hardware devices and install drivers. This can take a long time, and a lack of disk activity is not uncommon. Don't panic, just let Setup run and do its job. If it is inactive for more than an hour or so, it is probably not going to complete. At this point you may need to reboot.

11. A screen asks if you want to customize the system for regional settings. You can change the local language for the keyboard and display. Choose U.S. English unless you have already determined that all the other software you will be loading (including MetaFrame) supports another language.

12. Enter a name and organization. Click Next.

13. The licensing screen is the same as Windows NT. Choose either Per Server or Per Seat licensing. Click Next.

14. Enter the name for this computer and the Administrator password twice. Click Next.

15. A screen will ask you to select the desired components to install. Make the following selections: deselect Internet Information Server, as this computer will not be serving Web requests. Then select the following components:

   ■ Management and Monitoring Tools: This selection contains the SNMP agent service, the network monitor, and other utilities that are useful for troubleshooting.

   ■ Networking: This should already be selected by default.

   ■ Terminal Services: This is the actual service responsible for providing a remote desktop.

   ■ Terminal Services Licensing: This service is required if the above service is selected.

   The following selections are optional:

   ■ Remote Install: This service allows you to install Windows 2000 components on other servers. Only choose this if this is what you intend to do. We'll provide methods for updating servers in Chapter 14.

   ■ Remote Storage: Windows 2000 provides support for SANs. If you intend to use this type of remote storage, install this service.

   Click Next when you are finished with your selections.

16. Enter the date, time, and time zone and click Next.

17. You will now enter Terminal Services Setup. The first screen asks you to set the mode. You can choose optimization for Remote Administration, which has a minimal performance impact, or you can choose Application Server mode, which optimizes program response times. Choose Application Server Mode. Click Next.

18. Terminal Services Setup continues with the Compatibility settings screen. You can choose Windows 2000 compatibility or Legacy mode for compatibility with Terminal Server 4.0 applications. Unless you only intend to run new applications that are compatible with Windows 2000 Terminal Services, choose Legacy mode. Applications not written for Windows 2000 will find the former mode too restrictive and will not function properly.

19. On the Network Settings screen, wait while the network components install. Choose Custom and click Next.

20. On the Network Components screen, the default selections are Client for Microsoft Networking, File and Print Services for Microsoft Networking, and TCP/IP. Click TCP/IP and assign a static IP address, subnet mask, gateway, and DNS servers.

NOTE: Though it is possible to run your server with a dynamically assigned address, this choice can cause a variety of performance and compatibility problems. For example, WINS has been shown to exhibit performance degradation with dynamically assigned addresses. We have found that some WINS requests are lost completely in this case. Also, many applications that depend on a static IP address will have trouble if the IP address changes for any reason.

21. When prompted to enter a work group or domain, choose Workgroup for now, and enter some name. You will go back and add this server to the domain later, but it should not be part of the standard image.

22. The screen will now display status updates such as "Installing Components," "Configuring," and "Copying Files." Eventually Setup will proceed to the Performing Final Tasks screen where it will add Start menu items, register components, save settings, and remove temporary files. On the Completing the Windows 2000 Setup Wizard screen, click Finish and allow the system to reboot.

23. When the system boots, log in as Administrator using the password you assigned.

24. On the Windows 2000 Configure Your Server screen, it prompts whether this is the only server, or one or more are already on the network. Choose the latter and click Next.

25. Uncheck the box to "Show this screen at startup."

26. The tabs on the left of this configuration screen provide access to a variety of functions. You can register the software; set up Active Directory; configure your server as a File Server, Print Server, a Web or Media Server; or choose additional networking options, Application Server mode, Database Server, E-Mail Server, and some Advanced functions. For now, you are finished.

MetaFrame 1.8

MetaFrame version 1.8 is for Windows NT 4.0 Server, Terminal Server Edition. Windows 1.8a is also called MetaFrame for Windows 2000. Make sure you choose the correct version of MetaFrame for the underlying operating system you intend to use.

1. If you insert the CD-ROM into the CD-ROM drive of a computer running Terminal Server or Windows 2000, the Autorun feature will launch the installer. Click MetaFrame Setup in this case. Otherwise, use Windows Explorer to open the i386 folder on the CD-ROM, and run Setup.

2. The License Agreement screen will appear. Click Agree to continue.

3. Click Next on the Welcome screen.

4. Click Next on the Setting Up MetaFrame screen. The installation program will now begin copying files from the CD-ROM to the hard disk.

5. On the MetaFrame Licensing screen you have the option of licensing the software by clicking Add License Packs. Click Next for now. You will add licenses later.

6. The Network ICA Connections screen allows you to select protocols to be used for ICA. Unless you have a specific reason for doing otherwise, just choose TCP/IP. Click Next.

7. On the TAPI Modem Setup screen, click Next. If you intend to use a direct-dial ICA connection, configure it after the initial install.

8. The next screen illustrates how the client and server drive mappings will work. By default, client drives A:, B:, C:, and D: will be mapped to A:, B:, V:, and U: in an ICA session. This client drive mapping is so that the server drives C:, D:, E:, and so forth, can remain as they are. Click Next.

   The Server Drive Reassignment screen, shown in Figure 13-3, allows you to change the default drive mappings described in step 8. There is no reason to change the defaults here.

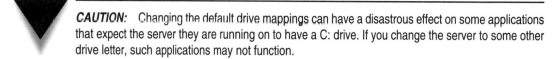

CAUTION: Changing the default drive mappings can have a disastrous effect on some applications that expect the server they are running on to have a C: drive. If you change the server to some other drive letter, such applications may not function.

9. On the System Reboot screen, click Finish.

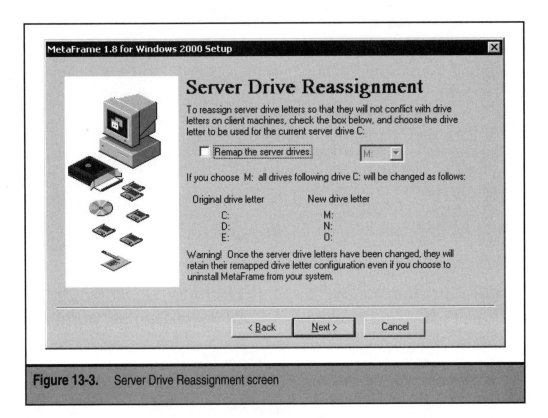

Figure 13-3.   Server Drive Reassignment screen

POSTINSTALLATION CONFIGURATION CHANGES

We have found a number of postinstallation changes to be beneficial to the production Corporate ASP. The changes are given in checklists below, and where one of these changes is optional, we state that fact. For each recommended change, we include an explanation and the Registry key and value in question. The explanation can include a URL to a technical note from a Web site that offers a great deal of detail on the setting. If the recommended change is not related to the Registry, we describe how to effect the change. Figure 13-4 shows the REGEDIT program and a sample key.

NOTE: Many of the listed Registry changes can also be made using the Citrix Client Configuration Manager or a standard application such as those found in Control Panel. The changes are presented here in Registry-key format in order to facilitate the construction of a script that will make all the changes in an unattended fashion. This will be discussed in more detail in Chapter 16.

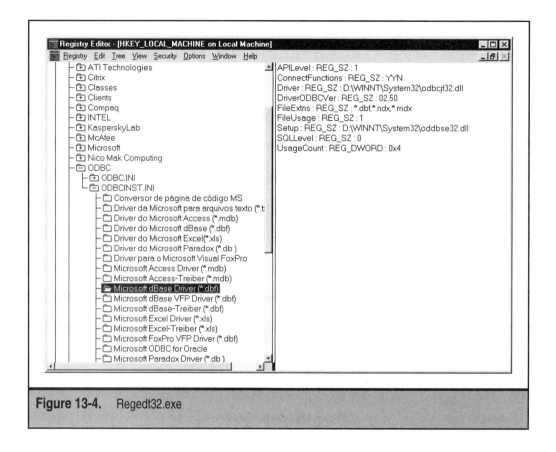

Figure 13-4.   Regedt32.exe

In the interest of brevity, we will abbreviate the Registry keys HKEY_LOCAL_ MACHINE as HKLM, HKEY_CURRENT_USER as HKCU, and CurrentControlSet will be CCS.

Generic Checklists for Changing the Registry

The following checklist will aid you in changing the Registry as safely as possible. You will need to modify the steps based on the requirements of a given key. In some cases, the keys listed will not exist and will need to be added. If they do exist, simply change the current value to the one indicated. In the few cases where a key should be deleted, it is clearly indicated.

In each case, begin by clicking Start > Run, and then type **regedit.exe** in the Open box. Then click OK and follow the steps for adding, changing, or deleting the key.

If Adding a New Key...

1. Find the Registry key above the key you wish to add, as in this example:

   HKLM\Software\Microsoft\Windows NT\CurrentVersion\

2. Click New > Key on the Edit menu.

3. Click the new Registry key, and click New > (String Value, Binary Value, or DWORD Value) from the Edit menu.

If Changing an Existing Key...

1. Locate the appropriate Registry key, as in this example:

   HKLM\Software\Microsoft\Windows NT\CurrentVersion\AeDebug

2. Click the Registry key, and then click Export Registry File on the Registry menu.

3. Enter a name and location for the saved Registry file, and then click Save.

4. Double-click the Registry key and change the value.

If Deleting an Existing Key...

1. Locate the appropriate Registry key, as in this example:

   HKLM\Software\Microsoft\Windows NT\CurrentVersion\AeDebug

2. Click Edit > Delete.

To restore a changed or deleted key, double-click the .reg file you created in the steps for changing an existing key, above.

I can't overemphasize the importance of standardized configurations. Before we started standardizing the Registry changes on our servers, we were prone to frequent blue screens. Now they are a rare occurrence.

—Jeff Doan,
Vice President Information Technology,
Pacific Gulf Properties

Operating System Configuration

This section describes changes to the operating system designed to increase performance and reliability in the Corporate ASP.

▼ Set the open file limitation fix. This is related to a CIFS limitation introduced by backward compatibility with older operating systems such as Windows NT 3.51 and Windows 95. When many Terminal Servers connect to the same file server, this fix is needed. See the Web site: http://support.microsoft.com/support/kb/articles/Q190/1/62.ASP?LNG=ENG&SA=ALLKB&FR=0.
Key: \HKLM\System\CCS\Services\Rdr\Parameters\
Value: MultipleUsersOnConnection
Type: REG_DWORD
Data: 0

NOTE: The "Rdr" key does not exist in Windows 2000, so the proper key is \HKLM\System\CCS\Services\Parameters\.

▼ Set UNC path fix. This problem occurs when user profiles are stored on a central server. A user creates a shortcut on one server and then logs into another. The shortcut appears, but prompts the user for a password. See the Web site: http://support.microsoft.com/support/kb/articles/Q195/8/87.ASP?LNG=ENG&SA=ALLKB&FR=0.
Key: \Software\Microsoft\Windows\CurrentVersion\Policies\Explorer\
Value: LinkResolveIgnoreLinkInfo
Type: REG_DWORD
Data: 1

▼ Set remote policy update (Part 1). This will allow system policies to be updated remotely. First, set the policy update mode to manual:
Key: \HKLM\System\CCS\Control\Update\
Value: UpdateMode
Type: REG_DWORD
Data: 2

▼ Set remote policy update (Part 2).
Key: \HKLM\System\CCS\Control\Update\
Value: NetworkPath

Type: REG_SZ
Data: <path to policy file>

▼ Set user and computer name. This is an incredibly useful change that replaces the text in the My Computer icon with the user's login name and the server he or she is logged on to. It can help greatly in troubleshooting by quickly locating the user in a large server farm.

First, delete the following value:
Key: HKCU\CLSID\{20D04FE0-3AEA-1069-A2D8-08002B30309D}
Value: My Computer

Then add the following value:
Key: HKCU\CLSID\{20D04FE0-3AEA-1069-A2D8-08002B30309D}
Value: leave blank
Type: REG_EXPAND
Data: %username% on %computername%

▼ Kill Dr. Watson. The good doctor pops up to aid in troubleshooting whenever an error occurs. In a Corporate ASP environment, this can cause a problem because the server can "hang," waiting for input from the user. See the Web site: http://support.microsoft.com/support/kb/articles/Q188/2/96.ASP?LNG=ENG&SA=ALLKB&FR=0.
Key: \HKLM\Software\Microsoft\Windows NT\CurrentVersion\AeDebug\
Value: Auto
Type: REG_SZ
Data: 0

▼ Set up native time synchronization. It is important for running scripts and reading logs that all servers conform to a consistent time base. From the Windows command prompt, type

net start w32time -automatic

▼ Maximize the number of Page Table Entries (PTEs). Normally Windows calculates the number of available PTEs based on the platform and available memory. We have seen this calculation turn out to be inaccurate, so we recommend setting it manually. Some experimentation may be necessary based on the memory available on your server. The value below was tested on a server with 2GB of RAM. See the Web site: http://www.jsiinc.com/TIP1000/rh1094.htm.
Key: \HKLM\SYSTEM\CCS\Control\Session Manager\Memory Management\
Value: SystemPages
Type: REG_DWORD
Data: 50000 (max value)

NOTE: The number of PTEs also depends on the type of processor. The above example was tested on Pentium II and Pentium III processors. Check with the manufacturer to determine the number of kilobytes per memory page for your server.

▼ Enable Quick Reboot for server. The server will often be rebooted in an unattended fashion for maintenance. This change will speed up the boot process.
Key: \HKLM\Software\Microsoft\Windows NT\CurrentVersion\Winlogon\
Value: EnableQuickReboot
Type: REG_DWORD
Data: 1

▼ Set License Manager for file and print services. The License Manager is not always accurate in enforcing the correct license count. We have found it easiest to disable it and rely on a stringent purchasing and asset tracking policy to ensure your company is in compliance with software license requirements.
Key: \HKLM\SYSTEM\CCS\Services\LicenseInfo\FilePrint\
Value: FlipAllow
Type: REG_DWORD
Data: 1

▼ Disable License Logging service. Windows NT 4.0 uses this service to enforce licensing, but it is possible to disable it. In Windows 2000, it is not possible to disable this service.
Key: \HKLM\System\CCS\Services\LicenseService\Start
Type: REG_DWORD
Data: 4

▼ Disable TS License Service. In Windows NT 4.0, this service is provided for informational purposes only. In Windows 2000 the service enforces the license count and cannot be disabled.
Key: \HKLM\System\CCS\Services\TermServLicensing\Start
Type: REG_DWORD
Data: 4

▼ Change SPOOL directory to the D: drive. This simple change is designed to ensure there is adequate space for the print spool files. You can set it to whatever drive and directory is appropriate.
Key: \HKLM\SYSTEM\CCS\Control\Print\Printers\
Value: DefaultSpoolDirectory
Type: REG_SZ
Data: D:\spool\printers (example)

▼   Disable printer pop-up message. Similar to Dr. Watson, the printer dialog can hang the server, asking for user input. See the Web site: http://support.microsoft.com/support/kb/articles/Q122/1/60.asp?LNG=ENG&SA=ALLKB&FR=0.
Key: \HKLM\SYSTEM\CCS\Control\Print\Providers\
Value: NetPopup
Type: REG_DWORD
Data: 0

▼   Disable printer error logging. Similar to the previous change, this one will cut down on the "background noise" written to the Event Log. See the Web site: http://support. microsoft.com/support/kb/articles/Q115/8/41.asp?LNG=ENG&SA=ALLKB&FR=0.
Key: \HKLM\SYSTEM\CCS\Control\Print\Providers\
Value: Event Log
Type: REG_DWORD
Data: 0

▼   Disable beep for printer. The beep is not appropriate for a multiuser environment.
Key: \HKLM\System\CCS\Print\
Value: BeepEnabled
Type: REG_DWORD
Data: 0

▼   Set System Event Log MaxSize to 1MB. This is a simple housekeeping measure to ensure the Event Log doesn't grow too large. Each key corresponds to a different log file (Event, Application, Security), but the Value and Data are the same.
Key: \HKLM\System\CCS\Services\Event Log\System\
\HKLM\System\CCS\Services\Event Log\Application\
\HKLM\System\CCS\Services\Event Log\Security\
Value: MaxSize
Type: REG_DWORD
Data: 1048576

▼   Set System Event Log Retention to When Needed.
Key: \HKLM\System\CCS\Services\Event Log\System\
\HKLM\System\CCS\Services\Event Log\Application\
\HKLM\System\CCS\Services\Event Log\Security\
Value: Retention

▼ Write debugging information to a file. The next few changes simply enable and define the Crash Dump feature.
Key: \HKLM\System\CCS\Control\CrashControl\
Value: CrashDumpEnabled
Type: REG_DWORD
Data: 1

▼ Write debugging information to D:\Memory.dmp.
Key: \HKLM\System\CCS\Control\CrashControl\
Value: DumpFile
Type: REG_SZ
Data: D:\Memory.dmp (example)

▼ Overwrite existing debugging file.
Key: \HKLM\System\CCS\Control\CrashControl\
Value: Overwrite
Type: REG_DWORD
Data: 1

▼ Automatically reboot after memory dump.
Key: \HKLM\System\CCS\Control\CrashControl\
Value: AutoReboot
Type: REG_DWORD
Data: 1

▼ Do not send an administrative alert after a memory dump. It is not necessary to broadcast a message upon reboot if an NMS is in use.
Key: \HKLM\System\CCS\Control\CrashControl\
Value: SendAlert
Type: REG_DWORD
Data: 0

▼ Write an event to the Event Log after a memory dump. This change will provide a simple audit trail in the event of a crash. It also is not needed if an NMS is in use.
Key: \HKLM\System\CCS\Control\CrashControl\
Value: LogEvent
Type: REG_DWORD
Data: 1

▼ Remove server from Network Neighborhood. This will prevent browsing to Terminal Servers. There is no reason to allow users to do this since there is no file storage on these servers.

Key: \HKLM\System\CCS\Services\LanmanServer\
Value: Hidden
Type: REG_DWORD
Data: 1

▼   Add the announcement of server comment. The comment field provides
    additional detail on a given server. Even though there are few situations
    in which browsing is allowed on Terminal Servers, this can be useful by
    providing additional detail. See the Web site: http://support.microsoft.com/
    support/kb/articles/Q231/3/12.ASP?LNG=ENG&SA=ALLKB&FR=0.
    Key: \HKLM\System\CCS\Services\LanmanServer\Lmannounce
    Type: REG_DWORD
    Data: 1

▼   Disable LMHOSTS lookup. This change forces name resolution to be done by
    DNS and WINS.
    Key: \HKLM\System\CCS\Services\NetBt\Parameters\
    Value: EnableLmhosts
    Type: REG_DWORD
    Data: 1

▼   Disable Alerter service. This will prevent inconvenient dialog windows.
    Key: \HKLM\System\CCS\Services\Alerter\
    Value: Start
    Type: REG_DWORD
    Data: 4

▼   Disable LM broadcasts. This prevents the server from participating in browser
    elections. See the Web site: http://support.microsoft.com/support/kb/
    articles/Q136/7/12.asp?LNG=ENG&SA=ALLKB&FR=0.
    Key: \HKLM\SYSTEM\CCS\Services\LanmanServer\Parameters\
    Value: Lmannounce
    Type: REG_DWORD
    Data: 0

▼   Set the Registry size limit. This change is designed to keep the Registry from
    growing too large.
    Key: HKLM\System\CCS\Control\
    Value: RegistrySizeLimit
    Type: REG_DWORD
    Data: 83886080

MetaFrame Configuration

▼ Increase the number of ICA listeners. The default value is insufficient for a busy server. See the Web site: http://206.103.132.14/texpert.nsf/ffe39dd1f6086af9852566a2004acbb8/a6672db5fdec3f0f85256720007398b0?OpenDocument.
Key: \HKLM\CCS\Control\Terminal Server\
Value: IdleWinstationPoolCount
Type: REG_DWORD
Data: 5

▼ Disable background wallpaper for ICA sessions. Unnecessary graphics can consume bandwidth.
Key: \HKLM\SYSTEM\CCS\Control\Terminal Server\WinStations\ICA-tcp\ UserOverride\Control Panel\Desktop\
Value: Wallpaper
Type: REG_SZ
Data: (none)

NOTE: The values under the above key exist under \HKLM\SYSTEM\CCS\Control\Terminal Server\WinStations\RDP-TCP\… in Windows 2000.

▼ Set low audio output (optional). Only make this change if you need to allow audio to be passed from the server to the client. We recommend disabling audio altogether.
Key: \HKLM\SYSTEM\CCS\Control\Terminal Server\WinStations\ICA-tcp\ AudioConfig\
Values: PCMOutputFormat, fEnablePCMGovernor, fDebugFlags
Type: REG_DWORD
Data: PCMOutputFormat: 1024, EnablePCMGovernor: 1, DebugFlags: 0

▼ Disable client audio mapping. Unless there is a strong business reason to use it, disable it. It can consume bandwidth to the client.
Key: \HKLM\SYSTEM\CCS\Control\Terminal Server\WinStations\ICA-tcp\
Value: fDisableCam
Type: REG_DWORD
Data: 1

▼ Disable client COM port mapping (optional). We recommend the next four changes in the interests of making the client as secure and low-bandwidth as possible.
Key: \HKLM\SYSTEM\CCS\Control\Terminal Server\WinStations\ICA-tcp\
Value: fDisableCcm

Type: REG_DWORD
Data: 1

▼   Disable client drive mapping (optional).
    Key: \HKLM\SYSTEM\CCS\Control\Terminal Server\WinStations\ICA-tcp\
    Value: fDisableCdm
    Type: REG_DWORD
    Data: 1

▼   Disable client printer mapping.
    Key: \HKLM\SYSTEM\CCS\Control\Terminal Server\WinStations\ICA-tcp\
    Value: fDisableCpm
    Type: REG_DWORD
    Data: 1

▼   Disable client LPT port mapping.
    Key: \HKLM\SYSTEM\CCS\Control\Terminal Server\WinStations\ICA-tcp\
    Value: fDisableLPT
    Type: REG_DWORD
    Data: 1

▼   Set Shadow Input on and Notify on. This will need to be set according to your
    company's privacy policy, but we like to notify people when we are shadowing
    their connection.
    Key: \HKLM\SYSTEM\CCS\Control\Terminal Server\WinStations\ICA-tcp\
    Value: Shadow
    Type: REG_DWORD
    Data: 1

▼   Don't inherit Shadow settings from the client. We recommend against allowing
    the server to inherit any settings from the client in order to enforce consistency.
    If you need to make an exception for a user, we recommend using the setting
    Inherit from User.
    Key: \HKLM\SYSTEM\CCS\Control\Terminal Server\WinStations\ICA-tcp\
    Value: fInheritShadow
    Type: REG_DWORD
    Data: 0

▼   Don't inherit disconnection from client.
    Key: \HKLM\SYSTEM\CCS\Control\Terminal Server\WinStations\ICA-tcp\
    Value: fInheritMaxDisconnectionTime
    Type: REG_DWORD
    Data: 0

▼ Don't inherit idle time-out setting from client.
Key: \HKLM\SYSTEM\CCS\Control\Terminal Server\WinStations\ICA-tcp\
Value: fInheritMaxIdleTime
Type: REG_DWORD
Data: 0

▼ Don't inherit broken or timed-out session from client.
Key: \HKLM\SYSTEM\CCS\Control\Terminal Server\WinStations\ICA-tcp\
Value: fInheritResetBroken
Type: REG_DWORD
Data: 0

▼ Adjust the 10-minute disconnection limit to your preference. We find 10 minutes to be a good working value. This affects the length of time a connection can be in a disconnected state before the "disconnection session" rule applies to it.
Key: \HKLM\SYSTEM\CCS\Control\Terminal Server\WinStations\ICA-tcp\
Value: MaxDisconnectionTime
Type: REG_DWORD
Data: 600000

▼ Reset timed-out or broken sessions. We recommend resetting the sessions to clear their resources from the server.
Key: \HKLM\SYSTEM\CCS\Control\Terminal Server\WinStations\ICA-tcp\
Value: fResetBroken
Type: REG_DWORD
Data: 1

▼ Set a four-hour idle limit. This is the amount of time a session can be idle before being disconnected.
Key: \HKLM\SYSTEM\CCS\Control\Terminal Server\WinStations\ICA-tcp\
Value: MaxIdleTime
Type: REG_DWORD
Data: 14400000

Desktop Settings

▼ Rename syncapp.exe. This prevents the creation of the briefcase for each user. The briefcase is not usable in a Terminal Services environment.

▼ Remove Dial-Up Networking from My Computer. Similar to the above change, there is no reason to give users access to this application. See the Web site: http://support.microsoft.com/support/kb/articles/Q166/2/99.ASP?LNG=ENG&SA=ALLKB&FR=0.

Key: \HKLM\Software\Microsoft\Windows\CurrentVersion\Explorer\
MyComputer\NameSpace\{a4d92740-67cd-11cf-96f2-00aa00a11dd9}\
Value: Dial-Up Networking
Type: Action
Data: Delete

▼ Delete automatic start-up of ICA bar (shown below). We like to reserve the use
of this application to administrators who know how to execute it from the
command line ("security by obscurity").
Key: \HKLM\Software\Microsoft\Windows\CurrentVersion\Run\IcaBar\
Value: icabar.exe /adminonly
Type: Action
Data: Delete

▼ Delete locally cached profiles file. Profile storage can eat a tremendous amount of disk space in a large network. Though there is no way to stop Windows from copying the profile from the PDC to the Terminal Server, you can make sure that the profile is deleted upon logout.
Key: \HKLM\Software\Microsoft\Windows NT\CurrentVersion\Winlogon\
Value: DeleteRoamingCache
Type: REG_DWORD
Data: 1

▼ Fix problem where shortcuts resolve to relative path. This ignores the relative path and forces shortcuts to resolve to an absolute path.
Key: \HKLM\Software\Microsoft\Windows\CurrentVersion\Policies\
Explorer\
Value: LinkResolveIgnoreLinkInfo
Type: REG_DWORD
Data: 1

▼ Configure My Computer to open Explorer. This prevents users from accessing undesirable areas through My Computer.
Key: \HKLM\Software\Classes\CLSID\{20D04FE0-3AEA-1069-A2D8-08002B30309D}\Shell\Open\
Value: Command
Type: REG_SZ
Data: Explorer.exe

Performance Optimization

▼ Set server service to maximize for net applications (Part 1). This change and the next optimize a variety of kernel parameters for running the server as an Application Server.
Key: \HKLM\System\CCS\Services\LanmanServer\Parameters\
Value: Size
Type: REG_DWORD
Data: 3

▼ Set server service to maximize for net applications (Part 2).
Key: \HKLM\System\CCS\Control\Session Manager\Memory Management\
Value: LargeSystemCache
Type: REG_DWORD
Data: 0

▼ Set level 2 cache setting to the actual size of the processor cache. The default value is 256. See the Web site: http://support.microsoft.com/support/kb/articles/Q183/0/63.ASP?LNG=ENG&SA=ALLKB&FR=0.

Key: \HKLM\SYSTEM\CCS\Control\Session Manager\Memory Management\
Value: SecondLevelDataCache
Type: REG_DWORD
Data: 1024 (or actual cache size)

▼   Don't page out NT kernel and drivers to disk. This setting limits unnecessary paging by the operating system. See the Web site: http://support.microsoft.com/support/kb/articles/Q184/4/19.ASP?LNG=ENG&SA=ALLKB&FR=0.
Key: \HKLM\SYSTEM\CCS\Control\Session Manager\Memory Management\
Value: DisablePagingExecutive
Type: REG_DWORD
Data: 1

▼   Increase number of possible connections. The default value can limit the number of clients that can connect to the Terminal Server and cause connection errors. See the Web sites: http://support.microsoft.com/support/kb/articles/Q232/4/ 76.ASP?LNG=ENG&SA=ALLKB&FR=0 *and*
http://support.microsoft.com/support/kb/articles/Q216/1/ 71.ASP?LNG=ENG&SA=ALLKB&FR=0
Key: KLM\System\CCS\Services\LanmanServer\Parameters\
Values: MaxWorkItems, MaxMpxCt
Type: REG_DWORD
Data: MaxWorkItems: 8192, MaxMpxCt: 1024

▼   Increase network performance parameters. The default values are the same as Windows NT and are not necessarily optimized for the high number of processes typical of Terminal Services. See the Web site: http:// www.jsiinc.com/TIP0100/rh0125.htm.
Key: HKLM\System\CCS\Services\LanmanWorkstation\Parameters\
Values: MaxCmds, MaxThreads, MaxCollectionCount
Type: REG_DWORD
Data: MaxCmds: 255, MaxThreads: 255, MaxCollectionCount: 65535

▼   The AdditionalCriticalWorkerThreads change can enhance application performance.
Key: HKLM\system\CCS\control\session manager\executive\
Value: AdditionalCriticalWorkerThreads
Type: REG_DWORD
Data: 16

▼ Delete the OS/2 and POSIX subsystems (optional). This prevents them from being loaded by certain commands or programs being executed. See the Web site: http://support.microsoft.com/support/kb/articles/Q101/2/70.asp?LNG=ENG&SA=ALLKB&FR=0.
Key: HKLM\SYSTEM\CCS\Control\Session Manager\ Subsystems\
Values: POSIX, Os2
Type: Action
Data: Delete

▼ Optimize updates to the file system. See the Web site: http://support.microsoft.com/support/kb/articles/Q150/3/55.ASP?LNG=ENG&SA=ALLKB&FR=0.
Key: HKLM\SYSTEM\CCS\Control\FileSystem\
Values: NtfsDisableLastAccessUpdate
Type : REG_DWORD
Data : 1

Network Connectivity

▼ Improve connectivity over inconsistent WAN links. This setting yields a benefit over most distributed networks. See the Web site: http://206.103.132.14/texpert.nsf/ffe39dd1f6086af9852566a2004acbb8/8174e0ca7ab4b7dd852567150053b781?OpenDocument.
Key: \HKLM\system\CCS\services\tcpip\parameters\
Value: TcpMaxDataRetransmissions
Type: REG_DWORD
Data: 10

Standard Operations

Anyone who has administered Windows NT knows that the best way to handle repetitive administrative tasks is with scripts. In Chapter 16, we will show you some useful scripts for setting file system security, performing daily administration, and other functions. In any case, you will need to make sure the Scheduler service is always running.

▼ Set Scheduler service to run automatically (Part 1). The Scheduler service is needed to run any scheduled event, such as an administrative script.
Key: \HKLM\System\CCS\Services\Schedule\
Value: ErrorControl, Start, Type
Type: REG_DWORD
Data: ErrorControl: 1, Start: 2, Type: 272

▼ Set Scheduler service to run automatically (Part 2).
   Key: \HKLM\System\CCS\Services\Schedule\
   Value: ObjectName
   Type: REG_SZ
   Data: LocalSystem

NOTE: In Windows 2000, scheduled jobs are created in the Control Panel under Scheduled Tasks.

FURTHER STANDARD IMAGE DEFINITION

In Chapter 14 we will discuss techniques for the rapid deployment and efficient change tracking of MetaFrame servers. Chapter 15 will go into some detail on the creation of a published application environment, how to configure the various clients to take advantage of the benefits offered by that environment, and some application configuration issues you may run into. Chapter 16 will focus exclusively on scripting techniques for system management and how to translate your corporate policies and operating principles into Windows system policies and definition of the user environment.

CHAPTER 14

Automation

All of your regional servers have been eliminated, and Windows terminals have replaced good portions of your PC desktops. Of those PCs that remain, most are running the ICA client and getting at least standard applications from a central data center. Much of the day-to-day tedium has been eliminated from your help desk and system administration staff with this new simplified system. Sound like paradise? Maybe not, but we hope it sounds more desirable than the alternative of distributed computing. Even in this server-based computing paradise, plenty of repetitive maintenance and administrative tasks will need to be performed. Such tasks might include generating new servers for the server farm, packaging and distributing applications, creating large numbers of users or groups, or checking available disk space on production shares. All of these inherently manual tasks can benefit from automation.

What is automation in this context? *Automation* is the process by which otherwise manual tasks are made to run automatically. *Automatically* can mean unattended or with dramatically less user input than the manual alternative. The added benefit of automation is that the process in question is done the same way every time. This can greatly aid in troubleshooting, managing configuration changes, and saving time.

> *It didn't take a genius to figure out that with the number of MetaFrame servers increasing, we would quickly be spending the bulk of our time building servers and installing applications. We turned to imaging to decrease the time to build servers; in some cases by a factor of 10.*
>
> —Sorin Badea,
> Director, Network Operations WEST,
> AvalonBay Communities

There is one important warning in the move toward automation. Make sure that the process being automated is well defined, well understood, and already works well in a manual fashion. If this is not the case, you risk turning a "dumb, slow" process into a "dumb, fast" process. In other words, writing a script to automate a repetitive task and thereby making it faster cannot mitigate the fact that the repetitive task has no consistency or makes no sense to the people who perform it.

The most common tool for automating tasks in a Windows NT environment is scripting. In this chapter we will discuss the built-in scripting facility Windows Scripting Host (WSH) as well as some third-party alternatives. We will also discuss the underlying technology that makes WSH function and the companion technologies that allow you to perform real work. One of the major subjects of automation is bulk server creation. The task of loading an operating system, implementing configuration changes, and loading an application is time-consuming and not very rewarding work once it has been well defined. We will discuss ways to use WSH to perform server imaging and application packaging and distribution tasks. We will introduce Citrix Installation Management Services (IMS) and show you how this product can be used to package and deploy applications. Finally, we will discuss popular commercial imaging products that can be used to perform bulk server creation.

WINDOWS SCRIPTING HOST

Windows NT has long been knocked as a serious operating system due to its lack of an automation interface, or native scripting ability—something taken for granted on other operating systems such as UNIX or VMS. This has spawned a host of third-party utilities—some native to Windows, such as WinBatch, Kixtart, and XLNT—and some ported from other platforms, such as Perl. Microsoft addressed this deficiency starting with Windows NT Service Pack 4 (or Windows NT, TSE SP3) and the introduction of Windows Scripting Host (WSH). WSH is now included in Windows 98 as well.

WSH is an object-oriented, full-featured, robust scripting language, but it seems that a lot of confusion still revolves around what it is and what it is not. In this chapter we will discuss the role of WSH and its related technologies in various automation tasks. It is not our intention to supply a primer on WSH script coding or Windows programming, but we will provide examples of code and refer you to sources for more information. The information presented here is based on our use of various scripting techniques for our clients. Much of the script work done for them is very specific to their environment; however, where we can provide a generalized example we do so.

What Is WSH?

WSH is an interpreter that executes script files, stored as plain text, in more than one language. With version 2.0, these languages include Wscript, a native scripting language, Jscript, which is based on Java, and VBScript, from Visual Basic fame. By far, most of the published examples you will find of WSH scripting are in VBScript. This is probably due to the fact that support for VBScript is pervasive throughout Microsoft's operating system and application products. We will stick to this convention with examples in this book.

WSH includes two executables: cscript.exe and wscript.exe. The former is used when the script requires no output or just simple text console output (though you can still initiate popup dialog boxes). The latter is used when a richer GUI is needed, as is the case when user input must be collected. The general form for running a script from the command prompt using either interpreter is as follows (assuming the script is written using VBScript):

```
C:\> cscript.exe <scriptfilename>.vbs
```

On the surface, WSH may seem inferior to some existing scripting technologies because it relies on knowledge of other Windows subsystems, such as Active Directory System Interface (ADSI) or Windows Management Instrumentation (WMI), to perform many common tasks. Other scripting languages, such as Kixtart, only require knowledge of the tool itself to accomplish the same tasks. Once you begin exploring WSH, however, you will find that its scope is much broader than any other scripting tool for Windows. Its reliance on and support of those other technologies was intentional. With ADSI, for example, you can write one script that is general enough to perform the same function on any server on the network by querying the same system layer as the Windows administration tools do. Some examples of the many things you can do with WSH include

▼ Reading and writing variables in most accessible areas of Windows, including Active Directory Services and the Registry

■ Dynamically creating shortcuts on a user's desktop

■ Mapping network shares and printers

■ Launching programs

▲ Accessing special folders, such as Desktop, Start menu, Favorites, and My Documents, directly

WSH is included in Windows 2000 and as part of IE5. If you have either of these, it is already installed on your system. If not, you can download it from the MSDN Web site at http://msdn.Microsoft.com/scripting/windowshost/download/default.htm. The Microsoft scripting home page can be found at www.msdn.microsoft.com/scripting.

> **TIP:**   The Windows 2000 Support Tools consist of several WSH scripts and COM objects for managing those systems. This is an excellent source of examples showing "deep" access into the operating system using WSH scripts.

Other Scripting Tools

As we mentioned before, there are a host of other choices besides WSH if you decide for some reason that it is not appropriate for your company. We mention two of the better choices below: Kixtart and Perl. Before you choose to standardize on some other scripting tool, you should be aware of the following facts:

▼ Because WSH uses COM objects, whose components are loaded into system memory, the commands run much faster than with other scripting tools.

■ Microsoft has built native WSH script execution into the Windows 2000 command processor. Due to this support, a WSH script can run very fast. It is unlikely that a third-party tool could optimize performance to this degree.

▲ Since WSH is a core technology for Microsoft, they will likely continue to enhance it until virtually all system functions can be addressed with this tool. Other tools may come close over time, but they will necessarily always lag behind in incorporation of new features available in WSH.

Kixtart

Kixtart is a logon script processing utility for Windows NT. It is freeware included in the Windows NT Resource Kit. The tool was originally intended to be a logon script processor, but it can be used as an enhanced batch processing language. It can perform many common functions.

Perhaps the most significant difference between a batch language like Kixtart and WSH is the concept of objects. WSH is a lightweight language that doesn't try to incorporate native functions to support everything that may be needed. Rather, it calls the same set of Win32 Application Program Interfaces (APIs) as the standard, graphical Windows utilities. Because of this, its capabilities are easy to extend and enhance as the core operating system changes and evolves.

Before WSH was available, we used Kixtart to great effect as a replacement logon processor, and even extended it to perform other system administration functions. The Kixtart home page is http://netnet.net/~swilson/kix.

Practical Extraction and Reporting Language (PERL)

Reportedly, Larry Wall invented Perl because he wasn't happy with the text-manipulation capabilities of the existing utilities available for UNIX. Perl is an interpreted scripting language like VBScript or Jscript, but its syntax is a combination of many sources, including the C language. It includes the popular and powerful text processing capabilities of the UNIX commands **sed**, **awk**, and **tr**, but it has evolved far beyond a simple text processor. Perl is extensible and has many published modules that are freely available on the Web from the Open Source community. There are modules for database access, scientific calculations, and even game programming, to name a few. The Perl community maintains www.perl.com as a central resource for developers.

ActiveState maintains the Windows version of Perl (www.activestate.com), and a version with support is available for a nominal fee. This version gives access to the Registry and can exchange information with other Windows programs in a similar way to WSH. Because of its text-handling capabilities, Perl is often chosen for developing Common Gateway Interface (CGI) programs, though it can handle binary formats as well. There are even compilers for Perl to speed program execution, though it is not as fast as a compiled C program. Overall, Perl is a solid choice for scripting in Windows.

Common Object Model (COM)

In order to understand COM, it is necessary first to understand the concept of an object. An *object* is simply some system component, somewhere on the network. Each object has a set of attributes that define it. For example, an order entry application written in C++, which is an object-oriented programming language, might have a "customer" object. That object would contain all of the information on a customer in the system. The name, address, and phone number as well as the customer's past order history may all be attributes of the object.

Each object uses *methods* to perform actions. Using our example above, the customer object might contain a method for querying the customer by last name. When this function is desired in a program, the programmer simply references the object, the method, and passes some information to be used in the query. It is not necessary to redefine the query every time because it is contained in the object. In addition to its self-description, a COM component consists of one or more *classes* that describe objects and the associated methods. Using COM, objects (or classes) and their methods and associated data are compiled into binary executables that are, in fact, files with a DLL or EXE file name suffix. An executable module can contain more than one class.

COM is this object concept applied to operating systems and networking. In this paradigm, the printing subsystem in Windows could be an object. It is not necessary to know the attributes of the printer or even the location of the print server on the network in order to print a letter. The COM component for the printing system contains that information.

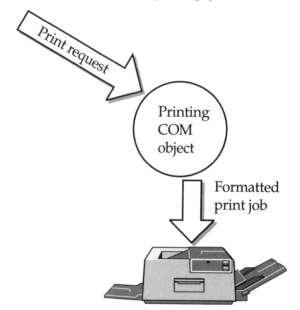

COM provides the necessary function of providing a common interface between components, licensing, and standard event services. It can also determine whether an outdated object can be removed from a system or what happened to an object that fails.

COM includes the ActiveX, COM+, and DCOM subsystems.

ActiveX

It can be said that ActiveX is Microsoft's answer to the Java technology from Sun Microsystems. An ActiveX control is roughly equivalent to a Java applet or JavaBean. Upon creating an ActiveX program, you have created a self-contained component that can be accessed using standard COM methods.

ActiveX components, called *controls*, can be seen in the file system as files with an OCX extension. OCX stands for "Object Linking and Embedding control," referencing the predecessor technology to ActiveX, OLE. OLE supports compound documents with elements from different programs. ActiveX extends this concept to a much broader scope.

The terms "COM object" and "ActiveX control" are often used interchangeably. Whatever the reference, such an object can be reused by many applications, reducing system complexity and increasing efficiency.

COM+

COM+ is viewed as Microsoft's answer to the approach known as Enterprise JavaBeans (EJB) endorsed by IBM, Oracle, and Sun. COM+ is an extension of COM and both an object-oriented programming architecture and a set of operating system services. A COM+ class has properties described in an interface. As with COM, the class and its interface are language neutral.

COM+ adds to COM a new set of system services for application components. Among the services provided by COM+ are

▼ The support of message-based transactions. This allows asynchronous communication between objects and provides tight integration with Microsoft Transaction Services (MTS).

■ A "publish and subscribe" service that functions similarly to a database trigger. One object's event can trigger the execution of a method in another object.

▲ A security service for transactions between objects that provides authentication and restricts execution of unauthorized methods or access to objects.

Distributed COM (DCOM)

DCOM is COM applied to a network of computers. DCOM provides objects that enable communication using a Remote Procedure Call (RPC). DCOM objects were intended to be used for distributed applications such as complex Web sites with multiple servers and data types.

DCOM is Microsoft's implementation of a system that provides similar capabilities to those defined in CORBA, the Common Object Request Broker Architecture. CORBA's development is controlled by the Object Management Group (OMG), and works across different operating systems. DCOM is necessarily Windows focused, but there are utilities available that bridge DCOM and CORBA˙components to provide an enterprise object model. To extend our previous printing example, it is not necessary to know the location of the printer or print server when using DCOM, as shown below:

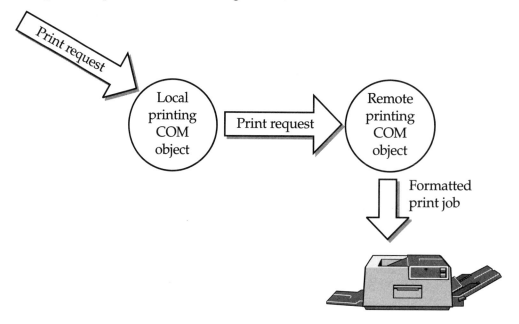

Related Technologies

The following technologies and Windows system services are what provide WSH with the ability and scope to perform so many functions. If WSH is the car, these technologies are the engine.

Active Directory Service Interface (ADSI)

Active Directory Service Interface (ADSI) defines a set of COM interfaces that let directory service client applications access services at the network directory layer. The current

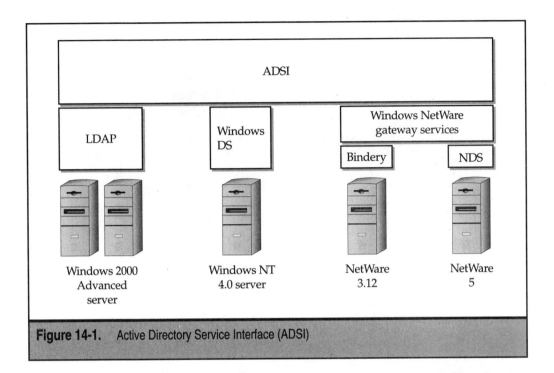

Figure 14-1. Active Directory Service Interface (ADSI)

directory services that ADSI can access include Windows NT, IIS, LDAP, NetWare Bindery and NDS, Exchange, and of course, Active Directory, as shown in Figure 14-1.

ADSI is the core technology accessed when writing WSH scripts that need to perform functions on an enterprise network, regardless of where the servers or other resources may be. ADSI provides a set of COM objects for access by WSH scripts and a set of low-level objects for access by C/C++ programs.

ActiveX Data Objects (ADO)

ADO is part of Microsoft's Universal Data Access Strategy (UDA). Essentially, it provides a COM interface to data sources on a network. ADO evolved from an earlier Microsoft technology, RDO (Remote Data Objects), that worked with ODBC to access relational databases. The support of nonrelational data support with RDO/ODBC was limited. ADO provides access to a wider array of data sources, and since it is a set of COM objects, it is abstracted from the physical location of the data.

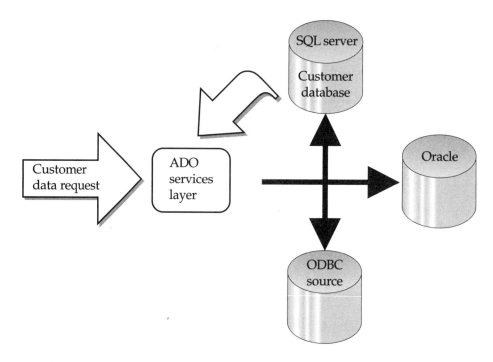

Active Server Page (ASP)

ASP is a Web technology used to extend the capabilities of standard HTML. ASP allows WSH or other scripts to be embedded in a Web page. If you are familiar with the Common Gateway Interface (CGI), ASP scripts are similar to CGI programs that execute on the server. ASP scripts can be used to tailor the Web page for the user based on input, or to populate Web pages with database content. ASP has the advantage of being compatible with most browsers since it is a server-side technology. ASP was originally a technology for IIS, but it has been adopted by other vendors and is now supported by many Web servers on Windows and other operating systems such as UNIX.

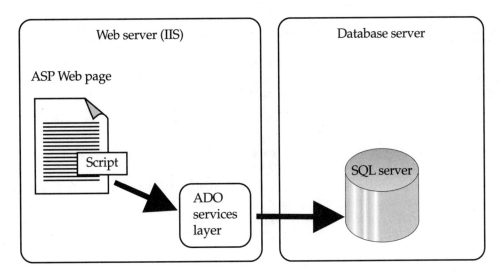

Collaboration Data Objects (CDO)

CDO is built along the lines of ADO, but instead of data sources, its focus is on messaging. CDO provides a set of objects that can be called by a script to provide e-mail or collaboration interfaces to systems like Microsoft Exchange. CDO also provides a scripting interface to the legacy Microsoft messaging technology MAPI (Messaging Application Programming Interface).

Windows Management Instrumentation (WMI)

WMI is to systems management what ADSI is to directory services management. Another core technology, the choice of where to look for a particular system service is often between ADSI and WMI. WMI is based on the Web-Based Enterprise Management (WBEM) initiative and the Common Information Model (CIM) adopted by the Distributed Management Task Force (DMTF). WMI abstracts the various network and system management services, such as the Desktop Management Interface (DMI) and SNMP. WMI has been available since the release of Windows NT Service Pack 4 and, like ADSI, is included as a standard feature in Windows 2000. The WMI resources page from Microsoft can be found at www.msdn.microsoft.com/downloads/sdks/wmi/whitepapers.asp. Numerous examples of WSH scripts—many using WMI—are available in the NT Resource Kit Supplement 4.

AUTOMATED SERVER CREATION

Since much of the work needed to create and maintain a user's desktop is mitigated by moving to server-based computing, the main job of building computers becomes that of server configuration. Although many organizations intend to standardize the build process, few can accomplish this goal by merely writing install instructions. The TSE build process, for example, would typically incorporate hundreds of manual steps and would thus be prone to installation errors and omissions. Over the years we have used many methods for accomplishing this important if onerous task. As the number and frequency of new servers and applications increases, you can quickly run out of hours in a day to get everything operating correctly, no matter how large the IT staff. The other problem is one of change control and consistency. Unless there is a standard method for building a server, a myriad of problems are bound to crop up. These can include DLL library conflicts, application version differences, application optional component differences, and driver conflicts. In this section we will introduce two methods to address this task: imaging and scripting. Though they are not mutually exclusive, they do have a different focus.

Imaging is the process by which a standard collection of software components is defined, tested, and certified. This collection includes the operating system, the applications, utilities, and any system configuration changes necessary to make the system work, as shown in Figure 14-2. A system image is often created using a third-party utility such as Norton Ghost or StorageSoft Imagecast software. These programs allow great flexibility in how the image gets loaded on a target system. Options include creating a self-loading image on a media set including a bootable floppy disk and CD-ROM, or creating a software distribution server in which the same image can be "multicast" to multiple target servers. Using such a product can speed up the loading process by orders of magnitude. The imaging method for bulk server creation has the following advantages:

▼   The imaging process requires no programming or scripting knowledge.

▲   Multicasting an image to multiple target servers saves time and is a standard feature of most server imaging products.

Limitations of imaging include

▼   An image is specific to each hardware type. Differences in NICs, video cards, array controllers, and manufacturer are difficult or impossible to handle within a simple image.

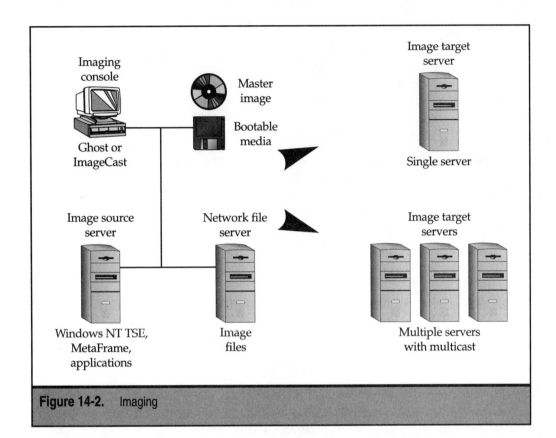

Figure 14-2.   Imaging

- ◼ It is difficult to track all the components and configuration changes that go into an image. For example, many large enterprise applications have many options that can be chosen during installation that affect how the application will run. Unless all of these options are recorded, there is no way to be sure which were chosen when the image was created.

- ◼ Imaging tools are not officially supported by Microsoft for NT servers.

- ▲ After the image is successfully installed on a target computer, information that is unique to the computer must be changed. This information includes the system identifier (SID), IP address, and so on.

NOTE: In addition to the above limitations, it is not currently possible to image servers running Windows 2000 in native mode due to the fact that the servers have a portion of Active Directory on them. Ghost gets around this by not cloning the server per se, but using the native Remote Install capability of Windows 2000.

Scripting the bulk server creation process involves the creation of recorded software packages that can be replayed on target servers, as shown in Figure 14-3. A package can simply be the standard application software setup program run unattended with a pre-defined answer file, or it can be a proprietary set of software components and system configuration changes created with a commercial software packaging program such as Citrix Installation Management Services (IMS). One server acts as a deployment host and contains the software packages. Windows Scripting Host can be used to replay the packages and make any needed configuration changes the same way on all servers. Optionally, a tool such as IMS from Citrix can be used to create application packages. IMS has its own facility for distributing these packages. The scripting method of bulk server creation has the following advantagess:

▼   One build can support different hardware types.

■   Microsoft supports scripting.

■   A high degree of flexibility for loading applications, service packs, utilities, and making configuration changes is possible with scripting.

■   A single application can be changed and deployed without significantly affecting the actual deployment script.

▲   It provides consistency at the OS level across all configured builds. This consistency helps provide stability for the entire environment.

Limitations include

▼   If anything other than a commercial package such as IMS is used, knowledge of scripting is required. Though we feel the effort is justified, learning VBScript or Jscript requires a higher level of commitment than simple batch programming.

▲   Areas of the operating system, such as the \wtsrv directory, must be granted read/write access for all users in order for the scripts to run. Though these security holes can be closed later, this must be taken into account during the server build process.

The two methods for building servers—using an imaging product and scripting—are not mutually exclusive. In fact, they can be used together quite effectively. We will discuss an example of this later in the chapter.

Imaging Products

We have used both ImageCast and Ghost in different client projects and have found them both to be feature-rich and reliable programs. Both programs have free trial versions with a built-in expiration feature. ImageCast can be found at www.innovativesoftware.com/home.asp. Ghost can be found at www.symantec.com/sabu/ghost/indexB.html.

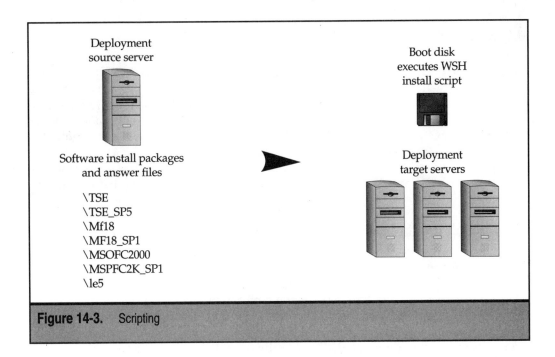

Figure 14-3. Scripting

Both products have unique features. However, a simple, generalized procedure for creating a disk image can be abstracted. First, to create a disk image, follow these steps:

1. Boot to the network with the boot floppy. This floppy is created manually or with a utility such as ImageCast's ClientBuilder. The boot disk will map a network drive for storing images.

2. Once booted, run the imaging client program from the floppy or from the mapped network drive.

3. Select Disk to Image from the client interface.

4. Choose a location on the network to store the file and proceed.

To load a disk image, follow these steps:

1. Boot to the network with the boot floppy from the target computer.

2. Once booted, run the imaging client program from the floppy or from the mapped network drive.

3. Choose Image to Disk from the client interface.

4. Choose the correct image file from the network drive and proceed.

5. Remove the boot disk while the target computer is being imaged so that it will reboot from the local hard drive once imaged.

Microsoft Support

To overcome some of the postinstallation configuration problems that can crop up, Microsoft has created a System Preparation Utility (SPU) for Windows NT. The release of these tools coincides with Microsoft's public endorsement of cloning technology. The Windows NT SPU provides each cloned PC with a unique system identifier (SID). It provides a Registry entry that Microsoft technical support can use to determine whether a system has been cloned. Refer to the Microsoft Web site at www.microsoft.com/ntworkstation to download this utility. Microsoft only "officially" supports workstation cloning. We have used these products many times with no trouble for server cloning. We also know firsthand of at least two major PC hardware manufacturers that use cloning products internally.

StorageSoft ImageCast Version 4.0 from Innovative Software

ImageCast is newer on the scene than Ghost but nearly as capable. It can create a disk image in stand-alone mode (as in the procedure described above), and it was the first tool to incorporate multicasting as a standard feature, as shown previously in Figure 14-2. ImageCast can manage the cloning of several target computers from one central console, and it can convert image files originally created with Ghost. It has an excellent boot disk creator called ClientBuilder. ClientBuilder runs as a "wizard" that takes the guesswork out of creating a boot floppy and choosing the correct protocol and network interface card drivers.

Norton Ghost Version 6.0, Enterprise Edition from Symantec

Ghost is the "old guard" in imaging products. It has been around a long time and is still arguably the best and most reliable utility for cloning computers. Version 6 now includes a multicast feature as well as native support for Windows 2000 Remote Installation Server. Ghost can be used to roll out Windows 2000 to PXE-Compliant (PC98) computers. The program includes some excellent utilities such as Ghost Walker, which can assign a compatible SID, and Ghost Explorer, which allows the selection of individual files and directories within an image file.

TIP: There is a potential problem with user profile corruption when the profile is dynamically loaded on a newly built server with time stamps newer than the profile. This same problem occurs on servers that were cloned or built manually. The work-around is to set the server's clock back to well before the profile was created, perhaps one year. After the first login as the Administrator, set the clock to the current date and time.

Using WSH to Build Servers

The main advantage of using WSH to build servers is the great flexibility in choosing configuration options, in making changes to system components such as the Registry, and in performing general system administration functions like moving files around or modifying policies or profiles. In this section we provide an outline for building a server using WSH techniques.

First you must designate a server as the deployment server. This server will contain all of the software and software installation packages for the target servers. Next, you will need to create a WSH script that can distribute the packages to the target servers, track the installation process, and make any necessary postinstallation changes.

NOTE: We begin this script outline assuming that the base operating system is already loaded. You have a few choices for accomplishing this. First, you can use the standard Windows NT unattended install facility. This operation is covered in detail in the Windows NT Deployment Guide available at www.microsoft.com/windows/downloads/bin/ntw/depguide.exe. The alternative is to use one of the imaging products we mentioned to partition the hard drive on the target and download the image. Upon reboot, the new target server can execute the WSH client script and begin to load other software. The one thing to keep in mind with these methods is RAID support. If the imaging product doesn't support your RAID configuration, it won't be able to partition the drive or push the image to the target server.

Outline of a Sample Bulk Server Creation Script

In Phase One, the script modifies the initial operating system install and installs MetaFrame.

1. Start with base Windows NT 4.0 Server, Terminal Server Edition with Service Pack 4. We intentionally start with SP4 so we can illustrate how to load a new Service Pack with WSH.

2. Wait for the server to start after the initial operating system image loads. You can write a routine that will detect whether the "server" service is running before executing the script.

3. Install MetaFrame 1.8. We've provided a sample VBScript code fragment below:

```
' ------------------------------------------------------------------
'                          Install MetaFrame
' ------------------------------------------------------------------
Function InstallMF18()
     On Error Resume Next
     Err.Clear
     WshShell.Run "change.exe user /install", 0, True
     WshShell.Run "e:\meta18\setup /u:e:\meta18\unattend.txt", 1, True
```

NOTE: On the line above, we see the MetaFrame setup program being run with a preformatted answer file.

```
     If(WshShell.RegRead("HKLM\Software\Microsoft\Windows\CurrentVersion
       \Uninstall\MetaFrame\DisplayName") = "MetaFrame 1.8")
     Then
```

```
          WshShell.LogEvent 0, "MetaFrame Install Successful"
    Else
          WshShell.LogEvent 1, "MetaFrame Install FAILED"
    End If
          WshShell.Run "change.exe user /execute", 0, True
End Function
```

4. Install MetaFrame 1.8 Service Pack 1.

5. Format the D: partition.

6. Read and set Registry values.

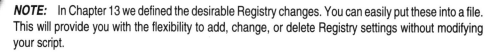

NOTE: In Chapter 13 we defined the desirable Registry changes. You can easily put these into a file. This will provide you with the flexibility to add, change, or delete Registry settings without modifying your script.

7. Set the system start setting to a five-second delay (boot.ini).

8. Make changes to the system's default settings. In this step you may want to

    Replace the default Start menu with one you have predefined.

    Relocate the Spool directory to the D: drive (which invariably has more space).

    Set desired system services to AutoStart. Such services include Time services (w32time) and the disk performance counter.

    Set the location and size of the swap file.

9. Change tracking using the Registry. You can have your script record progress by writing progress to the Registry. This is a useful way to track complex installations that require multiple reboots.

10. Enable autologon for the next phase.

11. Reboot.

Phase Two gets the system ready for production and installs any operating system service packs. It is usually a good idea to install these service packs as the last step.

1. Wait for the server to start after the initial operating system image loads.

2. Make final Registry changes. In this step you should

    Disable autologon.

    Change the Administrator password to the production value.

    Set Phase Two.

3. If you started the process of installing the operating system using Microsoft's unattended install, you will need to disable the autostart of that process.

4. Install Windows NT 4.0 Server, TSE Service Pack 5, as shown next:

```
'  ------------------------------------------------------------------
'                           Install Service Pack 5
'  ------------------------------------------------------------------
Function InstallTseSP5()
     On Error Resume Next
     Err.Clear
     WshShell.Run "change.exe user /install", 0, True
     If( WshShell.Run("e:\ms\sp5\update\update -u -z -q -o -n", 1, True) <> 0 )
     Then
          WshShell.LogEvent 1, "Terminal Server Service Pack 5 Install FAILED."
     Else
          Wscript.Sleep(5000)
          WshShell.LogEvent 0, "TSE Service Pack 5 Install successful."
     End If
     WshShell.Run "change.exe user /execute", 0, True
End Function
```

After these phases, the next phases will install the actual applications. We will discuss this in the next section.

APPLICATION PACKAGING

There are two basic approaches to application packaging that we have used with Terminal Services and MetaFrame and compatible applications. The first approach we will discuss is to use a commercial application packager such as Citrix Installation Management Services (IMS). IMS has its own method of recording changes to the Registry, INI files, and file system. IMS generates a package of program components and an associated installation script file that can be replayed on multiple MetaFrame servers.

The second approach is to use an *answer file*. In order for an application to get a compatibility certification from Microsoft, it must be able to be installed in unattended mode. Such applications carry the familiar "Windows NT Ready," or the Windows 2000 equivalent, on the packaging. The capability is also present in all newer Microsoft operating systems. An answer file contains predetermined responses to questions presented in the application's setup program. Answer files also often contain configuration options not possible when installing the application with a GUI.

Citrix Installation Management Services (IMS)

IMS not only facilitates the installation of applications on multiple MetaFrame servers, but it is also integrated with Load Balancing and the Published Application Manager. IMS requires at least three computers to function: a packager system for installing applications and creating packages; a file server for storing packages, installation scripts, and compatibility scripts; and a MetaFrame server to run Installer and receive the packages.

IMS can be used to install or uninstall an application and is composed of three components: Packager, published application enhancements, and Installer.

Packager

The Packager is responsible for "watching" the system while an application is installed and recording all changes. It can record changes to the Registry, individual INI files, file operations, and the creation of shortcuts, among other things. It runs as a background process while the application is being installed. When completed, the Packager's output consists of a package of files necessary to install the application and an installation script with a .wfs extension.

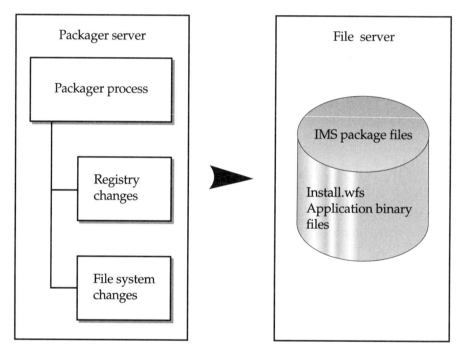

The configuration of the Packager server involves creating two bootable partitions. One contains a pristine copy of the operating system. This partition is referred to as the Backup Packager partition. The other partition contains a copy of the target operating system that will be used to record application changes. This partition is referred to as the Primary Packager operating system.

TIP: Make sure the Backup Packager partition is a fresh install—that is, no additional changes have been made to the operating system. It is also important not to make the server part of any domain. Doing so will cause undesirable Registry changes to be made.

The Backup Packager partition is used to refresh the Primary Packager partition after each application installation. The Packager application that runs on the Backup Packager partition has Backup and Restore functions to accomplish this.

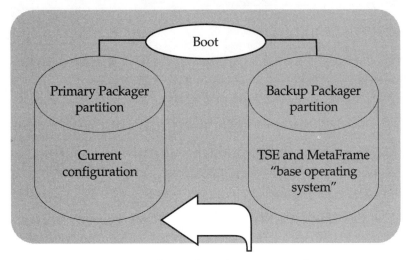

Restore after each package is created

Application Publishing Enhancements

These enhancements synchronize an application's published status with the application installation process. IMS installs or uninstalls an application based on whether it is published. This happens by simply using the Published Application Manager (PAM) to publish an IMS script file (.wfs) instead of an application.

Installer

The Installer is responsible for downloading packages and running installation scripts. The Installer resides on each MetaFrame server and "listens" for an install request coming from the PAM. In addition, the Installer gets a pointer to the application compatibility script so that script can be incorporated into the installation process.

Packaging an Application with IMS

The following checklist is the basic procedure for packaging an application with IMS:

1. Make sure the Primary Packager partition contains the same operating system as the target server.
2. Back up the Primary Packager partition from the Backup Packager partition in a clean state.
3. Create a directory on the file server to contain the packages.

4. Install the application software and allow the Packager program to record the changes.

> **TIP:** Only applications *not* requiring a reboot as part of the installation can be packaged.

5. Optionally, install any service packs or make other changes related to the application. These can all be part of the same package.

6. Optionally, allow Packager to merge changes from an application compatibility script.

7. Run the Packager application and stop the recording process. After the packaging has completed, you will be prompted for the following information:

   The name and path of the application executable.

   The package destination on the file server.

   The package description.

   Confirm settings.

8. Restore the Primary Packager partition by booting to the Backup Packager partition and choosing Restore from the Packager application menu.

Publishing an IMS Application Package

You can publish a package by running the Published Application Manager.

1. Select "Filter Servers by," and then choose to list servers with an IMS Installer and license.

2. Choose the server or servers from the Available list and click Add to add them to the Configured column.

3. The Installers on the servers chosen will begin installing the package as soon as you exit the PAM.

> **TIP:** You can monitor the installation's progress from the Citrix Server Administration window

Other Commercial Application Packagers

There are several commercial programs that include the ability to do remote or unattended software installations. ImageCast, for example, contains this ability, as do framework products such as Novell's ZenWorks and HP OpenView. You must decide whether such applications will add or detract from the overall complexity of your network and whether you have the personnel to support them. We prefer to keep it simple. IMS is sold and supported by Citrix and is integrated with Load Balancing and the Published Application Manager. The method of using answer files is supported by Microsoft as is using WSH to further distribute and customize the application deployment process.

Answer Files

The strategy behind using answer files is to take advantage of an application's inherent ability to be installed in an unattended fashion. Multiple applications and answer files can be automated with a simple WSH script. The advantage of this approach is that it is more generic and therefore less prone to obsolescence, and more likely to have the code survive the departure of an individual programmer. The code fragment for MetaFrame installation, shown earlier in the chapter provides an example of installing the product with an answer file from a WSH script.

SYSTEM ADMINISTRATION TASKS

Here, we've included code snippets that can be incorporated into scripts and used for some common, useful system administration tasks. In all cases, the language is Wscript; the system interface is WMI.

The following code can be used to list drive partitions with less than 30 percent free space:

```
Set DiskSet = GetObject("winmgmts:{impersonationLevel=impersonate}")
.ExecQuery("select FreeSpace,Size,Name from Win32_LogicalDisk where
DriveType=3")
for each Disk in DiskSet
If (Disk.FreeSpace/Disk.Size) < 0.30 Then
WScript.Echo "Drive " + Disk.Name + " has less than 30 percent free space."
End If
Next
```

This code will list stopped services:

```
Set ServiceSet = GetObject("winmgmts:{impersonationLevel=impersonate}")
# Change the StartMode below to find Manual or Auto services

.ExecQuery("select * from Win32_Service where State='Stopped' and StartMode='Auto'")
for each Service in ServiceSet
WScript.Echo Service.Description
next
if ServiceSet.Count = 0 Then WScript.echo "No stopped services found."
```

Use this final code snippet for collecting jobs with high CPU utilization:

```
set events = GetObject("winmgmts:{impersonationLevel=impersonate}")
.ExecNotificationQuery _ ("select * from __instancemodificationevent within 5 where
targetinstance isa 'Win32_Processor' and targetinstance.LoadPercentage > 50")
if err <> 0 then
```

```
WScript.Echo Err.Description, Err.Number, Err.Source
end if
WScript.Echo "Querying jobs with high CPU Utilization."
WScript.Echo ""
do
set NTEvent = events.nextevent
if err <> 0 then
WScript.Echo Err.Number, Err.Description, Err.Source
Exit Do
else
WScript.Echo NTEvent.TargetInstance.DeviceID WScript.Echo
NTEvent.TargetInstance.LoadPercentage
end if
loop
```

FURTHER READING

We have found the following books and Web sites to be invaluable in learning about WSH and related technologies. Many of these books approach the subject in the context of Web programming; however, much of the content can be abstracted for other purposes.

▼ *ADO 2.0 Programmer's Reference,* by David Sussman and Alex Homer (Wrox Press)

■ *ADSI ASP Programmer's Reference,* by Steve Hahn (Wrox Press)

■ *ADSI CDO Programming with ASP,* by Mikael Freidlitz and Todd Mondor (Wrox Press)

■ *Learning VBScript,* by Paul Lomax (O'Reilly)

■ *Professional ADSI Programming - Active Directory Services Interface,* by Simon Robinson (Wrox Press)

▲ *Windows Script Host Programmer's Reference,* by Dino Esposito (Wrox Press)

These Web sites are great sources of information. By their nature, they are more current than most printed material.

▼ Microsoft's Programmers Reference for WSH: www.microsoft.com/management/wshobj.htm

■ Microsoft's Developer's Network download site. Here you can find the current versions of WSH, ADSI, and other related technologies, as well as examples and sample programs written by Microsoft and others: msdn.microsoft.com/developer/default.htm

■ An excellent private site: http://wsh.glazier.co.nz

■   Clarence Washington's Windows scripting site: http://
     cwashington.netreach.net

▲   For add-on products that work with WSH: www.netal.com

Windows 2000 magazine often contains useful scripting and Windows architecture information. The same publisher also puts out the *Win32 Scripting Journal* in printed form
and on the Web at www.win32scripting.com.

CHAPTER 15

Application Services

One of the challenges of deploying MetaFrame and Windows Terminal Services is knowing how to use the myriad features and services to build a stable, high-performance Corporate ASP. During our careers, we have been called in many times to fix failed ASP implementation efforts. We've drawn many of our "best practices" out of this experience. We've had an opportunity to learn not only from our mistakes, but also from the mistakes of others. The potential complexity of a MetaFrame and Terminal Services deployment is largely eliminated by applying a rigorous methodology for testing, user education, and application selection, as described in Chapter 12. In this chapter we focus on the application deployment process. We will discuss the general installation and configuration of applications in a MetaFrame and Terminal Services environment, as well as provide specific tips and checklists for common applications. We will also discuss the proper configuration of the application-specific components of MetaFrame and Terminal Services.

ASP APPLICATION STRATEGIES

The idea behind building a Corporate ASP in the first place is to provide a way to distribute common applications to users that is low in cost and complexity but high in functionality and performance. It is important to keep this "end state" in mind when selecting or writing applications to be run in a Corporate ASP environment. An application that is not stable in a traditional distributed computing network isn't going to work better under server-based computing. In fact, it will probably exhibit new problems. It is also of critical importance to take the client environment into account. If you intend to reuse or deploy PCs or Windows terminals, the capabilities for each are quite different and will affect application functionality.

Application Features and Requirements

We have created the following list of features and requirements to aid you in the application selection process:

▼ Applications should be stable and perform well in a traditional, distributed computing environment.

■ Ideally, an application should execute in multithreaded fashion and make efficient use of memory and CPU resources when running in a multiuser environment. This would seem to preclude DOS and most 16-bit applications. We will provide a method, though, for dealing with these types of applications later in the chapter.

■ If possible, the application should have stated support from the manufacturer. With Windows NT 4.0 Server, TSE, this is hit or miss. Some manufacturers do have support; some do not. With Windows 2000, however, in order for a software package to be Windows 2000 ready, it must support execution under Terminal Services. As such, we expect multiuser support to become less of a problem over time.

■ The use of multimedia in applications should be kept to an absolute minimum. Sound, graphics, or video should be limited to mission-critical features only, because the cost of the extra network bandwidth consumed by these features must be justified.

NOTE: The Citrix VideoFrame product can be used for live video in a Corporate ASP. It has a very efficient protocol for distributing video to the client.

■ The application should make the most use of the Windows printing system and be as efficient as possible in the creation and distribution of print jobs. Here again, we issue a warning for very graphic-intensive programs. These programs typically generate very large print files that must travel over the LAN or WAN to the printer. This must be taken into account when planning for the management of the available bandwidth.

▲ Similarly, the application should make efficient use of network bandwidth if it requires back-end access to legacy host computers, databases, or Web servers. This type of client-server application should be run from the data center and access the back-end resource over a high-speed switch LAN. Avoid running these applications across a WAN link.

Application Optimization

We discuss the process of installing and configuring applications in later sections. But first, it is necessary to address some specific optimization issues for the following categories of applications.

DOS and 16-Bit Applications

In order for a DOS or 16-bit application to run under any flavor of Windows NT, a separate resource pool must be created for that program. This is due to the fact that such applications cannot share memory in the same way as 32-bit programs that were created specifically to run on Windows NT. This resource pooling program is called "ntvdm" for "NT Virtual DOS Machine." It uses the partitioning capability of the Intel architecture to create a virtual 8086 environment in which each DOS program can run. When you run a DOS or 16-bit Windows program on Windows NT and open the task manager, you will not see the program executable listed. Rather, you will see ntvdm.

```
Windows Task Manager                              _ □ ×
File  Options  View  Help

Applications  Processes │ Performance │

  Image Name              PID   CPU   CPU Time   Mem Usage ▲
  System Idle Process       0    99   39:14:15        16 K
  System                    8    00    0:00:38       212 K
  smss.exe                136    00    0:00:00       344 K
  csrss.exe               164    01    0:00:14     2,508 K
  winlogon.exe            184    00    0:00:07       440 K
  services.exe            212    00    0:00:05     4,904 K
  lsass.exe               224    00    0:00:11       532 K
  WS_FTP95.exe            300    00    0:00:04       352 K
  svchost.exe             388    00    0:00:00     2,472 K
  spoolsv.exe             416    00    0:00:01     2,748 K
  svchost.exe             476    00    0:00:11     5,728 K
  regsvc.exe              512    00    0:00:00       812 K
  ntvdm.exe               516    00    0:00:13     1,968 K
  mstask.exe              532    00    0:00:00     2,216 K
  taskmgr.exe             536    00    0:00:00     1,884 K
  wfica32.exe             652    00    0:02:01       688 K
  wfcrun32.exe            656    00    0:00:00     3,800 K
  explorer.exe            672    00    0:00:56     3,640 K
  msmsgs.exe              856    00    0:00:00     2,440 K ▼

                                           End Process

Processes: 21    │ CPU Usage: 1%   │ Mem Usage: 77856K / 310684K
```

Because these older programs cannot share resources, they do not scale well. We have seen environments in which an application was being migrated from an older 16-bit version to a newer 32-bit version. The 16-bit program took two to three times the resources of its newer 32-bit cousin. We realize that these older programs must often be run on the Corporate ASP, particularly as part of a migration effort. We will offer some tips on running them safely in the "Server Farms" section in this chapter.

DOS Program Keyboard Polling   Another feature of some DOS programs to look out for is keyboard polling. Most DOS programs were written to run in a single-user environment, and data entry screens typically do nothing until the user presses a key. In order to respond as quickly as possible, the program polls the keyboard, sometimes hundreds or thousands of times per second. In a multiuser environment this can wreak havoc with system performance. Even though Windows NT runs ntvdm to give such a program its own resource pool, it must still grant access to hardware components such as the keyboard, mouse, and video. In some cases, the keyboard polling can be adjusted to more reasonable levels by using a standard command like DOSKBD or a third-party utility like Clip2F or Tame. If the DOS program will not respond to limiting the keyboard polling, it should not be used in a Corporate ASP. We have seen a single, problematic DOS application consume 100 percent of the available resources on a MetaFrame server.

TIP: The DOSKBD (or other similar utility) can be run from the autoexec.nt file that is accessed for each DOS session. The autoexec.nt file is specified with the PIF editor. Issuing the following command at the command prompt can collect initial statistics on the DOS application:

```
DOSKBD /StartMonitor SOMEPROG.EXE
```

32-Bit Applications and the Registry

Just because an application is written to be 32-bit does not mean that it makes effective use of the Registry. It is important that such an application use the Registry to store its settings for a variety of reasons.

▼   Application packaging is made much simpler when it is known that all changes made by the installation process are in a particular group of Registry keys.

■   The application installation process in Terminal Services (**change user /install**) makes a copy of the Registry changes that an install program makes for each user (HKEY_CURRENT_USER). If an application uses an INI file or incorrectly writes user-specific information to the HKEY_LOCAL_MACHINE key, it is more problematic to get that application functioning in a multiuser environment.

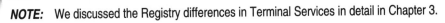

NOTE: We discussed the Registry differences in Terminal Services in detail in Chapter 3.

▲   Registry changes can be easily propagated between servers through a number of methods, as described in Chapter 14.

Custom Applications

There is nothing wrong with deploying custom applications in a Corporate ASP as long as you keep the environment in mind. Such applications should be 32-bit and should avoid hard-coded values for elements such as network paths or data sources. You should also keep in mind any library dependencies such as those required by Visual Basic. These libraries must exist on each server in the server farm.

As mentioned previously, an application should write all user-specific information to the HKEY_CURRENT_USER Registry key and all global system information to the HKEY_LOCAL_MACHINE key.

INSTALLING AND CONFIGURING APPLICATIONS

There are two basic methods for installing an application on a MetaFrame server. The recommended method is to use the Control Panel and run the Add/Remove Programs application. The other is to run the **change user /install** and **change user /execute** commands from a command prompt.

Using Add/Remove Programs

We have found that installing the application using Add/Remove Programs creates the "shadow key" properly in all cases. The Add/Remove Programs application monitors changes to the HKEY_CURRENT_USER key and saves them in the shadow key. This key is then propagated to each user, as shown in Figure 15-1, so that they may have unique settings for that application.

NOTE: Do not allow the system to reboot until after you click Finish in the Add/Remove Programs application. Doing so will ensure that the shadow key information is safely written.

Using Change User /Install

Using the command works well most of the time, but we have seen that in some cases shadow key information is missed. For example, there is a known problem installing Internet Explorer 4 in this manner, but it works perfectly if you use the Add/Remove Programs application. This method involves opening a command prompt, typing **change user /install**, installing the application, then typing **change user /execute**.

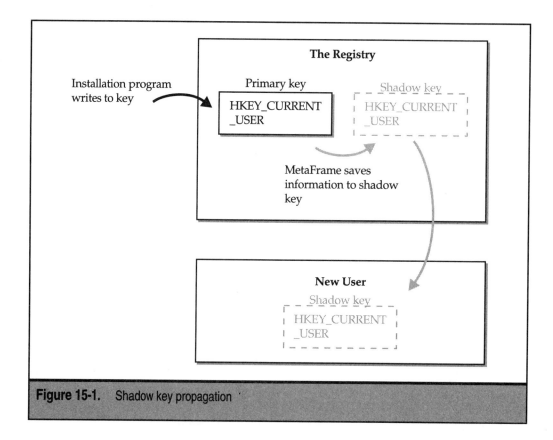

Figure 15-1.   Shadow key propagation

NOTE: If you use this method, make sure you do not allow the system to reboot without first issuing the **change user /execute** command. If you do not issue the command, the system may not properly record the changes to the Registry.

Application Installation Checklist

The basic procedure for installing an application under MetaFrame is as follows:

1. Make sure you are logged onto the test server console as a member of the local Administrators group.

2. Kill any remote sessions with the Citrix Server Administration utility.

3. Run the Add/Remove Programs application and select the application's setup program to begin installation.

4. Click Finish after the application is finished installing and before the server reboots.

5. If an application compatibility script exists, run it. Review the notes in the script and any "read me" notes on application compatibility, and perform any other necessary steps.

6. At this point this application is installed, and you can begin testing.

NOTE: Though you can uninstall an application with Add/Remove Programs, we don't recommend it. Citrix also provides uninstall scripts that reside in the %SystemRoot%\Application Compatibility Scripts\Uninstall directory. We recommend a strategy of using Windows Scripting Host (WSH) and possibly imaging products to create standard server images including packaged applications. If an application needs to be removed, simply restore the image that was current before the application package was installed. Alternatively, you can rewind an installation script that was played with WSH by creating a version that backs out all the changes that were made. Other methods can leave remnants of the application, in the form of leftover Registry changes or library files that can cause problems with the system or with other applications.

Postinstallation Changes

After installing an application on the MetaFrame server using the Add/Remove Programs application or the command-line method, other changes are often required to make an application perform well in a multiuser environment. Unless an application was written specifically with Terminal Services or MetaFrame in mind, it is likely that some postinstallation changes will be necessary to provide user-specific program settings, or library file locations, for example. An *application compatibility script* is a fancy name for a batch file that makes any changes to the operating system that are necessary for a specific application to function in a multiuser environment. There are two types of application compatibility scripts: install and logon.

Install Scripts

The two main functions of the install script are to remove any inappropriate changes to the HKEY_LOCAL_MACHINE Registry key, and to verify that the other logon scripts are correct. An install script will first verify that the root drive has been properly specified. If it has not, the script will open the ROOTDRV2.CMD file so you can specify it. If the root drive has been specified, it proceeds to correct inappropriate writes to HKEY_LOCAL_MACHINE as well as perform any other necessary cleanup work to make the application run correctly. Finally, it adds a call to the USRLOGN2.CMD file that will call the appropriate logon script for the application.

Logon Scripts

As the name implies, logon scripts are designed to correct problems with the user logon environment, either with the HKEY_CURRENT_USER key, the user's home directory, or user-specific application settings. The USRLOGN2.CMD batch file calls the application logon scripts. This script is called by the main logon file, USRLOGON.CMD. USRLOGON.CMD is responsible for creating the RootDrive variable used by all logon scripts to identify the user's home directory.

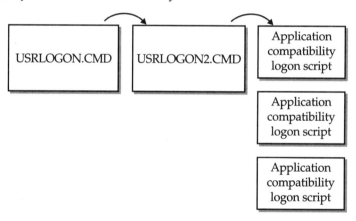

The RootDrive variable defines both the user's home drive and the home path and can be used instead of the UNC path defined in User Manager for Domains. Use of the drive letter is preferable because the user will not have access to directories above the directory where the home drive is mapped.

Installation Tips

Though it is impossible to provide installation tips for all common applications, we thought it would be appropriate to include a few to set expectations. There is a wealth of information about application configuration on the Citrix Web site (www.citrix. com/ support). We have found the online knowledge base to be particularly useful, as it contains many technical notes from other users on application difficulties and the methods used to fix or work around them.

The following examples show the format you should consider for application installation and configuration checklists. They are provided both as an example of the process of installing an application under MetaFrame and as a suggestion for your own record keeping.

Palm Pilot HotSync Installation Checklist

This is an example of an application in which a compatibility script is not available, and changes for the multiuser environment must be made manually.

NOTE: The following application checklist was created and tested using the Palm Pilot III and with both PCs and Windows terminals for clients. The HotSync application worked well where there was plenty of bandwidth between the client device and the MetaFrame server (over 1.544 Mbps) but exhibited synchronization problems in constrained bandwidth environments. We provide this example because the application was such a useful way to share data from a central server to mobile professionals in the field.

1. Go to the command prompt and type **net stop w32time**, or, alternatively, stop the time synchronization service in the Services application in the Control Panel.
2. Set the date back one year. Since HotSync uses time stamps to determine what to sync, this step is necessary to make sure all data is captured the first time it is run by a user.
3. Proceed to install the HotSync application.

NOTE: The next time the server is rebooted, the w32time service will start and automatically set the correct date.

4. Insert the HotSync application CD into the CD-ROM drive.
5. Go to the Control Panel and run Add/Remove Programs.
6. Browse to the \PALMSFW\DISK1 directory on the CD and select the Setup program. Click Next.
7. Click on Next in the Welcome dialog box.
8. Click on Next in the Pre-Install dialog box.
9. Change the destination folder by clicking on Browse. Type **D:\APPS\PALM** and press ENTER. The system will respond with a dialog box that reads "The folder d:\apps\palm does not exist. Do you want to the folder to be created?" Click on Yes.
10. Click on the Custom button, and then click on Next.

11. In the Select Components dialog, deselect Quick Tour and click Next.

12. Leave Synchronize with Palm Desktop selected and click Next.

13. In the Select Program Folder dialog, leave it as is and click Next.

14. To create a user account, type **Default User**. This will create a directory under D:\APPS\PALM named UserD. Click Next.

15. Click Next again.

16. Click on OK for Serial Port Setup, even though there is no cradle hooked up.

17. At the next screen choose Com1:, and then click on OK. The software will then install the files needed.

18. Choose No in the Perform Mail Setup dialog box.

19. Click Finish.

20. Return to Add/Remove Programs and click Finish.

21. Take HotSync out of the Startup group.

22. Make changes to the following Registry key as described below.

```
\HKLM\Software\Microsoft\Windows NT\CurrentVersion\Terminal
Server\Install\Software\U.S. Robotics\Pilot Desktop\Core
```

There will be two entries under Core. One is the HotSync path, and the other is the data path. The data path needs to change from D:\apps\palm to the user's home data path as specified in the RootDrive variable.

Checklist for Configuring an ODBC Data Source to Use with RMS

This is an example of multiple applications being installed and configured together. The checklist refers to other checklists that would provide detail on individual applications. This example is provided to show how certain applications will have interdependencies that must be taken into account in the installation process.

1. Install MDAC version 2.1, Service Pack 2. (Refer to MDAC installation checklist.)

2. Run the ODBC compatibility script.

3. Configure ODBC data source to access the database to be used for RMS. (Refer to ODBC for RMS configuration checklist.)

4. Copy the resulting rms.dsn file to the following directory on all MetaFrame server C:\program files\common files\odbc\data sources.

5. Install RMS and specify the data source set by rms.dsn. (Refer to RMS installation checklist.)

6. Set RMS not to record data for system processes (except print spoolers).

7. Set RMS not to record data for "system" user.

8. Add Read permissions for all users to \HKLM\software\odbc and all subkeys.

TESTING YOUR APPLICATIONS

In Chapter 18 we discuss the testing process in detail as it applies to the entire Corporate ASP deployment project. In this part of the chapter, we provide some examples of this testing methodology as it applies to applications.

Manage the Application List

Before launching into the application test process, it is important to have a controllable list of applications targeted for production. The list should be as small as possible but still have representative applications in any category that your company needs to use. What you want to avoid is a lack of standardization within a category. For example, a large organization may be using both Microsoft Office and Lotus SmartSuite. Make every effort to choose one application (or suite, in this case) for deployment in the Corporate ASP. It will reduce complexity, ease support, and cause less confusion to the user community.

Application Testing Procedure

Each application should go through two phases of testing—component testing and system testing—in order to assess how it functions running by itself and as part of a fully configured server. The strategy is to have as much breadth and depth of testing coverage as is practical, given the realities of most fast-paced corporate IT departments. The effort of creating and refining an application testing process is worthwhile. Over time, the IT staff will become fast, proficient, and confident at running the tests.

Component Testing

This phase of testing is designed to exercise an application running by itself in a multiuser environment. This can be especially important with applications that were not written specifically for this environment, do not have application compatibility scripts, or are older DOS or 16-bit applications.

Generic Functions The generic functions of the component test phase are functions that are common to most applications. Examples of generic functions are Execute (run the program), Exit, File-Print, File-Open, and Cut and Paste. Coverage of generic functions is important to ensure the application works as expected in a multiuser environment. One test list can be created that will cover every application slated for deployment, or at least broad categories of applications. Not every test on the list will apply, but running the test list is important nonetheless.

Specific Functions As the name implies, these are functions that are specific to each application. At least one test list should be created for each application to cover specific functions. Examples are running a custom macro in Microsoft Excel, creating a new project in Visual J++, and changing the color saturation in Adobe Photoshop.

System Testing

The system testing phase is designed to ensure that an application behaves predictably on a server loaded with other applications. This is also typically the phase that includes some load testing for performance. A system test involves running the following steps:

▼ Run the component tests again on a fully configured server. Such a server has all the applications slated for production deployment loaded, the network connected, and is participating in a domain, a server farm, and load balancing. The idea is to set up an environment that is as close to the production environment as possible.

■ Test necessary application integration functions—for example, database access through Microsoft Excel, cutting and pasting between applications, running a mail-merge macro in Microsoft Word, or running a custom client application that provides a front-end user interface to a legacy system.

■ Load test the application. Establish as many user sessions as are likely to be used in production. This can either be done literally, through scripting, or through a commercial testing application. Have several people run test lists on the application simultaneously.

▲ Test the application using all targeted client environments. This includes not only desktop PCs, laptops, and Windows terminals, if you plan to use them, but also different points in the enterprise network and over different types of network connections.

Anecdotal Testing

This is not an "official" test phase and is taboo in many formal testing processes. However, we have found that a period of "beating on the application" after all other formal testing has been done is often very useful. This type of undirected testing allows the testers to think "outside the box" and exercise functions that the test list creators may not have thought of. Anecdotal testing is no substitute for formal testing and should never be used as the sole testing method.

Test Lists

There is no secret to creating good test lists, but there is an art to it that can only be mastered with practice. The most important thing to remember is not to let best get in the way of better. In other words, it is better to start with a basic test list and make it better over time, than to delay the test process until you have the "perfect" test list. This elusive goal will never be realized without experience in the process. Table 15-1 shows a test list of generic functions that can be applied to Lotus Organizer or other applications. Table 15-2 shows a test list of functions specific to Organizer. You should feel free to adapt it to other programs or even modify its structure to fit your needs.

Sample Detailed Test List for Lotus Organizer 97

Lotus Organizer 97 is a personal information manager and a group-scheduling tool that displays information in an electronic notebook. Organizer can create a customized calendar to track meetings and appointments as well as manage to-do lists, long-range events, and anniversaries. Organizer's group-scheduling feature works with Lotus Notes 4.51. In addition to managing information in separate sections, Organizer lets you see important information in the calendar.

NOTE: Substitute the information in parentheses in the tables with information specific to the application being tested.

Step	Test (Generic)	Description	Expected Result	Result	Pass/Fail	Notes
1	Launch Method #1	Click App icon on the desktop.	App executes.	App executed.	P	
2	Launch Method #2	Click Start, Programs, (Program Group), (App Name)	App executes.	App executed.	P	
3	Open a (document)	Choose File, Open from the menu.	The default or last data directory is displayed.	The default directory was displayed.	P	Might want to run this test two more times to see which directory is displayed.
4	Print a (document)	Choose File, Print from the menu.	Current (document) prints in full.	Document printed.	P	
...						
24	Exit Method #1	Choose File, Exit from the menu.	App exits.	Exited	P	
25	Exit Method #2	Click the X in the upper-right corner of the main application window.	App exits.	Exited	P	This method is faster.

Table 15-1.   Generic Functions Test List 1

Step	Test (Specific)	Description	Expected Result	Result	Pass/Fail	Notes
1	Create an Entry Method #1	Double-click a blank area of an Organizer page; a dialog box appears. Enter your information, select the options that are appropriate for your entry, and click OK.	New entry is saved.	Entry saved.	P	
2	Create an Entry Method #2	Choose Create (menu) – Entry in, and then choose the type of entry you want to create.	New entry is saved.	Entry saved.	P	
3	Delete an Entry Method #1	Drag and drop your entry to the icon that looks like a wastebasket in the lower-left corner of your screen.	Entry is deleted.	Entry deleted.	P	
4	Delete an Entry Method #2	Select your entry and press the Delete key.	Entry is deleted.	Entry not deleted.	F	Possible keyboard mapping problem?
5	Edit an Entry Method #1	Double-click the entry and make your changes, then click OK.	Changes are saved.	Changes saved.	P	
6	Edit an Entry Method #2	Double-click an entry to edit it directly on the page	Changes are saved.	Changes saved.	P	

Table 15-2. Lotus Organizer Test List—Contact Entries

Step	Test (Specific)	Description	Expected Result	Result	Pass/Fail	Notes
7	Link an Entry	Click on the icon that looks like a solid chain in the toolbox, and click the first entry you want to link. Go to the second entry you want to link to, and click that entry. Click on the icon again next to either entry to move between the links.	Entries are linked.	Entries linked.	P	

Table 15-2.   Lotus Organizer Test List—Contact Entries *(continued)*

Pass or Fail Status

Once a test list has been run, a report of the application, test lists, tests run, and the status can be generated. It is up to you whether or not to deploy an application that has not passed particular tests, but we recommend that you have a healthy intolerance for error. It is not unreasonable to expect an application to pass all tests before being considered for production deployment.

Test Cycles

As shown in Figure 15-2, all test lists run on a particular application are considered one *test cycle*. It is very likely that not all tests will have passed. After the test cycle, fixes or corrections are made, and all test lists with failed tests are run again. Once all the failed tests have passed, a final run of the entire suite of test lists is advisable to make sure nothing new was "broken" during this phase. This is often refered to as *regression testing*. The cycle repeats until all tests pass or until the pass percentage meets your predetermined acceptance level. Once all tests have passed or met the goal, the application can be considered a candidate for production deployment.

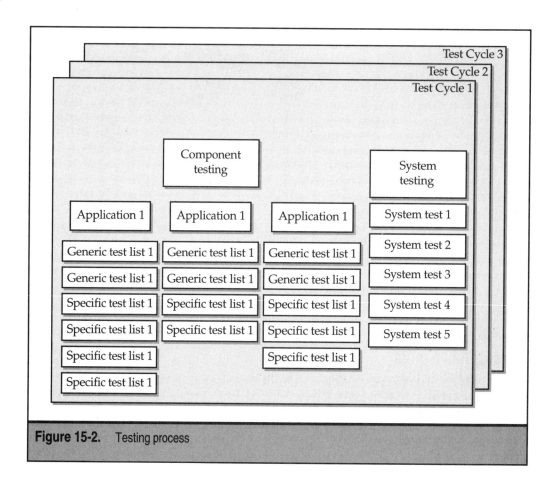

Figure 15-2.   Testing process

Production Deployment Process

Once an application has completed the testing process, it is time to manage its deployment into the production environment. Unless extensive load testing was done before deployment, we recommend putting the application on one or just a few servers to begin with and using the ICA pass-through capability to direct users to the new application, as shown in Figure 15-3. You should also consider having an "early adopter" user group that can begin using the application before it is deployed throughout the enterprise. A week or two of running the application in this manner can reveal any last-minute issues that were not discovered in testing, without unduly burdening the user community with problems.

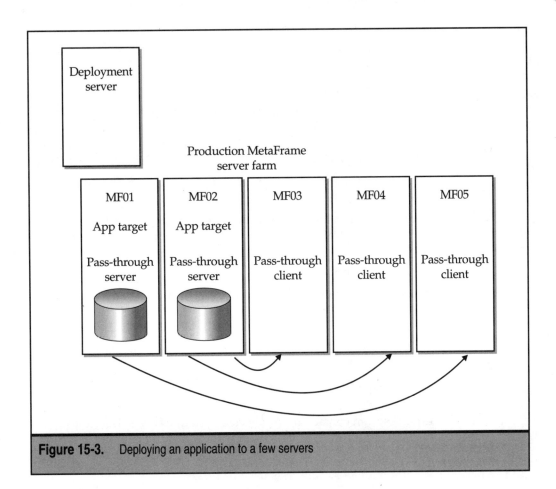

Figure 15-3. Deploying an application to a few servers

Sample Process Checklist for Application Deployment

The following checklist can provide a guideline for an application deployment process. You should modify it to fit your organization and established procedures.

1. A qualified request for application support by the Corporate ASP is received.

2. Verification that management has approved the application is completed.

3. A contact person for the application has been identified. This person will be the point of contact for communicating the application's status.

4. Review of the application's specifications and requirements is done.

   Is the software 32 bit?

   Are there Registry entries?

   If internally developed, are network paths hard-coded?

   Are there any system library dependencies?

5. Install application on test server. Document all steps of the install.

6. Perform any necessary software configuration for operation on TSE; for example, Registry changes, INI file settings, file or directory modifications.

7. Create specific function test lists. Determine suitability of generic function test lists and modify as appropriate. Create test lists for both component and system test phases.

8. Begin Test Cycle 1. Perform component testing.

9. Repeat component testing until all tests have passed, or pass percentage is acceptable.

10. Begin system testing. Add application to last good server image that includes other production applications and operating system modifications. Rerun component tests and add system tests.

11. As part of system testing, load-test the application. Test with a single user, usually contact.

12. Get five test users from contact to run selected system test lists. Determine whether further load testing is necessary or if results can be extrapolated from the five-user test.

13. Repeat test cycle until all system tests have passed.

14. Turn over testing documentation and certification to production IT staff for installation.

15. Install application on one or two production servers. Set up ICA pass-through to make the application available to the appropriate users. Monitor the server's performance to ensure that there are no utilization spikes or any other irregularities.

16. Survey users to see if application is performing properly.

17. Schedule production deployment using chosen distribution method (Windows Scripting Host, imaging, or IMS).

18. Deploy application.

19. After one week of production, survey a sample of users to see if application is performing properly.

SERVER FARMS

A *server farm* is simply a collection of MetaFrame servers that can be managed centrally. *Managed* is defined as making configuration changes that are common to all as well as defining application parameters that are common to all. Applications or desktops published on a server farm are seen in the Citrix Program Neighborhood as application sets, as shown below:

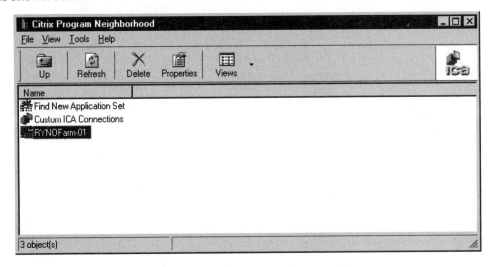

A server can be in most combinations of Windows NT workgroups and domains. Servers in the same or in different domains can be part of the same server farm, though a server can only be a member of one farm at a time. Users connecting to the farm must be in the intersection of all the concerned NT trust domains. You can use the Citrix Published Application Manager to move a server from one farm to another. Similarly, servers can be part of the same or different TCP/IP subnets.

A server farm does not depend on the Load Balancing Option Pack being installed, but load balancing is often applied to all servers within a farm. It is possible to have multiple server farms, each with its own characteristics, applications, and load balancing, but we don't recommend it unless there is a good business reason. We like to keep things simple, and managing multiple server farms can start to become complex.

Server Farm Configuration

Server farms are configured through the Citrix Published Application Manager (CPAM). You simply run the CPAM and set the scope of management to Citrix Server Farms. You will then be allowed to create or modify a server farm and add servers to that farm.

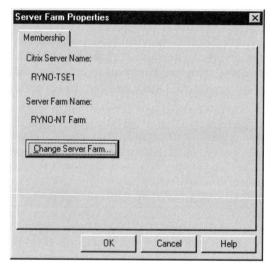

Server Farm Configuration Checklist

You can use the following checklist to configure a server farm.

1. Log onto the MetaFrame server console as the Administrator account that is in the Local Administrators group.
2. Run the Citrix Published Application Manager.
3. Click View and then Select Scope.
4. Click Citrix Server Farm and click OK.
5. Click View and then Select Server.
6. Click the server(s) you wish to add to the farm and click OK.
7. Click Configure and Server Farm.
8. Click Change Server Farm and click Next.
9. Type the name of the server farm in the appropriate field and click Next.
10. Click Yes to create the new farm.
11. Click Finish and then OK.

APPLICATION PUBLISHING

The Citrix Published Application Manager publishes and maintains applications on MetaFrame servers. The act of publishing an application makes that application available to an ICA client. The ICA client doesn't need to know on which server the application resides, only where the ICA browser is. The browser maintains information on published applications and the addresses, host names, or locations of all the MetaFrame servers.

The CPAM can publish an application using one of two methods. Each method involves setting a different management scope, either Citrix Server Farms or NT Domains. If the Server Farms scope is used, applications are added to the application sets available to Program Neighborhood clients automatically and are available for use immediately. If an application is published in the NT Domains scope, they are not automatically added to application sets. Rather, they are made available as individual applications. This capability is provided for clients that do not support Program Neighborhood.

Citrix Published Application Manager

In addition to allowing applications to be published to Program Neighborhood clients and other ICA clients, CPAM can require explicit user authentication or anonymous access. Explicit authentication requires the user to log onto the Windows NT domain successfully before running an application. The anonymous method requires no authentication security but is very useful for making applications available through the Internet.

Application Publishing Checklist

The following checklist can be used to publish an application.

1. Log onto the MetaFrame server console as the Administrator account that is in the Local Administrators group.

2. Run the Citrix Published Application Manager.

3. Click View and Select Scope. Set the management scope to Citrix Server Farm or NT Domain.

4. Select either the appropriate server farm or the appropriate domain for the application.

5. Click View and Select Server.

6. Click the server(s) from which the application is to be managed.

7. Click Application and New.

8. Type the name of the application and click Next.

9. Set the application type to Explicit or Anonymous and click Next.

10. Enter the name of the executable in the Command Line field and click Next.

11. Deselect "Maximize application at startup" and click Next.

12. Click Next to accept the default Citrix Program Neighborhood Client settings (if the Citrix Server Farm management scope was chosen in the beginning), or change the settings as appropriate.

13. Click Next to accept the default Neighborhood Administration features, or change them as appropriate.

14. Select the appropriate domain and click Next.

15. Select Domain Users and click the Add button. Click Next.

16. Make sure the correct "Server Farm\Server" appears in the Configured field and click Next.

17. Accept the default server or change as appropriate. Click Next.

18. Click Finish.

Multitiered Application Publishing

Occasionally it is necessary to publish an application that is not satisfactorily stable, purely for business reasons. We may not like it, but that is reality. If you need to do this, we strongly recommend that you have defined a "sunset period" in which the application will be replaced with a newer, more multiuser-friendly version. This period should be made known to the users and any concerned stakeholders.

Because such an application is not entirely stable, we recommend a slightly different approach to publishing it. This application, called "DOSBOMB" in Figure 15-4, is installed either on its own dedicated server or is installed with other problematic applications on the same server. The server is part of the farm, but the application is only published using this one server. The idea is to isolate and contain the problem and not compromise the stability of the entire server farm for the sake of one application.

Once that application is published on a single server, you will use the ICA pass-through capability to enable access to the other servers in the farm. This is done by installing the ICA client on the other servers and using Seamless Window to put a link to that application on the common desktop. In this scenario, when users get the desktop from any server in the farm, they will see the icon for the application. They will not necessarily know that the application is only installed on a single server.

Of course, it is not necessary to limit the install to one server if more are needed. The idea is to limit the servers listed as "publishers" to the absolute minimum and not to load that application on the common, mainstream servers containing most of the production applications. Using this methodology serves not only to minimize downtime for all users, but also to optimize performance, since such applications typically do not perform as well as newer, 32-bit applications.

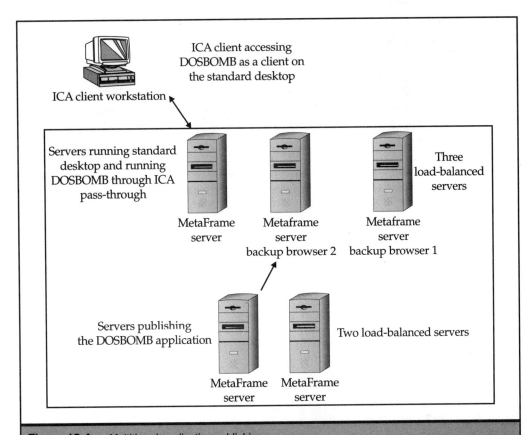

Figure 15-4.   Multitiered application publishing

NOTE: The ICA client is automatically installed on the server when MetaFrame is installed. It is located in the \%SystemRoot%\System32\ICA PassThrough directory.

Using the ICA pass-through capability, we created a standard desktop for all users, even though the applications were running on different servers. This was critical both from the standpoint of our administrators keeping their sanity by having a simple environment, and from the standpoint of isolating our legacy applications on their own servers.

—Sean Finley,
Deputy Director and Assistant VP,
Electronic Services Division, ABM Industries

LOAD BALANCING

Load balancing serves to balance the application publishing service workload among several servers. Load balancing utilizes the ICA browsing service to manage the list of available servers. When a client attempts a connection to an application that is load balanced, the ICA browser is contacted and asked for the least busy server that is publishing that application. The client is then routed to that server, and the connection is established. This least-busy status is a numerical index supplied to the master browser by each load-balanced server, and indicates the current load.

Once a session is established, it stays on the same server no matter how busy that server gets. If that server crashes for some reason, a user can log on and be routed to a different server that is publishing the desired application, as shown in Figure 15-5.

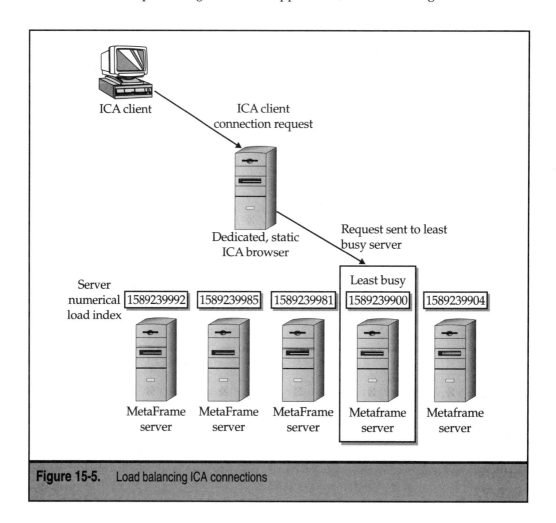

Figure 15-5.   Load balancing ICA connections

ICA Browser

As we stated previously, the master browser maintains the browse list of available MetaFrame servers. It receives updates from subordinate browsers that are also Meta-Frame servers. Though placing a master browser in each local network or subnet is probably overkill, it is necessary to keep this "overhead" in mind when ordering WAN connections.

The ICA browsing service can function over TCP/IP, IPX/SPX, or NetBIOS/NetBEUI. Each subnet needs one master browser for each of these protocols. If you only intend to use TCP/IP, it is possible to have one master browser and one group of subordinate browsers for the entire network.

Master Browser Elections

Master browser election is similar to the election process in the Windows NT domain model. A packet containing an election request can come from either a client or a browser and is sent in the following situations:

▼   The master browser fails to respond to a client request.

■   The master browser becomes unavailable.

■   A new browser is brought online.

■   The master browser fails to respond to a browser update.

▲   Two master browsers are detected on the same network for the same protocol.

When a browser receives the election packet, it determines which available browser meets the following ranked election criteria:

1.   Highest browser version number

2.   Statically configured as a master browser

NOTE: Configuring a server to act as a dedicated master browser can actually be a good practice. It speeds up the browsing and election process.

3.   Running on a domain controller

4.   Longest running browser

5.   Browser name

If the receiving browser has a higher rank than the issuer of the packet, the browser issues its own packet. If a server has a lesser rank, it passes the packet to the next server. If the packet passes all the way back to the original issuing server, that server becomes the new master browser.

NOTE: To illustrate the importance of keeping the browser election process in mind when designing the server farm, we will share a problem we had at a particular customer site. This customer has two MetaFrame servers that are accessible to the Internet through a firewall. When a third server was added, access from the Internet to all servers was suddenly blocked. After investigating that the firewall configuration had not changed and the proper UDP and TCP services were being passed, it turned out that the new server had become the master browser. We confirmed this with the **qserver** command that showed an "M" next to the name of the new server. Since the server had not been made accessible from the Internet, it effectively blocked access to the other two servers.

ICA Browser Design

It is possible to specify that every MetaFrame server is to participate in the ICA browsing process. This is done through the Citrix Server Administration utility. We have found that using this "default" methodology has some drawbacks. First of all, having the browser set to be completely dynamic means that each client has to "find" the browser each time a connection is requested. It also means that the entire election process must be followed in order to elect a new master browser if the old one is no longer appropriate. This can also affect performance. We recommend using a static master browser and the configuration shown in Figure 15-6. In this example, two MetaFrame servers can still become the master browser if the primary fails. The other MetaFrame servers will never try to become the master browser.

In order to optimize client traffic, the master browser is specified by host name in the ICA client. We also include two other browsers in the client list for added redundancy. Though the client does not browse the list in order, this method still decreases network traffic and the time it takes the client to connect.

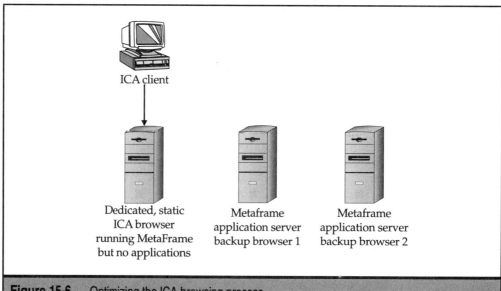

ICA client

Dedicated, static
ICA browser
running MetaFrame
but no applications

Metaframe
application server
backup browser 1

Metaframe
application server
backup browser 2

Figure 15-6.   Optimizing the ICA browsing process

We further recommend that the dedicated master browser not be a production MetaFrame server. In this way, the server can avoid the extra overhead of running client connections and concentrate solely on responding to browsing requests. This server should be set to accept logons from the Administrators group only.

TIP: If you have MetaFrame servers with both IP and IPX, but you have disabled the ICA browser service for IPX, Citrix utilities such as the Published Application Manager and Citrix Administrator will take a long time enumerating servers. To fix this, enable IPX on at least one server's ICA browser service, and the problem will disappear on all servers.

ICA Master Browser Configuration Checklist

This checklist assumes that the master browser is static and running on a server dedicated to that task.

1. Log onto the MetaFrame server console as the Administrator account that is in the Local Administrators group.

2. Run the Citrix Server Administration utility.

3. Click on the server to become a browser.

4. Click on the ICA Browser tab, and click "Hide from ICA client's server list."

5. Click "Do not participate in IPX network."

6. Click "Do not participate in NetBIOS network."

7. Click "Always attempt to become the Master ICA Browser."

8. Click Apply.

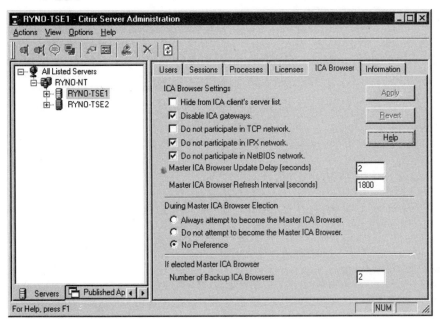

ICA Subordinate Browser Configuration Checklist

This checklist assumes that the subordinate browsers are also active MetaFrame servers.

1. Log onto the MetaFrame server console as the Administrator account that is in the Local Administrators group.
2. Run the Citrix Server Administration utility.
3. Click on the server to become a browser.
4. Click on the ICA Browser tab, and click "Do not participate in IPX network."
5. Click "Do not participate in NetBIOS network."
6. For two servers in the server farm, click No Preference.
7. For the remaining servers in the server farm, click "Do not attempt to become the Master ICA Browser."

NOTE: The previous two steps are a branch point in the checklist. The idea is to limit the number of servers on the network that will respond to the entire election process. By doing it this way, you will only have two servers—those marked as "No Preference," which will attempt to take over as master browser should the primary fail. The remaining servers will only attempt it should all three servers fail.

8. Click Apply.

ICA Gateways

Any time Citrix clients or servers need to contact servers on another network, an ICA gateway must be used. An ICA gateway acts to obtain a list of available servers, published applications, and server farms for a given network protocol on a given network. An ICA gateway is typically installed with at least two MetaFrame servers—one on either side of a router. We recommend also installing an ICA gateway on either side of the router for added redundancy, as shown in Figure 15-7. In a large enterprise network, further redundancy can be achieved by having more than one server act as an ICA gateway on each local network.

The ICA gateway does not necessarily need to run on a separate server. It can often be run on the same server as either a configured MetaFrame server acting as a browser or on your dedicated MetaFrame server running the ICA browsing service, as in Figure 15-7.

425

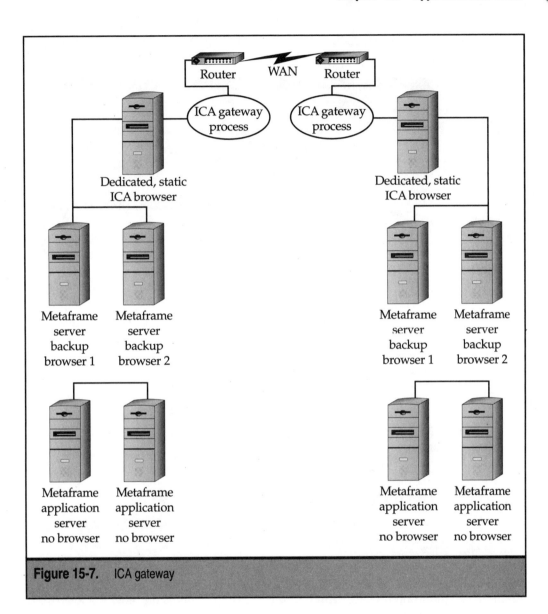

Figure 15-7. ICA gateway

The ICA gateway service is configured in the Citrix Server Administrator by clicking on the ICA Gateways tab when All Listed Servers is selected in the left panel.

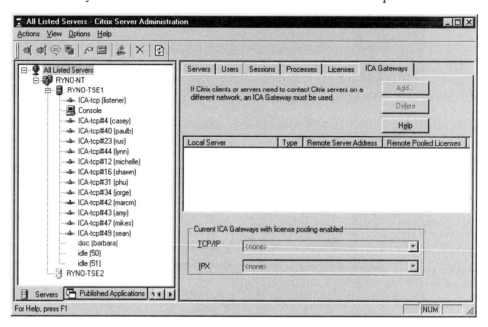

NOTE: As of MetaFrame 1.8 Service Pack 1, license pooling will also flow through an ICA gateway. In this way, licenses can truly be shared across the enterprise without regard to network architecture or geographic location.

ICA CLIENT OPTIONS FOR APPLICATION ACCESS

MetaFrame 1.8 accepts connections from two different types of clients: Citrix Program Neighborhood and Remote Application Manager.

Citrix Program Neighborhood

Program Neighborhood is used with Win32 clients and replaces the older Remote Application Manager. Program Neighborhood gives the client access to server farms, application sets, and published applications. The primary benefit of Program Neighborhood is that it requires very little configuration by the user to get started using an application. Program Neighborhood with some custom ICA connections is shown next:

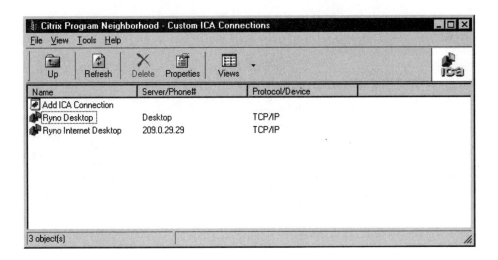

Remote Application Manager

The Remote Application Manager requires the user to configure an entry to run an application. It is still used on non-Win32 platforms such as DOS, Win16, UNIX, and Macintosh. Either client type can connect to a published application or directly to a desktop on a particular server.

Basic Configuration—Windows 32-Bit Client

One of the advantages of using MetaFrame for the Corporate ASP is the number of clients supported. Be that as it may, the most common client by a wide margin in any given network is the Win32 client. As such, we provide the following checklist as an example of how to configure this client, taking into account what we have discussed thus far in the chapter.

NOTE: This checklist assumes a manual installation and not one initiated by a script or by the software distribution function of a network management system such as Microsoft SMS.

The installation can begin from a set of two floppy disks or from a directory on a network file server.

1. Click Next on all screens with the option, accepting all the default settings until you get to the screen that requests client's name. Enter the user's Windows NT logon account name, and click Next.

2. Reboot when the installation has completed.

3. When the computer finishes with the reboot, double-click on the Citrix Program Neighborhood icon.

4. Double-click Applications Set Manager.

5. Double-click Custom ICA Connections.

6. Right-click in the blank area and select Properties.

7. Click the Default Options tab. Select the default options for all ICA connections. These include Encryption Level, Window Colors, and Window Size.

8. Click on the Connection tab and set options as shown below:

   Network Protocol: TCP/IP

   Server Group: Primary

   Click Add, type **icamaster**, and then click OK.

   Click Add, type **icamaster2**, and then click OK.

   Click Add, type **icamaster3**, and then click OK.

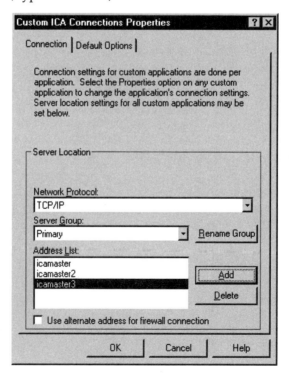

NOTE: The three "icamaster" servers specified above should correspond to the DNS host names of the dedicated master browser and the two MetaFrame servers with "No Preference" specified for browser elections.

9. Double-click Add New ICA Connection.

10. Select wide area network. Click Next. (This assumes your clients are not on the same network as the server, as is the case with a centralized data center.)

11. Click on Published Application.

12. In the pull-down window, find Desktop, and click Next.

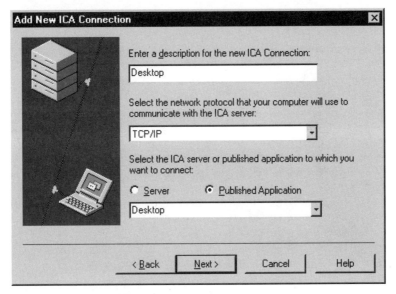

13. Select "View in a remote desktop window." Click Next.

14. Enter the encryption level to use, or check the box to use the server default (recommended). Click Next.

15. If desired, enter the user name, password, and domain. We recommend against this for security reasons. Click Next.

16. Change the window colors or window size, or accept the default. Click Next.

17. Click Finished.

18. An icon called Desktop will now appear in the CPAM window. Right-click on the icon and select Create Desktop Shortcut. Users will now be able to log onto the ICA desktop through an icon located on their local desktop computer.

Seamless Window

Sometimes it is necessary to limit a user to a specific application or small group of applications. If you choose to publish an application in a "desktop window," that application will appear to take up the entire screen when a user logs in. The Seamless Window feature of the Win32 ICA client was created in order to make access to individual published applications transparent to the user. These application icons appear just as any other icons on the user's PC desktop. The user doesn't necessarily know that the application is actually running on a server. With MetaFrame 1.8, all applications using Seamless Window on a user's desktops share a connection, so it is not necessary to log on again each time one of these applications is executed.

Seamless Window is an option in Program Neighborhood when configuring a connection to a published application.

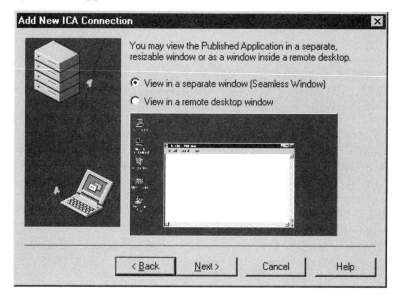

Auto-Update

MetaFrame includes the ICA Client Update Configuration utility that allows an administrator to manage the ICA client versions in use on the network. The database of the various ICA client versions is created when MetaFrame is installed and is located in the \%SystemRoot%\ICA\ClientDB directory. When a new client version for a particular type of client is placed in this directory, users with that client will see a notice the next time they log on. This notice will inform them that a new client is available. Depending on the settings in the Client Update Configuration utility, the user can choose to skip the update, or update at that time.

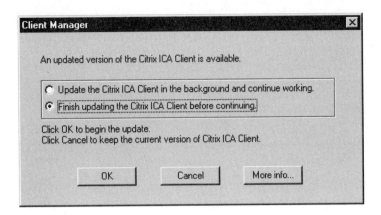

Once the update has been completed, the client will disconnect and reconnect using the new version. All Program Neighborhood settings and existing application sets and ICA connections are unaffected by the update.

Unattended Install

It is possible to do a fresh install of the ICA client without user interaction. In this way, the client software can be "pushed" to a PC without the need to send a technician to the desktop. The actual mechanisms used to accomplish this are wide and varied. You could execute the setup program from the user's Windows NT logon script, write a simple WSH script that will do it, or use a commercial software distribution package such as the one in Microsoft SMS. Whatever the method, the checklist below outlines the basic procedure.

NOTE: This checklist assumes a fresh install on a clean client system. This method only works with Program Neighborhood, not Remote Application Manager.

1. Create a setup.iss file and copy it onto Disk1 of the Program Neighborhood setup disks.

```
Sample Setup.iss file
[InstallShield Silent]
Version=v5.00.000
File=Response File
[Application]
Name=ICA Client
Version=4.0
Company=Citrix
[DlgOrder]
Dlg0=SdWelcome-0
```

```
Dlg1=SdLicense-0
Dlg2=SdAskDestPath-0
Dlg3=SdSelectFolder-0
Dlg4=SdShowDlgEdit1-0
Dlg5=MessageBox-0
Count=6
[SdWelcome-0]
Result=1
[SdLicense-0]
Result=1
[SdAskDestPath-0]
Result=1
szDir=C:\Program Files\Citrix\ICA Client
[SdSelectFolder-0]
szFolder=Citrix ICA Client
Result=1
[SdShowDlgEdit1-0]
Result=1
szEdit1=("")
[MessageBox-0]
Result=1
```

2. Make any necessary changes to the setup.iss file. Make sure the following value is unique for each client workstation: szEdit1=ICAClient. For Windows NT clients, you can do this by querying the %COMPUTERNAME% and %SYSTEMDRIVE% environment variables. For Win95/98 clients, these variables do not exist, so some other method must be used to generate a unique name. The following batch file, available from the Citrix support Web site, will query the PC and generate a unique name based on the above variables. It will also generate the setup.iss file and launch the ICA client setup program with the "-S" parameter to run in silent, or unattended, mode.

```
Sample icasetup.bat file
@echo off
ECHO Installing the Citrix ICA Client   Please wait...
echo [InstallShield Silent] > setup.iss
echo Version=v5.00.000 >> setup.iss
 . . .
```

NOTE: The remaining parameters preceded by an "echo" statement are the same as the sample setup.iss file listing above.

```
echo [SdAskDestPath-0] >> setup.iss
echo Result=1 >> setup.iss
REM The next two statements work only on Windows NT machines
echo szDir=%SYSTEMDRIVE%\Program Files\Citrix\ICA Client >> setup.iss
echo szEdit1=%COMPUTERNAME% >> setup.iss
if exist setup.exe Goto InstallIt
Echo.
ECHO The answer file Setup.iss was created but the Setup.exe file
ECHO does not exist in the current folder.  Setup did not complete.
Goto EndIt
:InstallIt
CALL SETUP.EXE -S
:EndIt
```

NOTE: There is an alternate method of making sure the client name is unique that avoids the need to obtain the variable ahead of time.

In the setup.iss file, if you set the line

```
szEdit1=" "
```

Leave a space between the quotes
then upon installation using setus /s, the wfcname.ini file will be created so:

```
[wfclinet]
clentname=
```

When the user makes the first connection to MetaFrame session, the file is updated with the NetBios machine name of the client.

CHAPTER 16

Profiles, Policies, and Procedures

In this chapter we will provide deployment tips on using Windows NT profiles and policies in a server-based computing environment. Usage is similar to a distributed environment, but there are some important differences. We assume the reader is familiar with Windows NT administration and thus knows how to create user profiles and system policies. However, we will provide a brief primer in the context of the discussion.

In the last section of the chapter we present the "best practices" for using profiles and policies. We focus on how to handle specific situations that arise when deploying a server-based computing infrastructure. The objective of this collection of methods is to provide the necessary flexibility to accommodate the application needs of different users and groups while maintaining the manageability and robustness that is required in this environment.

USER PROFILES

A Windows NT user profile is simply a Registry file that contains information about a specific user's environment and preference settings. The profile contains configuration information from different sources. First of all, it contains changes to the desktop environment such as background wallpaper, color schemes, shortcuts, and Start menu items. It also contains information from the system policy, which defines what a user is allowed to do on a local system or in a domain. There are two types of profiles: local and roaming.

Local Profiles

As the name implies, a *local profile* exists on only a single machine. In the world of server-based computing, this type of profile isn't useful for the average user, since it cannot traverse a load-balanced server farm. It could be used on a single server for a maintenance account of some kind but little else. A local Terminal Services profile is stored in the %SystemRoot%\Profiles\%UserName% directory as ntuser.dat.

Roaming Profiles

A *roaming profile* typically exists on a network share and is loaded from any server to which the user logs on. The user can log onto any server for which the profile is valid. This is the main type of profile employed in a server-based network. A roaming profile can either be *personal* or *mandatory*. The corresponding file has an extension specific to the type: .dat for personal and .man for mandatory.

Personal profiles were designed to allow users to make changes to their environment. These changes are then recorded in the locally stored profile. Once a user logs off, the profile is copied back to the network share from which it was originally loaded. This profile is then used the next time the user logs on.

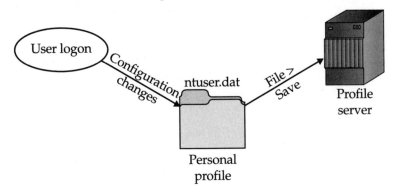

More than one user can use a roaming profile. Personal roaming profiles have the following advantages:

▼   User-specific application settings, such as default file locations and file history are saved to the profile.

▲   Users can customize the desktop environment. They can change colors, fonts, backgrounds, or the Start menu.

Limitations of personal roaming profiles include

▼   Profiles have no restriction on file size. This can lead to rapidly increasing disk space and network bandwidth utilization.

▲   Users are not prevented from making changes that may make their environment unstable or unusable.

Though personal roaming profiles were designed to allow users to make changes, it does not have to be so. We will describe methods for locking down the user environment, by using system policies and scripting, to prevent users from making unnecessary changes.

> *We chose to use roaming profiles because we found mandatory profiles too restrictive. We found that we could still lock down the roaming profiles enough to maintain the consistency of the desktop and other settings.*
>
> —Jason Womak,
> Network Services Manager, Kendall-Jackson Wine Estates

Creating a Roaming Profile

Before creating any user profile, you should first create a profile template that is appropriate for that user. An even better idea is to create a profile template that will represent a large group of users. To create a profile template, follow the checklist below:

1. Log onto the domain as Administrator and create a user that will represent the template. Give it a name that is easily identifiable as a template, for example __TemplateUser__. If the profile is to represent a group, include the group in the account name, for example __EngrUser__.

2. Assign the new user to the appropriate groups. Don't assign a profile for the template user yet. You will need to add the template user to the correct Administrative group to allow it to create a profile.

3. Log on as the new user.

4. Configure the desktop settings as desired. Customize the Start menu, remove icons, or make other related changes as appropriate.

5. Log off. At this time, a local profile will have been created and saved in the Profiles directory.

6. Log on as Administrator and remove the template user from any Administrative group.

7. Run the System application from Control Panel and select the User Profiles tab. You will see the template user profile in the list of local user profiles. Highlight this profile and click the Copy To button. Enter the location of the network share you have chosen to store profiles. Click the Change button and update the permissions with the correct group for this profile. This will assure that this profile can be reused. Click OK.

8. From Windows Explorer, go to the network share for profiles and make sure the file was created correctly. You will see the ntuser.dat and other files that define the profile. Once the template user profile has been created, it simply has to be copied for each user.

Mandatory Roaming Profiles

A *mandatory* roaming profile is a specific type of roaming profile that is preconfigured and cannot be changed by the user. Though this type of profile does have the advantage of enforcing a common interface and a standard configuration, it can be too restrictive for many common uses. This restriction is accomplished by preventing the user from saving any changes. A user can still make modifications to the desktop, Start menu, or other elements, but the changes are lost when she logs out.

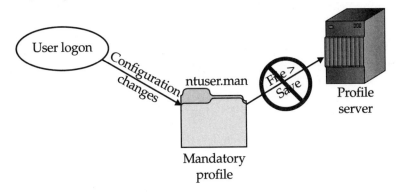

Like other profiles, the mandatory roaming profile is assigned in User Manager for Domains. This type of profile has a .man extension. Mandatory profiles are most appropriate for a *kiosk* user—a user with a very specific application requirement where a great deal of flexibility is not required. A kiosk user, for example, would be a user at a remote location who simply has to input his time into a custom application that automatically runs when he logs on.

Our recommendation regarding the use of mandatory profiles is that if you can tolerate their limitations in your environment, you should use them. Many problems associated with standard roaming profiles are avoided. Mandatory roaming profiles have the following advantages:

▼   Profile size is fixed and invariably small. This alleviates disk storage problems.

■   Profile traffic is cut in half since the locally cached profile is never stored on the profile server.

▲   No user settings are saved. This eliminates some service calls and avoids the problem of users inadvertently destroying their environment.

Limitations of the mandatory roaming profile include

▼   No user settings are saved. This lack of flexibility can lead to many different "standard" profiles being created to accommodate different needs.

▲   User-specific application settings, such as Internet Explorer history, are not saved with the profile. If such settings need to be saved, scripting is required for each setting.

Many of the same restrictions of mandatory profiles can be accomplished by using a personal roaming profile without compromising flexibility. Refer to the "Best Practices" section later in the chapter for tips on the best way to implement profiles.

Profile Mechanics

Two different profiles can be specified on a MetaFrame server. You set the profile in the User Environment Profile dialog, as shown in Figure 16-1.

▼ **User Profile Path**   This profile is only used when a user logs onto a regular Windows NT server.

▲ **Terminal Server Profile Path**   This profile is used when a user logs onto a server with Terminal Services running. If this field is blank, the profile specified in the User Profile Path is used in all cases.

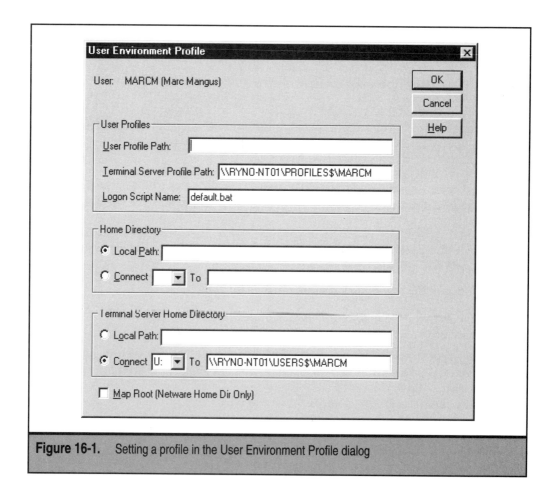

Figure 16-1.   Setting a profile in the User Environment Profile dialog

When a profile is loaded, it updates the HKEY_CURRENT_USER key in the Registry.

Home Directory

Similar to the profile path settings above, two home directories can be specified in User Manager for Domains. Home Directory specifies the user's home directory when logging onto a regular NT server; or if only this field has a path specified, it is used for any user that logs on. Terminal Server Home Directory specifies the directory used when a user logs onto a server running Terminal Services.

Profile Processing

Personal or mandatory roaming profiles are handled in almost the same way. Before we discuss the optimal way to implement profiles in a Corporate ASP, we will describe how they are processed. In the checklist below, the profile server is simply the server you have defined to store user profiles. It is not necessarily the PDC. The process is illustrated in Figure 16-2.

1. The user logs onto a server running Terminal Services.

2. The logon process checks to see if the user has a profile stored on the local server. If so, it is compared with the one on the profile server. If the server profile has a later time stamp, it is copied to the local server. If the time stamps are identical, the local copy is used. If the local one is newer, by default the user is asked which one he wants to use, but this behavior can be changed in the Registry.

3. If there is no local copy of the profile, the user's profile is copied from the profile server.

4. The file ntuser.dat contains the Registry information for the user's profile. It is loaded into the Registry in the HKEY_USERS hive. All logged-on users, along with the default user, can be seen by viewing this hive in REGEDIT.

5. Changes the user makes while logged on are stored in the Registry. In the case of a standard roaming profile, these changes are written to the local profile when the user logs out. In the case of a mandatory profile, these changes are discarded.

SYSTEM POLICIES

A *system policy* is a collection of Registry settings that define what a user or group of users have access to. A system policy can define many of the same things about the environment that a user profile does; the difference is in the order they are processed and how they are applied. Policies and the system policy editor (POLEDIT) were created to draw

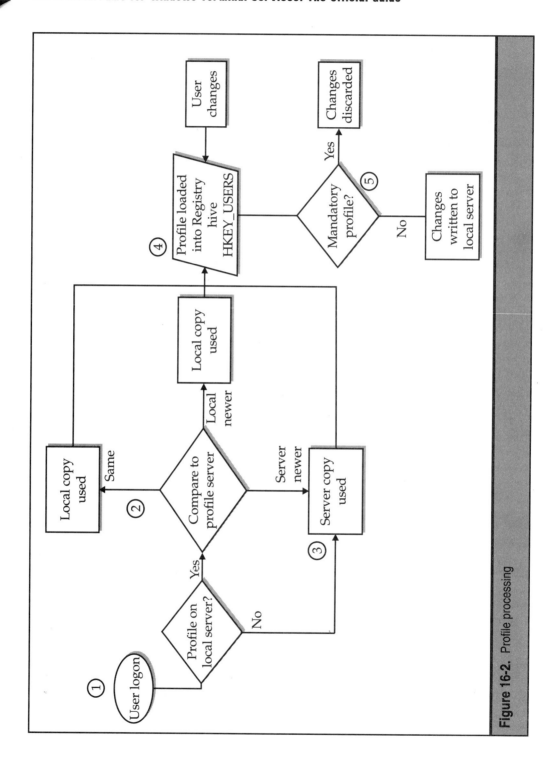

Figure 16-2. Profile processing

out certain commonly changed settings from the Registry and reduce the overall complexity of making changes to those settings. The policy editor is shown below:

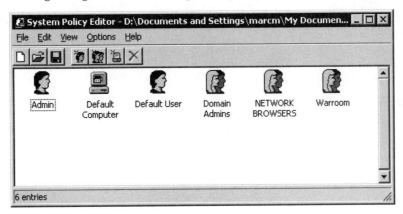

Unfortunately, if you use policies, as opposed to a script that makes all the appropriate Registry changes, you have more than one source for Registry changes. We use policies—mostly for ease of communication about certain settings with our customers and with Microsoft and Citrix. You can avoid the use of policies if you have a thorough understanding of the Registry and feel comfortable writing a script to make the same changes at the appropriate point in the logon process.

NOTE: The limitation of using scripting instead of system policies comes when you try to make changes to the Registry settings contained in the Local Machine section of a policy. Generally, this section is not available to a user logon script unless the user has permission to make changes to the Registry. It is possible to overcome this limitation with some creative use of Windows Scripting Host, but that could be the subject of an entire book. For the time being, we will continue to use system policies.

A system policy can be applied to an entire domain, a group, or a single user, and can be assigned in the following areas:

▼   **Control Panel**   Severely limits or denies access to the Display utility

■   **Desktop**   Limits or denies access to the background wallpaper and desktop color scheme

■   **Shell**   Controls certain items on the Start menu, desktop, and disables the ability for the user to shut down the system

■   **System**   Denies access to the Registry for a user and can be used to list specific applications that can be run

CAUTION: Defining a list of applications that can be run is more complex than it may seem. Most applications call other program elements (DLL or EXE files) after the program itself loads. If these items are not also listed, the execution will fail.

- ■ **Windows NT shell**   Allows an alternate location to be specified for desktop elements

- ▲ **Windows NT system**   Specifies the logon script and AUTOEXEC.BAT files to be run when a user logs on

In addition, policies can be set in the following areas on a server running Terminal Services. These new settings are stored in Windows NT Shell/Restrictions.

- ▼ Remove NT Security menu from Start menu

- ■ Remove Disconnect item from Start menu

- ▲ Remove Logoff from Start menu

NOTE: Profiles and policies work almost the same in Windows 2000. The main difference is that policies can be applied to an Active Directory container such as an Organizational Unit (OU). If all Terminal Services hosts are contained in the same OU, the same policy can easily be applied to them.

The Life Cycle of a Policy

Policies are stored as POL files when created by the system policy editor. The POL file looks a lot like any other Registry file with key/value pairs. By default, the server references ntconfig.pol located in the NETLOGON share. This reference can be found in the Registry, located at HKEY_LOCAL_MACHINE\System\CurrentControlSet Control\Update.

The policy file is created using POLEDIT. The POL file is stored to a network share. Optionally, if you wish to automatically distribute the policy, you can store it on the Primary Domain Controllers and Backup Domain Controllers. When a user logs on, the system checks the domain controller for an applicable policy. If it finds one, the POL file is sent to the MetaFrame server, and its contents are merged with the correct Registry root key.

When determining how to apply a policy, the system checks for one of three possible policy values:

- ▼ **On**   The policy is active and should be applied.

- ■ **Off**   The policy is inactive and should not be applied.

- ▲ **Leave as is**   Leave the current value for this policy in the Registry alone.

User- and group-specific policies are merged into HKEY_CURRENT_USER, and server-specific policies are merged into HKEY_LOCAL_MACHINE.

NOTE: Even if no specific policies are created, a default policy exists named ntconfig.pol. This policy has all values set to "leave as is."

If there is a policy file with the same name as the user logging on, it is used; otherwise, the default policy is used. If a named user policy does exist, it will override any group or computer policy. Group policies are additive, as they must be. If a user is in more than one group, all group policies for those groups are applied.

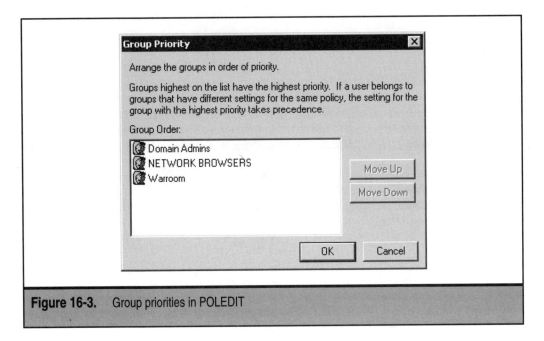

Figure 16-3.   Group priorities in POLEDIT

Since multiple groups can be assigned to a policy, they must be prioritized, as shown in Figure 16-3. Make sure that the Administrators group is always listed first. If different policies are assigned to different groups assigned to the same user, the policies are assigned in priority order. If the same setting exists in multiple policy files, the one with the highest priority is the one assigned to the user.

Policy Templates

A number of template policies are supplied that have the file extension .adm. They can be attached using Options > Policy Template in POLEDIT. The standard included policy templates are

▼ **winnt.adm**   Contains policies specific to Windows NT environments

▲ **common.adm**   Contains policy settings that apply to all Windows operating systems

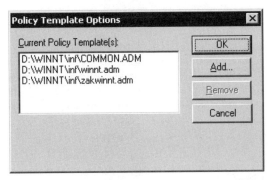

You can choose multiple templates to create a new policy. We recommend removing the ADM files from all servers and storing only the ones you intend to use on a central network share. This will prevent you from inadvertently using a template that may exist on only one MetaFrame server.

TIP: We recommend using common.adm, winnt.adm, and zakwinnt.adm to create system policies. We will refer to sections of these templates to address certain challenges. The zakwinnt.adm template can be found in the Zero Administration Kit for Windows NT Server 4.0.

It is possible to define your own template file. The syntax of the ADM file is fairly complex but is defined in Microsoft Article Q225087.

Here is an example of a user policy file that hides certain icons in the Control Panel:

```
File: cpanel.adm
CLASS USER
CATEGORY !!CPL_Icons
POLICY !!CPL_Access
KEYNAME "Control Panel\Don't Load"
VALUENAME "Access.cpl"ValueOn !!CPL_Hide ValueOff Numeric 0
END POLICY

POLICY !!CPL_AppWiz
KEYNAME "Control Panel\Don't Load"
VALUENAME "appwiz.cpl"ValueOn !!CPL_Hide ValueOff Numeric 0
END POLICY

POLICY !!CPL_Console
KEYNAME "Control Panel\Don't Load"
VALUENAME "console.cpl"ValueOn !!CPL_Hide ValueOff Numeric 0
END POLICY
END CATEGORY; Control Panel
[strings]
CPL_Icons="Control Panel Icons"
CPL_Access="Deny Access to Accessibility"
CPL_AppWiz="Deny Access to Add/Remove Programs"
CPL_Console="Deny Access to Console Properties"
```

Policy Distribution

To apply a policy to a specific machine, simply run POLEDIT and choose File > Open Policy. Open the policy file, and then choose File > Save. This is obviously not practical when you want to apply the policy to a large number of servers. Windows NT provides a method for doing just this.

Automatic Policy Distribution

Each domain controller has a share named NETLOGON. This share is actually the %SystemRoot%\System32\Repl\Import\Scripts directory. It was intended to contain user profiles, logon scripts, and other related data. You are free to place policy files in this folder.

In order to allow the other servers on the network to download the defined policy files in this share, you will need to make a change to the default computer policy on each server. This policy will prompt for a path for automatic policy updates.

1. Log onto the server you want to update and start POLEDIT.

2. Click on Open Registry from the File menu.

3. Double-click on the Local Computer icon. It will open a dialog showing the settings in effect on the local machine. Click on Network and then on System policies update.

4. Click on the Remote update policy.

5. Click on the drop-down box for Update mode. Select Automatic.

6. Exit and save.

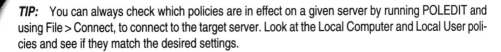

TIP: You can always check which policies are in effect on a given server by running POLEDIT and using File > Connect, to connect to the target server. Look at the Local Computer and Local User policies and see if they match the desired settings.

The problem with this method is that these policies will affect all compatible computers that use the domain controller. If your organization has a mixture of Windows NT Server, Workstation, Windows NT TSE, and Windows 2000 computers, they will all get these policy files. We recommend specifying an alternate location for the policy files that will only apply to the MetaFrame servers, as described in the next section.

Specifying an Alternate Policy Location

Follow these steps to load a policy file from another machine on the network:

1. Log onto the server you want to update and start POLEDIT.

2. Click on Open Registry from the File menu.

3. Double-click on the Local Computer icon. It will open a dialog showing the settings in effect on the local machine. Click on Network and then on System policies update.

4. Click on the Remote update policy, as shown in Figure 16-4.

5. Click on the drop-down box for Update mode. Select Manual and enter the network share containing the policies, and the name of the policy file in UNC format.

6. Exit and save.

Now when users log onto this server, the custom policy files will be used.

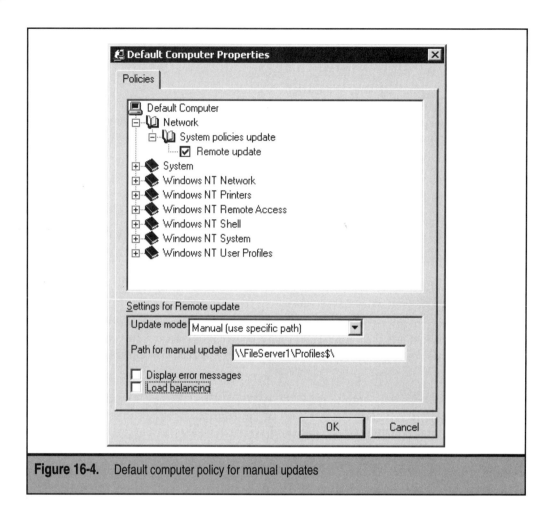

Figure 16-4. Default computer policy for manual updates

BEST PRACTICES

In our efforts to effectively deploy profiles and policies in a Corporate ASP, we have formulated our own list of best practices. Here, we define some of the major challenges you will encounter when implementing policies and profiles. Following this list, we show one or more solutions to each challenge.

▼ Limiting the profile file size to prevent high disk space and network utilization.

■ Locking down the desktop. Restrict users from making undesirable changes to their environment while providing the required amount of flexibility to make necessary changes. Such changes include custom data file paths and file history.

- Providing a consistent desktop across the enterprise in order to simplify administration and limit unnecessary help desk calls.

- Limiting local access. Politics, culture, and the composition of certain applications may necessitate local access, but in general, it should be limited. Local drive mappings, printers, or other devices compromise security, drive up network bandwidth utilization, and increase the number of support calls.

- Eliminating application features, such as animation or graphical splash screens, which will drive up network bandwidth utilization.

- Assigning application access based on group membership. The alternative is to have as many profiles as there are combinations of applications.

- ▲ Providing a minimum level of functionality if a user's profile becomes corrupt.

In order to overcome these challenges, we employ the strategies outlined below. After each problem statement, we provide a checklist or other instruction for making the necessary change.

Limit the Profile Size

All user changes and custom application settings are saved to the profile, which must travel back and forth across the network. The idea is to limit the file size and network utilization while providing a means to save necessary settings. There are several solutions to this problem.

First, don't save the locally cached profile to the profile server. To set this option in POLEDIT, use the following checklist:

1. Log into the server that hosts the policy file used for all computers running Terminal Services.
2. From POLEDIT, click File, and then click Open Registry.
3. Double-click Local Computer.
4. Click Windows NT User Profiles.
5. Click "Delete cached copies of roaming profiles," and then click OK.
6. Quit POLEDIT. Click Yes to save the policy changes to the Registry.

The second solution is to prevent certain folders from roaming with the profile. Even with the previous change, the profile information will still be stored to the profile server. This change will prevent certain application data from being saved to the profile server.

To set this option in POLEDIT, use the following checklist:

1. Log into the server that hosts the policy file used for all computers running Terminal Services.

2. From POLEDIT, click File, and then click Open Policy. If this is a new policy, click New Policy.

3. Double-click Default User.

4. Click Windows NT User Profiles.

5. Click "Exclude directories in roaming profile." (See Figure 16-5.)

6. Specify the directories, separated by semicolons, all relative to the root of the user's profile.

7. Quit POLEDIT. Click Yes to save the policy changes to the Registry.

A third solution: assign custom folders for common Windows NT paths. This will ensure that application configuration and user-settings data will be saved to the file server and not the profile server. To set this option in POLEDIT, use the checklist shown next.

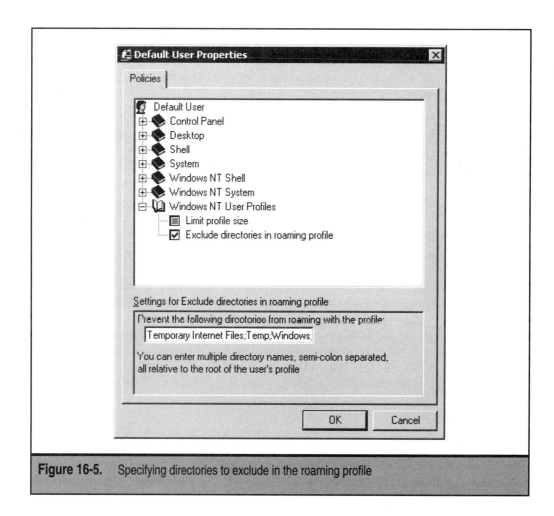

Figure 16-5. Specifying directories to exclude in the roaming profile

1. Log into the server that hosts the policy file used for all computers running Terminal Services.

2. From POLEDIT, click File, and then click Open Policy. If this is a new policy, click New Policy.

3. Double-click Default User.

4. Click Windows NT Shell, then Custom folders. (See Figure 16-6.)

5. Type in path values in UNC format for the following folders: Programs, desktop icons, Start menu, and Startup. We also recommend specifying a custom Start menu folder and path containing only what the user needs to see.

6. Quit POLEDIT. Click Yes to save the policy changes to the Registry.

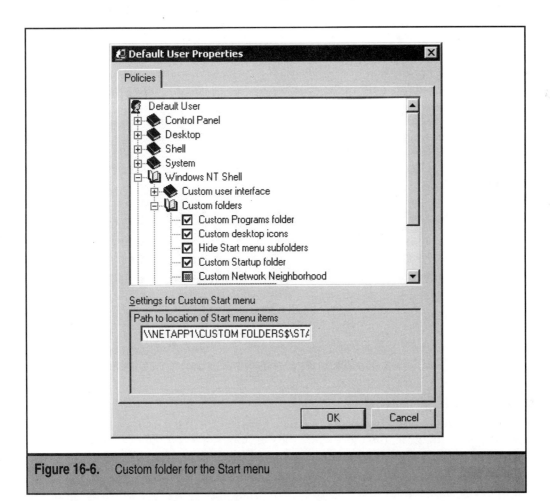

Figure 16-6.   Custom folder for the Start menu

For certain applications (like Internet Explorer), you can delete temporary files when the user logs out. This procedure will be specific to each application. The following checklist shows the procedure for IE versions 4 and 5.

1. From REGEDIT, set the following key and value:

    Key: HKEY_CURRENT_USER\Software\Microsoft\Windows\ CurrentVersion\ Internet Settings\Cache\Persistent
    Type: REG_DWORD
    Value: 0

2. Delete the following two keys. The system will re-create the correct path to the temporary files from the key set in step 1.

    Key: HKEY_CURRENT_USER\Software\Microsoft\Windows\ CurrentVersion\User Shell Folders\Cache

    Key: HKEY_CURRENT_USER\Software\Microsoft\Windows\ CurrentVersion\Shell Folders\Cache

A final solution for limiting the profile size is to disable the policy that detects slow network connections. When enabled, this policy prompts the user to either download the profile or use the locally cached copy. By default, after 30 seconds, it will download the profile. We have found the slow network connection to be inaccurate, and the dialog box causes unnecessary support calls. The Registry key in question is HKEY_Local_Machine\ Software\Microsoft\Windows NT\CurrentVersion\Winlogon, with a DWORD value 1 to always download the roaming profile.

To set this option in POLEDIT, use the following checklist:

1. Log into the server that hosts the policy file used for all computers running Terminal Services.
2. From POLEDIT, click File, and then click Open Registry.
3. Double-click Local Computer.
4. Click Windows NT User Profiles.
5. Click the option to always download the roaming profile.
6. Quit POLEDIT. Click Yes to save the policy changes to the Registry.

Lock Down the Desktop

Some organizations will be able to mandate more control of the user's desktop than others. Whatever the case, the more static the desktop, the fewer support calls will be received by the help desk relating to desktop configuration problems.

The first solution to this problem is to redirect the desktop folder and Start menu to a read-only folder. Similar to the checklist above, simply assign a path value that points to a read-only folder to the system policy part Default Users\Windows NT Shell\Custom Folders and the key "Custom desktop icons." Enter a path that points to a folder that has been set to read-only permissions for the user or group that will be accessing it.

Second, redirect the desktop to the user's home directory. In the case where configuration changes to the user's desktop must be allowed, you can still limit network traffic by always saving these changes to the user's home directory on the file server. Do so by specifying a path with the user's name as a variable in the same policy part specified in solution 1, for example, \\FileServer1\Users\%USER%.

Provide a Consistent Desktop Across the Enterprise

The first solution to the previous problem also accomplishes this goal.

Limit or Eliminate Local Access

The Citrix Connection Manager only allows you to enable or disable all local drive access. Instead of CCM, use the logon script with group membership and "net use" statements to grant access to local drives where necessary.

The following simple example is a portion of a user logon script written in Kixtart that checks for membership in the group "local-floppy" and then grants access to the local floppy drive through the ICA client. This same strategy can be used for mapping local COM or LPT ports as well.

```
Select
     Case ingroup("local-floppy")=1
          Net use A: \\Client\A
. . .
Endselect
```

Eliminate Undesirable Application Features

Many common applications, such as Microsoft Excel, have features that are not optimal for a Corporate ASP and are not much of a loss to users if removed. An example is the animated "paper clip" character that represents the help interface for all MS Office applications. Since it is an animation, it can consume precious bandwidth unnecessarily. All of the same help information is available by clicking Help on the Excel menu.

The MS Office suite comes with a policy template file, OFFICE9.ADM. Create a policy with this template that eliminates the animated help characters, as shown in Figure 16-7.

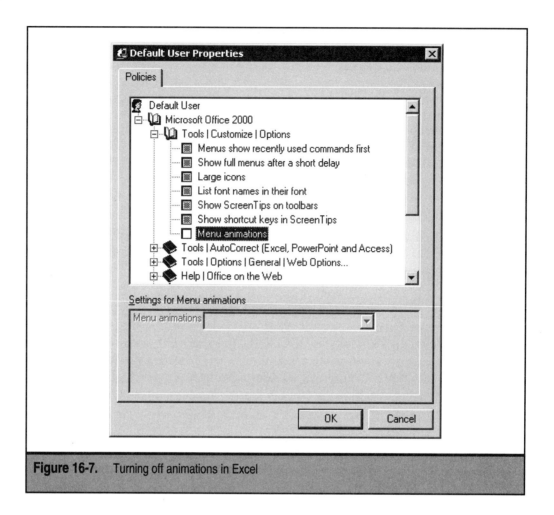

Figure 16-7.   Turning off animations in Excel

Assign Application Access Based on Group Membership

Typically, certain groups of users will have similar application requirements. The best way to assign application access is by creating groups based on applications, then adding users to them. Again, the ideal place to do this is the logon script. Any supporting operations such as copying configuration files and icons can be done at the same time. The example below is a logon script fragment written in Kixtart that assigns application access based on groups. This script could also be written using VBScript, PerlScript, or whatever language is standard in your organization.

```
Select
     ; Check for group membership for the "dosbomb" program
          Case ingroup("app-dosbomb")=1
     ; Substitute drive I: to appropriate location for the application
          Shell "%compspec% /c subst I: \\FileServer1\Corp-HQ$"
     ; Map drive J: to appropriate location for the application
          Use J: \\FileServer1\Corp-Common$
     ; Assumes common drives X: and Y: exist
          Shell "%comspec% /c copy x:\common\apps\dosbomb\*.* /s
          Y:\apps\dosbomb"
. . .
endselect
```

Provide Minimum Functionality in a Default Profile

The previous example shows application access based on group membership in the logon script. This same strategy can be used to map common drives, assign default printers, assign printers based on group membership, or make changes specific to certain applications.

Don't rely on the profile to set up a user's environment. Define critical resources in the logon script. This way, if a user's profile cannot be loaded for some reason, the default profile can be used with the settings made by the logon script. This will avoid downtime and allow the user to get work done with a minimum of interruption while any profile-related problems are resolved.

Change Control

In the examples and checklists presented in this chapter, we show the modification of policies, Registry keys, and profile settings. We thought it appropriate to mention here again the importance of testing these changes in a nonproduction environment first. We recommend not only testing them first, but also tracking any modifications to standard files through some kind of revision control system. This can be as simple as keeping a written change log or as complex as using revision control software such as RCS or PVCS. Whatever the case, the important thing is that all personnel involved with administering the system or making changes follow the same change control procedure and have easy access to the log.

CHAPTER 17

Printing

It may seem odd to devote an entire chapter to printing. Once you examine the differences between printing in a server-based computing environment and printing in a distributed environment, the reason becomes clearer. In a distributed network, many print servers are scattered throughout the enterprise. A user print request typically has only a short hop from the application to the printer. In a Corporate ASP, this is not the case. All computing resources are centralized. When a user somewhere out on the WAN needs to print something to a printer sitting right next to him, the print job must still traverse the WAN to reach the printer. This is not an ideal situation with regard to print performance or network bandwidth utilization.

In this chapter we will discuss ways to optimize this paradigm and mitigate some of its inherent problems and limitations. We will briefly explain how the ICA protocol handles printing and relate it to Windows printing in general. Finally, we will show how to optimize printing within a Citrix environment and how to accomplish the task outside the environment. Our deployment recommendations will incorporate logon scripts and general scripting, policies, and Citrix configuration changes designed to make printing as smooth as possible in your enterprise.

PRINTING PROTOCOLS AND TECHNOLOGIES

The combination of Terminal Services and MetaFrame yields a variety of printing options. We begin by briefly discussing the underlying technologies in order to make recommendations as to their best use.

Windows Printing

For a user to print in a Terminal Services environment, a printer must be defined in the client environment, and an appropriate printer driver must exist on the server. The client printer definition is stored in the user's profile, or it can be set up in the logon script. We will provide examples of this later in the chapter.

When Windows NT acts as a print server, printers are defined as shared resources. The definition includes the specification of a physical print device, a port, and a driver to use for formatting print jobs. The driver needs to reside upon the same computer that is generating the print request. If the driver does not reside on that computer, Windows NT can automatically download the driver. Windows NT can even store drivers for different versions of Windows and download them as needed.

Printer Drivers

If Windows is the car, then the printer driver is the engine. A print request goes to the driver and is formatted according to the native language required by the physical printing device. Microsoft supplies a large number of drivers on the distribution media for all of its operating systems. Microsoft drivers are thoroughly tested for the printers on the hardware compatibility list (HCL). If you could use those drivers exclusively, the

MetaFrame server would be incredibly stable. Unfortunately, new printers with new capabilities and new drivers are often needed. The problem arises with the way Windows NT loads and runs print drivers.

Versions of Windows NT, including NT 4.0 Server, Terminal Server Edition, load print drivers in the same execution space reserved for operating system kernel operations, as shown below:

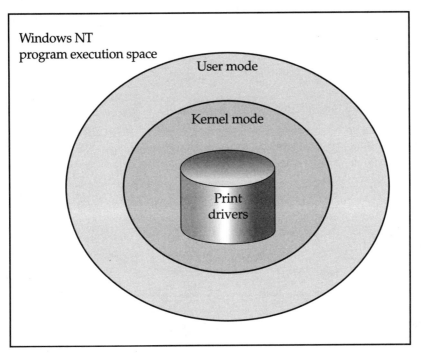

Components that execute in this space assume all of the other components are well behaved and that they use and release resources in a predictable way. Unfortunately, when it comes to print drivers written by third parties, this is not a valid assumption. Even drivers from major manufacturers often exhibit problems when installed on a multiuser platform. When Windows NT has a kernel mode component that exhibits problems that it cannot handle, it often crashes with a "blue screen of death" (BSOD) and a kernel error message. For this reason it is critical that only fully tested, well-behaved kernel mode drivers are loaded in the production environment.

Blue used to be my favorite color. Now I hate it.

—Anthony Lackey,
VP Electronic Services and CTO, ABM Industries

Windows 2000 supports a different driver-loading scheme. User mode drivers are loaded in the "user mode" execution space of the operating system, which is outside the kernel space, as shown here:

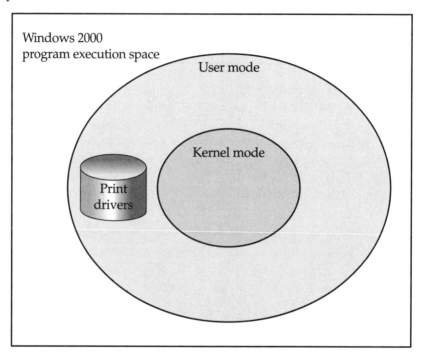

When a driver encounters a problem in this space, Windows deals with it just like any application. It can display Doctor Watson and terminate it, assign it a low priority if it stops responding, or simply allow it to run in a degraded mode. The point is that a server crash is far less likely than on previous versions of Windows.

If Windows NT automatically loads drivers from a print server to the server running Terminal Services, how do you make sure that only "good" drivers get loaded? There are two built-in mechanisms to help in addressing this question. The first deals with creating equivalent driver assignments with default autocreated printers and the second with creating a secure, trusted source for printer drivers.

NOTE: Windows 2000 maintains a high degree of backward compatibility with Windows NT. This means that if you load Windows NT kernel-mode print drivers on Windows 2000, they will still load in the kernel.

Default Autocreated Printers

MetaFrame automatically creates a user's printer when the user logs on. If the user happens to be running the ICA client on a PC, she also has the ability to install whatever printer driver she desires by default. If a user installs a "problem" print driver locally, then logs onto a MetaFrame server and attempts to print to it, many potential problems could ensue, ranging from slow performance to a BSOD.

Fortunately, a mechanism is available, in the form of a text file, to make disparate drivers appear equivalent to the operating system. If it appears that the same driver is on the client and the server, then no driver download takes place. The file is called WTSUPRN.TXT, and it resides in the %SystemRoot%\System32 folder. The file contains two columns—one for the client printer driver name, and one for the server driver name.

The file works as follows: A user installs an HP 4000 driver on his workstation. This driver has been known to cause a BSOD even on the latest version of Terminal Services in Windows 2000. The administrator knows this and researches a bit to find out that the standard Microsoft driver for the HP LaserJet 4 will work for basic printing on this printer. The administrator opens the WTSUPRN.TXT file and adds the following line:

```
"HP LaserJet 4000 Series PCL 5" = "HP LaserJet 4"
```

The administrator saves the file with an .INF extension. Now when the user attempts to print to his local printer, the driver on the Terminal Services server is used ("HP Laser-Jet 4," above), as shown in Figure 17-1. It is important that the same description of the printer is used in the file that is used in the client operating system, or the equivalency won't be found.

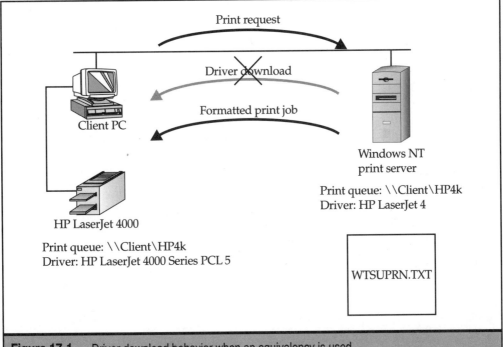

Figure 17-1. Driver download behavior when an equivalency is used

CAUTION: This printer-naming strategy has a limitation in that the advanced functions of a given printer are not likely to be available if you use an older or more basic driver.

Loading Drivers from a Trusted Source

A good way to limit which drivers are propagated between servers is to create a trusted source for print drivers. Only the Administrators group has write access to the directory on the computer containing the trusted drivers. If you want to set up a source for trusted drivers using Windows NT 4.0 Server, Terminal Server Edition including Service Pack 4 or earlier, use the following checklist. As of Service Pack 5 and with Windows 2000, having a trusted source for print drivers became the default behavior.

1. From REGEDT32, find the following key:

   HKEY_LOCAL_MACHINE\SYSTEM\CurrentControlSet\Control\Print\ Providers\LanMan Print Services\Servers

2. Add the following three values:

   Name: LoadTrustedDrivers
   Type: REG_DWORD
   Value: 1

   Name: TrustedDriverPath
   Type: REG_SZ
   Value: \\ServerName\\ShareName

   Name: AddPrinterDrivers
   Type: REG_DWORD
   Value: 0

   The first value setting of 1 tells the system to load drivers only from the second value setting that points to a share on the network. The third value controls the loading of drivers to nonadministrative users.

3. Driver files are stored in %SystemRoot%\System32\Spool\Drivers\W32x86\2. To populate the directory on the trusted share, first install the driver on another computer, and then copy the files to a "2" subfolder on the trusted share. For example, if the trusted share points to D:\TPD and the share name is "TrustedPrintDrivers," the subfolder would be D:\TPD\2, and the TrustedDriverPath Registry value would be \\ServerName\\ TrustedPrintDrivers.

Spooling

After a print file is generated by the printing system with the appropriate driver, it is saved to the spool directory on the same computer. This directory path is located in the following Registry key:

HKEY_LOCAL_MACHINE\SYSTEM\CurrentControlSet\Control\Print\Printers\
DefaultSpoolDirectory

By default, the key is set to %SystemRoot%\System32\Spool\PRINTERS. Even if a print queue is defined to point to a shared printer on the network, it must still spool locally. After the local spooler saves the file, it is moved across the network to the spool directory on the machine controlling the printer, as can be seen in Figure 17-2.

ICA Printing

ICA printing uses a combination of a local printer and a network print queue. The printer is controlled by components on the client and on the MetaFrame server. ICA printing

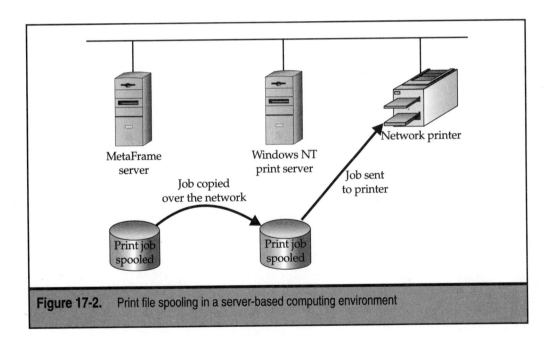

Figure 17-2.   Print file spooling in a server-based computing environment

works on the principle of port redirection or, more simply, printer mapping. *Printer mapping* occurs when a print queue accessible by the MetaFrame server is redirected to a printer connected to an ICA client. Client printer mapping is enabled by default for all supported transport protocols. It can be enabled or disabled with the Citrix Connection Configuration (CCC) program (see the following illustration). Client printer mapping settings can be changed using the CCC or, if you are changing them for a user or group, with User Manager for Domains.

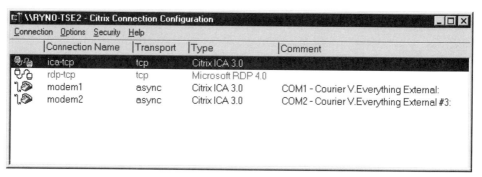

ICA printing functions by allocating bandwidth for a print job within an established ICA session. This can cause the normally small 20 Kbps ICA session to grow to be several times that size, as shown below. If the client and the server are connected over a LAN, this increased session size is not a problem. When connected over a WAN or dial-up session, however, the increased bandwidth can lead to performance problems if not taken into account in the network design. We will provide some recommendations for managing this issue in the "Best Practices for Enterprise Printing" section later in the chapter.

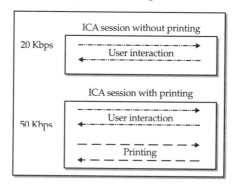

Client Printers

MetaFrame supports two options for creating client printers: *autocreate* and *manual*. An autocreated printer is mapped when a user logs on, and disappears when the user logs off. The advantage is clear: the printer definition only exists when it is needed. The disadvantage is related to drivers. The correct driver for whatever printer the user happens to have connected to the client may not exist on the MetaFrame server running the applications. A manually created client printer definition is persistent once created, but can have the same driver issues.

Autocreating Printers   Autocreating a printer refers to the process by which a user's printer is automatically mapped when the user logs on to a Citrix ICA session. The printer definition is not persistent. When the user logs off, the printer definition and corresponding icon are removed from the system. The feature is enabled in the CCC program. To enable autocreation, run the CCC program and choose the connection configuration for which the feature is to apply, for example, "ica-tcp." Click on Edit and then Client Settings. You will see several options for controlling how printers are created:

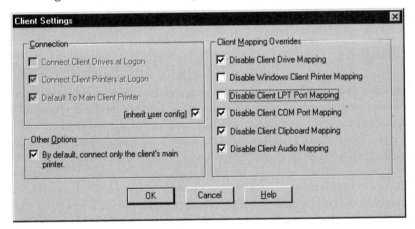

The "(inherit user config)" option allows the user to configure some of the printer settings, which are stored in the user's profile. If this option is checked, make sure that Connect Client Printers at Logon and Default To Main Client Printer are also selected. If either Disable Windows Client Printer Mapping or Disable Client LPT Port Mapping is selected, the printer will not be autocreated. Make sure that the latest drivers for the printers are installed on the client and that a compatible driver is installed on the MetaFrame server. You may need to define a driver equivalency, as described in the "Default Autocreated Printers" section earlier in the chapter.

TIP: If you want to grant regular users access to all autocreated printers, add the users to the Power Users local group on the MetaFrame member server and to the Print Operator local group on the Domain Controller.

Manually Creating Printers   Manually creating a client printer in Windows is nearly identical to creating any other type of network printer. The difference is the "Client Network" type available through MetaFrame. Use the following checklist to manually create a client printer. You may need to adjust the steps according to your specific client type, but the important step is to choose the client network for the printer.

From a Windows 9x client:

1. Choose Start > Settings > Printers > Add Printer.

2. Choose Client Network, then Client.

3. A list of available queue names will appear. Choose the appropriate one.

TCP/IP Printing

The third type of printing we will discuss is TCP/IP printing. TCP/IP printing utilizes the LPR and LPD protocols to provide print services and to send print jobs to remote machines. The advantage of this type of printing is that it is standards based. Thus, using LPR/LPD, a Windows computer can send or receive print jobs from a UNIX, VMS, or AS/400 system. The further advantage is that most hardware print servers, such as those available from Hewlett-Packard and Intel, have built-in support for these protocols.

LPD is a program that runs on the print host, or the computer acting as the print server. LPD spools print jobs and acts to assign processes and priorities for those jobs to be printed. LPR is the print client protocol used to initiate a print request, as shown in Figure 17-3. Microsoft includes support for TCP/IP printing in all Windows NT–based operating systems, including Windows 2000. The capability can be added to Windows 9x platforms through the use of a third-party utility such as NIPrint from Network Instruments (www.netinst.com) or Omni-Print from Xlink (www.xlink.com).

PRINTING IN A CORPORATE ASP

Creating a stable printing environment within a Corporate ASP is not as simple as plugging a printer into the back of a PC or connecting it to the network. Many things must be

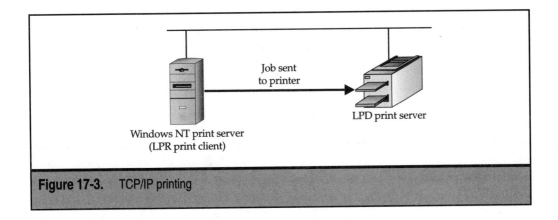

Figure 17-3. TCP/IP printing

considered before making the decision to support the printer in the environment. Since all print traffic must pass over the WAN from the data center to the user, it is important to examine any feature of a given printer that may affect performance or reliability in this scenario.

Printer Basics

There are literally hundreds of printers on the market, and it can be a daunting task to sift through the technical specifications, the marketing hype, and user requests to choose the right ones for your environment. Perhaps the most important factor in choosing a printer for the Corporate ASP is language support. The language used by the printer to render its output has a direct effect on the size of the print file. As we've stated, the size of this file is crucial to performance since it must travel to the user's printer from the data center over the WAN. The smaller and more compressible the job, the better the performance.

Fortunately, the majority of printers used in business—usually laser printers—support either the PCL or PostScript language, or both. Unfortunately, many people have nonbusiness printers in use that do not support either language. These printers are usually chosen because they are perceived to be inexpensive and can often provide color output. These printers are usually ink-jet printers. The ink-jet and DeskJet printers from HP use a rendering technology known as Printing Performance Architecture that we describe shortly. Other vendors such as Epson and NEC have their own equivalent technology that functions similarly with regard to server-based computing.

Another factor influencing performance in server-based computing is the type of data contained in the print file. If the print file is mostly text, network routers and switches will attempt to compress it as it travels over the WAN. With binary data, the possible compression is less.

TIP: Having the incorrect printer memory setting in the operating system can cause performance problems as well as garbled output. Take note of how much memory the printer has; then go to Start > Settings > Printers, and double-click the icon for the printer. Click Printer > Properties > Device Settings, and select Installed Memory. Make sure this setting is correct.

Printer Control Language (PCL)

HP invented PCL as a way to implement the same features across a number of different printers. It was originally intended for their dot matrix and ink-jet printers, but was applied to the first HP LaserJet in 1984 with PCL version 3. PCL commands take the form of escape sequences that are embedded throughout a print job. These device-independent sequences are translated into device-dependent graphics and fonts by the PCL formatter built into the printer.

The current version of PCL is version 6. There are four general types of commands:

▼ **Control codes** This is a command that initiates a built-in printer function, such as Carriage Return (CR) or Form Feed (FF).

■ **PCL** These commands are the escape sequences we referred to previously. The PCL command set grants access to all printer functions except those that deal with vector graphics.

■ **HP-GL/2** This is the vector graphic rendering command set.

▲ **PJL** These commands serve to control print jobs and printer communication. The features of PJL include the ability to return information about the printer model, allow language switching between jobs, or communicate job status with an application.

PCL is a good language to standardize on in a server-based computing environment. The language tends to optimize the size of output files, which is important when sending the job across the WAN. Jobs are in a binary format that is not as easily compressible as pure text.

PostScript (PS)

Invented by Adobe Systems in 1985, PostScript is an interpreted programming language rather than strictly a printer control language. It is device independent and enjoys wide industry support across a variety of print devices and operating systems. Because it is a full-blown programming language, PostScript has powerful graphics capabilities. PostScript is the de facto standard for high-end graphics publishing and can usually be found in more expensive printers or those intended for business use. PostScript files are composed of plain text commands that a PostScript-compatible printer turns into text and graphics. The print files tend to be smaller than both PCL or PPA files, and since they are text, they are more easily compressible over a network. PostScript is an excellent choice for a standard language in server-based computing. The general process for print language interpretation and rendering for both PCL and PostScript is shown in Figure 17-4.

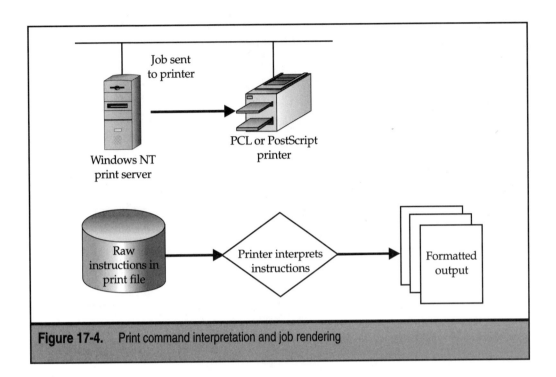

Figure 17-4. Print command interpretation and job rendering

Printing Performance Architecture (PPA)

HP invented PPA to offer a low-cost alternative to PCL and PostScript printing. By separating the various components required for a printer to render output, they achieved this goal. A PPA printer doesn't render a job itself. Rather, the computer running the application that requested the print job handles the bulk of the processing, as shown in Figure 17-5. The advantage is clear. HP can increase the capability of the printer simply by enhancing the rendering software. The disadvantage is that the print jobs tend to be several times larger than either PCL or PostScript. HP intends these printers to be for home use and thus will not support them on a network, even with an external JetDirect print server. We strongly discourage the use of this type of printer in a server-based computing environment. For more information about why this is the case, refer to the print performance test results in the section "Testing Printers" later in the chapter.

Text Printers

This class of printers includes dot matrix printers, line printers, band printers, or any other printer that is only rendering text or simple fonts. These printers typically have very small, text-based print files and simple drivers. As such, they work very well in a server-based computing environment.

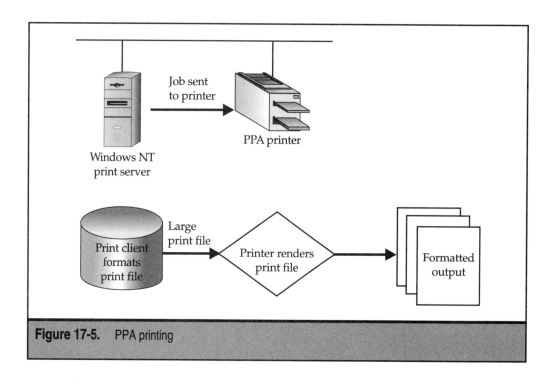

Figure 17-5. PPA printing

BEST PRACTICES FOR ENTERPRISE PRINTING

It should be obvious by now that designing an enterprise printing system for a Corporate ASP is not a simple exercise. In this part of the chapter, we give some practical advice in designing and deploying such a system with the dual goals of performance and reliability.

Printer Assessment

As with many of the other tasks presented in this book, an important first step is to take stock of the current state. If your company is like most large organizations we have encountered, you have hundreds of printers and dozens of brands spread throughout the enterprise. An important realization is that not all of these printers will be supported in the Corporate ASP.

ASP-Supported Printers

The best place to start when deciding whether a printer will work well within the Corporate ASP is with Microsoft's hardware compatibility list (HCL).

TIP: Microsoft maintains a searchable version of the HCL on the Web at the following address: www.microsoft.com/hcl/default.asp.

As we mentioned previously, the most reliable drivers are those supplied by Microsoft. The printers listed in the HCL have a driver, or at least an equivalent, included as part of any Terminal Services platform. You should create a table, like Table 17-1, that is easy for users and administrators alike to read and shows which existing printers will be supported.

In addition to defining which existing printers will be supported, you should keep a current list of which new printers will be supported. The Microsoft HCL can provide a good place to start here as well. If you find you need to support a printer not listed on the HCL, you simply need to test it to make sure it will work with Terminal Services and MetaFrame.

A useful technique to aid users in deciding which new printer to buy is to create a chart organized by the type of printing the user plans for the printer. These "profiles" can help users as well as your purchasing department, which can organize larger purchases and obtain deeper discounts. The profiles can be based on print volume, job complexity or composition, or other factors important to your users. A sample is shown in Table 17-2.

Laser Printers

Brother HL-730DX	Epson ActionLaser 1500	HP LaserJet 2
HP LaserJet 3	HP LaserJet 4	HP LaserJet 4 Plus
HP LaserJet 4/4M Plus PS 600	HP LaserJet 4/4M PS (300 dpi)	HP LaserJet 4L
HP LaserJet 4L/4ML Plus PS 300	HP LaserJet 4L/4ML PostScript	HP LaserJet 4M
HP Color LaserJet 4500		

Ink-Jet Printers

HP DeskJet 1600C	HP DeskJet 895	HP DeskJet 2000
HP DeskJet 2500		

Table 17-1. Sample List of Currently Supported Printers

	HP DeskJet 895cxi	HP LaserJet 1100xi	HP DeskJet 2000CN	HP LaserJet 2100TN	HP DeskJet 2500CM	HP LaserJet 4000N	HP LaserJet 4500N
User profile	Individual Color	Individual B&W	Small workgroup Color	Med. workgroup B&W	Med. workgroup Color	Large workgroup B&W	Large workgroup Color
List price	$399	$399	$999	$999	$1399	$1499	$2999
Network ready?	N	N	Y	Y	Y	Y	Y
Pages/minute B&W	4–11	8	12	10	11	17	16
Pages/minute Color	1–3	n/a	10	n/a	9	n/a	4
Monthly volume	3000	7000	5000	15000	12000	65000	35000
Memory, standard	2MB	2MB	2MB	8MB	20MB	8MB	32MB
Memory, maximum	2MB	18MB	2MB	40MB	76MB	100MB	208MB
8MB Mem upgrade	n/a	$27	n/a	$27	$19	$18	$18
16MB Mem upgrade	n/a	$46	n/a	$46	$27	$27	$27
32MB Mem upgrade	n/a	$64	n/a	$64	$54	$48	$47
64MB Mem upgrade	n/a	n/a	n/a	n/a	n/a	n/a	$64

Table 17-2. Sample List of New Printers Supported

NOTE: Users will be tempted to go to the corner computer store and buy the cheapest printer that they think will do the job for them. This practice should be discouraged. Every effort should be made to communicate to the users the importance of supportability, reliability, and performance.

Testing Printers

We have conducted numerous performance tests on a wide variety of printers in a server-based computing environment. Since PPA printers are inexpensive, you may find a lot of resistance from users against an outright ban on them. Table 17-3 shows the results of an actual test comparing the performance of an entry-level PCL printer versus a PPA printer. As you can see, the difference is dramatic. Once the users understand this, and all of the other benefits of server-based computing, they should be more receptive to the necessary restrictions.

The file used in the test is a 32-page Excel spreadsheet, 7618KB in size.

Printing Services

In the spirit of effective communication with users, you should also tell them how they can request support for a new printer and how printing services in general will be supported. We provide some examples for a printing service level agreement in Table 17-4.

Printer	Network	Time to Complete	Time to First Page
Brother HL-730DX	10 Mbps LAN	5 minutes, 18 seconds	20 seconds
	28.8 Kbps modem	28 minutes, 9 seconds	1 minute, 50 seconds
HP DeskJet 540	10 Mbps LAN	35 minutes, 41 seconds	1 minute, 20 seconds
	28.8 Kbps modem	1 hour, 45 minutes	2 minutes, 52 seconds

Table 17-3.   Print Performance Test Results

Service	Period	Response Time	Not Included	Description
Procurement	8 a.m. to 5 p.m. PST	Four hours to respond to request; three to five days to receive printer.	Ordering of nonstandard printers or consumables.	This is the purchasing process for obtaining a new printer based on a request from a user. It is the user's responsibility to obtain the proper approval for the purchase. Once purchased, the printer will be shipped out with the appropriate network hardware and will be installed by the user, the user's representative, or by a local technician dispatched by the help desk.
Support for new printer	8 a.m. to 5 p.m. PST	Four hours for tech to respond to request; up to one week to test and integrate new printer into environment.	Support for nonstandard printers or printers that do not work efficiently in the environment.	Once a user makes a request to support a new printer, either by e-mail or by calling the help desk, a technician will be assigned to integrate and test this printer. If this is a printer that the user currently has, the technician may ask that the printer, along with any drivers and documentation, be shipped to the help desk. If this is a new printer, the rules outlined under "Procurement" also apply.

Table 17-4. Sample Printing SLA

Optimized Print Client Architecture

There are a few different strategies to consider when deciding on an infrastructure for client printing in the Corporate ASP.

▼ **Scenario 1: printing within an ICA session**   In this scenario, the user has an autocreated or manually mapped printer (which can be done in the logon script) that uses the Citrix ICA port redirection function. The printing traffic is essentially encapsulated within the ICA protocol stream. The network bandwidth utilization of the ICA session increases to handle the additional load of the print job.

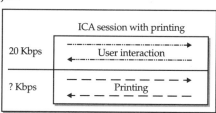

■ **Scenario 2: Windows printing** The user has a printer attached to a local PC, Windows NT-based Windows terminal, or a hardware print server with NetBEUI/NetBIOS printing capability. A print queue has been defined on the MetaFrame server that points to this local printer. The network bandwidth utilization is unregulated, and the Windows printing system takes as much bandwidth as needed in order to complete the request.

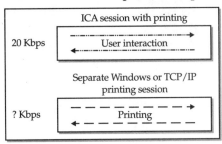

▲ **Scenario 3: TCP/IP printing** Similar to scenario 2, the user has a printer connected to the local PC, Windows terminal, or hardware print server. A queue has been defined with an LPR port that points to the local device. Again, bandwidth is consumed as necessary to fulfill the request.

In the above scenarios, we describe a printer attached to a local PC. If the PC is running a version of Windows NT, the setup is simple in all three cases. ICA printing is handled through the ICA client, Windows printing is supported, as is LPR. In the case of a Windows terminal, there are models that support LPR as well as Windows printing. Those that support Windows printing typically use the embedded version of Windows NT. In the case of a local PC running Windows 95 or 98, only ICA printing is supported well by default. Windows printing is of course supported, but performance suffers compared to the same PC running Windows NT. TCP/IP printing on Windows 9x systems requires third-party software.

Bandwidth Management

Bandwidth management is missing from all three scenarios above. In each case, it is possible for the print job to grow quite large and consume as much network bandwidth as is needed. In a large enterprise WAN with potentially hundreds of sites and thousands of printers, this unregulated bandwidth utilization can be disastrous to performance. In Chapter 6 we discussed both TCP rate control with the PacketShaper from Packeteer, and queuing with Cisco. Though either method of bandwidth management will have a beneficial effect on printing, TCP rate control allows a finer definition of how the bandwidth can be used. Similar solutions are available from NetReality (www.nreality.com) and Sitara Networks (www.sitaranetworks.com). Now we will examine the same three printing scenarios with bandwidth management in place.

▼ **Scenario 1: printing within an ICA session**   When the print job is streamed within an existing ICA session, it is not possible to "pull apart" the session and manage the bandwidth for printing separately. However, you can manage the total bandwidth for the session. With the PacketShaper, for example, you can either limit the amount of bandwidth that can be used for each session, for all sessions of a similar type, or prioritize the bandwidth used by a session. If this printing scenario is to be used, we recommend limiting the bandwidth used by each session to around 30 Kbps. This way, one user's print job will not affect other users' sessions directly. The print job will take longer to print, but only one user at a time will experience any delay.

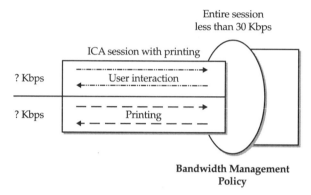

■ **Scenario 2: Windows printing**   If Windows printing is used, the printing session can be easily identified by the bandwidth management device and managed separately. You can define a policy and assign it only to printing. In this scenario, we recommend assigning per-flow limits to ICA traffic first in order to protect it, and then assign per-flow restrictions to the Windows printing traffic. You can limit the printing sessions' bandwidth to a low number, such as 40 Kbps, but allow it to burst higher if the bandwidth is available. This way, the ICA session traffic is protected, and the printing sessions are assigned whatever bandwidth is left.

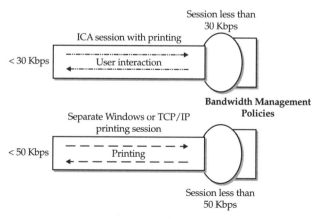

▲ **Scenario 3: TCP/IP printing**   Managing TCP/IP printing flows is the same as scenario 2. The bandwidth management device, such as a PacketShaper, can identify LPR/LPD traffic and assign the correct policy.

Hardware Print Servers

We have found hardware print servers to be a great solution for printing in a server-based computing environment. A device that supports a single printer and has built-in LPR/LPD support costs around $100 in volume. The device plugs directly into the network via Ethernet and to the printer through the parallel port. Some higher-end printers support this same functionality directly through a plug-in option card. Since they support a standard print protocol, network traffic can be more easily managed. An example network topology showing a hardware print server can be seen in Figure 17-6. Two print servers we have used successfully are the HP JetDirect and Intel NetPort Express.

▼ **HP JetDirect**   These units come in models that support one or multiple printers simultaneously on 10 Mbps or 100 Mbps Ethernet or on Token Ring. They support LPR/LPD, as mentioned, as well as NetWare and Apple printing simultaneously, and they feature a built-in Web interface for configuration. The server can be assigned a static IP address, or one can be automatically assigned through DHCP or BOOTP. We have found the units to be extremely reliable and consistent in how they function.

▲ **Intel NetPort Express**   This product has been around almost as long as the JetDirect. It is a solid choice for a hardware print server. The NetPort supports multiple protocols, including TCP/IP, NetBEUI and IPX.

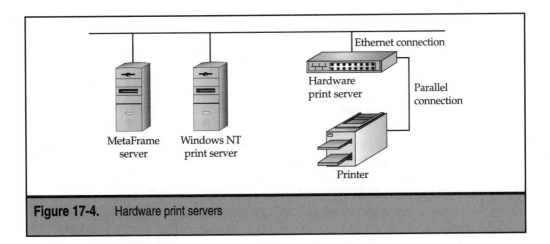

Figure 17-4.   Hardware print servers

Windows NT Print Servers

The design and deployment of the back-end print server architecture are just as important as those of the print client. The next few sections provide some tips and tricks on setting up a Windows NT print server.

Preinstallation

Dedicate a server to be the designated print host, and install Windows NT 4.0 Server or Windows 2000 Advanced Server. Before installing the first printer, make sure the following Registry values are set.

> **NOTE:** There is some duplication between the Registry values presented here and those in Chapter 13. This list of values is related specifically to printing. Those presented in Chapter 13 were examples of all the values you might potentially change in a Corporate ASP.

Each Registry change below is preceded by any relevant link to a Microsoft or Citrix support document as well as a brief explanation. The following changes should be made on the Windows NT/2000 print server.

▼ Increase the number of possible connections. The default value can limit the number of clients that can connect to the terminal server and cause connection errors. See http://support.microsoft.com/support/kb/articles/Q232/4/76.ASP?LNG=ENG&SA=ALLKB&FR=0 *and* http://support.microsoft.com/support/kb/articles/Q216/1/71.ASP?LNG=ENG&SA=ALLKB&FR=0.

Key: \HKLM\System\CCS\Services\LanmanServer\Parameters\
Values: MaxWorkItems, MaxMpxCt
Type: REG_DWORD
Data: MaxWorkItems: 8192, MaxMpxCt: 1024

■ Change SPOOL directory C:\winnt\system32\spooler to the D: drive. This simple change is designed to ensure adequate space for the print spool files. You can set it to whatever drive and directory is appropriate. See http://support.microsoft.com/support/kb/articles/Q123/7/47.asp *and* http://support.microsoft.com/support/kb/articles/Q137/5/03.asp.

Key: \HKLM\SYSTEM\CCS\Control\Print\Printers\
Value: DefaultSpoolDirectory
Type: REG_SZ
Data: D:\spool\printers (example)

■ Disable beep for printer. The beep is not appropriate for a multiuser environment.

Key: \HKLM\System\CCS\Print\
Value: BeepEnabled

Type: REG_DWORD
Data: 0

▲ Disable printer pop-up message. Similar to Dr. Watson, the printer dialog can hang the server while asking for user input. See http://support.microsoft.com/support/kb/articles/Q122/1/60.asp?LNG=ENG&SA=ALLKB&FR=0.

Key: \HKLM\SYSTEM\CCS\Control\Print\Providers\
Value: NetPopup
Type: REG_DWORD
Data: 1
Value: Eventlog
Type: REG_DWORD
Data: 0

Installing Drivers

After installation of any print driver, you must reinstall the current service pack and any Microsoft hot fixes you are using. Many drivers that are provided on the Windows NT CD have been replaced or updated by those found in the service packs. Manufacturers often incorporate out-of-date library files as part of their driver installation routines.

The following is a general-purpose checklist for installing printer drivers:

1. From the Start menu, select Settings and click Printers.
2. Double-click Add Printer.
3. Check My Computer in the Add Printer Wizard dialog box, and click Next.
4. Click Add Port. The Printer Ports dialog box appears. Highlight LPR Port in the drop-down list and click New Port. In the "Name or address if server providing lpd" field, enter the IP address or the host name of the printer. In the "Name of printer or print queue on that server" field, enter **raw**. Click on OK. Make sure the new port you created is checked.
5. Click Next, and the Print Driver window will appear. Click on Have Disk, and browse to the trusted location for your print drivers. Select your printer from the pop-up list, and click Next. Give the printer a name, and click Next.
6. On the share screen, choose to share the printer and click Next. Print a test page.
7. Reinstall any service packs or post–service pack hot fixes.
8. Reboot.

To add the printer to a MetaFrame server, use the following checklist:

1. From the Start menu, select Settings and click Printers.
2. Double-click Add Printer.

3. Check My Computer in the Add Printer Wizard dialog box, and click Next.

4. Click Add Port. The Printer Ports dialog box appears. Highlight Local Port in the drop-down list and click New Port. Enter the UNC name of the shared printer to which you want to print, for example, **Servername\Sharename**.

5. Make sure the new port you created is checked.

6. Click Next, and the Print Driver window will appear. Click on Have Disk and browse to your shared location for your print drivers (for example, \\ros-pratt2\sbc work files\print drivers). Select your printer from the pop-up list and click Next.

7. Give the printer a name and click Next to see the share screen. Share the printer, click Next, and print a test page.

8. Reinstall the service pack and any post–service pack hot fixes.

9. Reboot.

Once the printer is set up, the proper Registry key will be created for this printer. To more easily propagate this key to the other MetaFrame servers, it is possible to extract the Registry key and necessary files directly. To do this, use the following checklist:

1. Run REGEDT32 on the MetaFrame server with the printer defined. Select the following key:

   HKEY_LOCAL_MACHINE\SYSTEM\CurrentControlSet\Control\Print

2. With the Print subkey highlighted, select the Registry menu and select "Save key." (Do not select "Save subtree as.")

3. Save this file to disk as PRINT.KEY, and copy it to a file server.

4. From the same server, copy this directory with all its contents to a file server: %SystemRoot%\system32\spool\drivers\w32x86\2.

5. On each new MetaFrame server to which you would like to replicate these printer entries, perform the following steps:

   a. Connect to the file server where you saved PRINT.KEY and the \2 directory.

   b. Stop the Spooler service.

   c. Run regedt32.exe and highlight the following key:
      HKLM\SYSTEM\CurrentControlSet\Control\Print

   d. With the Print key highlighted, select the Registry menu, and select Restore.

   e. Select the PRINT.KEY file and click OK. You will see a warning stating that you are about to overwrite everything beneath the currently selected key. Make extra sure that you have the Print key highlighted and click OK. Close the Registry editor.

    f. Copy the contents of the \2 directory from the file server to the target server's %SystemRoot%\system32\spool directory.

    g. Start the spooler service and test your replicated printers.

Simple Redundancy

Once the print server is configured, you will need to ensure that it has some measure of redundancy. This could be a simple, fast way to rebuild the server and all of its printer drivers and Registry keys, or it could be a hot fail-over capability—you will have to decide.

Microsoft provides a tool to back up and restore the printer definitions on a server. It is called Printer Migrator (PRINTMIG.EXE), and it can be found in the Windows NT Resource Kit. Configuration data is written to a file called PM.CAB using the Microsoft Cabinet (CAB) file format. The file is saved to the default folder %SystemRoot%>\System32\Spool\Pm.

To perform a print server backup, use the following checklist:

1. On the Actions menu, click Backup.
2. In the Target Server box, type the NetBIOS name of the computer to back up. If you leave this box blank, Printer Migrator restores to the local computer.
3. In the CAB storage folder box, you can type the folder where the backup files will be stored. The default folder is <%SystemRoot%>\System32\Spool\Pm.
4. Click OK. Printer Migrator then writes the printer configuration data to the PM.CAB file.

To restore a print server, use the following checklist:

1. On the Actions menu, click Restore.
2. Type the filename of the PM.CAB file to be used for the restore in the File Name box.
3. Type the NetBIOS name of the destination computer in the Target Server box. If you leave this box blank, Printer Migrator restores to the local computer.

High Availability

If a higher level of redundancy is needed, you can use Microsoft Cluster Services or any of a number of third-party products to build a Windows NT server cluster. Products we have had success with are CoStandby Server and Octopus. CoStandby Server, formerly from Vinca, provides a bidirectional fail-over. Octopus is a file replication service that can track changes to the Registry or file system and duplicate them on another server. Both products are now owned by Legato Systems.

Non-Windows Print Servers

In the course of our investigations, we have evaluated a number of non-Windows print server solutions, most notably a LINUX server running Samba. As we discussed in Chapter 7, Samba is an open-source implementation of the CIFS file services protocol along with Windows NT authentication and printing services. It is possible to set up a LINUX server to act as the print host for a Windows-based network. Large companies such as Cisco have standardized on LINUX as a print server architecture. The advantage of this type of solution is in print performance and scalability. We have seen LINUX spool and serve multiple network print queues faster than Windows NT Server. The results are still out on whether this advantage exists over Windows 2000. The disadvantages to this solution are in administration, support, and driver availability. Unless your staff is already familiar with LINUX or UNIX, administering such a print host would be challenging. Built-in print driver support in LINUX is somewhat primitive. There are third-party print solutions available and shareware such as Ghostscript, but you will end up with a "roll your own" solution if you choose LINUX.

Our recommendation is to steer clear of non-Windows print servers unless you already have system administration expertise in the proposed platform or are willing to pay to obtain it, or you have a large number of non-Windows print clients that need to share printing with your MetaFrame servers. In the latter case, a hardware print server can probably do the job as we've already discussed.

Managing Printer Assignments

Users can get printer assignments through their profile or explicitly through the logon script. We recommend assignment through the logon script. This method enforces consistency and does not allow users to map to an inappropriate printer or become confused by what to do if they lose their printer assignment for some reason. Using this method also ensures that the users will be able to print even if their profile is deleted or becomes corrupted.

Standard Naming Convention for Printers

In order to manage a large number of users and printer assignments, it is necessary to come up with a standard naming scheme for printers and define user groups with printer access in mind.

Consider the format "Location-Printer Number." Using this format, the first printer defined at the location "CorpHQ" would be "CorpHQ-01." The next printer at the site would be "CorpHQ-02," and so on.

Assigning a Default Printer

With a naming standard defined, you must still come up with a scheme to make sure each user gets a default printer assignment. We discovered a method that works well but is kind of a "cheat." When creating a new user account, we put the name of the default printer in this field surrounded by parentheses "( )." This information can then be read in the logon script and used to map the default printer for the user. You can still use the Full Name field; just make sure the printer name is inside the brackets. An example of this function is shown below using Kixtart:

```
;set default printer
? "SETTING DEFAULT PRINTER" ?          ;display what is happening
$x=instr(@fullname,"(")                ;find the first bracket
$y=instr(@fullname,")")                ;find the second bracket
$z=($y-$x)-1                           ;find the # of characters
                                       ;between brackets
$printer=substr(@fullname,$x+1,$z)     ;find the printer name w/in the
                                       ;brackets
$nul=addprinterconnection("$printer")  ;adds default printer in case
                                       ;it doesn't exist
if setdefaultprinter("$printer")=0
      "Setting default printer to $printer"
else
      "Default printer not specified in user manager"
endif
return
```

Assigning a Printer Based on Group Membership

Most users need access to more than just their default printers. Which printers will be assigned to which users really depends on the organization. If you define the assignment based on a *site user group,* you can make sure each user will get a mapping to each printer at his or her particular site. Extending our example above, you first define a local group corresponding to the site name. In this case, the name is "CorpHQ." Since the group name is contained in the printer name, it is a relatively simple matter to create a loop and add the equivalent of a "net use printer" for each printer at the site. The following Kixtart code does just that.

```
;add all printers at a site
? "ADDING PRINTERS" ?     ;display what is happening
$x=0
:addprinter
$x=$x+1                   ;begin the section needed because there
                          ;is no for/next loop
$y=$x
if $x<10
      $y="0"+$x            ;add a "0" to printer names that are less
                          ;than 10 chars
endif                     ;end "for/next" section
```

```
if addprinterconnection("\\tfp-sf02\$printloc-$y")=0
      ? "Added Printer $printloc-$y" ?
      goto "addprinter"
else ?
endif
return
```

If you wish to make the list of assigned printers more granular, you can make the printer naming scheme, and therefore the logon scripting, more sophisticated.

CHAPTER 18

Deploying Terminal Services

This chapter covers the methodologies for migrating from a PC-based to a server-based computing environment. First we'll review the process of setting up a proof-of-concept pilot program. We next talk about expanding the pilot to a beta in order to identify and resolve any issues that arise in a small-scale production environment. We then cover expanding the beta to an enterprise-wide rollout of Terminal Services. Finally, we discuss postproduction processes of ongoing measurement and reporting, change control, upgrades, and changes to the environment.

PROOF-OF-CONCEPT PILOT PROGRAM

In Chapter 4 we discussed setting up a proof-of-concept pilot program as an important element in the design of a Corporate ASP. The pilot is also the first step in an enterprise rollout. It serves as a basic test of application performance using Terminal Services.

At first, the pilot program should be a nonproduction system designed to ensure that the desired applications perform together adequately over MetaFrame and Terminal Services. The next step is to expand the nonproduction pilot to a small production pilot with carefully selected participants running specific applications.

Pilot Platform

The pilot hardware should be representative of the hardware that will eventually be used in the data center to support the enterprise rollout. The pilot program should not be constrained by any difficulties or limitations in the existing network infrastructure. For instance, if the network backbone is causing latency issues, the pilot should be set up on a separate backbone. If a data line to a remote office frequently fails, then the remote office should not be part of the pilot program.

Application Selection

The objective is to load all applications to be hosted under the Corporate ASP as part of the proof-of-concept, nonproduction pilot program. That being said, most organizations have far too many applications to reasonably host together in a MetaFrame environment. During the infrastructure assessment and project plan design process, the appropriate applications are studied in great detail and are carefully selected for server-based computing. Since the pilot takes place before this assessment begins, you can pare down the applications to be hosted in this environment by following a few rules of thumb:

▼ *Use representative samples.* Applications should be a representative sample of the production suite.

■ *Eliminate duplications.* Look over the list of all applications to eliminate obvious duplications. For instance, if 90 percent of projected Corporate ASP users run Microsoft Office and 10 percent run Corel WordPerfect Office, you can reasonably assume that MS Office will win out as the new corporate standard under server-based computing.

▲ *Develop selection criteria.* Create a list with "must-have" and "should-have" features to help pare down the applications in the pilot program. For instance, a must-have feature would be that an application is stable under standard NT workstation. A should-have feature would be that the application is 32 bit.

Testing

The performance, stability, and interaction of the various applications individually and collectively under Terminal Services must be tested and evaluated. One way to do this is by using test lists.

The application information gathered during the infrastructure assessment can be used to prepare the test lists. The lists should include the attributes to be tested along with the expected outcomes. Record the actual outcome for each test and whether it passed or failed. In Chapter 15 we discussed application testing in some detail.

Expanding to a Production Pilot Program

Start with a prepilot survey geared to recording the current state of user performance, reliability, and satisfaction in a fat-client environment. Use the survey results to set expectations for the users about the performance under MetaFrame. Be sure they are prepared for the inevitable problems that the new environment will precipitate, as well as for any differences they are likely to encounter by running their applications in a server-based computing environment.

It is acceptable to ask "leading" questions in the survey to set expectations, but they should strive for quantifiable answers where practical. For example, instead of asking, "Does your PC crash on a daily basis?" you can ask, "How many times per day does your PC need to be rebooted?" The results should be tabulated and published to the users who participated. A good way to do this is by using the intranet site, as mentioned in Chapter 10. If such a site is already available, consider doing the survey online rather than with paper forms.

Selecting Applications

The objective of the pilot program is to prove the value of server-based computing by running crucial applications successfully in this environment. Misbehaving, but noncrucial, applications should not be included as part of the production pilot. They can be tested further for inclusion as part of the beta if their problems can be solved or isolated using a two-tier server farm, as discussed in Chapter 15.

TIP: You can use batch files or WSH (Windows Scripting Host) to remove or move icons from Corporate ASP applications that are currently run locally on a user's PC. This allows for a quick rollback in the event that the pilot program does not succeed.

The following are some minimum requirements for running an application in a production pilot program. These are suggestions to help get you started on your own list.

▼   The application is stable in the current distributed environment.

■   If it is a DOS application, it does not extensively poll the keyboard. This can cause huge CPU utilization on the MetaFrame server. You should consider replacing any DOS application with a 32-bit Windows version if possible.

■   If it is a 16-bit Windows application, consider replacing with a 32-bit application because the latter tend to use less memory and CPU resources.

■   If it is an older or custom application, make sure it doesn't use hard-coded pathnames for files. Since most paths need to be user specific in a multiuser environment, this can cause major headaches.

■   The application represents the most users possible. Using our previous example, we would want to test MS Office and not WordPerfect Office because the former represents 90 percent of the users.

▲   Applications with back-end integration requirements (such as database or terminal session connectivity) have upgraded to the latest version. We have found that many applications that fit this description, such as IBM Client Access or various reporting packages, work fine in a multiuser environment but *only* if you use the latest version.

Testing and Evaluation

Start with the test lists defined in the pilot program for component and system testing, and layer in tests aimed at the production environment. Such tests would include a larger number of users running the applications, competing network traffic, reconnection to a user session, use of shadowing to support an application, and the effect on applications of backing up and restoring data.

Determine what performance data needs to be collected and how to collect it. System management tools such as Citrix RMS can be useful here, as well as user surveys. One of the best testing methods at this stage is simply saturation: let the users pound away at the applications, and see what they come up with.

Selecting the Participants

The production pilot program should include a larger sample of users than the nonproduction pilot, but the number should remain relatively small. The exact number will be based on the size of your organization and the complexity of your application environment. Ideally, the users selected should be representative of the users who will participate in the Corporate ASP, but they should also be friendly to the project. We have found that keeping the number of participants in the production pilot between 5 and 10 users, and no more than 50 for large companies, seems to work best.

Choose which categories of users will participate in the pilot, keeping in mind that you are looking for a representative mix of the ultimate Corporate ASP participants. A small pilot, therefore, might still include thin-client-only, mobile, and hybrid users. As discussed in Chapter 4, we recommend including at least one Windows terminal as part of the pilot, if possible, in order to get across the point that this is a new way of delivering applications. Of course, a Windows terminal can only be used when all required applications for a user or group are accessible over MetaFrame.

Location of users is also important. If users in remote offices will be part of the pilot program, the network's wide-area infrastructure needs to be very sound. Remote office users should be trained ahead of time not to engage in excessive bandwidth utilization practices such as copying data from a local hard drive back to the data center server, or downloading MP3 files from the Internet connection via the MetaFrame server farm. Alternatively, you should have a method to limit the bandwidth available to users. We've already discussed TCP rate control and custom queuing as two common methods. We've summarized these and other requirements as follows:

▼ Choose a small but representative mix of users. The users selected should access different groups of applications from different types of clients.

■ Use this opportunity to test key parts of your infrastructure with server-based computing. Choose users in major regional offices, telecommuters, and VPN users.

■ Choose users who are open to the Corporate ASP concept. Demanding users are fine as long as the demands are reasonable, but avoid high-maintenance users.

▲ At this stage, choose users who are computer literate and can make the "paradigm shift" necessary to participate fully. We are not saying they have to be programmers or system administrators, just experienced users who have some command of their current desktop.

Customer Care

We discussed customer care in detail in Chapter 12. It is crucial to alert the help desk and to put special mechanisms in place for expediting any problems users encounter. A sour experience during the pilot program, even among friendly users, could end up poisoning the entire Corporate ASP project. On the other hand, if users receive fast and competent responses to issues that arise, they are more likely to start an early, strong, favorable buzz about the new technology. A good technique is to have a "triage" process in which the help desk can quickly categorize a pilot call from a normal production call and route it appropriately. After a call is identified and routed to the first tier of support, it should go directly to the pilot implementation team. This is an excellent method for keeping the team in tune with the users and making continuous, incremental improvements to the pilot environment.

Training Techniques

It is important for the ultimate success of the project to formulate a training plan for all employees involved, including users, help desk technicians (all levels), and administrators. Some suggestions are provided below:

▼ **Users** If your organization, like many, is already using a Windows desktop environment, moving to a Corporate ASP will not represent a large functional difference to users. We recommend integrating a short orientation, perhaps 15 to 30 minutes, into the user migration process. The user should be oriented, the data migrated, the client installed, and the client device configured all during the same visit by a deployment technician.

■ **Help desk** The people fielding technical support and administrative requests must not only understand the basics of server-based computing, but they must also be trained in how to do whatever they do now in the new environment. Creating users, adding them to groups, and giving them access to file storage and applications are different tasks in MetaFrame and must be the subject of training. The deployment team is a good source of targeted information on these operations, so build time in the schedule to have them give input into the training plan.

▲ **System administrators** These individuals usually represent the smallest group and need the most training. They will eventually receive calls from other groups and are responsible for solving problems in production. You should build money into the budget for the training programs offered by Citrix and Microsoft. Specifically, the Citrix Certified Administrator (CCA) and Microsoft Certified System Engineer (MCSE) should be considered for administrators.

Controlling the Pilot Program

A carefully implemented pilot program is likely to be successful, but this very success leads to quick requests for enhancements. It is important not to cave into pressure from users to introduce new variables, such as additional applications, as part of the pilot. Do not stray from your pilot plan until after the initial testing is complete. If adjustments such as adding applications must be made before a beta implementation, the initial proof-of-concept testing offline should be repeated and then the new server image introduced to the users. Don't assume that since the production pilot worked with 10 applications that it is acceptable to add an 11th. Everything must be tested before being deployed. Also realize that your deployment team is limited. If you are forced to spend a lot of time testing new applications or features at the last minute, it is likely to have an impact on the schedule.

Creating a Variance Process Define a variance process before the pilot that defines the handling of scope creep. You can publish this process as part of the user survey or other communication given to the pilot users. Decide who needs to approve requests for additional applications or pilot participants, and have a mechanism ready to handle this process. We've found such requests often come from management members who outrank the deployment team. If you *must* implement a change, be ready to clearly and concisely communicate the impact it will have on the deployment schedule, resources, and cost.

Handling Objections to Server-Based Computing   Despite careful pilot participant selection, some users may still object to the concept. Be prepared to do a quick sales job that shows them both the personal and corporate benefits of migrating to a Corporate ASP environment. If you run into unreasonable or unfounded objections, be ready to pass them to the proper management members. The executive sponsor for the pilot is an excellent choice to help handle objections. Another important tool is to have the facts at hand regarding any objection. We've found that users sometimes couch objections in terms sympathetic to their case that do not always reflect the facts. For example, a user may go to his manager and say, "The pilot team says I can't have the printer on my desk anymore." In reality, the pilot team published a list of compatible printers, and this user's printer wasn't on it. Be ready to tell this user and his manager how they can get a compatible printer or what to do as a work-around.

Assessing Performance

Document your expectations of the pilot program before you begin. Decide up front upon the success metrics for the pilot. Take measurements of application performance in the current distributed environment, and compare these to performance under server-based computing. For example, the time it takes to launch Microsoft Word can be measured in both environments. (It should be faster under server-based computing.) Other examples include the time it takes to print a certain document or to open a specific file.

In addition to the user-oriented metrics mentioned, include *system* and *cost* metrics. An example of a system metric is the time it currently takes to support a regional file server when it fails as compared to the time it takes to fix a file server in the data center. An example of a cost metric would be the cost of flying a technician to the site where a problem is occurring as opposed to having a technician handle the problem at the data center.

After the pilot, create a report on whether success metrics were met. Document any problems encountered along with their solutions. Document any open issues or new questions raised by the pilot, along with the actions being taken to resolve them.

EXPANDING THE PILOT PROGRAM TO A BETA

A beta deployment, while conceptually still a pilot, should represent users and environments that will be part of the enterprise rollout. The beta will be invaluable as a mechanism for discovering and resolving major performance issues before going to enterprise production. It should not be implemented until after the design for the enterprise rollout is well under way and the funds for the entire project have been justified. Even so, a poorly performing beta could end up killing the project, and it is therefore essential that the beta be implemented with the same high level of diligence used in the pilot phases. You should also try to make the beta implementation as nondisruptive to the current production environment as possible by running as many services in parallel as possible. For example, if you intend to run a new network backplane and a new enterprise-class file server for the Corporate ASP, leave the old systems online as you bring up the new systems. Users can then move from the old to the new system incrementally. This also serves the purpose of "leaving yourself an out." The smooth running of your business is more important than this project. If something doesn't go right, be able to go back to a known, reliable state.

Customer Care During Beta

As with the pilot program, responsiveness to users' problems will greatly influence their opinions about the project. Enhance the help desk and call center staff for quicker turnaround.

In the spirit of having no secrets from the user community, a published outage log should be created for users via an intranet Web site or through an internal electronic forms application such as Microsoft Exchange or Lotus Notes. Encourage users to let IT know about any system outages or problems. Also provide a forum for beta participants to provide feedback unrelated to problems. This can help increase user satisfaction.

Now is the time to refine the support process and be ready for production. Help desk personnel, along with system administrators, should be trained and ready for the demand. If you intend to deploy system management servers or a network management framework tool that integrates with your help desk system (as discussed in Chapter 10), they should go through final implementation at this point.

Maintenance Window

As with a mainframe environment, a maintenance window should be scheduled once a production server-based computing environment is in place. During this time, the deployment team and system administrators will perform tasks that require a significant portion of the infrastructure to be offline. Such activities include hardware and software upgrades, switching over network connections or carrier lines, or troubleshooting and correcting problems before they cause a production outage.

The maintenance window should be scheduled during the least disruptive time. If an organization is international in scope or works 24×7, it may be difficult to set aside a regular time slot, but it should be done if possible. During the implementation process of both the beta and the enterprise deployment, the maintenance window will likely need to occur more frequently than after project completion. It is important to user acceptance to avoid unscheduled downtime whenever possible. Since Corporate ASP users are completely dependent on the network for their processing, unscheduled downtime will create unhappiness and loss of productivity.

TIP: If you have a 24×7 operation, you can schedule maintenance items such as hot fixes and service packs without undergoing systemwide downtime. This is accomplished by disabling the logon to a particular server or group of servers in your farm the day before your scheduled maintenance. The next day, you are free to perform your maintenance and then bring the server or group of servers back online. You can repeat this process until all servers are upgraded.

Unscheduled Nonemergency Maintenance   Some organizations might not be able to, or may not wish to, have a regularly scheduled maintenance window. In these situations, carefully created procedures should still be utilized to ensure minimal disruption to the organization. For instance, the policy may be to give users at least three days notice before nonemergency maintenance will be performed. Scripting can be created to send out initial e-mails to the affected parties explaining the nature of the maintenance, the likely effects, and the projected duration. A reminder e-mail might be sent again a few hours before the maintenance begins.

Emergency Maintenance   Sometimes, with or without regular maintenance windows, emergency maintenance procedures will need to take place. Again, policies should be developed ahead of time to let affected users know about the maintenance with as much time as possible in order to minimize disruption to their work. Keep in mind that the maintenance can potentially affect the work of hundreds or thousands of Corporate ASP users.

The rigorous testing done in the pilot and beta phases is intended to keep unscheduled downtime to an absolute minimum. In cases where it does happen, make sure the help desk has emergency response procedures in place. One option is to include a recorded message explaining the situation, the expected resolution, and the projected service restoration time. The idea is to avoid burdening the help desk or technicians with a lot of user calls reporting the same, known problem when they should be concentrating their efforts on restoring service.

Infrastructure Assessment

The beta should utilize the same hardware slated to be part of the enterprise rollout. The network infrastructure now plays a crucial role. A network problem that goes unnoticed or is tolerated under a PC-based computing environment is likely to be amplified many times under a server-based computing environment. For example, one organization we worked with had Novell servers with malfunctioning routing. Users did not notice it when running in fat-client mode. When they became completely dependent upon MetaFrame servers, the routing problems quickly became intolerable.

One intended outcome of the infrastructure assessment is to identify any network or infrastructure issues and resolve them before a beta rollout. Some problems, though, are likely to be missed. IT should be prepared to resolve them quickly as they show up. Users should understand that a beta is still an expanded pilot and that bugs will have to be worked out.

Adequate Bandwidth

Ensure that bandwidth will be adequate to remote offices where users will be part of the beta. User counts should be verified. Bandwidth management tools should be utilized if possible. Take into consideration any additional traffic required during the transition period, and order the bandwidth accordingly.

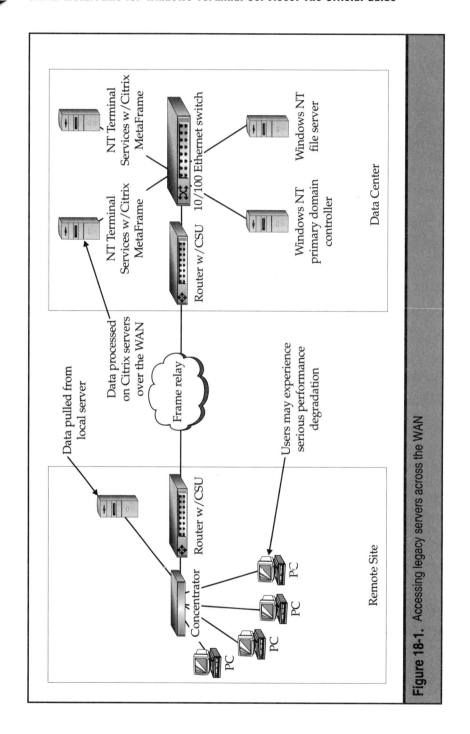

Figure 18-1. Accessing legacy servers across the WAN

Local Legacy System Access

In an enterprise server-based computing rollout, we recommend putting databases adjacent to the MetaFrame server farm. During the beta, though, this may not always be possible. Remote users may require access to local servers or host systems, but their sessions are now running on the MetaFrame server farm at headquarters. As Figure 18-1 shows, this means that users are accessing local servers across the WAN. Depending upon the databases and WAN bandwidth, they may experience much slower performance than they are used to. The beta participants should have their expectations set accordingly, along with the knowledge that it is a temporary problem that will be eliminated once the enterprise rollout takes place.

The other reason that legacy systems need focused attention is that they tend to be expensive or special purpose and cannot easily be run in parallel as the server-based computing project plan may dictate. These systems usually need to be "cut over" rather abruptly as they move from the old to the new environment. A separate, detailed project plan to accomplish this is required, as is a separate project team to address the special needs of these systems.

Local File Sharing

During the beta, remote users may still be allowed to share files locally. During the enterprise rollout, this practice should be eliminated wherever possible. The beta is the perfect time to start making the transition.

CD-ROM Sharing

If users at a remote site need to share CD-ROMs, this can be done using a small CD-ROM server or even a PC with sharing enabled. We recommend against this if it can be avoided because it is difficult to support centrally. If CD-ROMs must be shared, place a CD-ROM server at the data center nearest the user, and use groups and scripting to give the user access to the volumes as part of the login process.

Application Considerations During Beta

Make sure that all of the applications to be run in the Corporate ASP are part of the beta. Some selection criteria include

- ▼ The total number of people who need to run the application
- ■ How often the users require access to the application
- ▲ How many users would have to remain on PCs instead of Windows terminals if you do not migrate the application

> *Properly documenting and testing key procedures during the beta process is one of the fundamental elements to a successful large-scale Corporate ASP deployment. The documents Westaff developed were an indispensable tool, which allowed us to efficiently create over 1100 user accounts for over 260 locations. It also enabled us to maintain consistency among all accounts and helped us complete our rollout one month ahead of schedule.*
>
> —Rob Hutter, NT Systems Manager, Westaff

Some applications may have exhibited troublesome signs during the pilot, but it might take a beta to see how they really perform under a production environment. In this case, the problematic applications should be layered into the beta one at a time in order to minimize disruption to other applications and to users' perceptions of the Corporate ASP's reliability.

Apply the same rigor for testing these new applications before deploying them as part of the beta as you would if deploying them in your enterprise production environment. The beta is your last chance to work the kinks out of the testing and deployment process before going live.

User Selection During Beta

The beta should be a microcosm of the Corporate ASP. As with the pilot phases, users should be friendly to the concept of server-based computing. Users can be layered into the beta until all categories and groups of users are represented.

Also be sure to get an accurate count for the number of users in remote offices. If the number is too low, the bandwidth ordered will not be sufficient. As with the production pilot, users should also be aware that they will be participating in a beta and are likely to have some performance and reliability issues come up.

Testing During Beta

The test lists prepared for the pilot program should be updated for the beta and utilized again. In addition, appropriate infrastructure tests for bandwidth and redundancy should be performed, and their results evaluated. The beta period is the time to hone a healthy intolerance for error. If a system is not performing as expected, it should be fixed immediately. After all, garbage doesn't smell better with age.

Service Level Agreements

In Chapter 10, we introduced the concept of a service level agreement (SLA) and how to use SLAs for the Corporate ASP. You can also apply SLAs effectively to the deployment process. They can be used to provide the pilot and beta users with the proper expectations for system stability, performance, and help desk response times, for example. It is important both to set service level agreements and to manage them. For instance, a beta user may have a problem with her newly installed ICA client. This affects her ability to participate in the beta, but it does not affect her ability to do work. The associated SLA for help desk response should reflect this by allowing enough time for overburdened technicians to respond to more critical problems first.

Incorporate What You Learned from the Pilot Program

Now is the time to review the information collected during the pilot. Help desk call logs, user requests and comments, performance metrics, application changes performed, and system administration logs all provide a wealth of information and a platform for improvement during the beta phase.

Beta Assessment

IT must honestly assess whether the beta environment meets the production scope requirements. If not, adjustments must be made either to the technology or to the scope. Sometimes, the beta will have outcomes exceeding expectations that might also lead to scope reevaluations. For example, an organization originally intending to deploy only a couple of applications may determine that users are eager to run all of their applications from the Corporate ASP. If this is the case, the beta should reflect any changes before the enterprise rollout occurs.

ENTERPRISE ROLLOUT

All contingencies must be completed before the start of the enterprise rollout. Data centers and network upgrades should be complete. Equipment staging should be ready. Rollout teams should be ready to be deployed.

User Training During Rollout

Ensure high attendance for training sessions through management e-mails and user incentives. Be creative. Include project marketing along with the training sessions in order to reinforce initial project acceptance. Use rainbow packets, desk-side orientation, and videos. If your help desk charges users per incident, establish a grace period for free support during the conversion. As discussed previously, the amount of training necessary is likely to be limited to a short orientation to the new environment. Of much greater importance is effective marketing to get the users to embrace the change as something positive.

Expanding Service Level Agreements

Beta SLAs should be expanded to fit the conditions appropriate to a production rollout. For example, you may want to intentionally set the help desk response to a short period—say, one hour—for newly converted users, to make sure any initial problems are solved quickly.

Creating a Deployment Guide

For a large enterprise conversion to server-based computing, creating a deployment guide can be very helpful in making the process go smoothly. This is particularly important if you have a large number of remote offices requiring multiple implementation teams. Though the audience for such a guide is technically proficient, it is important to have a guide for reasons of consistency. If deployment technicians are allowed to carry out the migration their own way, it will be that much more difficult to troubleshoot problems as they arise. The deployment guide should include the following sections:

▼ **User communication FAQ**   Arm the deployment technician with answers to common questions encountered during the pilot and beta stages. This type of FAQ will help tremendously with conflict resolution and will help maintain a professional image for the technician.

■ **Contact information**   List the appropriate contacts and phone extensions for IT staff to support specific issues, including desktop migration, printer setups, wide area network problems, and Windows terminals. The escalation paths for different types of problems should be clear.

■ **Data migration procedure**   Spell out the specific steps for migrating data. Figure 18-2 shows a copy of the data migration procedure that ABM Industries used for their remote offices.

Checklist and Procedures

Data Migration Procedure (all desktops)

1. Determine if total amount of data to be copied from all sources is less than 20MB (C:\ & H:\). If so, skip to WAN-Based File Copy Procedure below.

2. Determine the file system type of the PC. DOS/Windows 3.x should be FAT16. Windows 9x should be FAT32 and Windows NT should be NTFS. Choose the appropriate boot disk for the PC.

3. Determine the number of hard drives and the number of partitions on each hard drive. The easiest way to do this is with the DOS FDISK program.

4. Attach Jaz drive to user's PC and insert the floppy chosen in step 2 in drive A:. Reboot the PC.

5. After boot scandisk will run on the C: drive. When the A:\ prompt appears run scandisk.

Figure 18-2.   ABM's data migration procedure guidelines

- **Client installations**   The deployment guide should include detailed instructions for installing each type of ICA client you intend to deploy. Each installation method should include a checklist and any relevant screen shots to make the procedure clear.

- **Desktop device configuration**   Include a table showing all categories of users and their associated devices, such as hybrid PCs, laptops, and Windows terminals. Include a list of the appropriate equipment for each category of user, such as a monitor or network card. Include IP and DNS setup as well as things like how to set up LPD printing on Windows terminals.

- **Shadowing users**   Support personnel can use shadowing to take control of users' PCs or Windows terminals for troubleshooting purposes. Show how to set up shadowing, including screen prints for each step.

- **VPN or Internet dial-up connectivity**   If remote users are connecting to the data center through a WAN or VPN, explain how to set up the VPN client software on a PC, configure the Windows terminal's SecureICA functions, or whatever is appropriate to your environment.

- **Printing**   Recap which printers are supported and which ones will work with bandwidth management devices, if appropriate. If printers are not supported, include instructions about the proper procedures to take when such a printer is encountered during deployment.

- **IP address scheme**   A workable IP addressing scheme needs to be implemented if it hasn't been already. If DHCP is to be used, explain how to configure the client to take advantage of it.

- ▲ **General migration issues**   Include answers to problems that the implementation team may encounter, such as what to do if a user scheduled for migration is absent or if a user's PC is not operating properly under MetaFrame.

Creating Migration Databases

A large migration involves a large number of employees, all requiring current information. Developing databases to sort and track this information will significantly enhance the process. Making this database available in some ubiquitous fashion, such as Web publishing, will help assure its adoption and currency. Below are some ideas for different aspects of the deployment process that you should consider tracking in this way.

Locations Database

List every location and pertinent information, including current status, data connectivity status, number of users, type of users, and the implementation team assigned. The implementation, WAN, and procurement teams should update this database as part of their normal process. For example, after a user is installed, the deployment team member can connect to the locations database from the user's new client and enter the information that the user has been installed and any asset information on the equipment assigned to that user.

Change-Management Database

Track everything that changes at the data center, including new applications, printer drivers, and all unscheduled downtime. This enables much better troubleshooting of modifications causing problems. Significant changes in the field, such as large bandwidth increases, premise router changes, and the like, can also be entered here for all to see.

Survey Databases

User surveys taken at the various deployment stages can be entered and the results tracked in a database.

Migrating Headquarters

Converting users at headquarters to a server-based computing environment is much easier than migrating remote offices. The planning design document should cover most of the contingencies you are likely to run up against when migrating headquarters. The close proximity of these users to IT and the lack of bandwidth variables make it relatively easy to identify and remedy problems. For these reasons, it is generally advisable to migrate headquarters before migrating users at remote offices, even though the latter may have the greater need. As always, new users should be added to the Corporate ASP in layers in order to minimize disruptions caused by unexpected problems.

Client Operating System Upgrades

Although the MetaFrame client will operate with nearly any client, from DOS to NT to LINUX, some organizations prefer to standardize on one operating system platform to make administration easier. In this case, the operating system can be migrated as part of the implementation process. Since the result will be users accessing their applications from the corporate data center, individual PC issues are a minor concern in terms of project success.

User Data Migration

It is possible to write scripts to migrate data off users' local PCs and transfer it to a centralized file server. This can be accomplished through batch files or with WSH (Windows Scripting Host).

Desktop Application Migration

In the pilot program, we recommended leaving local applications in place and moving, or removing, icons. In a production environment, we recommend eliminating Corporate ASP applications from local PCs altogether in order to ensure that users operate only in the intended server-based computing environment. There are many methods for uninstalling applications. Microsoft SMS 2.0 has this capability, or you can "roll your own," using scripting tools such as WSH, as mentioned in Chapter 14.

Planning for Remote-Office Migration

The project design document will almost certainly focus on the corporate data center and users at headquarters. Although remote offices and their users can be categorized in broad terms, the project plan is not likely to encompass specific implementation details if a large number of remote facilities are part of the project. In these cases, we recommend creating a separate implementation plan for the actual server-based computing rollout.

Assess Remote-Office Infrastructure

Completing a detailed assessment of the remote-office networks and environments enables much better planning and, consequently, a much smoother implementation. A good tool for this is a site survey. You can assess the infrastructure, the number of users, equipment, and any other special needs in the survey. As we will discuss later in the chapter, you will have several teams available for doing field deployments. During the inevitable periods when the team members are not in the field due to scheduling, have them perform the surveys.

NOTE: You may already have a tool in place, such as Microsoft SMS, that is capable of doing hardware inventory across the WAN. This is useful but is not a substitute for a site survey. Use the polling results from SMS during the survey as part of the discussion with the people on-site, but don't treat it as gospel. Not all hardware you are interested in will respond to a poll, and you need to be as accurate as possible.

Determine Time Constraints

Since implementing a Corporate ASP is usually very economically advantageous, time is often the biggest project constraint. Establish guidelines to ensure that project timelines are met. Communicate these time limits to users before the implementation in order to help gain their support in making the migration successful. Make the time limits part of the SLA for the implementation team, and manage them. This means collecting accurate data and publishing the results to the team. Then discuss what can be done to improve problem times.

Implementation Team Follow-Up   Create a way for the implementation teams to check on the status of each time-critical item remotely. One method to accomplish this follow-up is to create an intranet site that can be accessed once the user is online.

System Implementation Time Limit   Set a maximum amount of time that an implementation team member can spend on any single system to ensure that an office can be migrated in a reasonable amount of time. For instance, you may determine that converting a user to server-based computing should take no more than an hour. If a conversion runs over an hour, the user is given a Windows terminal in addition to her PC, and her existing data is not migrated to the data center. Though this is obviously not ideal, it will keep the project on track and eliminate huge costs that can result from schedule delays.

PC Preparation Time Limit   Set a limit, tied to the conversion time limit, on how much time to spend preparing a PC for migration. For instance, if the conversion time limit for a PC is an hour, you may wish to set a 30-minute time limit on preparing the PC.

Communication Lines   If a new or upgraded WAN was put into place, confirm that the line was installed, and test connectivity before the implementation team's arrival at a remote office. Do not, under any circumstances, rely on the telecommunication provider's word that the line is in and working. Test it yourself.

User Accounts   Set up user accounts in NT a minimum of one day before the installation. The help desk, in cooperation with the field deployment teams, should do the set up.

Remote-Office Data Migration

In a typical conversion from PC-based to server-based computing, data will be migrated from PCs and remote-office servers back to the corporate data center. Remember that the migration process can take longer than planned due to unexpected problems such as delays in the WAN implementations, conflicts in employee work schedules, and delayed shipments of hardware.

User Training for Remote-Office Migration

Users should first be shown preliminary marketing materials and videos so that they know what to expect. The implementation team's responsibilities should include a brief user training session. Users should sign forms indicating that they have received training prior to the implementation team's departure.

In some organizations, the ability of a Corporate ASP to deliver computing capabilities inexpensively means that it will sometimes be a user's first experience with networking services, or even with using a computer. In these cases, extra thought needs to go into the training of using the PC, applications, and network in order to save the help desk from a deluge of calls.

Desktop Data Migration

There are many techniques for migrating data from PCs back to the data center, depending upon the infrastructure and service level agreements. It is important to come up with a universal method where possible. If a wide area network has sufficient bandwidth to copy files to the data center, this methodology will be the easiest to use. Your first impulse might be to copy the user data over the network to the data center. In a large, distributed organization with many offices, this could quickly cripple the network. Sometimes simple methods are the best ones. After trying many sophisticated methods, we've found the following works well:

1. Tell the users that they will have access to their current working files immediately, and the rest of the data on their hard disks in 48 hours, as part of the deployment SLA.

2. Make sure the users' accounts and login environment are ready.

3. From the users' desktops, copy their working files across the network to the data center. The data allowance for this copy should be small—perhaps 5MB to 10MB maximum. Most users will have far less data than this.

4. Using a prepared boot disk and a parallel-attached backup device such as a Jaz drive, reboot the PC and copy the contents to the removable media.

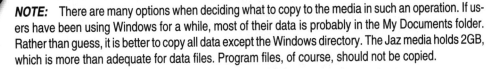

NOTE: There are many options when deciding what to copy to the media in such an operation. If users have been using Windows for a while, most of their data is probably in the My Documents folder. Rather than guess, it is better to copy all data except the Windows directory. The Jaz media holds 2GB, which is more than adequate for data files. Program files, of course, should not be copied.

5. Send the removable media via overnight shipping to the data center.

6. Provide a brief orientation. When users log in, they should immediately have access to their working files and new applications.

7. Within 48 hours, load the removable media at the data center and copy the files into the users' directories.

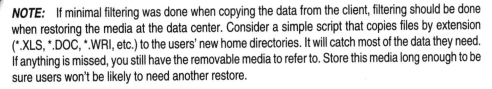

NOTE: If minimal filtering was done when copying the data from the client, filtering should be done when restoring the media at the data center. Consider a simple script that copies files by extension (*.XLS, *.DOC, *.WRI, etc.) to the users' new home directories. It will catch most of the data they need. If anything is missed, you still have the removable media to refer to. Store this media long enough to be sure users won't be likely to need another restore.

At ABM Industries, our engineers worked in conjunction with ABM personnel to form six migration teams. We used Jaz drives to back up data from PCs, and tape drives to back up data from servers. We sent the drives and tapes back to the data center by overnight delivery, where they were restored to ABM's Network Appliance Filer. We had an SLA in place that guaranteed users access to their information within 48 hours of conversion to the new environment.

Migration of Server Data   Data can be moved to the data center before the rollout via backup tapes. Anything that changes after that date can be moved over the WAN. Any modern backup program can do backups based on the "archive bit" of the file that is set each time a file is written to tape. A full backup of the server can be done and sent to the data center before the deployment team arrives. After all the users at that site have been converted, a differential backup (only changed files) is run and sent via overnight delivery to the data center. Those files are then restored as soon as possible. This scheme works because any file the user is currently working on is copied to the data center over the WAN for immediate access as part of that user's migration process.

Rogue Applications

Even the best planning often does not prepare implementation teams for what they face in the field. When unexpected applications are discovered, the project manager should be immediately notified, particularly if the users are scheduled to be converted to run in thin-client mode only. A decision can then be made about whether to allow access to the applications locally, or to halt the rollout and do the preparatory testing required to host the applications over the Corporate ASP. One technique is to migrate what you can at that office but leave one or two PCs and the local file server just for running the problem application. Establish a "sunset period" in which the equipment will be removed and the application will no longer be available or supported.

Remote-Office Migration Teams

A project with many remote offices will likely require several teams to ensure a successful migration within a reasonable time period. These might include one or more implementation teams, a WAN team, and a procurement team.

Implementation Teams

Enough implementation teams should be chosen to meet the timelines for data migration.

Choosing Team Members   Desirable qualities for team members include both technical skills and training capabilities. Personality and training skills generally outweigh technical skills. Making the implementation process very simple can compensate for the lack of technical skills in implementers. On the other hand, superior technical skills do not compensate for the lack of interpersonal skills. When implementers do a good job explaining the server-based computing system, the users are more understanding when inevitable problems occur. The individual team member should be armed with skills for conflict resolution and must be familiar with the support and escalation process. Team members must also be people that the users will trust and want to work with.

Consultant/IT Staff Mix   If using a consulting company to help with your migration, we recommend using a mix of internal and external consultants on each team. This provides expertise and objectivity combined with internal IT and organizational knowledge. It also provides a good, informal method of transferring knowledge from external experts to internal staff.

Facilitating Effective Teamwork   It is important that the implementation teams work together and share their experiences in order to avoid making the same mistake twice. Facilitate this practice by giving each team member a cell phone and two-way radio, by giving each member access to the corporate e-mail system, and by having members of the project management team join each implementation team for part of their trips. Scheduling weekly teleconferences for all members can be particularly useful in helping to avoid making repetitive mistakes and for sharing ways to improve the implementation process among all teams and members. These conferences can also be a forum for sharing good news and quickly improving methods when problems occur.

The Road Kit   The material that each deployment team member will carry makes up the *road kit*. It should be well stocked, and the procedures for replenishing it should be simple and understood by team members before they visit the first site. Using our example methods described in the chapter, a road kit might contain a boot disk, Jaz drive, laptop, overnight courier materials, Ethernet cables, crossover cables, an extra floppy drive, and several blank Jaz disks.

WAN Team

The WAN team orders data connections and bandwidth upgrades. They confirm the installation of these lines. They order and ship any required routers or bandwidth management devices to remote sites before the implementation, or make sure the telecommunication provider does so.

Procurement Team

Responsible for the overall logistics of the project, the procurement team orders and ships the equipment. They should check to ensure receipt of the equipment at least one week before installation. The procurement team also updates the remote office surveys to reflect the new equipment and properly tracks the asset on the company's books after it has been installed. They should also process equipment returns and have the ability to quickly respond to mistakes and make sure the deployment team and the site have the equipment they need.

Deployment Challenges

Every server-based computing implementation will face unique challenges depending upon the existing environment, project scope, and technology utilized. Some issues will be impossible to anticipate. Others are fairly common and include travel, printing, local file sharing, CD-ROM sharing, and access to legacy systems from remote locations.

TIP: Do not make assumptions. When replacing a user's PC with a Windows terminal for one of our clients, the implementation team encountered a particularly irate user. The implementation team member could not get the new terminal to communicate with the existing monitor despite hours of troubleshooting. The team leader finally discovered that the monitor had never worked. The user neglected to tell the installer because he wanted to see if the new Windows terminal could fix it.

Travel

Extensive remote-office implementations require dealing with issues such as travel arrangements and scheduling. Covering large geographical regions may necessitate a great deal of travel, which may in turn limit the number of willing participants on implementation teams. In addition, last-minute scheduling changes can quickly eat up the travel budget. Careful planning and control are essential in managing this project cost.

Bad Tapes or Backups

It is best not to rely on existing backup tapes. The safest procedure is not to wipe out any hard drives or recycle existing PCs until you are sure that all required data is off the PCs, on the new servers, and the users have had the opportunity to confirm this and sign off on the operation.

Printing

Printing is such a major challenge that we devoted Chapter 17 to it. In general, try to standardize as much as possible on the printers used. In particular, try to limit the print drivers to those supported natively by Windows NT 4.0 TSE or Windows 2000, depending on which operating system you are using. Some printers simply will not run well under Terminal Services. Replacing these printers before the migration will eliminate the added pressure on the implementation teams of ordering new ones on-site.

Data Line Procurement

Anticipate problems in getting WAN connectivity completed according to installation promises. Plan to do more work up front in order to ensure that the data connectivity is complete before installation. Even when a local exchange carrier (LEC) confirms that a data connection is complete, take the time to test it yourself. We've seen miscommunication between an LEC and a national telecommunication carrier cost a project weeks of time and thousands of dollars.

PCs

Even the easy task of installing the Citrix MetaFrame client can become arduous when migrating thousands of users. The easiest migration of all sometimes is simply to give users a Windows terminal.

Inaccurate Site Surveys

Most organizations depend on user surveys to determine the type and state of equipment in remote offices. Impress upon the survey respondents how crucial it is for them to report this information accurately in order to avoid costly implementation delays and potential downtime. If your organization already has a tool in place that does hardware inventories, such as Microsoft SMS or HP OpenView, make sure the data is current. If possible, confirm critical items shown in the inventory, such as site routers or servers, with a phone call.

Internal Selling

In Chapter 4 we talked about creating internal videos and other marketing tools to help sell the Corporate ASP concept. Use e-mail, management meetings, press releases, and "at-a-glance" documents to communicate the Corporate ASP concept and the implementation procedures to users. Do not depend on local management to share the concept.

TIP: Do not oversell the Corporate ASP. Set realistic expectations. Make sure users know the benefits, but also let them know about any problems or limitations they can expect to encounter, particularly in terms of performance and reliability, during the implementation period.

POSTPRODUCTION MANAGEMENT OF THE CORPORATE ASP

Your Corporate ASP is now rolled out. Your users are happy, and your IT staff has joined the swelling ranks of server-based computing evangelists. These final sections discuss ongoing measurement and change control, and upgrades and changes to the environment.

Continue Measurements

During the beta and the production deployment, you established service levels for your Corporate ASP. These service levels represent an agreement between the IT staff and the user community. Part of the agreement is that the IT staff will manage the system to meet certain established metrics and goals. The data needed to establish whether these goals are being met needs to be collected diligently and continuously. For example, if part of the SLA is 99.99 percent system uptime, every blue screen or other server outage needs to be recorded, as well as major network disruptions for a given region or data center.

Publish Results

The collected data does no good unless the appropriate people review it. There should be a policy of no secrets between the IT staff and the user community. Establish a reporting cycle as part of the SLA. It may not be critical for a user to see daily status, but it may be appropriate to display quarterly or monthly SLA results. This will depend on your corporate culture and what your internal reporting capabilities are.

Establish a Corporate ASP Steering Committee

A technique for keeping IT staff and the user community focused on continuous improvement is to create a committee made up of both groups. The user representatives should be as diverse as the reach of the server-based computing project. If the Corporate ASP is multinational, a representative from each major region or country should participate. The exact scope and responsibility of the committee will depend on your corporate culture, but it should at least evaluate and recommend changes to the server-based computing environment.

Provide a Forum for Feedback "Outside the Box"

The help desk will record user problems and outages. In addition, you should provide a way for any employee of the company to give suggestions or constructive criticism. This input should be reviewed and evaluated by the steering committee. We've found that brilliant suggestions sometimes come from the most unlikely places.

Make Facts-Based Decisions for the Future

Collecting and reporting on established SLAs and keeping the users involved will provide invaluable information for making decisions about the future of your company's Corporate ASP. Even after a successful rollout, there may be factions within the company that remain unconvinced as to the value of server-based computing. Having facts to back up a recommendation to expand the infrastructure or add applications can mean the difference between ultimate success or failure of the environment.

Establish a Server-Based Computing Lab

To maintain a high quality of service, it is necessary to maintain a lab environment where new versions of software and hardware can be evaluated and tested. This lab does not need to be on-site. In fact, manufacturers often allow their facilities to be used for this purpose, as long as you agree to share the results. Regularly check the Web sites of Microsoft and Citrix for the latest information on changes and upgrades. The Citrix knowledge base, in particular, is an excellent place to find this kind of information. Since your Corporate ASP environment is now tested and stable, any change must be rigorously evaluated and tested before deployment.

Share Your Experiences

After getting the proper clearance from management, seek out other companies that have undergone similar server-based computing deployments, and offer to share information. Even if a nondisclosure agreement is necessary, the result will be an enrichment of the server-based computing environment at each company. Participate in server-based computing-related forums and events from Citrix and Microsoft to keep up on the latest developments and share your experiences. Finally, seek out peers on the Internet, in discussion groups, chat rooms, e-forums, or other areas.

Corporate ASPs are an emerging technology. Manufacturers of server-based computing hardware and software are eager to help you publicize your success by writing and publishing success stories. In this way, you can help contribute to the growing momentum behind this new and tremendously exciting industry.

APPENDIX A

Creating a Corporate ASP Financial Analysis Model

Every organization's financial analysis will involve unique variables and methods of calculation, but you can use the model presented in this appendix as a framework for creating your own Corporate ASP financial evaluation. This model defines a method for identifying common costs and savings involved when migrating to enterprise server-based computing.

BUILDING A SPREADSHEET MODEL

We recommend creating a spreadsheet that calculates both expected server-based computing costs and savings over a three-to-five-year time frame. The savings come from reducing the costs involved in a PC-based computing environment. For instance, if your organization's policy is to upgrade your PCs every 12 months, then the cost of purchasing and installing the PC becomes a yearly savings under server-based computing.

It is not necessary to be creative when financially justifying a Corporate ASP project. The hard quantifiable savings alone should easily pay for the project and also provide a good return on investment. We recommend quantifying soft savings, such as reduced user downtime, and then listing these savings independently of the return on investment (ROI) calculation. Although the value of certain benefits from implementing a Corporate ASP can exceed that of the combined savings, we still recommend listing benefits separately as well. Taking this conservative approach makes a very strong statement to management about the overwhelming value of the project. It also helps the feasibility committee defend against anyone who tries to poke holes in the financial analysis.

An effective financial model utilizes a multidimensional spreadsheet that isolates the different variables involved. This makes the spreadsheet both easy to follow and easy to adjust for different assumptions. We recommend creating a spreadsheet with four tabs: Demographics, Logistics, Costs, and Report.

Information entered into the Demographics, Logistics, and Costs sections will come from assumptions and research by the feasibility committee. The Report section will show the results of calculations derived from information entered into the other three sections.

In order to simplify the model, do not bother listing costs that are equivalent under both server-based and PC-based scenarios. For instance, if you plan to purchase new NT file servers regardless of whether you build a Corporate ASP or not, do not list the cost of these servers in your financial model.

TIP: RYNO Technology developed an Excel-based Total Cost of Ownership (TCO) calculator that you can download from their Web site at www.ryno.com. The "Questions" tab lets you put in your own estimates for factors such as your cost of a PC, the number of years before you will replace it again, and the number of average servers in your remote offices. The "Reports" tab calculates your estimated five-year savings by deploying server-based rather than PC-based computing technology.

Demographics

The number of users and remote offices participating in the Corporate ASP project are identified and categorized. Figure A-1 shows a Demographics spreadsheet example.

Number of Users

Whether employees or contractors, the number of expected Corporate ASP users should be estimated and categorized as to what degree of Terminal Services they are likely to require. Common categorizations include thin client, mostly thin client, and minimal thin client.

▼   **Thin client**   These users will run their entire desktops from the Corporate ASP. They will either use Windows Terminals or PCs configured as Windows Terminals with local drive mapping disabled.

■   **Mostly thin client**   These users run the majority of applications from the Corporate ASP, but may still run some applications locally. Users requiring unique applications and certain laptop users often fall into this category.

■   **Minimal thin client**   These users primarily operate in fat-client mode and will use server-based computing selectively. This group might include headquarters employees who use fat-client PCs at work, but who like to dial

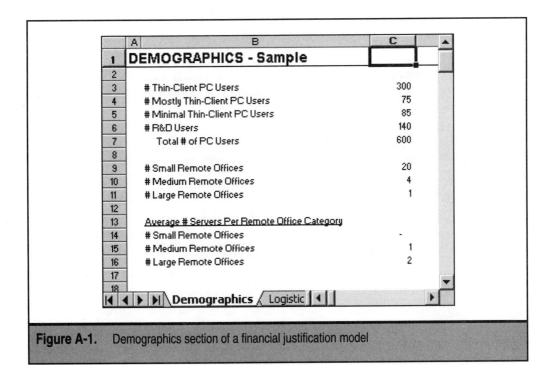

Figure A-1.   Demographics section of a financial justification model

into the network from home. It might also include salespeople who are often on the road, but who need to access corporate applications and databases. It might include remote fat-client users who simply like to save time by accessing their e-mail through MetaFrame rather than downloading it.

▲ **Other** This category will differ by organization. It might include R&D engineers who want to run Windows applications on their UNIX workstations. It might include customers who run applications as anonymous Internet browsers utilizing Citrix NFuse. Or it may be limited to a single company executive who insists on continuing to run the majority of his applications on a Mac.

Remote Offices

The composition of remote offices will have a big impact on the design of the server-based computing architecture. We recommend different categorizations such as home office, small office, medium office, large office, jumbo office, and regional office. Some general parameters follow, though of course they will be different for almost every organization.

▼ **Home office** The home office is the new branch office. Telecommuters typically dial into the network or come in through the Internet. They sometimes use their own PCs and sometimes use company-issued PCs or laptops. If the organization implements a server-based computing environment, telecommuters are good candidates for inexpensive Windows terminals.

■ **Small remote office** Generally, these offices range from one to five users and have only low-bandwidth connectivity to headquarters, if any.

■ **Medium remote office** These offices range from 5 to 14 users. They will sometimes have their own file and e-mail servers. Limited bandwidth connectivity is often in place.

■ **Large remote office** These offices range from 15 to 39 users. They often have their own servers and will sometimes have their own network administrators on staff. They frequently have high-speed bandwidth connections to headquarters.

■ **Jumbo remote office** These offices range from 41 to 200 users. They almost always have multiple servers and often have local network administrators in addition to high-speed bandwidth connections.

▲ **Regional office** These offices have over 200 users along with IT support staff on-site.

Logistics

The Logistics spreadsheet section is for making assumptions about how usage and growth variables will impact users and equipment. Where appropriate, the logistics should reflect the specific user or remote-office categories defined in the Demographics section. Figure A-2 shows a Logistics spreadsheet example.

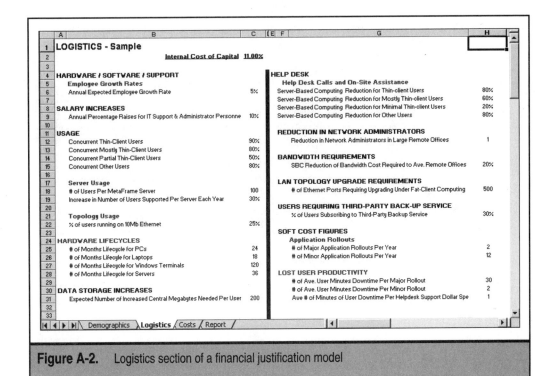

Figure A-2.   Logistics section of a financial justification model

Internal Cost of Capital

The feasibility committee should obtain the organization's internal cost of capital from finance. This figure will be used to calculate the present value of both project costs and savings.

Employee Growth Rate

The expected employee growth rate should be obtained from management. For simplicity, we usually assume that this growth rate will apply across the board to all categories of employees and to all locations. Of course, you may wish to fine-tune your spreadsheet with more specific calculations if appropriate.

Salary Increases

List the expected annual percentage salary increases for both IT support and administrator personnel.

Usage

A Corporate ASP environment often enables economies in licensing, infrastructure requirements, and support because the number of concurrent users tends to be less than the number of total users. In some cases, this discrepancy can be very large. A multinational manufacturer based in California, for instance, saves a great deal of money on Citrix MetaFrame licenses because their users around the world operate in different time zones.

▼ **Concurrent users by category**   List the expected concurrency percentage for each category of users.

■ **Server usage**   Calculate the number of users per MetaFrame server, which will enable you to calculate the total number of servers required in the Report section.

■ **Increase in supported users each year**   As servers continue to become more powerful, they will be able to support much larger numbers of users. Estimating this percentage enables you to more accurately forecast the number of new and replacement MetaFrame servers required in the years ahead, which will continue to fall relative to the number of users accessing them.

▲ **Topology usage**   List the percentage of users running on 10MB Ethernet .

Hardware Life Cycle Estimates

In order to build a realistic financial model, the feasibility committee should estimate life cycles for PCs, laptops, Windows terminals, and servers. These figures should reflect the number of expected months of use for each device.

▼ **Personal computers**   The average realistic PC life cycle in most organizations seems to range between one and two years, though some organizations keep them considerably longer.

■ **Laptops**   The average laptop's life expectancy is generally around two-thirds that of PCs.

■ **Windows terminals**   Since Windows terminals tend to have mean times between failure measured in decades, and since processing takes place on the MetaFrame servers, the Windows terminals' expected life cycle should easily exceed the time frame of the financial analysis.

▲ **Servers**   The life cycle for servers tends to range between two and three years. The increasing power of servers should also be considered because it means that fewer servers can handle more employees. This makes it more economically compelling to centralize computing.

Data Storage

If appropriate, an estimate should be made for the increased centralized storage that will be required for each category of user once users become Corporate ASP clients.

Reduction in Help Desk Calls/Personnel

The feasibility committee should estimate the impact a Corporate ASP will have in reducing either help desk support calls or in support personnel—depending upon how their organization accounts for this expense. For instance, IT may already charge users $100 per month for both phone and technician support. The feasibility committee might estimate that under server-based computing, support calls will decrease by the following amounts per category of user: thin client, 80 percent; mostly thin client, 60 percent; minimal thin client, 20 percent; other, 80 percent.

Reduction in Network Administrative Personnel

This figure should reflect the lower number of administrators that will be required as a result of eliminating servers in remote offices.

Bandwidth Considerations

Estimate bandwidth requirements for both a PC-based and server-based computing environment. These will depend upon the applications utilized, the size of the remote offices, and the extent to which users are full thin-client users.

LAN Topology Upgrade Requirements

PC-based computing's inexorable demand for higher bandwidth to the desktop makes it reasonable to assume that most organizations will be forced to upgrade their existing 10MB Ethernet or Token Ring topologies to 100MB Ethernet over the next few years. Identify the number of ports in your existing network topology that would require upgrading to maintain a PC-based computing environment.

Third-Party Backup Subscriptions

The majority of PC-based computing environments allow users to maintain data on their local hard drives. If IT already backs up this data, then the additional storage discussed earlier in the chapter may not be required. If users are required to back up their own hard drives, then include this time as a soft cost for lost productivity. If a third-party service is utilized, include the percentage of users who subscribe to this service.

Soft Cost Figures

Soft costs are those costs that are harder to quantify, but still can clearly impact the organization.

Application Rollouts   The estimated number of application upgrades or rollouts will be used to calculate their costs, assuming that excess personnel or contractors are required to accomplish them. If your organization simply forgoes most application upgrades because of the huge cost of performing them within a PC-based computing environment, then having the latest software can be identified separately as a server-based computing benefit on the Report spreadsheet section.

▼ **Number of major application rollouts per year**   Rollouts of new application packages or operating systems

▲ **Number of minor application rollouts per year**   Software version upgrades

Lost Productivity

Estimate the amount of user productivity lost each year due to PC-based computing limitations such as inaccessibility to required corporate data and from downtime.

▼ **Number of average user minutes downtime per rollout**   The expected length of downtime suffered by users for both major and minor rollouts

■ **PC upgrades**   The expected downtime users undergo when they receive a new PC

▲ **Help desk delays**   The expected lost productivity time while waiting for the help desk to resolve a PC problem

Costs

Estimated costs for both the existing PC-based computing environment and the proposed Corporate ASP are entered into the Costs section of the spreadsheet. Figure A-3 shows a Costs spreadsheet example. Where appropriate, modify costs to reflect the specific user category as defined in the Demographics section of the spreadsheet.

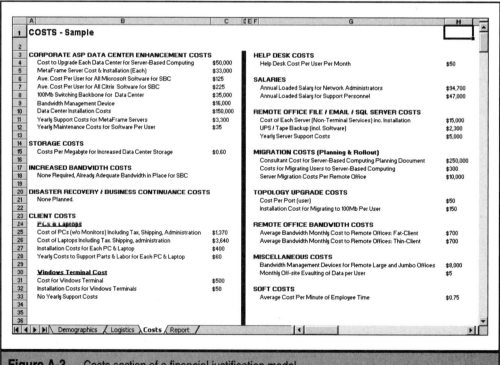

Figure A-3.   Costs section of a financial justification model

Corporate ASP Data Center

As discussed in Chapter 5, building a Corporate ASP will involve configuring one or more data centers to support enterprise server-based computing. This is likely to require a more robust and redundant architecture than that of most existing PC-based computing environments. You may be able to upgrade your existing data centers, or you may wish to build new ones or to co-locate them with a third-party service such as AT&T, Exodus, or Sprint. The feasibility committee needs to choose a preliminary strategy, including the number of data centers, and assign appropriate costs for the model.

MetaFrame Servers   Include both the cost and installation expense for each server.

Windows 2000 Software   Microsoft licenses Windows 2000 on the basis of total number of users. See Chapter 3 for licensing details.

Citrix Software   Citrix software is licensed on a concurrency basis, as explained in Chapter 2. In addition to the basic MetaFrame licenses, most organizations also purchase load-balancing software, Resource Management Services, Installation Management Services, the ICA Encryption Option, and sometimes the VideoFrame product. You should get a complete quote from your Citrix reseller, but the estimated street price for the spreadsheet model is $225 per concurrent user.

LAN Backbone   As discussed in Chapter 6, a Corporate ASP data center requires a very robust LAN backbone. This usually means a minimum 100MB switching configuration and may include FDDI or gigabit switching for larger implementations.

Bandwidth Management   If you have remote offices, you may want to consider utilizing bandwidth management, as discussed in Chapter 6. One good solution is to use a bandwidth management device. These units can easily pay for themselves by increasing the utilization of available bandwidth from a typical 40 percent to as much as 80 percent.

Installation   Ensure that enough money is allocated to properly install all of the data center components. Remember that much of the work may have to be done in off-hours in order not to disrupt your current environment.

Maintenance and Support   Include estimated costs for both annual maintenance and support of hardware and software.

Storage Costs

Estimate the cost per megabyte for required increased data center storage to support the Corporate ASP users. An estimate of 60 cents per megabyte is probably reasonable.

Increased Bandwidth Costs

Although the bandwidth costs to remote offices may fall under server-based computing, the data center bandwidth requirements are very likely to increase.

Disaster Recovery/Business Continuance

The feasibility committee needs to determine the extent to which the Corporate ASP will include disaster recovery and business continuance. The associated costs should then be entered into the spreadsheet.

Client Costs

The cost for PCs and laptops includes sales tax, shipping, and administration. Software operating system costs are included along with annual hardware support costs. A realistic installation cost should reflect the hours it takes to configure each device. For most organizations, this ranges between three to eight hours per PC or laptop.

The lack of any moving parts makes the installation and annual support costs for Windows terminals minimal.

Help Desk Support Costs

Some organizations will show help desk costs as reductions in the number of support personnel required. Others might already have an assigned monthly support cost per user, as discussed in the "Logistics" section earlier in this appendix.

Salaries

Include annual loaded salary costs for administrators and support personnel.

Remote-Office Server Costs

Servers in remote offices will usually be eliminated under a Corporate ASP scenario. It is therefore important to estimate the costs for these servers, including ancillary equipment such as tape backups, tape backup software, uninterruptible power supplies and software, network O/S software, and network management software. Include costs for installing new servers along with the costs for annual server maintenance.

Migration Costs

Estimate the costs for migrating PC users to server-based computing desktops, including the cost of migrating the data to the corporate data center. Four hours for migrating each PC is probably a reasonable figure. Include the estimated cost to migrate information from remote office servers back to the corporate data center. Also include the cost for preparing the project definition and planning documents, as well as the infrastructure assessment.

Topology Upgrade Costs

This is the cost for upgrading from an older topology, such as 10MB Ethernet or Token Ring, to a 100MB or switched 10MB topology. For a rough estimate, figure $50 per port (user), assuming correct cabling is in place; otherwise, add $150 per cable drop.

Remote-Office Bandwidth Costs

Compare the cost of bandwidth required for a PC-based computing environment with the cost for providing adequate bandwidth connectivity for a server-based computing environment. Both figures will depend upon the size of remote offices and the bandwidth medium. Using the Internet or a VPN is likely, for example, to be much less expensive than using a dedicated leased line or frame relay connection. Server-based computing could either reduce or increase the bandwidth cost to a remote office depending upon the number of users and applications required. Effective using of an ERP application in a remote office, for instance, may require much higher bandwidth under PC-based computing than under server-based computing.

Miscellaneous Costs

This category includes the miscellaneous additional costs for both the server-based and PC-based computing environments. Examples include costs for bandwidth management devices for the larger offices and the cost of using a third-party service to back up user hard drives.

Soft Costs

The cost of employee time shown on a minute or hourly basis should be entered into this part of the spreadsheet.

Report

The Report section pulls together all of the information from the Demographics, Logistics, and Costs sections of the spreadsheet. The end result is a net present value estimate for building a Corporate ASP and for the savings it is expected to generate over a three-to-five-year time frame. The present value of the total savings can then be divided by the present value of the total cost of the project to show the expected return on investment (ROI) for the Corporate ASP initiative.

We like to list the categories in the first column and then the summarized costs for the ensuing years in the following columns, as seen in Figure A-4, which shows an example of a Report spreadsheet section.

Demographics Summary

We find it useful to recap the total number of expected concurrent employees by year, along with the number of expected MetaFrame servers required. Since technology is likely to accelerate faster than your employee growth rate, the number of servers required each year should actually decline.

Corporate ASP Costs

These costs summarize the costs of all of the different components involved in constructing and maintaining a Corporate ASP.

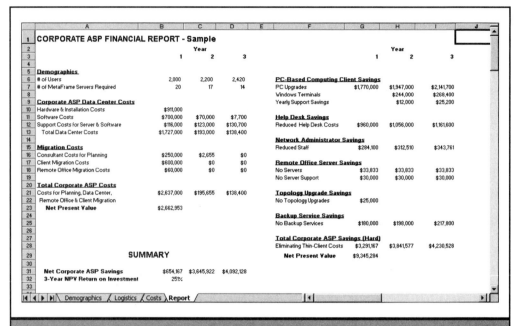

Figure A-4. Report section of a financial justification model

TIP: You may wish to break down costs and savings on a per user basis in order to analyze the impact of a Corporate ASP from a different angle.

Data Center Costs   In the sample shown in Figure A-4, we consolidate the costs by hardware and installation, software, and support costs.

Migration Costs

Migration costs include the project definition, infrastructure assessment, and planning costs, as well as the client migration costs and remote-office migration costs.

Corporate Savings

As mentioned earlier in the chapter, the Corporate ASP savings equate to the money not spent that would have been required to sustain a PC-based computing environment.

PC and Laptop Savings   This section summarizes the expected savings from less frequent upgrades of PCs and laptops. The figures come from multiplying the total cost of the laptop or PC by (12 / device life cycle). For instance, suppose a PC costs $2500 including taxes, installation, shipping, and administration. If your company policy is to replace PCs every 18 months, then your annual savings by going to server-based computing will be $2500 × (12 / 18) = $1667 per PC. If appropriate, the annual maintenance savings for PCs and laptops should also be reflected in this category.

Windows Terminal Savings   These are savings that result from being able to purchase less expensive Windows terminals rather than PCs for new users.

Yearly Support Savings   These are the savings that result from using Windows terminals rather than PCs for new users.

Help Desk Savings

The amount of decreased help desk support required under a Corporate ASP should be summarized by showing a decline in either the monthly charge per user or in a reduced salary cost for help desk personnel.

Network Administrator Savings

This figure reflects the savings from no longer having to maintain network administrators on staff each year to manage remote office networks, as would be required in a PC-based computing environment.

Remote-Office Server Savings

These savings result from no longer having to upgrade and maintain remote-office servers. The annual savings from not having to upgrade the servers are calculated in the same manner as the savings from not upgrading PCs and laptops.

NOTE: We assume here that all servers in remote offices will be eliminated under a Corporate ASP model. This may not always be the case, depending upon factors such as the size of the office and bandwidth availability.

Topology Upgrade Savings

These savings result from not having to upgrade the network topology to support increased PC-based computing bandwidth demands. They are calculated by multiplying the cost per port, obtained from the Costs spreadsheet section, by the percentage of existing outdated topology, obtained from Logistics, by the total number of thin-client users, obtained from Demographics.

Backup Savings

Any hard backup savings such as the money that will no longer be required for third-party backup services are reflected here. Any soft backup savings are quantified apart from the ROI calculation.

Summary

Subtract the Corporate ASP costs from the anticipated savings to show the net Corporate ASP savings each year.

Calculate the expected ROI of a Corporate ASP by subtracting the net present value of the ASP costs from the net present value of the ASP savings. Then divide this figure by the net present value of the ASP costs.

Soft Savings

Show soft savings apart from the ROI calculation, and include savings from reduced user downtime and inaccessibility to required corporate data.

Benefits

List the expected benefits from implementing a Corporate ASP along with the financial report. It might even be appropriate to quantify some of them, but excluding them from the ROI calculation should still leave a project savings easily large enough to justify the Corporate ASP implementation.

TIP: The Tolley Group prepared an Excel-based Total Cost of Application (TCA) calculator that you can obtain from a Citrix Solutions Network (CSN) member. A local CSN member can be found on the Citrix Web site at www.citrix.com. The TCA uses industry averages to let you determine your estimated savings from deploying specific applications through a server-based computing methodology. This is a different approach for calculating server-based computing savings that focuses on the value obtained from much more effective application deployment.

APPENDIX B

Creating a Corporate ASP Subscription Billing Model

In most organizations, IT expenses are often allocated on the basis of somewhat arbitrary criteria, such as a percentage of sales. On the other hand, commercial ASPs such as FutureLink or Corio must charge their customers fees that are clearly based upon usage of their application hosting services. A Corporate ASP enables an IT department to apply a similar billing model to their organization's internal customers. This should result in greater accountability that can lower overall IT expenses. In this appendix, we give an example of one strategy for creating a subscription billing model.

MONTHLY SUBSCRIPTION FEES

IT can charge users a monthly subscription fee structured like a cable company bill. Each user and each remote office is charged a basic monthly fee for utilizing the Corporate ASP. Additional fees cover supplementary applications, services, and changes. Account change fees help to ensure that users remain conscious of the administrative costs their requests for system modifications entail.

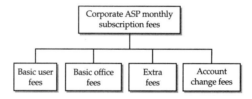

Basic User Fees

Basic user fees are monthly charges for products and services necessary for a user to access the Corporate ASP. For example, a department with ten user accounts would be charged a basic monthly fee for each of the ten named users to receive help desk support and the necessary hardware, software, and disk space.

▼ **Help desk support** The basic user fee should include a charge for help desk support. Since a Corporate ASP both greatly simplifies the user computing environment and allows help desk personnel to "shadow" user sessions, this charge should run as much as 80 percent less than it would in a PC-based computing arrangement.

■ **Network device** Users require a PC, laptop, Macintosh, UNIX Workstation, or Windows terminal in order to access the Corporate ASP. Although it probably makes more sense to let departments pay for their own equipment, IT does need to set a price for access.

■ **Disk space** The basic subscription fee should include a certain amount of disk space in the corporate data center.

▲   **Basic software suite**   Users will have access to the standard corporate software suite such as Microsoft Office and e-mail. This suite should include virus-protection software and all licensing costs for accessing Terminal Services and MetaFrame.

Basic Office Fees

The monthly basic office fee covers the expense of putting a remote office onto the Corporate ASP. The charges might be categorized by size of office, as described in Chapter 6, and shown here:

Office Type	Number of Users	Basic Monthly Fee	Shared Disk Space
Small	1–5	$ 50	500MB
Medium	5–14	150	1GB
Large	15–30	250	2GB
Jumbo	41–200	900	10GB

▼   **Shared disk space in the corporate data center**   Remote offices may require shared disk space in excess of the amount for individual users.

■   **Bandwidth**   The monthly fee should include the cost of connectivity as well as the cost of bandwidth management and support.

■   **Printing**   Large remote offices often have print servers, and small offices use print management hardware at the corporate data center. The basic office fees should cover basic printing, using corporate standard printers.

▲   **Administrative support**   The monthly fee can also include a basic level of administrative support for each office.

Extra User Fees

As with a cable company, IT can tack on additional charges for additional services. The following table shows an example of basic and additional monthly subscription fees.

User Subscription Fees	Amount
Basic user fee	$150
Includes PC or Windows terminal, network and MetaFrame software licensing, MS Office, e-mail, antivirus software, 200MB data center storage	

User Subscription Fees	Amount
Additional user fees	
Laptop	$50
Extra 100MB storage	10
Each extra 32-bit application	10
Local printer (Terminal Server–supported drivers)	5

Some of the categories of additional fees are as follows:

▼ **Nonstandard software**   Users requiring access to nonstandard corporate applications should pay additional fees. DOS or 16-bit applications requiring separate MetaFrame servers will be more expensive.

■ **Hardware types**   It generally costs a little more to maintain and support a PC configured as a Windows terminal than it does to support a genuine Windows terminal. A laptop user who runs applications both locally and through the Corporate ASP will likely require significantly more support. IT can tack on additional charges depending upon the type of hardware utilized and the degree to which the user operates in complete thin-client mode.

■ **Additional disk space**   IT can charge users extra for additional data storage requirements.

■ **Local devices**   Local devices such as printers and scanners can be charged appropriately.

▲ **Access from home**   A small charge might be levied for employees who want to work from home as well as from the office, though server-based computing makes this process relatively painless. IT may instead choose to bundle this service as part of the basic monthly user fees in order to encourage working from home.

Extra Office Fees

IT can charge extra fees to remote offices requiring additional storage space or printing requirements beyond the basics. New users or application changes also fall into this category.

Account Change Fees

In order to help foster computing efficiency throughout the organization, IT may wish to charge remote offices or departments for each account change. An account change is a new account setup or an addition or deletion to a user or office account. For example, adding or deleting a specific application to a user or group desktop would be an account change. An account change would also take place if an office decided to increase or decrease its shared disk space at the data center.

USING RESOURCE MANAGEMENT SERVICES FOR SPECIFIC USAGE BILLING

Citrix Resource Management Services (RMS) may be used to supplement the monthly subscription fee model by billing users for some applications per minute of connection time. It also enables billing by memory utilization and/or processor utilization. A semiconductor manufacturer, for example, might utilize a common manufacturing application requiring a huge amount of RAM per user. RMS can add a supplemental fee for the inordinate amount of server resources that manufacturing users consume.

RMS enables billing by user or by cost center using the Windows NT Domain structure, or you can create your own cost center assignments. Billing reports can be constructed to show resources used, session start time, session elapsed time, and applications executed. Figure B-1 shows a screen print from an RMS report.

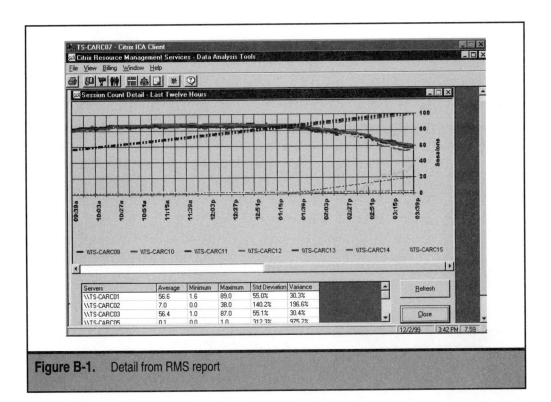

Figure B-1.   Detail from RMS report

Index

B

E

F

G

H

O

P

Q

R

routing
> gateway routing and, 216
> remote access and, 213–214

Routing and Remote Access Service (RRAS), 213–214

Routing Information Protocol (RIP), 133

RPCs (Remote Procedure Calls), 377

RRAS (Routing and Remote Access Service), 213–214

RSVP (Resource Reservation Protocol), 155

S

salaries
> costs report and, 518
> logistics and, 513

SAM (Security Account Manager), 245

Samba, 172

SAP (Service Advertising Protocol), 133

scalability, network design and, 127

scope creep, 490–491

scripting
> application compatibility scripts and, 46, 72
> install scripts and, 404
> logon scripts and, 404
> server creation and, 384, 387–388

SCSI. *see* Small Computer Storage Interface (SCSI)

Seamless Window, 35, 430

Secure Sockets Layer (SSL), 312

SecureICA
> application publishing and, 43
> encryption with, 261
> remote access and, 216–217

security, 230–266
> application publishing and, 42–43
> auditing and, 261–264
>> file system and, 264
>> Registry and, 261–262
>> tools for, 264
>> user accounts and, 262–263
> Citrix security and, 260–261
> concepts of, 238–244
>> firewalls, 238–242
>> VPNs, 242–244
> connectivity and, 310
> Corporate ASP preparation and, 92
> Corporate ASP project plan and, 98
> file security and, 74
> management of, 278–279
> models for, 235–238
>> data centers and, 236
>> regional offices and, 236–237
>> security zones and, 235–236
>> small office/home user and, 238

overview of, 230–235
> areas of exposure, 234–235
> server-based computing and, 230–235
> what are you protecting, 233
> physical security and, 118
> products for, 264–266

Security Account Manager (SAM), 245

security, Microsoft, 245–260
> account management and, 255–257
> application security and, 260
> file system and, 257–259
> NT domain authentication and, 245
> Registry and, 248
> Terminal Services and, 248–254
> Windows 2000 authentication and, 246–247

seismic dangers, 118

server backbones
> costs of, 517
> data center components and, 18
> infrastructure upgrades and, 331
> Terminal Services design and, 94

server-based computing. *see* Corporate Application Service Providers (ASPs)

server farms
> application services and, 415–416
>> configuration of, 416
>> overview of, 415
> MetaFrame and, 411
> Terminal Services design and, 94

server hardware, configuration. *see* hardware, configuration of

servers
> automated servers and
>> imaging products and, 384–386
>> overview of, 382–384
>> WSH and, 386–388
> capacity of, 106
> costs of, 517
> data migration and, 503
> life cycle estimates and, 514
> print servers and
>> hardware print servers, 477
>> non-Windows print servers, 482
>> Windows NT print servers, 478–481
> server usage and, 514

Service Advertising Protocol (SAP), 133

service level agreements (SLAs)
> areas of responsibility and, 269
> beta testing and, 496–497
> defining, 269
> enterprise backups and, 270
> enterprise rollout and, 497
> establishing, 334
> post-deployment management and, 508
> printing and, 474
> SMEs and, 280–281